America and the Black Body

America and the Black Body

Identity Politics in Print and Visual Culture

Edited by
Carol E. Henderson

Madison • Teaneck
Fairleigh Dickinson University Press

Associated University Presses
2010 Eastpark Boulevard
Cranbury, NJ 08512

The paper used in this publication meets the requirements of the American National Standard for Permanence of Paper for printed Library Materials Z39.48-1984.

Library of Congress Cataloging-in-Publication Data

America and the black body : identity politics in print and visual culture / edited by Carol E. Henderson.
p. cm.
Includes bibliographical references and index.
ISBN 978-0-8386-4132-3 (alk. paper)
1. American literature—19th century—History and criticism. 2. American literature—20th century—History and criticism. 3. Blacks in literature. 4. Body, Human, in literature. 5. Race in literature. 6. African Americans in literature. 7. Blacks—Race identity. 8. African Americans—Race identity. I. Henderson, Carol E., 1964–
PS217.B55A64 2009
810.9′3552—dc22 2009006783

PRINTED IN THE UNITED STATES OF AMERICA

For
My Grandparents
Mr. Elvin Henderson Sr., July 6, 1897–April 8, 1986
Mrs. Bertha Mitchell Henderson, March 6, 1904–August 6, 1983
Mr. Roscoe Marbley Sr., July 5, 1918–May 23, 2000
Mrs. Mable Young Marbley, June 1, 1924–March 2, 2006

And
My Parents
Mr. Willie B. Henderson Sr., April 3, 1936–
Ms. Barbara Marbley Henderson, October 6, 1945–

Whose ancestral dignity,
Ordained purpose,
And audacious spirit
Imagined an America with me *in it . . . their hard work is my legacy.*
I have been bought and paid for.

Contents

Preface

THIS PROJECT EMERGED OUT OF A GRADUATE COURSE I TAUGHT IN the spring of 2005 called "Imag(in)ing America: The African American Body in Literature." In it, we explored how superficial and metaphoric differences between various groups of human beings restructured the ideological figurations of "race" in the Americas. Aware that race is an ever evolving idea, never fixed but intimately tied to the social, cultural, and political landscape of America's ideals' systems, we concerned ourselves with America's struggles to define itself—indeed its national and physical body—through the site of the Other, and in our case, through the site of the black body. As our class discovered in many of our discussions, these "dialogues," which constitute the cultural and theoretical essence of America's developing discourse on "difference" shape the racial imaginings of our culture, and as such, provide a segue into the implicit and explicit historical and social development of American identity. Moreover, we found that the discursive practices of nineteenth and twentieth century American authors reflected this national angst in their writings. Exploring such subjects such as slavery, emancipation, Jim Crowism, and gender politics helped us to navigate through the murky waters of unfair and unethical practices directed at African Americans, women, and immigrants, whose black and foreign bodies placed them outside the borders of national belonging in the Americas.

Little did we know that three months later, our deliberations about nationality, race, and class would be revisited—live and in living color—in the tragedy of Hurricane Katrina. The televised images of tens of thousands of U.S. citizens stranded on roof tops and in the Louisiana Superdome for days, without water, food, or suitable shelter—amid festering floodwaters and accumulating debris and sewage—made painfully clear to the world America's inability to move past race. From the nationally perpetuated *faux-pas* of African American citizens being considered "refugees" in their own country, to the media's recontextualization of desperate victims as looters (if black) and survivors (if white), Katrina unearthed a bevy of social ills and myths that have continued to haunt the American, and I would argue, global racial memory. At the center of these contentious and volatile social storms is the racial imaginings of a nation unable—or unwilling—to move past its ignominious relationship with black people.

This collection honors the spirit of these and many other discussions of national belonging as our diverse group of scholars explore the deployment of racial formations of difference in visual culture and in the body of literature written by a wide array of authors who helped to develop the generic representations of the black body. These representations are multifaceted: from the phenomenological depictions of the body vis-à-vis inanimate objects, to the legal, social, and scientific uses of material/cultural artifacts that seek to represent the black body in public spaces vis-à-vis the literary marketplace and the court room. This collection is broader in scope than most. Other collections tend to narrow their focus of the black body to gender and/or sexuality exclusively (black men or black women and the body), and of these, many of the collections look at African American authors and/or literature exclusively. Few collections, if any, cross-pollinate the perspectives of the black body in literature from white and black authors—placing Ralph Waldo Emerson's "The Over-Soul" in dialogue with W. E. B. DuBois's *The Souls of Black Folk*, or William Dean Howells's *An Imperative Duty* in conversation with Jessie Fauset's "The Sleeper Wakes," for example, provides a fascinating tapestry of the ways in which American identity, and in some cases global identity, is accessed and assessed through the site of the black body. Such investigations underscore issues of race, class, and gender that consider the representations of the black male and the black female body in theory and cultural studies, as it also reveals the invisible ties that connect white men and women's identities to these racial imaginings.

In the end, we hope this project will alter the landscape of the discussion of race matters in the United States, as we also provide a set of touchstones relevant to the human experience in America. This is the spirit out of which this project was birth, and the context from which my own imaginings of self sprang. My grandparents and parents, each one a laborer in the vineyard of America's promise, experienced the highs and lows of the American dream. Their journey—often forged in social discord—gave little but yielded much in constituting the true spirit of America. Their spiritual strivings represent the essence of a people that continue to imagine an America with them in it despite the overwhelming circumstances that shape their lives. The seeds they have sown are manifested in the meditative reflections of their granddaughter and daughter. The other writers in this volume join me in saluting their ancestral spirit as we, too, imagine an America along the contours of their embodied and inspirited personage.

Acknowledgments

Any project of this magnitude requires the energies and generous support of those individuals committed to academic excellence. To thank them all here would require a volume separate from this one, but I would like to acknowledge the special contributions of a few individuals who went above and beyond the ordinary limitations of the present to see this project to the end.

First, I want to thank the contributors to this volume who generously gave of their time and talents to explore the phenomenon of America's fascination—obsession—with the black body. Your steadfast belief in the spirit of rigorous intellectual inquiry—your willingness to stretch the comfort zones of your academic circles to embrace the dialogue contained herein has humbled this scholar. Thank you for taking the journey with me and seeing the project to its conclusion. I hope this volume honors your commitment and stands as a testament to the wonders of scholarly inquisition.

Secondly, I would like to thank Harry Keyishian, director of Fairleigh Dickinson University Press, whose generous spirit and sure wisdom nurtured this book along. Your patience and keen eye were a comfort during a difficult stage in this project. He, along with my colleague Don Mell, assured me that this volume would make a tremendous contribution to American Studies. Any setbacks encountered would be for scholarly gain. I thank them for their encouragement and their confidence that this volume would see the light of day. I would be remiss if I didn't thank Christine A. Retz, whose editorial gifts and technical expertise make this project presentable. Your attention to detail is admirable.

That said, I would also like to thank the English department at the University of Delaware for a research developmental grant. These funds were instrumental in helping me to secure copyrights for the four essays reprinted in this study. Likewise, I want to acknowledge Thomas A. Robinson, J.D., and Diane Grosse, Rights and Permissions Manager at Duke University Press, Kate Johnson of Georges Borchardt, Inc., and Dr. Charles Johnson for their wonderful collegiality in securing copyright permission. Their prompt attention to my requests and concerns are gratefully acknowledged here.

I would also like to thank Media Services at the University of Delaware, particularly Becky Rothwell, for assistance in getting printed materials to typeset. Thomas Butts at Office Max in Newark, Delaware was a godsend during the final stages of this project. His technical expertise saved me weeks of typing, and for that I am forever grateful. To the editorial staff at Fairleigh Dickinson University Press—thank you for nurturing this project as if it were your own. These pages are a tribute to your spirit of excellence, and it has been a pleasure to work with you.

Lastly, I would like to thank my church family at Bethel AME Church for their prayers and spiritual support. Your smiles, kind words, hugs, and gestures of love were a warm blanket on a rainy day. I cherish you. And to my husband Leroy and my son Kelsey, thank you for allowing me the room to fulfill my earthly purpose. My love for you can not fill these pages. Only my heart knows the depth of my gratitude for you. Thanks for being in my life. And finally to my grandparents, Mr. and Mrs. Roscoe Marbley Sr., Mr. and Mrs. Elvin Henderson Sr., and my parents Mr. Willie B. Henderson Sr. and Ms. Barbara J. Henderson: thanks for lighting the way.

Introduction: Bordering on the Black Body: Text and Subtext in America's Literature and Culture

Carol E. Henderson

> How does one come to accept and affirm a body so despised by one's fellow citizens?
>
> —Cornel West, *Race Matters*

IN HER PROVOCATIVE PRESIDENTIAL ADDRESS FOR THE AMERICAN Studies Association, then President Mary Helen Washington poses a question for her audience that is relevant to the collection proposed here. "What happens to American Studies if you put African American Studies at the center?"[1] That is, how does the study of America look when the formerly marginal topics and/or theoretical issues of African American Studies become part of the mainstream culture of intellectual inquiry in American Studies? Washington's question is an interesting one. Her methodological approach presupposes an institutional challenge to the "possessive investment in whiteness"[2] that so prevalently frames "traditional" American Studies programs and scholarship—those investments that, more often than not, exclude ethnic cultural voices—or at the very least, frame these voices in the imaginary conundrum of one-dimensional cultural representations that reinscribe and/or reinforce the cultural myths of white supremacy. Washington's philosophical considerations direct attention to the "prophetic allegory"[3] of our current social reality on race politics, and these critiques also function as a subtext for the parallel universes that exist in the academy. Here, the daily indignations and humiliations of intolerance become enabled by the tokenisms of a number of educational institutions who deploy a few ethnic studies scholars within select departments in effort to "spice up" the college curriculum without rethinking the framework of American Studies on the whole. As Washington points out:

> While those in American Studies were lighting out for the territory, on the pioneer trail from East to West, [we] Black Studies [were] following other itineraries: the triangular slave trade, the underground railroad, and the Great Migration . . . while American studies scholars were still immersed in *Virgin Land*, *The Machine in the Garden*, and Turner's frontier thesis, we were reading Lerone Bennett's *Before the Mayflower*, Malcolm X's speeches, the essays and stories in *Black World*, [and] John Hope Franklin's *From Slavery to Freedom*.[4]

Placing emphasis on the varying approaches to what it means to be "American," Washington identifies the organizing principles of the American Studies community. In this community, small gestures of preclusion create unmediated dialogues of belonging that reveal the true nature of nation building within the institutional life of the academy. It is in the shadow of these conversations that practice and principle meet as the authority to establish a discernable American identity rests in determining the representations of this identity in signs and symbols, in laws and literatures, in cultural and social practices.

Washington's meditations point up the paradoxical nature of speaking one's difference while acknowledging the social and cultural institutions that fashion, and likewise mythologize these differences. As critic Stuart Hall reminds us, cultural identity is not a fixed reality, but an ever-evolving production—a positioning of selves within the fragmented sutures of history and culture. In these sutures, social forces stake claims to fields of representation in the racial economy of Western culture. Hence, there is always "a politics of identity, a politics of position," a place of struggle.[5] It is here that we see the vertiginous encounters with "otherness," circumscribed in the flesh of peoples defined by the body. Socially the natural body is coded as a fleshly field of dreams—a projected and imagined representation of identity formations that reinvest the political and cultural objectives of the dominant power structure. Explicit in this line of inquiry are the enduring legacies of the "already-already known" dialogues on race and their implications for identifying systems of subjugation within the universal community of human dwellers. These "dialogues," which constitute the cultural and theoretical essence of America's developing discourse on "difference," shape the racial imaginings of our culture, and as such, provide a segue into the implicit and explicit historical and social development of American identity, particularly as it relates to the "black" body. Historical reflection will demonstrate that the black body has been a crucial apparatus in the development of a cultural discourse that color codes power within the dynamics of social remembrances. It is these remembrances that constitute the basis of

U.S. history, and as such, posits the black body and its flesh as a literal and figurative repository of these memories. As critic Hortense Spillers suggests, the social pathology of cultural and critical discourses makes the black body an interlocking contradiction of various possibilities—it is at once "a thing," becoming *being* for the dominant society, and its flesh serves as a primary narrative: its woundedness, its tears, scars, openings, ruptures and lesions a template of the Western world's hieroglyphic language.[6] Thus what is at stake in these discussions is the self-fashioning of these memories recorded on the flesh as the relationship between the aesthetic and the political become contested sites of resistance for the rematerialization of national and communal identities.

The shape these identities take, however, has as much to do with those referential systems of discourse that map the ideologies of "whiteness" onto the black flesh, as it does with the currency of "blackness" that undergirds the architectural formations of U.S. primacy. As social activist bell hooks makes abundantly clear, long before explorers defined the borders of what we now know as the United States, they had developed images of blackness and African people that would validate their ideas of racial superiority, "their political imperialism, their will to dominate and enslave."[7] The brilliance of this system is its simultaneity—the ways in which the black body and its identity are seized upon and made markers for the grounding of social limits. By default—and design—white America gains its footing in establishing preeminent power. It is in its signs and wonders, the literature, print and visual media, social and jurisprudence and/or juridical law—all become devices for augmenting incalculable control of the black body. In short, the system reproduces itself in ways that, as writer Toni Morrison demonstrates, necessitated the nation develop "coded language and purposeful restriction to deal with the racial disingenuousness and moral frailty at its heart."[8] Thus the complex and varied social meanings formed around these resilient markers of native and foreign beings situated in this "Africanist/Americanist" dialogue direct attention back to the structures that form these identities through textual and sociological dimensions of representations that conjure up coded performances of race. These *manifested* images form the basis of a currency of race that constantly reinvents itself at every level of our social stratum.

This domination—its colonial fallout—is expressed in the critical exercise of normalization that constructs difference within the categories of knowledge commonly known in the West. According to Stuart Hall, the traumatic character of colonialism rests in the power to make one see and experience him or herself as the Other. "It is one thing to position a subject or set of peoples as the Other of a dominant discourse," writes Hall. "It is quite another thing to subject them to that 'knowledge,' not only as a matter of imposed will and domination, [but also] by the power of inner compulsion and subjective con-formation to the norm."[9] This "conformity to the norm" breeds systems of nihilistic behavior and self-destruction that results in high incidents of violence, incarceration, unemployment and undereducation in some segments of the African American community. In others, the contempt for self is bore out in the twisted logic and/or lavish lifestyles that has some African American people refusing to love and respect their own bodies. As Cornel West reminds us, white supremacist ideology is based foremost on "the degradation of black bodies in order to control them." This system is best sustained "by convincing them that their bodies are ugly, their intellect is inherently underdeveloped, their culture is less civilized, and their future warrants less concern than that of other peoples."[10]

This troubling dynamic forms the basis of poverty and despair and generates a cultural division that not only reinforces but escalates the explosive racial tensions of American life. As Ralph Ellison aptly stated some thirty-five years ago,

> Since the beginning of the nation, white Americans have suffered from a deep inner uncertainty as to who they really are. One of the ways that has been used to simplify the answer has been to seize upon the presence of black Americans and use them as a marker, a symbol of limits, a metaphor for the "outsider." Many whites could look at the social position of blacks and feel that color formed an easy and reliable gauge for determining to what extent one was or was not American.[11]

This is a slippery slope, though, as Ellison reminds us. The irrefutable presence of African Americans and other immigrants in the United States raises concerns about not only the legitimacy of "the white man's value system, but arouses the troubling suspicion that whatever else the true American is, he is also somehow black."[12]

The chapters in this collection will explore the parameters of this "identity" formation—its coded restrictions, its denotative and connotative meanings—through the signs and bodies that have come to represent the figurative and literal manifestations of America's grammar within the body of literature written on and about race and culture. Such an examination will reveal the intricate balance American social and political discourse has had to maintain to promote the ideals of "whiteness" using manifestly different criterion for disavowing blackness. American literature has been a primary tool of this cultural apparatus. But as the first section of this volume will demonstrate, the fields of science, law, and economics were also instrumental in shoring up the ornamental trappings of a racialized aesthetic. In "Race Matters: Texts and Contexts," the authors engage in a number of critical and theoretical fields in an effort to apprehend the cultural practice of "writing" the national body vis-à-vis the black body in our nation's public forums and printed materials. In "Narrating African American Subjectivity," Richard Schur traces the enabling hierarchies of legal discourse that "infused and affected legal thought even when legal discourse omitted specific mention of race." Employing the use of literary techniques like storytelling and autobiography by legal scholars such as Derrick Bell and Patricia Williams, Schur argues that these authors were successful in pointing out the unconscious racialization of legal discourse through their use of African American subjects as rhetorical figures. However such a linkage proves problematic, in Schur's estimation, undermining the very reasoning behind such discussions as the visible and nonvisible properties of whiteness become reified in these dynamics.

In "Distorted Images in Travel Literature: An Exploration of the Subjugation of Blackness in the Western World," Katrina Dyonne Thompson suggests that the function of travel journals as popular literature in the early republic served to solidify the image of the black body as deviant in the public sphere, and thus the journals help to set the foundations for race in the United States of America. Travel journals represented the "National Geographic" of its day, according to Thompson, and as such, should be viewed as a viable source for the critical assessments of perverted images of otherness despite their biased presentations. The material relevance of these cultural artifacts is found in the manner in which they create the exotic African body, revealing, to a large degree, the inextricable tie between travel and global expansion, representation, and exploitation.

Allison E. Francis expands Thompson's trajectory of the culture of nonfictional accounts of the development of America's early life to include an analysis of "The Culture of Sentiments and the Black Female Body in the Nineteenth-Century Literary Marketplace." In her chapter Francis argues that black women's participation in the abolitionist circuit in 1840s North America afforded Afro-Caribbean writers such as Mary Prince and Mary Seacole, and other African American writers like Harriet Jacobs and Harriet Wilson the opportunity to reinvent themselves through the act of telling their stories. "By fleshing out their experiences on paper," writes Francis, "black writers were, in effect, circulating themselves in the literary marketplace in a daring and novel way by imagining textual bodies that would supplant their literal ones." This textual body stands as a counter to the known socially deviant black body constructed under slavery's gaze, making "familiar" to the white American and British reading audiences the plight of disenfranchised blacks.

Francis's correlation between the economics of the flesh and the economy of the flesh points up the fundamental difficulty of interrogating the mythological and philosophical dualism of the body complexion and the body incarnate. It is the body complexion that allows the United States and its global communities to build systems of inclusion and exclusion along the borders of the flesh. At stake are those properties of whiteness and blackness that govern material forces and class interests within the infrastructure of U.S. social order. But these systems begin with ideas—ideas primarily sustained by the ideological reading of the black body in the white mind. In "Emerson's Platonic Influence," Elizabeth Schroeder investigates the intersections of racial thought and philosophical inquiry in her analysis of Emerson's prose and poetry. Schroeder concludes that Emerson's notions of power, proportionality, and the aesthetics "lionizes and silences" the black body through a variety of tactics and rhetorical strategies that form not only his race-based notions of the aesthetics, but also influence his Western philosophies on power and beauty. "Such a transformation of bodies helps pull beauty and power back to certain white male bodies," writes Schroeder, "that embody the proportion necessary for Emerson to remain at the top of this hierarchy. Such a self-radiating space securely places political power and beauty in the hands of the white male."

Schroeder's appraisal of Emerson's philosophical politics align themselves nicely with David Krell's "The Bodies of Black Folk: From Kant and Hegel to DuBois and Baldwin." In his chapter Krell traces the intellectual and artistic development of African American philosophers whose studies abroad help to shape not only their scholarly pursuits but also their global perspectives of blackness in America. At first glance, this evaluation may not seem unique. It is logical to assume that black minds and white minds have always communicated across racial, cultural, and civic barriers irrespective of time or place. But Krell situates his interrogation of these minds—W.E.B. DuBois and James Baldwin, Immanuel Kant and Georg Hegel more specifically—in their generally bleak account of black bodies and Africa. In Krell's estimation, these *bodies* disturb Hegel's philosophy of nature in a way that complicates the essentialist notions of the European intellectual tradition, yet as Krell concludes, "European study remains an essential part of the education of black folk in our time." As such,

W.E.B. DuBois and James Baldwin's exploration of the souls of black folk in the Americas enjoins itself to the intimate proximity of European culture's inestimable value of blackness.

Krell's global examination of the ways of black and white folk reveals a breathtaking attention to ideologies of "whiteness" that influence social interactions amongst groups of people. At the center of this interaction is the black body—imagined and imaged—in the seamless stories of folk culture that give life to the resilience of American racism. Yet embedded in this web of ever-changing intellectual rationalizations are those gestures of resistance subtly interwoven in the discursive practices of African American writers. In part two, "Mutual Relations: Race, Gender, Formation," the authors extend the time-centered analyses of the previous section to chronicle the conscious and unconscious desires and/or fears that undergird the discursive and visual practices of representation of race and gender, its performance, and interpretation in African American and American literatures. In "The Sentimental Slave Body in Frederick Douglass's *The Heroic Slave*," Therese Rizzo explores the tenuous connection that exists between white women and the slave population in one of Douglass's most critically neglected pieces of writing. Here, Rizzo charts Frederick Douglass's appropriation of the sentimental tradition in order to unveil the complex merge between the racialized (black) slave body and the domesticated (white) female body. According to Rizzo, *The Heroic Slave* maneuvers Sentimentalism's hyperfeminized domestic landscape to explore issues of masculine angst and racial oppression. Such an examination not only reveals the violence inherent in plantation life (a given in some respects), but it also makes known the physical threat of surveillance of the sexualized and gendered racialized body in the domestic space. Douglass positions the black male body as a form of cultural mulatto-ism, according to Rizzo, who uses white domesticity and its illusive promise of safety as a vehicle to narrate the dangers to black masculinity.

Extending the paradigmatic structure of Rizzo's analysis, Henry B. Wonham determines in "Writing Realism, Policing Consciousness" that surveillance of the black body in the city reveals the conscious and unconscious fears of self-identity in writers like Henry James and William Dean Howells. Howells, in particular, was "decidedly squeamish about representing the self in Jamesian terms as a form of process," according to his most avid critics and, according to Wonham, entertained the image of a free-floating consciousness that found its residence in the black characters that peopled his fiction. This psychological materiality—projected in the "alien" clothing and bodily gestures of blacks in Boston—became a way to channel Howells' outward anxieties about self. As Wonham concludes, "Howells' infrequent but charged representation of blackness is one of several literary strategies that make this region of the mind, or this image of the self, accessible to his imagination." This black presence functions as an "enabler" according to Wonham, a "projection of the not me," using Toni Morrison's idea of the Africanist presence, "mirroring forth an image that Howells cannot approach directly."

Wonham's astute assessments of Howells' fiction, most notably his novel *An Imperative Duty*, underscore the ethical and aesthetic cost associated with the sense of terror that awaits a self that has no bearings. Howells's fictional black body becomes the vehicle for representing that presence that haunts so much of American Literature, and it also becomes the site of a reflexive meditation on the self. In "Genealogical Ambiguity and Racial Identity," Marina Fedosik investigates the degrees of agency present in the passing narratives of Kate Chopin and Jessie Fauset. Pointing to M. Giulia Fabi's assertion that white-authored representations of the tragic mulatto differ distinctly from African American representations of miscegenation and passing, Fedosik argues for a reevaluation of the bodies of female passing adoptees that complicates known studies of racial purity. In Fedosik's estimation, the fluidity and vulnerability of the passing adoptee's body encourages angst and anxiety when reestablishing familial ties through marriage. In each instance blackness is seen as something to be examined and identified—and the knowledge of who is black and who is not becomes a powerful and dangerous weapon in undermining America's racial hierarchy within the space of these texts. Analogously childbirth and the child's body serve as a rite of passage into the white world for these women, restructuring notions of whiteness and blackness within the American body politic.

Who or what makes an American within the national/international body politic drives the critical discussion of the third part, "Body/Language: Visions and Revisions." Here, the conventionality of the racial paradigms posited in sections one and two give way to the reenvisioned aesthetics of the body and its language. Authors Laura Doyle, Carol E. Henderson, Simone Drake, and Charles Johnson, reassess the theoretical shifts in texture and technique that shape the body's language in the American body politic. The often-contentious atmosphere created by these public "discussions" constitute the cultural and theoretical essence of America's developing discourse on "difference," shaping the racial imaginings of our culture. Black bodies undergo constant transformation in this space as the continuous interplay of history, culture and power, collides with the production of a new black subjectivity. Such grounding can pervert the natural impulse for ownership of one's person. These dispossessed bodies, fractured representations of the American ideal, presuppose "possession" as a staple of imagined possibilities that recontextualize the parameters of identity formation.

In "The Body against Itself in Faulkner's Phenomenology of Race," Laura Doyle unfolds the history of Anglo-America through the violent internal rupture of the Civil War. In this context, bodies that form the post-bellum nation in the United States, "be they native American, immigrant, or ex-slave, likewise suffer betrayal from within—exiled physically from home and past yet haunted by them in memory." It is this haunting that enfolds Doyle's evaluation of William Faulkner's *Light in August.* Doyle argues that the fundamental slippage of self-coherence in the novel mirrors "the ontological rupture of the racialized body in the South, which itself reiterates the traumatic crossing of liberty and slavery in the nation's body." Thus the real and the imagined, the verifiable and the undefinable properties of national belonging become projected onto the black and white bodies in Faulkner's text, revealing the collapse of the national body into itself as the "ghostly witnesses in the ongoing spectacle of bodies, race, and violence in the South" become ensnarled in the complicated legacies of history.

It is this history that frames the discourse for Carol E. Henderson's reading of the Emmett Till murder in "Policing the Racial Divide: The Body, The Nation, and the Emmett Till Murder." As Henderson argues, Till's murder stands at the crossroads of America's cultural debates over segregation and desegregation, freedom and neo-slavery, as the battered frame of this fourteen-year-old boy signaled to the world the ugly realities of racial hatred in the South—and the cost of pseudo-freedom. But more than that, Till's murder brought to the forefront society's barely repressed fears of black male sexuality and masculinity. The interplay between fact and fantasy, mythmaking and mythological fulfillment, or, as is the case in the Till murder, the *perceived* threat of acting upon or acting out this racial fantasy, underscores the ways in which the black male body is fashioned as Other, sexualized, and demonized. It is the *suggestion* that "little black boys grow up to be big black men" that amplifies white male and white female anxiety in this case, particularly as it relates to the issue of miscegenation. This subtext underwrites the cultural narrative of this murder as notions of manhood become inextricably tied to the "preservation" of nation, honor, and white womanhood.

In "A Space Beyond Beulah: Assessing the Mixed Race Body," Simone Drake troubles the relationship between geography and mixed-race bodies in her examination of Danzy Senna's short story, "The

Land of Beulah." Drake argues that the "future face of America" is ubiquitously represented in the multiple representations of otherness evident in Senna's text. Using Paul Gilroy's *Against Race: Imagining Political Culture Beyond the Color Line* (2000) as a critical canvas, Drake suggests that U.S. racial geographies are mapped on the mixed-race and black bodies of the inhabitants of Beulah in such a restrictive manner that complicates rather than fosters the postracial racial state Gilroy seeks. According to Drake, "race both matters and is rendered impotent" in Beulah, becoming not the marker for postracial identity strategies, but rather a reminder of a past that haunts the present racial formation of the imagined American state.

Such reconsiderations of racialized identities shape the focus of the last chapter of this book, "A Phenomenology of the Black Body." Taking as its subject the dynamic constructions of whiteness and blackness, Charles Johnson returns our gaze to the black male body while he interrogates the unfamiliar realm of knowing and being that forces each of us to renegotiate socially assigned roles daily. As Johnson points out, "before we can talk intelligently about the 'black experience' of the body . . . we must first get clear on what is essential to all experience—the correlate of consciousness and its content." It is this content that shapes a racial experience fraught with myths and painful realities. This chaos fuels the ambiguities that bracket the sociological and scientific theories concerning race and distorts the self-image of the individual who inhabits this "black body." It is this self-consciousness that must contend with the pathological feelings of self-perception that sees the peripheral vision of the body as skin and as social being. "[Frantz] Fanon is correct," writes Johnson. " 'not only must the black man be black; he must be black in relation to the white man'. . . . because it is from whites that the intention, the 'meaning' of the black body comes." Citing his own personal experience at a bar, Johnson laments, "I sit at the bar, ignoring the Others; but the body is acutely aware of them, knows immediately when someone outside my peripheral vision has stood up. It is intense, as though consciousness has shifted to the skin's seen surfaces."

Johnson's explorations into these theories of race and race consciousness redirect attention to the phenomenological experiences of the black body.[13] This body is a moving signifier, a canvas of convergent ideologies that says more about America than America is willing to say about itself. Our experiences as human beings can be best understood in the expressions of symbols, signs, stereotypes, and myths that revolve around this body—a body that lays bare the angst and anxiety of cultural identities built on the fragile multiplicities of a myriad of self-images. It is in these moments of reflection that the true character of America emerges—mythical, constant, ever changing. And it is in these moments that we must determine what it is to be human irrespective and yet respective of our differences and our geographical locations. Our loyalty to life depends on it. Our commitment to humankind makes it a matter of life and death.

Notes

1. Mary Helen Washington, "Disturbing the Peace: What Happens to American Studies If You Put African American Studies at the Center?" Presidential Address to the American Studies Association, October 29, 1997." *American Quarterly* 50, no. 1 (1998), 1.
2. George Lipsitz, as quoted in "Disturbing the Peace," 21.
3. This is Washington's term that she develops with critic Kevin Meehan during their many hours listening to the 1997 album *Octoroon* by Laura Love, and evaluating the 1996 movie *Lone Star* (directed by John Sayles). As Washington sees it *Lone Star* functions as a "prophetic allegory" for three reasons: first, it shows the system of white supremacy as a system of decay. Second, it projects a forward-thinking, but not utopian vision of new multicultural social institutions—society as what one character calls "a damn menudo." Finally, *Lone Star* insists that personal cross-cultural experiences only become comprehensible and liberatory when they are connected to a relevant institutional history. ("Disturbing the Peace" 11–12).
4. Washington, "Disturbing the Peace," 2.
5. Stuart Hall, "Cultural Identity and Diaspora," 299.
6. Hortense Spillers, "Mama's Baby, Papa's Maybe: An American Grammar Book," 67.
7. bell hooks, *Black Looks*, 2.
8. Toni Morrison, *Playing in the Dark*, 6.
9. Stuart Hall, "Cultural Identity and Diaspora," 299.
10. Cornel West, *Race Matters*, 123.
11. "What America Would Be Like without Blacks," 110–11.
12. Ibid.
13. Johnson's definition of phenomenology is a good one: for every object there is always a corresponding subject. Likewise Johnson argues that "consciousness is always consciousness *of* something" (Ibid., 224).

Works Cited

Ellison, Ralph. "What America Would Be Like without Blacks." In *Going To The Territory*. New York: Vintage Books, 1986.

Hall, Stuart. "Cultural Identity and Diaspora." In *Everyday Theory: A Contemporary Reader* edited by Becky McLaughlin and Bob Coleman, 295–306. New York: Pearson and Longman, 2005.

hooks, bell. *Black Looks: Race and Representation*. Boston: South End Press, 1992.

Morrison, Toni. *Playing in the Dark: Whiteness and the Literary Imagination*. Cambridge, MA: Harvard University Press, 1992.

Spillers, Hortense J. "Mama's Baby, Papa's Maybe: An American Grammar Book." *Diacritics* 17, no. 2 (Summer 1987): 65–80.

Washington, Mary Helen. "Disturbing the Peace: What Happens to American Studies If You Put African American Studies at the Center?: Presidential Address to the American Studies Association, October 29, 1997." In *American Quarterly* 50, no. 1 (1998):1–23.

West, Cornel. *Race Matters*. New York: Vintage, 1993.

America
and the Black Body

I
Race Matters: Texts and Contexts

Narrating African American Subjectivity through the Body: Critical Race Theory and Legal Discourse

Richard Schur

ANGLO-AMERICAN JURISPRUDENCE, ESPECIALLY SINCE THE ENLIGHTenment, has sought to create putatively objective legal doctrines that operate without respect to a particular person's identity or standing in society. Some commentators have characterized this shift as one that has moved from status to contract because law has moved away from imposing a social hierarchy and allowed individuals to determine social relationships based on their preferences or desires. Despite this general trend toward creating legal doctrines based on abstracted notions of personhood, race along with gender, has continued to shape legal discourse. Law permitted race-based slavery through 1865 and sanctioned race-based segregation until the 1950s. As Ian Haney Lopez demonstrates in his analysis of immigration, courts applied the rights of citizenship to white (male) bodies while they excluded bodies found to be nonwhite from citizenship and/or denied them the full exercise of their rights.[1] As the scholarship of Haney Lopez and others documents, African Americans, Latinos, and Asian Americans consistently challenged their exclusion from and special status within legal discourse. During the Civil Rights Movement, numerous racial and ethnic groups sought to expand existing doctrines to include historically marginalized groups. Movement lawyers persuaded courts to adopt innovative strategies for realizing the egalitarian impulses of Anglo-American law by crafting specific remedies for African Americans, Latinos, and Asian Americans who had long suffered from acts of individual and institutional discrimination.

During the 1970s, courts began moving away from constructing remedies for racism and racial hierarchy—both historical and ongoing. In cases such as *Milliken vs. Bradley*[2] and *Bakke vs. Regents of California*,[3] the United States Supreme Court limited the kinds of integration strategies that could be created.[4] Increasingly, the courts argued, as they did in *Bakke*, any mention of race was impermissible because "when a State's distribution of benefits or imposition of burdens hinges on ancestry or the color of a person's skin, that individual is entitled to a demonstration that the challenged classification is necessary to promote a substantial state interest."[5] The Court held that the system of admissions for medical school at issue in *Bakke* failed to meet this strict test and, in effect, demanded a colorblind or neutral methodology for making judgments and allocating resources.[6]

In the 1980s, legal scholars began questioning why legal discourse retreated from questions of racial equality during the post–civil rights period.[7] Influenced by the burgeoning of postmodernism and poststructuralism, many white legal scholars, primarily associated with critical legal studies (CLS), concluded that legal reasoning was indeterminate due to the malleability of legal language, the instability of the fact-value distinction, and the commitment to legal process over substantive equality.[8] These scholars expressed deep skepticism about rights discourse as well. For CLS, rights discourse offered merely a fundamental contradiction because those who most need it are the ones failed by current institutional arrangements and legal doctrines.[9] Peter Gabel, in a famous dialogue with Duncan Kennedy, asserts that rights "don't exist" and that they ought to be "trashed."[10] For Gabel and Kennedy, rights discourse constitutes an overbroad, abstract strategy to resolve the forces of alienation and dehumanization, which civil rights activism sought to remedy.[11] They advocate abandoning formal legal analysis in favor of developing human relationships and communal ties as more fruitful avenues for addressing the persistence of inequality.

Although they initially join in the conferences and conversations associated with CLS, legal scholars of color soon found that "racial power was exerting itself within CLS."[12] These scholars developed an alternative forum and discourse, critical race theory (CRT), to discuss issues of racialized power, which CLS tended to ignore.[13] They identify a number of themes and/or methods, which highlighted their critique of CLS: intersectionality,[14] multiple consciousness,[15] interest convergence thesis,[16] anti-essentialism,[17] and storytelling.[18] Between 1987 and 1997, CRT flourished within the legal academy.[19] Although numerous positions existed within the movement, CRT primarily focuses on exploring how racial subjectivity infused and affected legal thought even when legal discourse has omitted specific mention of race. Contra CLS claims, the civil rights movement failed to realize its ultimate vision, not because legal reasoning was indeterminate and thus alienating, but because lawyers, judges, and lawmakers' commitments to objectivity, neutrality, and legal process masked and enabled racial hierarchy and oppression.

Deconstructing the aspiration for a colorblind jurisprudence, CRT sought to revise CLS's approach to resolving social and cultural conflict. They engage not in abstract epistemological theorizing but articulated how the lived experience of racial minorities influenced the application of legal principles and doctrines.[20] In a seminal article entitled "A Critique of Our Constitution Is Color-Blind," Neil Gotanda illustrated the difference between CRT and CLS methodologies by moving away from exploring indeterminacy to focusing on how racial subjectivity shapes and affects legal reasoning. He shows how the desire for colorblindness requires judges to ignore the lived experiences of historically marginalized people and forces them to disembody and universalize their claims within ahistorical and decontextualized categories,[21] even as private decision making rests upon unspoken and invidious racialized thinking.[22] Gotanda argues that integration and assimilation became goals for legal activists within the civil rights movement precisely because they emphasize the homogeneity assumed by universal liberal constructs[23] and matched the cultural assumptions of many judges and legislators.[24] Tracing its historical and theoretical origins, Gotanda concludes that legal discourse has failed to remedy racism because it understands race as a physical description, rather than as a source of domination and power.[25] Against CLS, Gotanda attempts to show that it is not the general failure of legal reasoning and doctrines, but the unconscious racial biases upon which they are based that limited the gains of the civil rights movement.

In order to challenge colorblindness as jurisprudential value and respond to CLS's indeterminacy critique, the founding figures from CRT turned to literary techniques, especially storytelling and autobiography. They sought to deploy literary tropes to demonstrate how unspoken racialized assumptions continue to guide legal reasoning and infuse legal discourse with a black perspective. Across ethnic, racial, doctrinal, and linguistic boundaries, CRT increasingly argued that scholars of color spoke in a unique or distinct voice, which could counter unconscious racialized and gendered assumptions within legal discourse.[26] Derrick Bell, Patricia Williams, and Richard Delgado pushed literary techniques the furthest by building numerous essays, articles, and books around short stories, autobiographical writings, and dialogues. Others introduced or punctuated their analyses by referencing personal anecdotes.[27] Not all CRT scholars use such techniques,[28] nor did all CRT theorists rely on minority voice as a primary element of their legal criticisms.[29] Jerome Culp, however, astutely noted that CRT could not escape questions of subjectivity and authorship because scholars of color and others cannot "find a neutral place to observe how race interacts with legal decision-making."[30] Their critics, especially Richard Posner, Daniel Farber, and Suzanna Sherry, frequently reduced CRT to "voice scholarship" in order to avoid addressing CRT's concern that personal bias impeded the realization of liberal legal theories' ideals.[31] While most CRT writers share the concern with recuperating the goals of liberal theory, they frequently differ over what strategies would best accomplish that goal.

Once CRT advocated identifying and reconstructing legal subjectivity, the presence of a body marked as black (or as any other historically marginalized group) became a common strategy to represent epistemological gaps within legal reasoning. Borrowing a civil rights-era slogan from SNCC (Student Nonviolent Coordinating Committee), Mari Matsuda asks CRT: "where is your body?"[32] In its original meaning, the question references how middle-class African Americans participated in civil rights demonstrations by violating unjust laws in order to protest them. For CRT, the question emphasizes that debates over abstract legal doctrines have all too frequently replaced the protests of an earlier era. Without actual protesting bodies, CLS and other thinkers influenced by postmodernism could elide the experiences and struggles of historically marginalized people in favor of theoretical critiques.[33] Through literary techniques that emphasized the experiences of nonwhite people, CRT attempted to demonstrate that people "are all characters in a narrative. . . . We just fool ourselves into thinking otherwise."[34]

By plotting actual bodies within legal discourse's accounts of social relations, CRT sought to illustrate how race tends to shape cultural relations and legal decisions. The use of real and/or fictionalized bodies enabled CRT to create metaphors that could represent the ongoing irony of African American experiences within legal discourse, notwithstanding the civil rights revolution of the 1950s and 1960s. This chapter identifies and explores three significant textual moments that affected the development of and have become emblematic of CRT analysis: (1) Derrick Bell's story about Geneva Crenshaw traveling back to 1787 to persuade the Constitution's drafters to outlaw slavery; (2) Bell's appropriation of Jesse B. Semple, Langston Hughes's creation, to inject class within contemporary discussions of race; and (3) Patricia Williams's account of her exclusion at a lower Manhattan Benetton store and her subsequent difficulty in writing about and analyzing this encounter for legal audiences.[35] Using Gerard Genette's idea of the paratext, especially as developed by Beth McCoy, this chapter explores Bell and Williams's use of African American bodies as rhetorical figures that affect their meaning and interpretation of their texts.[36] Engaging in a specifically literary critique, as opposed to the typical legal or cultural studies lenses typically applied to their work, I will argue that this literary strategy of deploying black bodies, either as fiction or autobiography, allows CRT—not simply Bell and Williams—to offer a necessarily partial opening to engage in multicultural conversation about race.[37] In this analysis, the African American body offers both a potentially knowable metaphor for readers of multiple racial identities and provides a limit on the transferability of the knowledge produced through the act of writing.[38]

Critics have long identified narrative as a key tool for struggling against stereotypes and racism.[39] In 1926, W.E.B. DuBois told a gathering of the National Association for the Advancement of Colored People (NAACP) that "all Art is propaganda and ever must be . . . [and] whatever art I have for writing has been used always for propaganda for gaining the right of black folk to love and enjoy."[40] More recently, Henry Louis Gates, Jr., has written that "the ultimate form of protest, certainly, was to register in print the existence of a 'black self' that had transcended the limitations and restrictions that racism had placed on the personal development of the black individual."[41] Based on his analysis of slave narratives and autobiographies, Gates, in effect, claims such self-portraits possess a greater purpose than merely creating a historical record. Rather, he argues that these writers must use their bodies and their stories to fashion a public self, a subject position otherwise unavailable within dominant cultural discourses.

In his classic study of African American narrative, *From Behind the Veil*, Robert Stepto echoes Gates and argues that constructing one's self through literacy and narrative has proven a fundamental feature of the "Afro-American quest for freedom."[42] Stepto, however, asserts that African Americans have preferred the label storyteller over that of storywriter because the former emphasizes the transfer of knowledge between persons.[43] African American writers distrust writing and narrative because "the principal unreliable factor in the storytelling paradigm is the reader (white American readers, obviously, but blacks as well)."[44] In other words, as much as African Americans may want to challenge racial inequalities through their work, these writers are equally aware that readers filter and interpret their words through a preexisting matrix of ideas, biases, and values. Stepto's analysis of African American writing commences with the slave narrative to provide an overview of the relationship between the narratives and their authenticating documents.[45] In relation to Bell and Williams's work, Stepto's analysis offers some potentially surprising analogs to the slave narrative: (1) CRT texts must (still) negotiate the assumptions readers bring to their texts; (2) African American bodies cannot speak for themselves as the writer must make the bodies intelligible for both characters in their narratives and their readers; and (3) an abundance of authenticating documents and/or frames must be deployed to aid the characters and readers in decoding the meaning of the black body.

While many critics have either praised or condemned CRT in large part based on the work of Bell and Williams, few have examined the elaborate framing devices they deploy to stabilize the historical ambiguity of black bodies. CRT's analysis of race's effects on legal reasoning follows from their insight that color blindness, or a veil of racial ignorance, can sometimes reinforce racial hierarchy. Blackness need not be explicitly mentioned nor physically present to shape public policy and legal decision making. It merely must be referenced through a metaphor or proxy. CRT attempts to examine how such metaphors or proxies operate within legal discourse and thus undo the supposed rationality of law. By reintroducing black bodies into legal analysis, Bell and Williams seek to reveal the unspoken but all too real ways legal discourse is complicit with racism and white supremacy. However before introducing these black bodies, which will illustrate the irrationality of legal discourse, they offer an endless array of prologues, introductions, and additional texts. These framing devices reveal Bell and Williams's concern that their stories and the African American bodies within them will be misunderstood and serve as guides for the reader's understanding.[46]

And We Are Not Saved, Bell's first book of fictional dialogues, exemplifies the extensive use of framing devices as part of its literary strategy. It relies on a preface, introduction, and a prologue to prepare the reader for stories that follow.[47] These texts explain why Bell began writing fiction, offer a brief historical overview of the civil rights and post–civil rights eras, and provide background on the characters that appear in the dialogues. Bell creates an alter ego for himself, a black law professor who worked in the civil rights movement. Geneva Crenshaw is Bell's first interlocutor. She is a brilliant lawyer from the civil rights movement who disappeared from public view but has returned as would be prophet from the mysterious Curia with a series of tales about the current state of African Americans. In his second book, Bell introduces the reader to Jesse B. Semple, a revisionist version of Langston Hughes's famous character who imparted working-class wisdom to a member of the black bourgeoisie. Interestingly Bell embeds his most graphic, thought-provoking, and challenging stories within dialogues. In other words, he does not directly present the events through objective descriptions or first-person narratives, but conveys them through the interpretative conflicts between Bell's alter ego and either Crenshaw or Semple.

In *The Alchemy of Race and Rights*, Patricia Williams also layers a number of subtitles, section headings, and introductory chapters to guide the reader through her main argument. Her first chapter, although it operates more like a preface, describes vividly how her own racial subjectivity will inevitably affect her analysis throughout the book and that many readers will criticize her work for failing to meet the standard of objectivity demanded by legal scholarship.[48] Her second chapter explains how her interest in contract law follows from her attempt to understand her family history, especially as contract law shaped how owners treated her ancestors. Interwoven with this personal narrative, Williams discusses how contemporary legal discourse has failed to adequately remedy race's influence on social and cultural relations.[49] These two chapters serve as necessary foundations to guide the reader's understanding of the infamous Benetton incident, which will be discussed and analyzed below.

Gerard Genette, a French literary critic, identifies such framing devices as "paratexts" and has noted a large number of subordinate textual elements that, despite their apparently generic or formulaic nature, play a profound role in shaping a text's meaning. He eloquently describes their role in protecting the text's integrity:

> More than a boundary or a sealed border, the paratext is rather a *threshold*, or—a word Borges used apropos of a preface—a "vestibule" that offers the world at large the possibility of either stepping inside or turning back. It is an "undefined zone" between the inside and the outside, a zone without any hard and fast boundary . . . a zone not only of transition but also of *transaction:* a privileged place of . . . pragmatics and . . . strategy, of influence on the public, an influence—whether well or poorly understood—is achieved and the service of a better reception for the text.[50]

For Genette, paratext allows a writer to shape how the book will ultimately be understood, and provides a context for it to be read. In addition, the paratext serves as the threshold that allows the reader to leave his or her own experience and enter that of someone else. This, in turn, underscores how reading (along with literacy and intellectual growth) operate as a series of transactions in which writers exchange their experiences for a place in the reader's mind or consciousness.

While Genette is primarily interested in offering a history of the apparatus surrounding books, Beth McCoy has argued that "paratext has been deployed to transact white power."[51] Examining fugitive slave narratives, the O. J. Simpson case, contemporary fiction, and the public display of lynching photographs, McCoy has concluded that "the liberal subject exists largely as an effect of paratextuality."[52] In other words, the liberal subject does not exist in and of itself, but is the product of how texts, including statutes, contracts, constitutions, citizenship papers, etc., transform some bodies into legal subjects/objects. For McCoy, legal discourse operates like a book's paratext to define the meaning of bodies, especially those marked as black. To challenge the subordination of black bodies requires a reworking of the paratexts that define those bodies, according to McCoy. For this reason McCoy encourages scholars of African American culture to look to paratextual spaces for evidence of resistance to racism.[53]

Anticipating McCoy's critique, CRT argues for creating a more reciprocal relationship between the body and the paratexts that authorize its transformation into a legal subject.[54] By turning to literary techniques and using black bodies as metaphors and symbols, Bell and Williams illustrate how the framers founded the legal subject through racial categories and how contemporary social relations continue to racialize the legal subject. They both ultimately conclude that legal discourse must revise its account of a decontextualized (i.e., without race, gender, class, sexuality, etc.) legal subject in order to realize the dreams of freedom and equality.

In his chapter "The Chronicle of the Constitutional Contradiction," Bell transports Geneva Crenshaw back to the Constitutional Convention of 1787 to challenge the founders to create a document that would create and protect the rights of African Americans. In this article, I am less concerned with the nuances of Bell's argument than his use of Crenshaw's appearance, "a tall stranger—a stranger who was not only a woman but also, all too clearly, black."[55] The founders' response to her then structures the historical and contemporary dialogues described.[56] Crenshaw's arrival at the Constitutional Convention is greeted initially with "shocked silence" before "the chamber exploded with shouts, exclamations, oaths."[57] Various founders raise calls to "eject the Negro woman," question her authority to "interrupt" the proceedings, and accuse her of "inserting" herself in their conversations.[58] These seemingly gratuitous comments do not ostensibly further Bell's primary claims "that the matter of slavery will not be settled by [their] compromises"[59] and that "no one could have prevented the Framers from drafting a constitution including provisions protecting property in slaves."[60] Known primarily as a racial realist who emphasizes how material conditions shape legal decisions, Bell generally eschews overly ideological or theoretical analysis, despite his use of imaginative hypothetical situations that can involve time travel and space aliens. The inclusion of these phrases, however, signals the importance of metaphors and symbols within his critique of legal discourse. In this instance, Crenshaw's body serves as a metaphor for the absence of African American subjectivity from the Constitution despite the ubiquity of African American bodies within the revolutionary period and the lives (and livelihoods) of the founders. It also underscores Crenshaw's critique, borrowed from William Wiecek, that the Constitution "resorts to euphemisms like *persons* to keep out of the Constitution such words as *slave* and *slavery*."[61] Despite the universal language deployed by founding fathers, liberal legal theory cannot escape how distinct racial subjectivities give meaning to Constitution's abstract formulations.

The body of Geneva Crenshaw provides the catalyst for exploring how political, economic, and social relations defined legal discourse and undermined the very ideals the Constitution claimed to inaugurate.[62] Bell, as a founding figure of CRT, uses her body as a metaphor to represent what eventually becomes "Gotanda's critique of the colorblind constitution," or what CLS might term "the fundamental contradiction." Crenshaw's appearance reveals the central political divide that would otherwise be unspoken or downplayed. For Bell, legal discourse cannot be reduced to a wholly impersonal or rational discussion in which participants adopt a false "veil of ignorance" where they try to dehistoricize and decontextualize their perspectives and arguments. Such abstract conversations allow people to avoid their biases, which nonetheless shape how they apply liberal legal theory to discrete situations. To punctuate this point, Bell revels in portraying some of the founder's bigoted views: "'Woman!' A delegate shouted from the rear of the room. 'Explain to us how you, a black, have gotten free of your chains and gained the audacity to come here and teach white men anything.'"[63] If he does not engage in storytelling and fictional dialogues, traditional discursive structures would not allow Bell to make such claims about the founder's biases without substantial evidence and documentation. Because such biases were commonplace and generally assumed, the evidence supporting this claim may be fragmentary and poorly preserved. In addition, law's traditional focus on doctrine, original intent, or textual meaning avoids any sustained engagement with the cultural politics.

A curious element of the chronicle focuses on the delegate's efforts to remove Geneva from their meeting. Although protected by a mysterious force field "composed of thin vertical bars of red, white, and blue light," the founders tried to attack her with their bodies, swords, and rifles.[64] By attempting to remove her from the convention, the delegates seek to eliminate her concerns about liberal legal theory's limitations. Their actions do provide some comic relief, but they also reinforce the relationship between the body and legal criticism. Crenshaw's body, not her actual arguments, become the initial focus of the delegates. It is only once they become convinced that they cannot destroy or intimidate her, that they begin listening to her. They do continue to engage in her debate, explaining why they cannot prohibit slavery. At the moment when it appears as if Crenshaw might be persuading some delegates to move away from enshrining a compromise on slavery within the Constitution, the local militia is summoned and fires a cannon at her, which returns her to contemporary times.[65] The reader is forced to conclude that her visit could not change the course of history even if her body's presence caused a minor (fictional) controversy.

This opening chronicle sets the paradigm for Bell's other narratives and serves as an important model for later CRT writers. Bell introduces Geneva Crenshaw in order to make concrete the absences at the center of legal discourse. In effect, her presence legitimates and authorizes CRT's primary criticisms of liberal legal discourse. Without the fictional accounts of her attempt to intervene both physically and intellectually in the Constitutional Convention, Bell would struggle to represent the epistemological gaps that limit law's ability to realize its potential for liberating African Americans. Bell seems to reverse McCoy's description of the liberal subject being a discursive effect of paratextuality. Instead Bell suggests that the body becomes a necessary paratext for writing and reading about racial subjectivity. Without Geneva's bodily intrusion, slavery's challenge to liberal theory is either incoherent or unpersuasive. By resorting to the body as a literary symbol, Bell suggests that it provides the paratextual authority to create a persuasive argument. However, Bell's decision to embed the events within a series of frames suggests some ambivalence in using the body to authorize a particular critique. In other words, the various frames to *And We Are Not Saved* work to specify and limit the play unleashed by his use of the body as symbol and metaphor. Within this and the other chronicles, the message relies on the speaker's (fictional) body for its authenticity and rhetorical power even as he carefully constructs his text to protect it from alternate or unfriendly interpretations.

In his second book of stories or allegories, *Faces at the Bottom of the Well*, Bell again offers a preface and an introduction, in which he explains the characters and the writing style.[66] He also explains the historical factors shaping existing white attitudes that caused him to write the book: (1) statistics cannot adequately describe the ongoing effects of racism; (2) whites generally have no specific connection to black life and culture; (3) whites still generally believe that physical and intellectual laziness is a primary cause for the inability of Africans Americans to achieve higher levels of economic and educational success; and (4) modern discrimination operates through different mechanisms than pre–civil rights era discrimination.[67] Bell lists these (and other) reasons to support his conclusion that "Black people will never gain full equality in this country" and that by acknowledging it African Americans can perform "an act of ultimate defiance."[68] Despite his seemingly pessimistic conclusion, Bell nonetheless engages in an innovative synthesis of short story writing and legal criticism. By using Geneva Crenshaw, his alter ego, and Jesse Semple, a new character created for this and later books, Bell, in effect, attempts to personalize his critique of American culture and connect his (white) audience to likable, hardworking, intelligent African Americans who continue to face discrimination. Extending his analysis beyond either the black-white or male-female binaries, Bell deploys the persona of Jesse Semple to include an analysis of social class to contrast textual accounts of black life with lived experience, and to identify the tension between symbolic and materialist-based activism.

Unlike the chronicles in *And We Are Not Saved* that offer a relatively free and open dialogue among equals, *Faces at the Bottom of the Well* initiates a direct exploration of social class within the African American community. Semple serves as the narrator's driver, picking him up from the airport on his way to an elite college where Bell's alter ego will present a speech on Martin Luther King's legacy. Before their dialogue begins, the narrator is perusing another manuscript from Geneva Crenshaw.[69] By setting the scene in this way, Bell implicitly compares the forms of knowing offered by both Crenshaw and Semple. Although they challenge dominant legal discourse, the original chronicles tended to mimic or borrow heavily from legal discourse's normative assumptions and relate conflicts with law's structure of analysis. Semple, described as "dark-skinned, thin, and probably in his fifties"[70] and as "1960s-style militancy in a working-class black man with graying hair,"[71] offers a corrective to the overly-bourgeois or intellectual concerns addressed in the first chronicle. His body, especially how it labors, provides a crucial paratext, authorizing the "truth" of his legal-cultural analysis. At one point, Semple tells the narrator: "That's wrong, man. Look! . . . You are a brother able to afford a limo for a trip to Westchester that most people make by train, you carry your clothes in Hartmann luggage, and you dress like you are related to the Brooks Brothers—but you need to get off quoting the old folks and open your eyes to what is going down right around you in the here and now."[72] Through this quotation and others, Bell argues that not only race but also class shapes how people view the world. By including Semple as a living character and voice within his dialogues, Bell attempts to provide a working-class perspective to his analysis and to legal discourse more generally. He must use Semple's actual body in order to make vivid and persuasive his viewpoint.

The appropriation of Langston Hughes's famous interlocutor is not accidental or incidental. The opening chapter of *Faces at the Bottom of the Well* begins and ends with quotations from Langston Hughes, which serve as paratexts authenticating and regulating the meaning of Bell's text. Hughes has been known as a poet of the people and Semple, one of his most famous characters, frequently engaged in discussions with an unnamed narrator, Hughes's alter ego,[73] and provided home-spun wisdom to counter his middle-class and frequently idealistic view of American life. Hughes used Semple to signify on middle-class values and myths, especially to criticize dominant views of working-class existence. Most of these stories were initially published in black newspapers and represent a discursive sphere that was and remains invisible to most whites—so much so that Bell and/or his editors felt the need to explain the origin of Semple through a footnote. Bell's use of Semple connects his innovative writing strategies to both literary and African American discourses, thus suggesting that the limited lens by which dominant legal discourse views and understands American life, reflecting its general lack of knowledge of African American culture. Bell, however, does not offer a simple distinction between oral and textual traditions that privileges lived experience and orality as purer forms of knowledge. Such a move would merely reduce Bell's Semple to some sort of noble savage. Bell takes pains to represent his driver as literate and highly educated about African American life no matter his current occupation. Bell's Semple relates how his "mother loved Langston Hughes" and that he has "read all the Langston Hughes books."[74] Semple also tells the narrator that he needs to read the work of John Hope Franklin, Vincent Harding, Mary Berry, Nathan Huggins, Eugene Genovese, Leon Litwack, and C. Vann Woodward.[75] Through his appropriation of Hughes's character, Bell is able, in effect, to signify on many legal scholars and judges who make arguments and decisions about race in America without significant knowledge of African American culture.

Like the chronicles and his other stories, Bell's characters eventually explore a particular issue or topic. In the chapter "Divining our Racial Themes" where he introduces Semple, the narrator and Jesse discuss the efficacy of 1980s- and 1990s-style legal activism. They begin by discussing the impact of Dr. Martin Luther King Day on many working-class African Americans. Semple argues that "a holiday for Dr. King is another instance—like integration—that black folks work for and white folks grant when they realize—long before we do—that it is mostly a symbol that won't cost them much and will keep us pacified."[76] Later, Semple continues: "the fact is, though, that most whites and lots of black folks rely on symbols to support their belief that black people have come a long way since slavery and segregation."[77] Through these and other comments, Bell uses Semple to articulate his main message about the limited gains African Americans have made in achieving equality. Instead of affecting the material conditions of most African Americans, post–civil rights era activism has primarily favored symbolic actions, which has allowed supporters to keep their bodies and social positions safe because the requested changes have not affected a radical transformation of American political, economic, or cultural life. For Semple, Bell (and his alter ego) and Geneva Crenshaw function as symbols because whites view their achievements as indices of how far society has come even though their success is not representative of the general financial well-being of African Americans in general.[78] By placing these critiques in Semple's body/voice, Bell deploys Semple as paratext to further persuade his readers of claims that he has made elsewhere.

Again, as noted above, Bell is not unaware of the irony in his choice of rhetorical devices: he is using Semple as symbol to deconstruct the potentially negative affects of a politics of symbolism. Although Bell is clearly cautious about the value of legal discourse for affecting change because it prefers symbolic rather than material victories, he nonetheless is not without hope. By returning to the folk wisdom espoused by Langston Hughes, Bell is attempting to "reassess the worth of racial assumptions on which, without careful thought, we have presumed too much and relied too long."[79] This particular dialogue concludes with Semple reminding the narrator: "Don't forget your roots, brother."[80] One way of interpreting this warning is that the narrator cannot forget the difference between symbolic and material victories. On a deeper level, this call for cultural memory serves as a necessary reminder that bodies do not exist independent of ethnic or racial communities, discursive regimes such as law and literature, or the paratexts that shape its meaning. By opening the book with a conversation with a limousine driver, Bell invites the reader to misread Semple as an illiterate or uneducated African American male to make the point that despite his use of bodies, they can be misread. Of course, Bell quickly tries to remedy any confusion or errors by educating the reader through footnotes and jarringly didactic dialogue at times. Like his many introductions, prologues, and prefaces, Bell appears to want the literary freedom to use bodies as symbols or metaphors, but also realizes their insufficiency as representations and works to define or regulate their meaning.

In addition to engaging in storytelling and creating dialogues, CRT also emphasizes autobiography as a necessary supplement to legal analysis. Perhaps more than anyone else, Patricia Williams develops a strategic and innovative synthesis of autobiography and legal critique. At the narrative center of *The Alchemy of Race and Rights* in a chapter entitled "Death of the Profane (a commentary on the genre of legal writing)," Williams relates her exclusion from Benetton, a trendy store then engaged in a multicultural advertising campaign.[81] She begins by noting that Manhattan stores installed buzzer systems in the late 1980s to regulate who could enter them. Williams then describes how at 1:00 pm on the Saturday afternoon before Christmas, a Benetton employee told her through the window of a crowded store that it was closed. Filled with a "diffuse, even self-destructive" rage, Williams wrote down her initial response in her journal. Adding an additional layer of (fictional?) paratext, Williams claims that her book, in effect, reprints her original response to the events.[82] She then tells how she printed up a similar version (another paratext), which she proceeded to post on the offending Benetton's website.[83] The second round of versions occurs when Williams's attempts to write about these events for a law review symposium on Excluded Voices (more paratexts). Ironically the editors tried to edit her body out of the story because they "told her that they were not in the habit of publishing things that were unverifiable." Williams caustically responds that perhaps the "testimony of an independent white bystander" as required by the United States Supreme Court during the early 1900s would suffice. After removing all descriptions of her body from the story, an editor told her that "any reader will know what you must have looked like when standing at that window."[84] Even though the law review's editors thought her body merely served a stylistic function, Williams convinced them to maintain the reference to her race.[85]

The chapter then describes a third attempt at telling the story for another conference, this one focused on Equality and Difference. This (para)text, actually included in *The Alchemy of Race and Rights*, offers an eloquent and race-neutral critique—voiced in the third person—of how colorblind jurisprudence offers a "phantom room" that cannot adequately respond to the history of American discrimination. Her speech culminates with an impassioned defense of affirmative action.[86] She later learns that a local newspaper (another paratext) turned her argument upside down and quoted her as saying that "affirmative action promotes prejudice."[87] The chapter ends with a list of questions (another paratext) she receives from audiences when she discusses the Benetton event and her attempts to write about it. In effect, the uncomprehending audience gets the last word about the story.

As much as these stories testify to her struggle to narrate her subject-position, they also vividly exemplify the central paradox in relying on the body as proxy or metaphor for racial subjectivity. According to Janis Greve, Williams deploys her physical presence to illustrate her absence from legal discourse and the general epistemological gap within legal criticism, which omits discussions of race, racism, and racialization through its commitment to colorblindness. Greve argues that her use of writing to "seize back her private body from social usurpations of blackness" undermines the "very fluidity she insists upon as an embodied writing subject."[88] Despite her attempt to ground her legal critique in her experience, Williams finds that her body constitutes an unverifiable, unstable, and potentially unreadable object even as she attempts to stabilize its meaning through numerous explanatory texts. For Greve, Williams's attempt to capture in print a "(dis)embodied subject" presents the "problems of self-construction" that haunt cultural-legal criticism grounded in the body.[89]

Despite the dangers, Williams must risk representing the body as symbol or metaphor because it offers a necessary antidote to the abstract theorizing of CLS. Through her many personal stories, Williams attempts to show how CLS's portrayal of rights discourse as alienating and impersonal actually "dismisses a little too highhandedly and patronizingly the value of that discourse to people of color."[90] Williams, according to Jon-Christian Suggs, argues that "the deconstruction of rights by CLS is accomplished from a privileged, experiential base that is not that of Blacks and does not describe their relationship to civil rights."[91] By transforming herself and the bodies of friends, relatives, and students into symbols and metaphors, Williams shows how rights allow individuals to create affirming bonds and how rights might provide hope amid the ongoing racism and racialization of the post–civil rights era. While CLS theorists may imagine a world unburdened by legal indeterminacy, Williams uses her experiences to illustrate how indeterminacy, as well as race, class, and gender, help shape social interactions as much or even more than legal discourse.

Williams's Benetton story, in its many iterations, explores the links between legal discourse and everyday culture. Unlike Bell's concerns about the Constitution and the meaning of the Martin Luther King holiday, *The Alchemy of Race and Rights* explores the ordinary and potentially invisible way legal discourse infects market exchanges and the ability of individuals to participate in mass culture. The image of Patricia Williams peering into the Benetton window seems absurd and tragic simultaneously. With considerable wit and insight, Williams reveals the layers of meaning with the experience. The story's power resides in her ability to make readers feel her disappointment, disbelief, and rage as she encourages them to view the situation through her eyes and her body. Williams also shows how normative legal discourse seeks to elide her body from her analysis as a precondition for entering the discussion. Mimicking the analogical form of legal reasoning and moving from the particular to an abstract and general rule, her body and her experiences slowly recede in the various retellings. Even as Williams uses her body to vivify the scene and engage (white?) readers, her comic retelling of her efforts to publish versions of it in law reviews allows her to share her doubts about writing through the black body even as her book offers one last attempt to narrate her experience and intervene in legal discourse.

Like Bell's fantastic stories, Williams's use of autobiography becomes a model for other CRT writers. Despite her inability to control her story, Charles Lawrence, Mari Matsuda, Adrienne Davis, and others deploy anecdotes and other autobiographical writings to enrich their own articles and essays. Williams's writing, however, stands out because, per Jesse B. Semple's concern about Martin Luther King Day, she always articulates the link between symbolic and material concerns. The Benetton story is primarily a materialist one, focusing on how the marketplace unconsciously incorporates racism and racialization in its operation. For the people represented by Semple, this story connects ordinary events with their macroeconomic context and the ongoing relative poverty of Black America. Because of Benetton's multicultural advertising campaign, the story also speaks to the kind of symbolic concerns important to many middle-class African Americans. By balancing these concerns, Williams succeeds in using the black body to represent the needs of multiple aspects of the African American community.

As emphasized throughout, this chapter is less interested in evaluating CRT's criticism of CLS and legal discourse than evaluating the writing method by which it is accomplished. Halle Porsdam identifies their inclusion of nontraditional elements as offering "tools of unreason," which can supplement and improve traditional legal analysis.[92] She concludes that these tools allow Bell and Williams to inaugurate a new genre of legal writing, which in turn becomes the basis for CRT.[93] With their use of bodies and paratext to interrogate legal discourse, Bell's and Williams's writings seem more connected to the rhetoric found in Booker T. Washington's *Up From Slavery*, W. E. B. DuBois's *The Souls of Black Folk*, and the writings of Langston Hughes than Porsdam suggests. Porsdam's description of black bodies as "tools of unreason" and "supplements" to deconstruct legal discourse seems to misunderstand how bodies have long needed and relied on paratext for determining their relation to the law.[94] For Bell and Williams, black bodies have always underwritten the cultural logic that grounds legal discourse, even if those normative assumptions went unspoken. Numerous writers of African descent, from Olaudah Equiano to Langston Hughes, engage in legal criticism, which has never been accepted and adopted by legal discourse. Rather, their writing borrows strategies from other African American texts, which remains invisible to legal discourse only because of its disciplinary blinders.

Through their extensive use of explanatory materials and paratexts, both writers attempt to define the black body's meaning even as they signal their awareness about the potentially problematic nature of their symbolic and metaphoric use of those bodies. Recalibrating the traditional link between paratext and the liberal subject, Bell and Williams use black bodies to demonstrate how substantive arguments cannot be easily severed from the person making the claim. In other words, the body cannot be dismissed and legal discourses cannot operate solely through the rational function of abstract principles. Explanatory and authorizing paratexts do shape the ultimate meaning of any court decision or law review article. For CRT, law failed to realize the dream of freedom and equality not because legal reasoning is insufficient but because the people engaging in those deliberations and discussions could not extricate themselves from the operation of racism and racialization. The invisible paratext of whiteness blinded many CLS thinkers how race undermines the putatively colorblind operation of law. African American writers, such as Ishmael Reed[95] and Langston Hughes, and CRT scholars, including Richard Delgado[96] and Margaret Chon[97] have long noted that using the African American body is not a foolproof strategy to transform social relations even if it can bring awareness to the presence of racism in American culture. Producing autobiographical and fictional stories, however, did offer an effective tool for fighting the growing criticism of the rights discourse CLS scholars used during the 1990s.[98] By reintroducing "bodies" to legal analysis, CRT demanded, in effect, that the writer's race join the other information that publishers used (institutional affiliation, title, other publications, etc.) to define and determine a work's meaning, importance, and potential bias. Their reliance on black bodies, however, makes clear that they did not believe the black body could speak for itself or that it could achieve racial justice where commitment to legal principles could not. Rather, they sought to create the discursive space where lawyers, judges, scholars, and cultural critics could better identify the relationship between legal text and the body as paratext, and between liberal legal theory's aspirations and the limits caused by the lingering racism of the post–civil rights era.

While CLS sought to develop a complete description or model to describe how power operates through legal discourse, CRT possesses a different goal. CRT attempts to explore how legal discourse might help people negotiate the racism and racialization after more than 350 years of white supremacy in the Americas. For CRT, the post–civil rights era presented the challenge of opening the lines of communication between the historically marginalized and their oppressors. Despite some members' pessimism, CRT also wanted to develop an approach based upon existing institutional frameworks to create remedies for the problems presented by a formally desegregated but not integrated social structure. In this chapter, I have argued that CRT uses black bodies in a symbolic or metaphorical manner to emphasize how texts and discourses gain meaning by the paratexts that regulate their interpretation. Gerard Genette's characterization of paratexts as "thresholds" or "vestibules" offers a compelling explanation for CRT's deployment of black bodies. Black bodies, such as Geneva Crenshaw, Jesse B. Semple, and the narrative rendering of Patricia Williams, serve as a bold counterstatement to CLS's overly theoretical texts, and are a vivid textual reminder of the gap between dominant and minority cultures. Bell's and Williams's use of black bodies constitute metaphorical "thresholds" toward interracial communication and understanding. The bodies have entered the conversation, but still remain marginalized from the general terms of that discussion. In this sense, these black bodies fit Genette's description of paratexts as undefined zones because they simultaneously exist within and without the existing legal framework. In addition, the use of black bodies in dialogue—completed or frustrated in the case of Crenshaw and Williams—suggests the potential and eventual transfer of knowledge from African Americans to dominant society if it can welcome this new perspective and listen to it. In the meantime, these bodies remain in an undefined zone. As undefined zones and paratexts, their use of embodied black voices accentuate the future possibility of achieving the liberal legal ideals of creating free and equal citizens whose race, gender, and social class is irrelevant. CRT's effort to inject black bodies into legal discourse reminds CLS that the real failure is not of legal indeterminacy but the persistence of racism.

On another metaphorical level, any plaintiff must have standing to challenge a governmental practice or commence a lawsuit. The doctrine of standing is built upon the idea that an actual person who is harmed must present him or herself to the court. With the steady rise of corporations, partnerships, other business forms, and interest groups since the nineteenth century, its origin in requiring the physical presence of an actual claimant has become increasingly metaphorical. By reintroducing the black body into the scholarly debates about rights discourse, CRT offers a corrective to the abstract theories scholars use to understand legal debates. Using the body as paratext should remind legal scholars that their bodies matter. In other words, when CLS argued to "trash" rights discourse, CRT, through Bell, Williams, and others, respond by asking where are their bodies and do they have standing to raise this claim? Deploying the body as paratext helps minority writers regulate (as best they can) their reception and assert their heightened standing in questions over the value of rights discourse. Both Bell and Williams recognize the limitation of their strategy, but nonetheless still find it necessary to use the black body to ground their claims for social justice and to defend their right to speak truth to power.

Notes

1. Haney Lopez, Ian. *White by Law: The Legal Construction of Race* (New York: New York University Press, 1998), 40.
2. *Milliken vs. Bradley* 418 U.S. 717 (1974).
3. *Bakke vs. Regents of California* 438 U.S. 265 (1978).
4. *Milliken v. Bradley* held that multidistrict school desegregation plans violated the Constitution. *Bakke* held that quota-based systems for affirmative action violated the equal protection clause.
5. *Bakke vs. Regents of California*, 320.
6. [6.] Ross notes that the turn in post–civil rights era legal discourse shifted when the United States Supreme Court shifted from focusing on the harms endured by African Americans to the relative guilt of white perpetrators. Thomas Ross, *Just Stories: How the Law Embodies Racism and Bias* (Boston: Beacon Press, 1996) 40–49.
7. Girardeau Spann, *Race Against the Court: The Supreme Court and Minorities in Contemporary America* (New York: New York University Press, 1994), 19.
8. David Kairys, "Introduction," in *The Politics of Law: A Progressive Critique*, ed. David Kairys (New York: Pantheon, 1990), 3–7.
9. Mark Kelman, *A Guide to Critical Legal Studies* (Cambridge: Harvard University Press, 1987), 275 and 289.
10. Peter Gabel and Duncan Kennedy, "Roll Over Beethoven," *Stanford Law Review* 36 (January 1984): 34, 37.
11. Ibid., 48–49.
12. Kimberlè Crenshaw, "Critical Race Studies: The First Decade: Critical Reflections, Or 'A Foot in the Closing Door,'" *University of California at Los Angeles Law Review* 49 (June 2002): 1357.
13. This article focuses on legal iterations of critical race theory. While the term, critical race theory, has been broadly deployed in literary and cultural studies, this article focuses more narrowly on CRT's development within law schools because this strand has a clear genesis, its members clearly identified with it and read one another's work, and it allows me to define the term carefully. At times, Cornel West, bell hooks, and Henry Louis Gates have identified themselves and been named as critical race theorists, but they have eschewed any clear institutional association with the movement. Although my analysis might have some implications for understanding and analyzing their work, I have not applied it to their writing.
14. Kimberlè Crenshaw, "Mapping the Margins: Intersectionality, Identity Poli-

tics, and Violence Against Women of Color," *Stanford Law Review* 43 (July 1991): 1241–99.

15. Mari Matsuda, "Multiple Consciousness as a Jurisprudential Method," in *Where is Your Body?*, ed. Mari Matsuda (New York: New York University Press, 1996), 3–20.

16. See Derrick Bell, "*Brown v. Board of Education* and the Interest Convergence Dilemma," *Harvard Law Review* 93 (1980): 518–33.

17. See Angela Harris, "Race and Essentialism in Feminist Legal Thought," *Stanford Law Review* 42 (February 1990): 581–616; and Richard Delgado, *The Rodrigo Chronicles: Conversations about America and Race* (New York: New York University Press, 1995), 106–34.

18. The remainder of this chapter explores this theme. Readers should first look to Bell 1987, Bell 1992, Delgado 1995, and Williams 1991 as these are the primary examples upon which my analysis is based. Critical race theory literature is full of examples of stories and storytelling.

19. During the second half of the 1990s, Latino Critical Theory (LatCrit) and other forms of "outsider jurisprudence" burgeoned and have continued what CRT began. See Francisco Valdes, "Foreword—Posed at the Cusp: LatCrit Theory, Outsider Jursiprudence, and Latina/o Self Empowerment," *Harvard Latino Law Review* 2 (Fall 1997): 1–59.

20. Clevis Headley, "Black Studies, Race, and Critical Race Theory: A Narrative Deconstruction of Law," in *A Companion to African-American Studies*, ed. Lewis Gordon and Jane Gordon (Malden: Blackwell, 2006), 357.

21. Jerome Culp demonstrates one absurd consequence of colorblindness as a jurisprudence is that African American judges might be required to recuse themselves from civil rights cases because they might be affected by the decision even if there does not appear to be a countervailing force to persuade white judges to do the same even if they, too, live in communities marked by race. Jerome Culp, "Toward a Black Legal Scholarship: Race and Original Understandings," *Duke Law Journal* 41 (February 1991): 39–105.

22. Neil Gotanda, "A Critique of Our Constitution is Color-Blind," *Stanford Law Review* 44 (November 1991): 16–21.

23. See also Gary Peller, "Race Consciousness," in *After Identity: A Reader in Law and Culture*, ed. Dan Danielsen and Karen Engle (New York: Routledge, 1995), 67–82.

24. Gotanda, "A Critique of Our Constitution is Color-Blind," 56.

25. Ibid., 68.

26. John Calmore, "Critical Race Theory, Archie Shepp, and Fire Music: Securing an Authentic Life in a Multicultural World," *University of Southern California Law Review* 65 (July 1992): 2168–79. Robert Chang, "Toward an Asian American Legal Scholarship: Critical Race Theory, Poststructuralism and Narrative Space," *California Law Review* 81 (October 1993): 1289–14. Margaret Chon, "On the Need for Asian American Narratives in Law: Ethnic Specimens, Native Informants, Storytelling, and Silences," *UCLA Asian Pacific American Law Journal* 3 (Fall 1995): 5. Culp, "Toward a Black Legal Scholarship," 97–98. Margaret Montoya, "Celebrating Racialized Legal Narratives," in *Crossroads, Directions, and a New Critical Race Theory*, ed. Francisco Valdes, Jerome Culp, and Angela Harris (Philadelphia: Temple University Press, 2002): 243–44.

27. Charles R. Lawrence, "The Id, the Ego, and Equal Protection: Reckoning with Unconscious Racism," *Stanford Law Review* 39 (January 1987): 317–18.

28. Robert Chang and Adrienne Davis, "Defining the Voices of Critical Race Fem-

inism: The Adventure(s) of Blackness in Western Culture: An Epistolary Exchange on Old and New Identity Wars," *University of California at Davis Law Review* 39 (March 2006): 1233.

29. For examples of influential CRT work that does not assume or posit the voice of otherness, see Guinier 1994, Spann 1994, Haney Lopez 1998, and Harris 1990.

30. Jerome Culp, "Autobiography and Legal Scholarship and Teaching: Finding the Me in the Legal Academy," *Virginia Law Review* 77 (April 1991): 546.

31. Richard Delgado, "Crossroads and Blind Alleys: A Critical Examination of Recent Writing About *Race, Crossroads, Directions, and A New Critical Race Theory*," *Texas Law Review* 82 (November 2003): 130; Chang and Davis, "Defining the Voices," 1213.

32. Matsuda, "Multiple Consciousness," 78.

33. This question also offers a subtle but biting critique of CLS for abandoning social activism for abstract theorizing.

34. Delgado, "*The Rodrigo Chronicles*," 210.

35. Examples of the use of black bodies to illustrate legal critique pervade (CRT) writing. In a seminal article, Peggy Davis introduced the concept of "microaggression" to legal discourse. A microaggression asserts racialized power through everyday conversations, exchanges, and/or encounters (Davis 1989, 1556–1557). Davis uses conversations on an elevator or remarks by clerks to customers as examples of micoaggressions. Legal discourse would characterize these as insignificant events for which there is no remedy. For Davis such interracial interactions maintain white supremacy precisely because white people cannot see the harms produced by their actions. Because it analyzes such claims individually and attempts to de-race them, legal discourse is blind to the claim and thus delegitimizes the experiences of historically marginalized people. To remedy this, Davis contends that legal decision making must include black voices and consider the perspectives of African Americans (Davis 1989, 1577). In another influential article, Regina Austin subverts the Constitution's recognition of discrete protected classes (i.e., gender, race, or ethnicity) to show that such abstract categories do not exist independent of specifically marked bodies. Austin examined *Chambers v. Omaha Girls Club*, in which an unmarried black woman, Crystal Chambers, was fired for becoming pregnant, to demonstrate how neither a gender nor race-based analysis could be easily applied to the case's facts (Austin 1989, 555–56). Neither race nor gender alone accounted for the potential "danger" ascribed to Crystal Chambers, according to Austin. Rather, it was a pregnant and black female body that produced the employer's fear and anxiety. It should also be noted that Richard Delgado (1995) created a black body of Italian/American descent to complicate the simplistic black-white binary that pervaded legal and cultural discourses during the 1980s and 1990s.

36. Gerard Genette, *Paratexts: Thresholds of Interpretation*, trans. Jane Lewin (New York: Cambridge University Press), 1997; Beth McCoy, "Paratext, Citation, and Academic Desire in Ishmael Reed's *Mumbo Jumbo*," *Contemporary Literature* 46, no. 4 (2005): 604–35. Beth McCoy, "Race and the (Para)Textual Condition," *Publications of the Modern Language Association* 121, no. 1 (January 2006): 156–69.

37. Discussions of Bell and Williams typically analyze their work for their main message or critique (Porsdam 1999, 107–32; Suggs 1990; Taylor 2005; Delgado 2005). Some studies do consider Williams's use of the body as a literary strategy, but they tend to either isolate her from CRT (Greve 2001) or consider her approach within a very different disciplinary context (Prendergast 1998).

38. By approaching the African American body as a paratext for CRT texts, this essay both borrows from and criticizes Foucault's influential essay "What is an Au-

thor?" in which he describes the author-function as a way for discourses to define the meaning of a text and regulate its circulation. In this case, the writer/character's body shapes the text's cultural meaning. Unlike Foucault's description, this racial paratext does not always facilitate the transfer of knowledge. Rather, it reminds the reader of how their racial identity affects their ability to engage in certain kinds of legal-cultural criticism. Foucault argued that the author-function, in effect, freed the text. In my analysis, CRT deploys African American bodies precisely to combat the free play of signification, ground their theoretical critique, and challenge CLS's endless abstractions about the functioning of power, without locating or specifying their analysis.

39. Following Alain Locke, Zora Neale Hurston, Langston Hughes, and others, alternative theories exist about the role of literature in African American culture. I am not suggesting that this is the only possible purpose for narrative and fiction, only that a popular—if not dominant—position within African American cultural criticism has coalesced around the idea that narrative can challenge racism and racial discrimination.

40. W.E.B DuBois, "Criteria of Negro Art," in *African American Literary Theory: A Reader*, ed. Winston Napier (New York University Press, 2000), 22.

41. Henry Louis Gates, Jr., "On Bearing Witness," in *Bearing Witness: Selections from African-American Autobiography in the Twentieth Century*, ed. Henry L. Gates, Jr., (New York: Pantheon, 1991), 3.

42. Robert Stepto, *From Behind the Veil: A Study of Afro-American Narrative*, 2nd Ed. (Urbana: University of Illinois Press, 1991), 196.

43. Ibid., 199–201.

44. Ibid., 202.

45. Ibid., 4–6

46. Although beyond the scope of this chapter, CRT's cautious use of raced bodies within their writing may exemplify what Gayatri Spivak calls "a *strategic* use of positivist essentialism" (Spivak 1988, 205). Spivak acknowledged that activists may need to use such reductive strategies in order to build class or cultural consciousness. The various paratext deployed by Williams and Bell might reflect a certain ambivalence, the kind that Spivak acknowledges, in their use of strategic essentialism.

47. Bell, *And We Are Not Saved*, xi–25. Law reviews published a number of the chapters as articles prior to the release of the book version.

48. Williams, *The Alchemy of Race and Rights*, 3–14.

49. Ibid., 15–43.

50. Genette, *Paratexts*, 1–2 (italics in original).

51. McCoy, "Race and the (Para)Textual Condition," 157.

52. Ibid., 159.

53. McCoy, "Paratext, Citation, and Academic Desire," 632.

54. This intervention probably extends well beyond legal discourse. During the 1980s and 1990s, scholars from numerous disciplines began identifying their racial and/or gender position in the introductions and prefaces to ground their analysis. bell hooks's forays into autobiography certainly follow this general pattern. In a related vein, Henry Louis Gates, Jr., has discovered what he claims is the first novel by an African American woman, Hannah Craft's *The Bondwoman's Narrative*. Gates and others then published a second book that tried to identify the real identity of Hannah Craft with the ostensible purpose of using the truth about her body to shape our understanding of the words, events, and themes of the novel. Throughout the public dialogue about this found book, her body has served as a key element in determining the value and meaning of the text.

55. Bell, *And We Are Not Saved*, 26.

56. Although there is little evidence suggesting an intentional relationship, Bell's narrative shares some similarities with Octavia Butler's *Kindred.* In *Kindred,* Dana, an African American woman living during the 1970s, gets transported back in time to antebellum Maryland to save her master/ancestor from danger and thus ensure her eventual birth. During the course of these mysterious events, Dana must act as slave to fit within the Southern social structure. Like Crenshaw, Dana finds how deeply entrenched slavery, as both social and ideological systems, is for whites and African Americans. She also finds herself developing a "slave consciousness" despite being raised free. In both fictions, African American women return to the past and try to "right" American history, but encounter numerous political, social, economic, and cultural obstacles.

57. Bell, *And We Are Not Saved,* 27.

58. Ibid., 27–28.

59. Ibid., 29.

60. Ibid., 43.

61. Ibid., 34.

62. Ibid., 50.

63. Ibid., 35. Although beyond the scope of this essay, Geneva's gender is a crucial element of her embodiment. It is not simply her race, but her gender that offends the founders. By implication, the Constitution not only furthers racial inequality, but gender inequality as well. In addition, this and other chronicles contain a certain amount of sexual tension in the relationship between Geneva and Bell's alter ego as there are some significant suggestions that the narrator is attracted to Geneva. Bell also includes a chronicle about the fate of educated black women and their inability to find marriage partners (Bell 1987, 198–214). Patricia Williams finds Bell's analysis problematic (Williams 1991, 197–201). Gender, intersectionality, and other axes became central CRT concerns.

64. Bell, *And We Are Not Saved,* 27.

65. Ibid., 41–42.

66. Bell, *Faces at the Bottom of the Well,* ix–xiii.

67. Ibid., 4–6.

68. Ibid., 12.

69. Ibid., 15.

70. Ibid., 16.

71. Ibid., 18.

72. Ibid., 21–22.

73. In later short stories, the narrator is named Boyd.

74. Ibid., 17. To further emphasize Semple's book learning and, by implication, the invisible literacy of the black working class, Bell frequently references the "pile of books on the floor" of the car (22).

75. Ibid., 19–20.

76. Ibid., 18.

77. Ibid., 20.

78. Ibid., 26.

79. Ibid., 14.

80. Ibid., 30.

81. Williams, *The Alchemy of Race and Rights,* 44–51.

82. Ibid., 45.

83. Ibid., 45–46.

84. Ibid., 47.

85. Ibid., 48.

86. Ibid., 49–50.
87. Ibid., 50.
88. Greve, "Legal Bodies, Racial Bodies," 201.
89. Ibid., 215.
90. Porsdam, *Legally Speaking*, 210.
91. Suggs, "Epistemology and the Law," 158.
92. Porsdam, *Legally Speaking*, 126.
93. Ibid., 126.
94. McCoy, "Paratext, Citation, and Academic Desire," 609.
95. Ibid., 616.
96. Delgado, *The Rodrigo Chronicles*, 210–11.
97. Chon, *On the Need for Asian American Narratives in Law*, 23–28.
98. Recently Richard Delgado (2003) and Kevin Johnson (2004) sparred in the law reviews about the future of CRT. Central to this debate was Delgado's claim that LatCrit had become too involved in discourse and symbols and forgotten the material effects of racism. Delgado argued for a return to CRT strategies, methods, and theories. Although he did not advocate explicitly for renewing attention on writing style and strategy, I hope this chapter points out that perhaps Delgado was, in part, lamenting the relative disappearance of black and other bodies of color from the writing. Those bodies, I would argue, provided the medium by which CRT and LatCrit can balance materialist and symbolic claims.

Works Cited

Austin, Regina. "Sapphire Bound!" *Wisconsin Law Review* (May/June 1989): 539–78.

Bakke vs. Regents of California 438 U.S. 265 (1978).

Bell, Derrick. *And We Are Not Saved: The Elusive Quest for Racial Justice*. New York: Basic Books, 1987.

———. "*Brown v. Board of Education* and Interest-Convergence Dilemma." *Harvard Law Review* 93 (1980): 518–33.

———. *Faces at the Bottom of the Well: The Permanence of Racism*. New York: Basic Books, 1992.

Butler, Octavia. *Kindred*. 25th Ann. Ed. Boston: Beacon Press, 2003.

Calmore, John. "Critical Race Theory, Archie Shepp, and Fire Music: Securing an Authentic Life in a Multicultural World." *University of Southern California Law Review* 65 (July 1992): 2129–30.

Chang, Robert. "Toward an Asian American Legal Scholarship: Critical Race Theory, Poststructuralism and Narrative Space." *California Law Review* 81 (October 1993): 1243–1323.

Chang, Robert, and Adrienne Davis. "Defining the Voices of Critical Race Feminism: The Adventure(s) of Blackness in Western Culture: An Epistolary Exchange on Old and New Identity Wars." *University of California at Davis Law Review* 39 (March 2006): 1189–234.

Chon, Margaret. "On the Need for Asian American Narratives in Law: Ethnic Specimens, Native Informants, Storytelling, and Silences." *UCLA Asian Pacific American Law Journal* 3 (Fall 1995): 4–32.

Crenshaw, Kimberlé. "Critical Race Studies: The First Decade: Critical Reflections,

Or 'A Foot in the Closing Door.'" *University of California at Los Angeles Law Review* 49 (June 2002): 1343–73.

———. "Mapping the Margins: Intersectionality, Identity Politics, and Violence Against Women of Color." *Stanford Law Review* 43 (July 1991): 1241–99.

Culp, Jerome. "Autobiography and Legal Scholarship and Teaching: Finding the Me in the Legal Academy" *Virginia Law Review* 77 (April 1991): 539–59.

———. "Toward a Black Legal Scholarship: Race and Original Understandings" *Duke Law Journal* 41 (February 1991): 39–105.

Davis, Peggy. "Law as Microaggression." *Yale Law Journal* 98 (June 1989): 1559–77.

Delgado, Richard. "Crossroads and Blind Alleys: A Critical Examination of Recent Writing about *Race, Crossroads, Directions, and A New Critical Race Theory.*" *Texas Law Review* 82 (November 2003): 121–51.

———. "Derrick Bell's Toolkit—Fit to Dismantle that Famous House?" In *The Derrick Bell Reader*, edited by Richard Delgado and Jean Stefancic, 446–58. New York: New York University Press, 2005.

———. "The Ethereal Scholar? Does Critical Legal Studies Have What Minorities Want?" *Harvard Civil Rights and Civil Liberties Review* 22 (1987): 301–322.

———. *The Rodrigo Chronicles: Conversations about America and Race.* New York: New York University Press, 1995.

DuBois, W. E. B. "Criteria of Negro Art." In *African American Literary Theory: A Reader*, edited by Winston Napier, 17–23. New York: New York University Press, 2000.

Foucault, Michel. "What is an Author?" Translated by Donald Bouchard and Sherry Simon. In *Language, Counter-Memory, Practice: Selected Essays and Interviews by Michel Foucault*, edited by Donald Bouchard, 113–38. Ithaca, NY: Cornell University Press, 1977.

Gabel, Peter, and Duncan Kennedy. "Roll Over Beethoven." *Stanford Law Review* 36 (January 1984): 1–54.

Gates, Henry Louis, Jr. "On Bearing Witness." In *Bearing Witness: Selections from African-American Autobiography in the Twentieth Century*, edited by Henry L. Gates, Jr., 3–9. New York: Pantheon, 1991.

Genette, Gerard. *Paratexts: Thresholds of Interpretation.* Translated by Jane Lewin. New York: Cambridge University Press, 1997.

Gotanda, Neil. "A Critique of Our Constitution is Color-Blind." *Stanford Law Review* 44 (November 1991): 1–68.

Greve, Janis. "Legal Bodies, Racial Bodies: Autobiography and Autonomy in Patricia Williams's *Alchemy of Race and Rights.*" In *Bodies of Resistance: New Phenomenologies of Politics, Agency, and Culture*, edited by Laura Doyle, 195–216. Evanston, IL: Northwestern University Press, 2001.

Guinier, Lani. *The Tyranny of the Majority: Fundamental Fairness in Representative Democracy.* New York: Free Press, 1994.

Haney Lopez, Ian. *White By Law: The Legal Construction of Race.* New York: New York University Press, 1998.

Harris, Angela. "Race and Essentialism in Feminist Legal Thought." *Stanford Law Review* 42 (February 1990): 581–616.

Headley, Clevis. "Black Studies, Race, and Critical Race Theory: A Narrative Deconstruction of Law." In *A Companion to African-American Studies*, edited by Lewis Gordon and Jane Gordon, 330–59. Malden: Blackwell, 2006.

Kairys, David. "Introduction." In *The Politics of Law: A Progressive Critique*, edited by David Kairys, 1–9. New York: Pantheon, 1990.

Kelman, Mark. *A Guide to Critical Legal Studies.* Cambridge, MA: Harvard University Press, 1987.

Lawrence, Charles R. "The Id, the Ego, and Equal Protection: Reckoning with Unconscious Racism." *Stanford Law Review* 39 (January 1987): 317–88.

Matsuda, Mari. "Multiple Consciousness as a Jurisprudential Method." In *Where is Your Body?*, edited by Mari Matsuda, 3–20. New York: New York University Press, 1996.

McCoy, Beth. "Paratext, Citation, and Academic Desire in Ishmael Reed's *Mumbo Jumbo.*" *Contemporary Literature* 46, no. 4 (2005): 604–35.

———. "Race and the (Para)Textual Condition." *Publications of the Modern Language Association* 121, no. 1 (January 2006): 156–69.

Milliken vs. Bradley 418 U.S. 717 (1974).

Montoya, Margaret. "Celebrating Racialized Legal Narratives." In *Crossroads, Directions, and a New Critical Race Theory*, edited by Francisco Valdes, Jerome Culp, and Angela Harris, 243–50. Philadelphia: Temple University Press, 2002.

Peller, Gary. "Race Consciousness." In *After Identity: A Reader in Law and Culture*, edited by Dan Danielsen and Karen Engle, 67–82. New York: Routledge, 1995.

Porsdam, Helle. *Legally Speaking: Contemporary American Culture and the Law.* Amherst: University Massachusetts Press, 1999.

Prendergast, Catherine. "Race: The Absent Presence in Composition Studies." *College Composition and Communication* 50, no. 1 (September 1998): 36–53.

Ross, Thomas. *Just Stories: How Law Embodies Racism and Bias.* Boston: Beacon, 1996.

Spann, Girardeau. *Race Against the Court: The Supreme Court and Minorities in Contemporary America.* New York: New York University Press, 1994.

Spivak, Gayatri. "Subaltern Studies: Deconstructing Historiography." In *In Other Worlds: Essays in Cultural Politics*, 197–221. New York: Routledge, 1988.

Stepto, Robert. *From Behind the Veil: A Study of Afro-American Narrative.* 2nd Ed. Urbana, IL: University Illinois Press, 1991.

Suggs, Jon-Christian. "Epistemology and the Law in Four African American Fictions." *Legal Studies Forum* 14, no. 2 (1990): 141–62.

Taylor, George. "Racism as Original Sin: Derrick Bell and Reinhold Niebuhr's Theology." In *The Derrick Bell Reader*, edited by Richard Delgado and Jean Stefancic, 433–45. New York: New York University Press, 2005.

Valdes, Francisco. "Foreword—Posed at the Cusp: LatCrit Theory, Outsider Jurisprudence, and Latina/o Self Empowerment." *Harvard Latino Law Review* 2 (Fall 1997): 1–59.

Williams, Patricia. *The Alchemy of Race and Rights.* Cambridge, MA: Harvard University Press, 1991.

Distorted Images in Travel Literature: An Exploration of the Subjugation of Blackness in the Western World

Katrina Dyonne Thompson

Introduction

THE INITIAL IDEALS AND CHARACTER ASSESSMENTS OF BLACK Americans developed during the nation's formative years and resulted in blacks becoming outcasts in a society dominated by whites.[1] Blacks were often categorized as savages, comical musical minstrel figures who were oversexualized, immoral, and intellectually and culturally underdeveloped. These misconceptions contributed to the emergence of negative racial images infused in the culture and history of North America.[2] Although the literature concerning the role of slavery in the construction of the black body is robust, there is very little written on the numerous stereotypes that developed prior to them reaching the shores of the New World. These misappropriations of the black body within the continent of Africa from the first contact with whites reveal the societal values constructed to foster a human chattel system.

European and African contact rapidly progress with the inception of the Atlantic slave trade, which began in the fifteenth century and continued until the nineteenth century.[3] Europeans ventured to the Western regions of Africa for three main reasons: missionary work, commerce, and scientific expedition. However, the primary interest of Europeans was for material gain, chiefly for precious minerals and textiles that could be sold in other markets.[4] The use of slave labor in the mining of these materials in the developing colonies in the New World was a profitable commerce that resulted in continual contact between Europeans and Africans. While in Africa, Europeans observed and recorded their experiences. Many of these first-hand accounts were written in journals that provide clear evidence of the misrepresentation of the black body. This chapter examines the development of African and African American stereotypes in the United

States through an exploration of the journals of European travelers of the fifteenth through nineteenth century in Africa. These journals reveal Europeans (and later North Americans) frequently mischaracterizing Africans in order to justify purging their land of resources, converting them to Christianity, or, ultimately, enslaving them.

The "Other" Defined

Travel journals described Africans of several distinct societies as the antithesis of Europeans—the exotic Other—in their physical and cultural characteristics.[5] Psychologist Perry Hinton argues that there are three main components that assist in defining and understanding the creation of the Other in society.[6] The first component is that a group of persons must be identified by specific characteristics, such as skin color or hair texture. Europe has a long history, prior to the Renaissance era, of associating the color black with evil and negative attributes. Thus the skin complexion of Africans set them apart as different or unusual according to European standards. Additional differences include geographical location, culture, languages, and manner of dress, all of which contribute to the identification of the African people as the Other. The second element is to develop a set of additional characteristics to the out-group. The construction of the traits of savagery, cannibalism, inhumanness, innate musical and dance abilities, and heathenism were only a few of the characteristics created by Europeans to fulfill this component. Often white explorers did not understand the diverse customs throughout the vast region, therefore resulting in the perception that African music and dance was an uncivilized, pleasure activity. While white explorers accurately recognized music and dance as the centerpiece of many African cultures, they frequently misrepresented Africans' musicality as a sign of their innate joviality and simple-mindedness.

The last component entails identifying all persons in the "out group" as having the assigned characteristic.[7] European "reports about Africans were limited to description of their observable physical and cultural characteristics . . . all serving to paint a picture of ignorant savages."[8] These misrepresentations of West African music and dance culture are but one example of the manner that blacks were distorted and subjugated in travel journals. Africans were homogenized, therefore reducing their diversity of languages, traditions and histories into a single group of black bodies. These depictions of Africans were spread throughout the Western world courtesy of the accounts of European explorers beginning in the fifteenth until the nineteenth century.

West African Performing Arts Culture

Music and dance were distinct elements of many of the societies in West Africa. The personal narrative of Olaudah Equiano, a captive from the empire of Abyssinia off the Western coast of Africa, specifically recognized the role of the performing arts within his culture.[9] His narrative offers one of the earliest first-hand accounts of an African captive within the slave trade. Although Equiano spent many chaotic years outside of Africa, he still possessed a memory of the performing arts of his homeland. "We are almost a nation of dancers, musicians, and poets," Equiano writes, describing his native society to eighteenth-century readers.[10] His recollection of the rich culture of West African music and dance traditions portrays the importance of these arts in society, but his recollections are also representative of their significance throughout the diverse region.

Music and dance were interrelated aspects of West African societies either for recreational purposes or for performance of ceremonies or rituals.[11] The specific social role of music and dance varied according to group association, but it was an element of the social order that served an explicit cultural purpose. For example, music and dance were used as diversionary tactics to outwit enemies in times of battle, for marriage ceremonies, royal rituals, as spirit mediums and to commemorate births. Music and dance held a functional role in West African culture.[12] The structured nature of music and dance in society was evident in Equiano's description: "The assembly is separated into four divisions, which dance either apart or in succession. . . . The first division contains the married men . . . the married women . . . dance in the second division. . . . The young men occupy the third; and the maidens the fourth.[13] This statement details a ceremonial procession, and it reflects the organized and refined character of music and dance. Although interconnected, music and dance represented different components and roles within the diverse ceremonies of West Africa.

"Every great event, such as a triumphant return from battle, or other cause of public rejoicing, is celebrated in public . . . with song and music suited to the occasion."[14] Equiano recognized the functional usage of music and dance for specific ceremonial rituals in West African culture.[15] This complex structure of the performing arts of West Africa was manipulated by early European explorers. White Europeans and later North Americans misinterpreted the active, elaborate role of music and dance. These distorted observations were chronicled for public consumption through the publication of travel journals. Evaluating the distorted observations of white explorers reveals the misrepresentation of blackness and black people that developed and continued in the New World.

Distorted Observations

European explorers had the most lasting effect on the distorted image of the African but were not the creators of the stories. Prior to European exploration there were several myths that centered on Africa and its inhabitants. Scholar Margery Perham commented that travel journals created an illusion of pre-European Africa as "complete and anarchic savagery."[16] Europeans' initial impressions of Africa came from the classical works of Greeks, Romans, and Muslim explorers.[17] Their accounts formed the foundation of European knowledge and point of view of Africa and its inhabitants. They also were the first travel journals to represent the African as the exotic Other.

For instance, the earliest travel writer, Herodotus of Halicarnassus, a Greek researcher and storyteller from the fifth century BC, was the first to record his observations on the interior of Africa. Herodotus is known as the "Father of History" but equally deserved the title of "Father of Travel Literature."[18] His writings have been proven erroneous but they were still quite influential in establishing a basic understanding of the historical knowledge of Africa and its inhabitants. Herodotus wrote Africans "eat locusts and snakes, share wives, and speak no human language, but rather screech like bats."[19] He went on to say that wild animals inhabited Africa with men that had "dogs' heads, and those with no heads [had] eyes . . . in their chests."[20] Although Herodotus work was inaccurate, it set the precedent for European's initial impressions of Africa as uncivilized and exotic.

Travel narratives were fertile ground for the misrepresentation of African culture. The performing arts culture was one of the areas often mischaracterized and distorted in the written works of early explorers from the continents of Europe and North America.[21] European travelers often ignored the ritualistic purpose of African music and dance and instead inferred the musicality of Africans as an intrinsic trait of the black race. The creation of the innate performer reverberated in travel journals. These distortions reduced black bodies to the role of servant, prostitute, and entertainment in the New World.[22] Blacks were forced into a subjugated class where they were sexually abused and forced to entertain whites through the institution of slavery. Thus the distortion of the performing arts culture of West Africans within travel journals contributed to the negative ideals associated to the black body.

As a negative ideal, the innate performer trait was assigned to black people and distributed through travel journals. The neglect of complex and diverse representations of African culture played a role in performing arts' use as a tool to subjugate blackness. One popularly read travel journal was *The Golden Trade*, in which Richard Jobson states, "There is, without doubt, no people on the earth more naturally affected to the sound of musicke then these people."[23] The belief that blacks were "naturally affected" by music resulted in Africans being identified by specific characteristics that reasserted their Otherness in European society. The innate attribute of music and dance assigned to Africans contributed to their placement as entertainer or amusement. Such designations reduced them to physical rather than intellectual beings. These descriptions were purposely placed on the black body in order to subjugate Africans while justifying the assertion of white dominance within the institution of slavery that was developing in the New World.

Richard Jobson's assessment of West Africa was only one instance of the numerous published works that misrepresented the performing arts culture of blacks. French Dominican priest Jean-Baptiste Labat also simplified his assessment of the music and dance culture by recording that Africans "only love their pleasures . . . are excessively lazy, flee work as if it were the worst thing in the world; if hunger did not force them, they would never cultivate their land. . . . They love to dance."[24] Labat diminished the character of Africans to that of a child-like, simple group that was barely able to survive life due to their "natural" disposition. This idea was reiterated in other travel journals as well. Each felt Africans needed to be placed in slavery in order to aid them in their moral and mental development and to prevent slothfulness. In the nineteenth century, English explorer Richard Burton wrote that blacks were "unprogressive and unfit for change . . . devotedly fond of music. This love of tune has invented nothing but whistling and the whistle."[25] Burton's assertions that Africans were "unprogressive" fit well within the European collective that believed that the enslavement of blacks was justified. These perspectives deformed a tradition filled with rituals and order and transformed it to a negative myth that enhanced the otherness of the black body. Blacks became subjugated through written word and this image was created and consumed by whites throughout Europe and North America.

The depictions of West Africa often reflected the motives of the respective European explorer. Missionaries presented an image of Africa as a place with "human sacrifice, highly sexual religious ceremonies, wicked excess of polygamy, and lascivious dances with a childlike ignorance."[26] The manufacture of the naturally inclined dancer and singer contributed to the missionary assertion that blacks were immoral uncivilized beings. Therefore the negative representations of Africans, in part, fueled missionaries' desire to convert Africans.

The missionaries had a great interest in religiously converting and "civilizing" the inhabitants of the African continent.[27] Europeans believed that it was their duty to assert "order, self-discipline, self abnegation, sexual restraint, and Christianity" throughout West Africa.[28] The protestant religion was brought to Africa by missionaries from Britain and the Netherlands. Catholic missionaries came from France, Spain, and Portugal.[29] One Wesleyan missionary, Reverend R. M. Macbriar writes, "All these people . . . are capable of civilisation . . . It must be a Christian civilisation."[30] The Christian missionaries were culturally arrogant, believing that Christianity in Africa would liberate the African from the "bondage of sin, fear, and superstition."[31] Africanist scholar James S. Coleman writes,"Tropical Africa had a special attraction for the missionaries. The heathen was his target, and of all human groups, the Africans were believed to be the most heathen."[32] The missionaries received this erroneous perception from earlier travelers and their writings, and these missionaries continued the tradition of constructing negative images of the black body. Missionaries were critical of African religion, social customs, institutions, and polygamous ways, often condemning their lifestyles of possessing "barbarous superstition."[33] In order to further support their expeditions, many missionaries asserted that Africans possessed an immoral nature.

Missionaries were "representatives of European 'civilization and morality' . . . and were not only spokesmen for their god, but keepers of the European culture as well."[34] They entered the land with the intentions of casting a negative light upon the culture and history of Africans, placing them as the Other, while validating European hegemony. Missionaries legitimized the use of Africans as slaves and the slave system as a positive institution that could civilize and Christianize African captives. One slaver stated that in his opinion, he was a "kidnapper doing God's service." The slaver later said that he was, "instrumental in the salvation of more souls, than all the missionaries in Africa" through the placement of Africans into the slavery system.[35]

Analogous to other outside white explorers, missionaries often analyzed the performing arts aspect of African cultures in their journals. These accounts often revealed an innate relationship between black women and lascivious behavior, creating an idea of the oversexualized black female. The manner in which African women dressed was of constant concern in travel journals with great emphasis on the stark differences in custom. Henry Hawks, an English merchant, wrote in the early sixteenth century, "The wild people go naked, without anything upon them. . . . The women ware the skinne of a deere before their privities and nothing else upon their bodies."[36] Such assessments fostered inappropriate views of African and European women. Black women were viewed as lewd and immoral while white women were seen as chaste and virtuous. Such misguided attitudes bled over into missionaries perceptions of African dance culture. To many of the missionaries, the dances of the Africans were "licentious, lustful, indecent, and provocative."[37] The majority of the spectators that created these assessments were white men who had a completely different view of dance. The sensuous movements of the West African women, their vibrant polyrhythmic hip shaking motions while dancing, were often interpreted as evidence of their heathenish, lustful, uncontrollable ways. Therefore European and North American explorers believed that blacks needed to be restrained. The misinterpreted dancing and singing of West Africa contributed to the idea that black females were lascivious beings that could not control their lustful ways. Black women were often physically and sexually exposed to white male explorers (slaver). As one foreign traveler wrote about sub-Saharan Africa, "the women much given to lust and uncleanenesse, specially with straungers, which among them is no shame."[38] This statement set the stage for sexual assaults from white males toward black females due to their belief that African women were specially attracted to European explorers. This idea contributed to the belief that black women could not be raped since blacks desired sexual relations with whites.

The travel journal deliberately created the libidinous, immoral black female body through its misrepresentation of African cultures. Whites perverted black bodies to rationalize their degraded position in the Atlantic slave trade. Many travel journals that were absorbed by the reading public were biased and Eurocentric in their review of African cultures, but there were a small portion of Europeans that attempted to understand and depict an accurate view of the diverse regions.

In the sixteenth century, European explorers began to travel to Africa to conduct scientific research. The scientific exploration was often sponsored by a variety of learning societies in order to discover more about this unknown continent.[39] The London-based Association for Promoting the Discovery of the Interior Parts of Africa, known as the African Association, was a group that developed specifically for scientific explorations of the African continent. They were an alliance of aristocrats and wealthy business men that professed devotion to an unbiased scholarly view of the interior of West Africa.[40] Mainly composed of wealthy men, the organization formed with a "desire for definite, scientific knowledge of this great continent," therefore funding the "chosen man to find out the facts."[41] The purpose of these types of scientific organizations was to establish legitimate commercial and diplomatic contact, but they were still plagued by the existing myths of Africa formulated by earlier European explorers. Although members of the group attempted to counter many of these preexisting myths, some maintained ideological stereotypes that severely affected the images of Africans and their descendents.[42] Interestingly the antislavery movement was accelerated by these explorers as they attempted to present an unbiased view of Africans. One Danish physician, Paul Isert, wrote that proponents of slavery should "travel in the African interior . . . to be cured of their prejudices."[43] This innovative approach to Africa and its inhabitants did not affect North America with the same velocity as Europe, and allowed for slavery and the distortion of the black body to become a culturally intrinsic aspect of the New World foundation. The African Association was the first that tried to accurately understand the diversity of African cultures within the western regions. These explorers were, in many ways, pioneer anthropologists that did not attempt to disrupt the daily activities of African people in their various societies. These groups entered the continent subsequent to the missionaries and slave traders and tried to have a "general desire" for "human inquiry." Since travel journals were the main supply of knowledge and history of this unknown land, their efforts to validate the culture and the customs of Africans was a heavy task. Travel journals distributed negative cultural characteristics of blacks that became a part of the European consciousness. These stereotypes created a challenge for the African Association wherein they were unable to combat a long history of black misrepresentation and abuse.

Slavery Validation and Justification

Europeans created an accepted vision that validated the commencement of an African based human chattel system in the New World.[44] This vision was the stereotypical view of the Other that presented Africans as jovial, oversexualized music and dance performers. White slave owners utilized the accepted vision to mentally create a hierarchy in which whites dominated blacks. This system assisted in maintaining an idea that one group is superior to another, therefore validating the dominant group's self-asserted position. Whites attempted to create an accepted vision of the black body as immoral, oversexualized, lazy, docile, and innately happy that would validate slavery while it also asserted the hegemony of whites in society.

Whites needed to create and believe in the subordinate state of the African for two reasons: to commodify the African and to justify their pursuits of colonies and people under the power of Europe, and later North America. With these ideals, Africa was rendered the subject of Europe's projections, positive or negative. French scholar Hèlène Cixous states, "I saw how the white superior, plutocratic, civilized world founded its power on repressions of populations who had suddenly become invisible."[45] Throughout the world Europeans asserted hegemony through forced physical subjugation and consistently emphasized difference or Otherness. Scholar Mary Louis Pratt in, *Imperial Eyes*, referred to the encounter space between non-Europeans and Europeans as contact zones that were an active part of cultural formations for an imperialistic region attempting to establish its rank through nationalist, ethnocentric manners.[46] The rise of English nationalism and the New World's need to define itself contributed to white Europeans' desire to be primarily focused on difference, establishing themselves as normative of the standard.[47] Recognizing Africans by their black skin placed them as the Other and contributed to the development of race in the social development of a New World culture. This New World's development of a cash crop and a desired free labor system resulted in the region being founded on principles of the African Other and the white standard.

Constructing Race

The foundation of race was centered on the ideals of difference and the creation of the Other.[48] The earliest record of the use of the word "race" entered the English language in 1508 in a poem by William Dunbar, *Dance of the Seven Deidly Sins*. The author referred to race in the verse, "And bakbyttaris of sindry racis," within the section on the sin of envy.[49] The word race was randomly mentioned throughout the sixteenth century but in the seventeenth century became associated with a term used that classified humans.[50] The term race evolved over time according to geographical space and culture. The word was used by the Spanish during the fifteenth and sixteenth centuries and described the "caste or quality of authentic horses" that were recognized through an iron brand on their body.[51] In the sixteenth century, the Spanish heavily influenced Europe and were active in the African slave trade. During this time, the Spanish began to use the term *race* to refer to the populations they discovered through their travels.[52] The exploration of foreign land and acquisition of power through their imperialistic pursuits led directly to the classification of new groups.

The English adopted the term *race* from the Spanish and used it to identify and characterize people that they discovered and exploited throughout their exploration. Travel journals were used to introduce to public favor, a part of the globe that was virtually unknown to the rest of the world. Whites assigned drastically different characteristics to Africans according to "their color, their lack of Christian faith, and their social customs."[53] This led to the formation of the concept of a single homogenized group.[54] Travel journals depicted blackness as a separate race of inferior and uncivilized beings. The continual distortion of African music and dance contributed to the misrepresentation of the black race. The term race was often applied to the black body but it only represented one dynamic of this social construction. It was apparent that Europeans were being associated with normality and power that began early within the slave trade and continued to be an element of the development of whiteness. European imperialism and assertions of hegemony over unknown land and people was the predecessor to the development of the concepts of whiteness that later thrived in North America. Travel accounts set the foundation for the expectation of blackness while they also framed a context for whiteness throughout the Western world. These written accounts were quite influential not only because of their technological innovations, but also because of their circulation via literary and nonliterary mediums during the time. Exploring the preponderance of these accounts and its place in the shaping of Western thought and ideology helps contribute to the understanding of its weight in structuring the development of race and racial stereotypes.

The Publication of Blackness

Travel journals were a popular form of literature and media in the developing New World economy. They were the first major source that illustrated and distributed images of Africa and its inhabitants to the Western world. Travel literature brought great voyages of discovery to an anticipating audience, and it also broadened community to several areas of the world in massive collections and translations that consistently crossed national boundaries in one form or another. Travel journals circulated to literate and illiterate populations an erroneous image of Africa to European (and Euro-American) society in various mediums of art including literature and theater. The illiterate populations were able to hear remnants of the propaganda of travel journals through their oral folk culture in music, stories, and art. For example, in 1493 a painting titled, *The Archers' Festival in the Garden of their Guild*, displayed a black musician performing for Europeans, and a painting in 1529, *Drummer at the Entrance of the Emperor*, portrayed a black-skinned drummer.[55] These observations of travelers created images of Africans that were actively disseminated among the populace.

Analogously, high quantities of publications regarding Africa and its inhabitants from the perspective of European travelers greatly infiltrated the development of the New World. The new synchronic novelty of developments within printing allowed for a disbursement of knowledge of the unknown outside world to other substantial groups of people. Scholar Benedict Anderson wrote that "Between 1500 and 1800 an accumulation of technological innovations . . . mediated through print-capitalism, was making this type of imagining possible."[56] Thus the sixteenth century was an age of transformation in European life. During this time of geographical exploration, the world ideas of *manifest destiny* for the Christian West collided with the new technological revolution of printing.[57] In some instances, the advances in print technology directly affected the formation of outside cultures and histories in a fundamental manner. For example, the method in which records were duplicated, knowledge transmitted, and information stored and retrieved all directly shaped and affected the perceptions of African cultures. With these new technological innovations, culturally supercilious and ethnocentric observations of African peoples were given credence in Western culture by the printed word.

Marshall McLuhan in the book, *Understanding Media*, argued that during the shift from an oral to a written culture, the human mental processes changed.[58] His argument was that the printed page narrows the dimensions of reality thus causing a more lasting effect on the reader. Such reasoning explains the long-term influence the travel journals of the sixteenth century had on African and later African American culture, history, and future. With the printing revolution there was a rise in the availability of reading materials, thus allowing a larger audience to be exposed to these myths. The transition from an elitist society, where few people had access to books, to a broader general public having open access to a variety of literature caused a change in writing style. The writers, including the travel journalists, found a need to appeal to the masses with interesting, sometimes mythical stories. The rise of the printing revolution and its effect on the European world (including North America) would not have been as influential without the rise of literacy during the century.

In 1533, half of England was semi-literate to literate.[59] Norman Bennett recognized that "Africa was but a blank canvas for Europe's imagination."[60] The culturally arrogant and ethnocentric observations of these explorers were given immortality in Western culture by the printed page.[61] Regardless of the known biases in these documents, they were the main intellectual source of information concerning the history and culture of Africa during the inception of the Atlantic slave trade.

The image of Africa and its inhabitants were plagued with pervasive myths that were distributed to the public through these writings. These misrepresentations manipulated and perverted the images of Africans and their culture, and they were distributed throughout distant lands and its people. Additionally these myths justified the assertion of European hegemony, therefore setting the foundation for tenets of race and racism in the New World. These images reflected the European's personal feelings of superiority between the conquerors and the conqueror. Through these travel accounts, Europeans created "domestic subjects of Euroimperialism" therefore allowing for the subjugation of Africans in the European (and North American) public sphere.[62]

Conclusion

In this relationship, between the African and European, a growing disparity in power was created and, consequently, Africa's true culture, history, and tradition were often hidden to the Western world. The misrepresentation of African culture paved the way for the establishment of the institution of slavery and centuries of mistreatment of Africans and African Americans by Europeans or Euro-Americans. Through records that testified to the Africans' "nature," European travelers created a negative image of blacks to the western world that ultimately laid the foundation for the conception of racial hierarchy that was so prevalent at the time. This hierarchy placed whites safely at the top as a physically, intellectually, and morally superior race, while blacks were relegated to the bottom.

In the end, these racial stereotypes followed enslaved Africans to the New World and sustained the institution of slavery for over two centuries. Moreover, the happy dancing and singing African presented in early travel journals transformed into the happy darky on the plantation, and later the Sambo or Coon in the minstrel show, therefore revealing the stability of these racial stereotypes over time. In tandem, the lascivious, oversexualized African woman became the Jezebel in the plantation society and mentally justified for white males their continual onslaught of sexual attacks against the black female body. Travel journals had a fundamental role in the consumption of negative images of the black body in popular culture. Black stereotypes are currently ingrained in American entertainment. Blacks are continually being cast in roles that distort black realities and confirm racial stereotypes. The distortion of music and dance in Africa, through travelers' words, directly led to the commodification of the black body and offered justifications for slavery for some, resulting in further injustices toward black people.

Notes

1. William L. Van Deburg, *Slavery & Race in American Popular Culture* (Madison: University of Wisconsin Press, 1984), xi.
2. Deburg, xi.
3. Africa is an immense territory with an intricate, multidimensional development contingent on the geographical location. Every section of the land was influenced and developed at its own pace and in a distinct manner. The main area of interest in this work is West Africa because of its complicated, intertwined history with the Western world, specifically North America. According to Basil Davidson's *West Africa before the Colonia Era: A History to 1850*, West Africa is a term coined in Europe by Europeans and refers to a specific region of land but has no geographical meaning. It basically constitutes lands and the offshore islands about 20 latitude north of the equator and 15 longitude eastward or the large area south of the Sahara Desert. The broad term of Europe pertains to those persons from the continent of Europe. Euro-American represents those persons that migrated to the New World from Europe prior to the Revolutionary War.
4. J. D. Fage, "Slaves and Society in Western Africa, c. 1445–c. 1700," *The Journal of African History*, 21, no. 3 (1980): 296.
5. T. Carlos Jacques, "From Savages and Barbarians to Primitives: Africa, Social Typologies, and History in Eighteenth-Century French Philosophy," *History and Theory*, 36, no 2 (May, 1997): 212.
6. The three components of the "other" comes directly from the work of Perry R. Hinton, *Stereotypes, Cognition and Culture* (Hove and East Sussex: Psychology Press, 2000), 7.
7. Hinton, 7–12.
8. Jacques, 212.
9. Olaudah Equiano, *The Interesting Narrative of The Life of Olaudah Equiano or Gustavus Vassa, The African, Written by Himself*, ed. Angelo Costanzo (Canada: Broadview Literary Texts, 2001), 48.
10. Equiano, 48–50.
11. J. H. Kwabena Nketia, *The Music of Africa* (New York: W.W. Norton, 1974).
12. Akia Euba, "The Potential of African Traditional Music as a Contemplative Art," *Black Orpheus 3.1*, (1974); and Kofi Agawu, *African Rhythm: A Northern Ewe Perspective* (Cambridge: Cambridge University Press, 1995).
13. Equiano, 47.
14. Ibid., 48.
15. The purpose of this section is to discuss the progressive character of music and

dance throughout many regions in West Africa, but the reader must recognize that the complexity of this artform and its culture are broader than described in this section. To read further on the diversity of music and dance as an artform please refer to: Eric Charry, *Mande Music: Traditional and Modern Music of the Maninka and Mandinka of Western Africa* (Chicago: University of Chicago Press, 2000); Bilial Abdurahman, *Tradition African Musical Instruments* (New York: Ethno Modes Forkloric Workshop); and Thomas Hale, *Griots and Griottes: Masters of Words and Music* (Bloomington: Indiana University Press, 1998).

16. Margery Perham and J. Simmons, eds., *African Discovery: An Anthology of Exploration* (Evanston, IL: Northwestern University Press, 1963), 16.

17. William B. Cohen, *The French Encounter with Africans: White Response to Blacks, 1530–1880*, (Bloomington: Indiana University Press, 1980), 1.

18. K.H. Waters, *Herodotus, the Historian: His Problems, Methods, and Originality* (Norman: University of Oklahoma, 1985); Percy G. Adams, ed., *Travel Literature through the Ages: An Anthology* (New York: Garland Publishing, Inc., 1988), 3. Herodotus is considered the "Father of History" and was one of the earliest writers to say anything about the interior of Africa. He visited Egypt and Libya in the fifth century BC and recorded his experiences while also documenting the layout of the land. For several centuries there was little added to the tales of Africa reported by Herodotus.

19. Herodotus, *History*, Bk IV, chs. 171–94, trans. J. Enoch Powell (Letchworth, Great Briatin: Temple University Press 1912), 341–48.

20. Herodotus, 341–48.

21. Travel journals reviewed that contain references to the performance arts culture in Africa are as follows: John Ogilby, *Africa: Being Accurate Description of the Regions of Aegypt, Barbary, Lybia, and Billendulgerid, The Land of Negroes, Guinee, Aethiopia, and the Abyssines; With All the Adjacent Island* (London: T. Johnson, 1670); El Hage Abd Salem Shabeeny, *An Account of Timbuctoo and Housa Territories in the Interior of Africa*, trans. James Grey Jackson, reprint, (London: Cass, 1976); Thomas Astley, *A New General Collection of Voyages and Travels; Consisting of the Most Esteemed Relations, which Have Been Hitherto Published in Any Language; Comprehending Everything Remarkable in Is Kind, in Europe, Asia, Africa, and America*, ed. John Green (London: Printed for T. Astley, 1745–47); Richard Hakluyt, *The Principall Navigations, Voyages and Discoveries of the English Nation, Made by Sea or Ouer land, to the Most Remote and Farthest Distant Quarters of the Earth at Any Time within the Compasse of These 1500 Yeeres: [yeeres]* (London: George Bishop, 1589) Text-fiche; Paul Erdmann, *Letters on West Africa and the Slave Trade: Paul Erdmann Isert's Journe to Guinea and the Carribeen Islands in Columbia* (1788) translated from the German and ed. Selena Axelrod Winsnes (New York: Oxford University Press, 1982); Thomas Birch Freeman, *Journals of Various Visits to the Kingdom of Ashanti, Aku, and Dahomi in Western Africa*, 3rd ed. (London: Cass, 1968). These travel journals mainly represent works reviewed but not directly quoted in this chapter's text. They were provided as further evidence of the continual reference to Africans association to music and dance.

22. In the theatrical realm, the tall tales of European explorers were seen throughout many areas of life in England and later transported to the New World. In William Shakespeare's work, *Othello* (1604), Africans are viewed as cannibals that eat each other, and have men whose heads grow beneath their shoulders. The manifestations of these black representations in theater production reinforce the stereotypes that were prevalent in European society. These plays also assist in the validation of the institution of slavery through representations of blacks as beast of burden in several plays. In 1588, a line in the play *Tamburlaine, Part Two* by Christopher Marlowe, states, "With naked Negroes shall thy coach be drawn." Another writer, Thomas

Lodge, displays blacks in a similar fashion by stating in *Wounds of Civil War*, "in his chair triumphant of gold, drawn by four Moors before the chariot." These dramas were an active part of society and introduced or reinforced the stereotypes of Africans while also validating the ideals behind the slavery system. Theater had a major impact on society because it visually displayed a belief system to persons of all ages and backgrounds that Africans were inferior, thereby creating a social system for their proliferation. Furthermore, these plays were often performed in the New World. In *Black People in the British Empire: An Introduction*, Peter Fryer examines the history of black people in England. Fryer states black people held three principle capacities in society, in addition to their literary portrayals as servants, prostitutes, and court entertainers. These roles fall under the submissive, heathen, or entertainer spectrum. These scenes of blacks as entertainers and servants supported the continuation and justification of the slavery system that existed in England and continued in the New World.

23. Richard Jobson, *The Golden Trade or A Discovery of the River Gambra, and The Golden Trade of the Aethiopians* (Teignmouth: E. E. Speight & R. H. Walpole, 1623), 105–8.

24. Jean-Baptiste Labat, *Nouvelle relation de l'Afrique occidentale: contenant une description exacte du Senegal & des païs situés entre le Cap-Blanc et la Riviére de Serrelionne jusqu' á plus de 300 lieues en avant dans les terres . . . Avec l' état ancient et present des compagnies qui y font le, 5 vols.*, 1728.

25. Richard F. Burton, *Wandering in West Africa, from Liverpool to Fernando Po* (New York: Dover, 1863).

26. Philip D. Curtin, *The Image of Africa, British Ideas and Action, 1780–1850*, 1, (Madison: University of Wisconsin Press, 1964), 327.

27. The perception and ideas of the European missionaries have been reviewed in great detail in many scholarly texts and articles. For further readings on missionaries in Africa see Roland Oliver, *The Missionary Factor in East Africa* (London: Longmans, 1952); J.F.A. Ajayi, *Christian Missions in Nigeria 1841–1891* (London: Longmans, 1965); R. L. Rotberg, *Christian Missionaries and the Creation of Northern Rhodesia* (Princeton: Princeton University Press, 1965); M. W. Murphree, *Christianity and the Shona* (London: Athlone, 1969); and H. W. Mobley, *The Ghanian's Image of the Missionary* (Leiden: Brill, 1970). I should note here that Christian missionaries were not the first group to enter to convert the African populations. Muslims entered and converted several regions in the continent during their earlier explorations.

28. Cohen, 33.

29. Norman R. Bennett, *African and Europe: from Roman times to the Present* (New York: Africana Publishing Co., 1975) Rev. Dr. J. Lewis Krapf, *Travels, Researcher, and Missionary Labours, During An Eighteen Years' Residence in Eastern Africa: Together with Journeys to Jagg, Usambara, Ukambani, Shoa, Absennia, and Khartum; and a Coasting Voyage From Mombaz to Cape Delgado* (London: Trubner and Co., Paternoster Row, 1860). The Portuguese and Spanish were the first of the European group that often connected their exploration activities to converting people to Catholicism. Missionaries were some of the most influential visitors, often learning local languages to assist them in their pursuits. Such Portuguese missionaries that left influential travel journals include: Antonio da Coinceicao, "Tratado," English translation, "Treatise on the Cuama Rivers," in D. N. Beach and H. de Noronha, "The Shona and the Portuguese 1575–1890" (2 vols.: Harare, 1980), 1:196–229 Francisco Monclaro, "Account of the Journey Made by Fathers of the Company of Jesus with Francisco Barretto in the Conquest of Monootapa in the Year 1569," in Theal/RSEA, 3:202–53.

30. Quote found in A. F.R.G.S., *Wandering in West Africa From Liverpool to Fernando Po.*, (London: Tinsley Brothers, 1863),178.

31. Ibid.; Toyin Falola, ed., *African Cultures and Societies Before 1885*, v. 2 (North Carolina: Carolina Academic Press, 2000).

32. Gabriel Almond and James S. Coleman, eds., *The Politics of the Developing Areas*, (Princeton: Princeton University Press), 1960, 278.

33. Almond and Coleman, 33. This work gives great explanation on the superstitions of Africa and proclaimed that "Polygamy exists on every part of the coast" of Africa contributing to the "heathenish" ideals of the region.

34. Kariamu Welsh Asante, "The Jerusarema Dance of Zimbabwe," *Journal of Black Studies* 15, no. 4 (June 1985): 381–403.

35. T. J. Bowen, *Adventures and Missionary Labours in Several Countries in the Interior of Africa from 1849 to 1856*, 2nd ed., (London: Frank Cass & Co. Ltd.,1968), 18.

36. Richard G. Cole, "Sixteenth-Century Travel Books as a Source of European Attitudes Toward Non-White and Non-Western Culture," *Proceedings of the American Philosophical Society* 116, no. 1 (February 15, 1972): 66.

37. Bowen, 384.

38. Jan Huygen van Linschoten, *Discours of Voyages into East and West Indies* (Amsterdam: Theatrum Obris Terrarum, 1974), 202.

39. Ali A. Mazrui, "European Exploration and Africa's Self-Discovery," *The Journal of Modern African Studies*, 7, no. 4 (1969): 663.

40. Mary Louise Pratt, *Imperial Eyes: Travel Writing And Transculturation* (London: Routeledge, 1992), 69–70, 10.

41. Exerpts from *The Proceedings of the Association for Promoting the Discovery of the Interior Parts of Africa, London*, 1790. Found in an archival collection of works in a published text, *West African Explorers*, C. Howard, ed., (London, New York and Toronto: Oxford University Press, 1951),74–75; Records of the African Association 1788–1831. Ed., *Robin Hallet for the Royal Geographical Society*, (London: Nelson, 1964).

42. Pratt, 69–70.

43. Found in Pratt, 71.

44. Sander Gilman, *Difference and Pathology: Stereotypes of Sexuality, Race, and Madness* (Ithaca, NY: Cornell University Press, 1985), 16–27.

45. David Wood and Robert Bernasconi, eds., *Derrida and Difference* (Coventry, England: Parousia Press, 1985).

46. Pratt, 43.

47. Alden T. Vaughan and Virginia Mason Vaughan, "Before Othello: Elizabethan Representations of Sub-Saharan Africans," *The William and Mary Quarterly*, 3rd Ser., 54, no.1 (January 1997): 21.

48. Audrey Smedley, *Race in North America: Origin and Evolution of a Worldview*, (Boulder, CO: Westview Press, 1999), 37.

49. Smedley, 38; and Peter Osborne and Stella Sanford, ed., *Philosphies of Race and Ethnicity* (New York: Continuum, 2002).

50. Smedley, 38; and Michael Banton, *Racial Theories* (Cambridge: Cambridge University Press, 1998).

51. Banton, 60–65.

52. Banton, 62.

53. Cohen, 27.

54. Cohen, 27.

55. A copy of these paintings may be found in Peter Fryer's, *Black Africans in Renaissance Europe* (London: Pluto Press, 1988), 36–38. There are several other paintings depicted throughout the text displaying black-skinned persons performing in music and dance.

56. Benedict Anderson, *Imagined Communities: Reflections on the Origin and Spread of Nationalism*, (London: Verson, 1983), 188.
57. Cole, 59–67.
58. Marchall McLuhan, *Understanding Media: The Extensions of Man* (New York: The MIT Press, 1964), 178; and Glenn Wilmott, *Modernism in Reverse*, (Toronto: University of Toronto Press, 1996).
59. Bennett, 169.
60. Jacques, 201.
61. Richard G. Cole, "Sixteenth-Century Travel Books as a Source of European Attitudes Toward Non-White and Non-Western Culture," *Proceeding of the American Philosophical Society* 116, no. 1 (February 15, 1972): 59.
62. Pratt, 4 and The term public sphere was first introduced in *Jürgen Habermas, The Structural Transformation of the Public Sphere—An Inquiry into a Category of Bourgeois Society*, trans. Thomas Burger (Cambridge, MA: MIT Press, 1991). Habermas defined the public sphere as "a network for communicating information and points of view," which becomes public opinion.

Works Cited

Abdurahman, Bilal. *Traditional African Musical Instruments.* New York: Ethno Modes Folkloric Workshop, 1987.

Adams, Percy G. *Travel Literature and the Evolution of the Novel.* Lexington: University of Kentucky Press, 1983.

Ajayi, J. F. A. *Christian Missions in Nigeria 1841–1891.* London: Longmans, 1965.

Almond, Gabriel, and James S. Coleman, eds. *Politics of the Developing Areas.* Princeton, NJ: Princeton University Press, 1960.

Anderson, Benedict. *Imagined Communities: Reflections on the Origin and Spread of Nationalism.* London: Verson, 1983.

Asante, Kariamu Welsh."The Jerusarema Dance of Zimbabwe," *Journal of Black Studies* 15, no. 4 (June 1985): 381–403.

Astley, Thomas. *A New General Collection of Voyages and Travels; Consisting of the Most Esteemed Relations, which Have Been hitherto Published in Any Language; Comprehending Everything Remarkable in Is Kind, in Europe, Asia, Africa, and America.* edited by John Green. London: Printed for T. Astley, 1745–47.

Banton, Michael. *Racial Theories.* Cambridge: Cambridge University Press, 1998.

Bennett, H. S. "The Production and the Dissemination of Vernacular Manuscripts in the Fifteenth Century." *The Library, fifth ser.*, 1, no. 3–4 (1946, 1947): 1947.

Bennett, Norman R. *African and Europe: From Roman Times to the Present.* New York: Africana Publishing Co., 1975.

Bowen, T. J. *Adventures and Missionary Labours in Several Countries in the Interior of Africa from 1849 to 1856.* 2nd ed. London: Frank Cass & Co. Ltd., 1857.

Burton, Richard F. *Wandering in West Africa, from Liverpool to Fernando Po.* New York: Dover, 1863.

Caillié, Réné. *Travels through Central Africa to Timbuctoo; and across the Great Desert to Morocco; Performed in the Years, 1824–1828.* 2 vols. London: Frank Cass, 1968.

Chambers, E. K. *The Elizabethan Stage* 4 vols. Oxford: The Clarendon Press, 1923.

Charry, Eric. *Mande Music: Traditional and Modern Music of the Maninka and Mandinka of Western Africa.* Chicago: University of Chicago Press, 2000.

"Christianity and Native Government of Uganda," *The Church Missionary Review*, 72 (1921): 306.

Clarkson, Thomas. *An Essay on the Slavery and Commerce of the Species, Particularly the Africa.* London: J Philips, 1785.

Cohen, William B. *The French Encounter with Africans: White Response to Blacks, 1530–1880.* Bloomington: Indiana University Press, 1980.

Cole, Richard G. "Sixteenth-Century Travel Books as a Source of European Attitudes toward Non-White and Non-Western Culture," *Proceedings of the American Philosophical Society* 116, no. 1 (February 15, 1972).

Curtin, Philip D. *The Image of Africa, British Ideas and Action, 1780–1850 Vol. 1.*Madison: University of Wisconsin Press, 1964.

Davidson, Basil. *West Africa before the Colonial Era: A History to 1850.* Essex: Addison Wesley Publishing, 1998.

Deburg, William Van. *Slavery & Race in American Popular Culture.* Madison: University of Wisconsin Press, 1984.

Dupuis, Joseph, esq. *Journal of a Residence in Ashantee.* London: Printed for Henry Colburn New Burlington Street, 1824.

Equiano, Olaudah. *The Interesting Narrative of The Life of Olaudah Equiano or Gustavus Vassa, The African, Written by Himself* edited by Angelo Costanzo. Canada: Broadview Literary Texts, 2001.

Erdmann, Paul. *Letters on West Africa and the Slave Trade: Paul Erdmann Isert's Journe to Guinea and the Carribeen Islands in Columbia.* Translated from the German and edited by Selena Axelrod Winsnes. Oxford: Oxford University Press, 1788, 1982.

Erickson, Peter. "Representations of Blacks and Blackness in the Renaissance," *Criticism*, no. 35 (1993): 199–527.

Euba, Akia. "The Potential of African Traditional Music as a Contemplative Art," *Black Orpheus 3.1*, (1974), and Agawu, Kofi, *African Rhythm: A Northern Ewe Perspective.* Cambridge: Cambridge University Press, 1995.

Fage, J. D. "Slaves and Society in Western Africa, c. 1445–c. 1700," *The Journal of African History* 21, no. 3 (1980): 296.

Falola, Toyin, ed. *African Cultures and Societies Before 1885* Vol. 2. North Carolina: Carolina Academic Press, 2000.

Freeman, Thomas Birch. *Journals of Various Visits to the Kingdom of Ashanti, Aku, and Dahomi.* 3rd ed. London: Cass, 1968.

Fryer, Peter. *Black People in the British Empire: An Introduction.* London: Pluto, 1988.

Gilman, Sander. *Difference and Pathology: Stereotypes of Sexuality, Race and Madness.* Ithaca, NY: Cornell University Press, 1985.

Habermas, Jürgen. *The Structural Transformation of the Public Sphere—An Inquiry into a Category of Bourgeois Society.* Translated by Thomas Burger. Cambridge, MA: MIT Press, 1991.

Hakluyt, Richard A. 1589. *The Principall Navigations, Voyages Traffiques and Discoveries of the English Nation, Made by Sea or Overland, to the Most Remote and Farthest Distant Quarters of the Earth at Any Time within the Compasse of These 1600 Yeares: [yeers].* London: George Bishop, Text-fiche, 1589.

Hale, Thomas. *Griots and Griottes: Masters of Words and Music.* Bloomington: Indiana University Press, 1998.

Hallet, Robin. *The Penetration of Africa: European Exploration in North and West Africa to 1815.* New York: Frederick Prager, 1965.

Herodotus. *History*. Translated by J. Enoch Powell. Letchworth, Great Britain: J. Enoch Powell Temple Press, 1912.

Hinton, Perry R. *Stereotypes, Cognition and Culture*. Hove: Psychology Press, 2000.

Howard, Cecil, ed. *West African Explorers*. London: Oxford University Press, 1951.

Jacques, T. Carlos. "From Savages and Barbarians to Primitives: Africa, Social Typologies, and History in Eighteenth-Century French Philosophy," *History and Theory* 36, no. 2 (May, 1997): 212.

Jobson, Richard. *The Golden Trade or A Discovery of the River Gambra, and The Golden Trade of the Aethiopians.*Teignmouth: E. E. Speight & R. H. Walpole, 1623.

Khaldun, Ibn. *The Muqaddimah: An Introduction to History*. Translated by Franz Rosenthal Princeton, NJ: Princeton University Press, 1969.

Krapf, Rev. Dr. J. Lewis. *Travels, Researcher, and Missionary Labours, During An Eighteen Years' Residence in Eastern Africa: Together with Journeys to Jagg, Usambara, Ukambani, Shoa, Absennia, and Khartum; and a Coasting Voyage From Mombaz to Cape Delgado*. London: Trubner and Co., Paternoster Row, 1860.

Labat, Jean-Baptiste. *The Memoirs of Pere Labat 1693–1705*. Translated by John Eaden. London: F. Cass, 1931.

Mazrui, Ali A. "European Exploration and Africa's Self-Discovery," *The Journal of Modern African Studies* 7, no. 4 (1969): 661–76.

McLuhan, Marshall. *Understanding Media: The Extensions of Man*. New York: MIT Press, 1964.

Mobley, H. W. *The Ghanian's Image of the Missionary*. Leiden: Brill, 1970.

Murphree, M. W. *Christianity and the Shona*. London: Athlone, 1969.

Nketia, J. H. Kwabena. *The Music of Africa* New York: W.W. Norton, 1974.

Ogilby, John. *Africa: Being Accurate Description of the Regions of Aegypt, Barbary, Lybia, and Billendulgerid, the Land of Negroes, Guinee, Aethiopia, and the Abyssines; With all the Adjacent Island*. London: T. Johnson, 1670.

Oliver, Roland. *The Missionary Factor in East Africa*. London: Longmans, 1952.

Park, Mungo. *Travels in Interior Districts of Africa*. Edited by Kate Ferguson Marsters. Durham: Duke University Press, 2000.

Perham, Margery, and J. Simmons, eds. *African Discovery: An Anthology of Exploration*. Evanston, ILL: Northwestern University Press, 1963.

Pratt, Mary Louise. *Imperial Eyes: Travel Writing And Transculturation*. London: Routeledge, 1992.

Rotberg, R. L. *Christian Missionaries and the Creation of Northern Rhodesia*. Princeton, NJ: Princeton University Press, 1965.

Sandford, Stella, and Osborne, Peter, ed. *Philosophies of Race and Ethnicity*. New York: Continuum, 2002.

Shabeeny, El Hage Abd Salem. *An Account of Timbuctoo and Housa, territories in the interior of Africa*. translated by James Grey Jackson. Reprint. London: Cass, 1976.

Shakespeare, William. *As You Like It*. Edited by Samuel Thurber, Jr., and Louise Wetherbee. Norwood, Mass: Norwood Press, 1922.

Smedley, Audrey. *Race in North America: Origin and Evolution of a Worldview*. Boulder, CO: Westview Press, 1999.

Twitty, Michael. "The Persistence of Memory," *The Journal of Negro History* 85, no. 3 (Summer 2000): 176–82.

Van Linschoten, Jan Huygen. *Discours of Voyages into the East and West Indies.* Amsterdam: Theatrum Obris Terrarum, 1974.

Vaughan, Alden T.. and Virginia Mason Vaughan. "Before Othello: Elizabethan Representations of Sub-Saharan Africans," *The William and Mary Quarterly.* 3rd Ser., 54, no. 1 (January 1997): 21.

Waters, K. H. *Herodotus, the Historian: His Problems, Methods, and Originality.* Norman: University of Oklahoma Press, 1985.

Winterbottom, Thomas Masterman. *An Account of the Native Africans in the Neighborhood of Sierra Leon.* 2nd Edition. Edited by John D. Hargreaves and E. Maurice Backett. London: F. Cass & Co., Lt., 1969.

Wood, David, and Robert Bernasconi, eds. *Derrida and Difference.* Coventry, England: Parousia Press, 1985.

The Culture of Sentiments and the Black Female Body in the Nineteenth-Century Literary Marketplace

Allison E. Francis

IN "OF THE ASSOCIATION OF IDEAS," DAVID HUME OFFERS A USEFUL framework for approaching the process of narration: "[i]t follows that in narrative compositions the events or actions which the writer relates must be connected together by some bond or tie. They must be related to each other in the imagination, and form a kind of *unity* which may bring them under one plan or view, and which may be the object or end of the writer in his first undertaking" (1955, 35). Hume argues that literary production requires purpose, intent and "unity," a gesture that effectively centers the narrative for the writer and eventually, for the reader.

If nineteenth-century literary production is read under Hume's rubric, then sentimentality provided this unifying gesture that offers a means of organizing an author's narrative in a manner that appeals to early American and British reading audiences, and ensured a text's marketability. One could argue that the purpose of certain nineteenth-century literature, such as conduct manuals, etiquette books, and/or slave narratives was to effect social change. However, the intent to achieve financial independence for the writer (or at least to alleviate, temporarily, certain pecuniary difficulties) through the act of telling also was an acceptable intention.

Accordingly my concern here lies in examining how nineteenth-century black female writers in the Caribbean and the United States exercise Hume-ian purpose, intent and unity in order to effect social change. To illustrate my argument, I will refer to two representative texts from the English-speaking Caribbean: Mary Prince's *The History of Mary Prince: A West Indian Slave* (1831), and Mary Seacole's *Wonderful Adventures of Mrs. Seacole in Different Lands* (1857), and two texts from the United States: Harriet A. Jacobs's *Incidents in the Life of a Slave Girl* (1861), and Harriet E. Wilson's *Our Nig or, Sketches From the Life of a Free Black in a Two-Story White House North* (1859). Each of these texts employs the unifying culture of sentiments and makes use of the literary marketplace. Mary Prince, born in Bermuda, narrated her *History* to English abolitionist Susanna Strickland, a family friend of Thomas Pringle, who became Prince's editor and secured her freedom after she ran away from her West Indian slave owners when they brought her to London (Prince 1993). Despite her early memories of living alongside her parents and siblings, Prince eventually was sold away from her family and subjected to one cruel master after the other, who abused and continually overworked her in crowded dairies, harvest fields, and the unforgiving salt ponds of Turk's Island. Harriet A. Jacobs, born in Edenton, North Carolina, also revisits her family life in her slave narrative, and details her fortunate ability to form relationships with her relatives and an admirably cohesive slave community, despite her debilitating slave status. Using anecdotal material as well as her own experiences, Jacobs, writing under the pseudonym "Linda Brent," exposes the terrible, but well-documented "incidents" of African American slave girls who found themselves accountable to licentious masters and their jealous wives.

The narratives of Mary Seacole, a freeborn Jamaican, and Harriet Wilson, a freeborn Northern African American, offer alternative views on what constitutes a nineteenth-century black woman's role in the so-called free societies of England, Jamaica, and New England, respectively. Seacole's worldly travels took her to the wilds of Panama and California where she established hotels and cafeterias for gold seekers and canal workers regardless of color or ethnicity. Seacole also traveled throughout the war-torn European landscapes of Turkey, Ukraine, and the Crimea, dispensing medicine and basic food supplies to homesick English soldiers. Unlike Seacole's entertaining memoirs, Wilson's fictively structured narrative is a thinly veiled account of Wilson's harrowing experiences as the indentured servant "Frado" for the "Bellmont family" in the North. But like Seacole, Wilson's strong work ethic led her to secure odd jobs as a seamstress, hat-maker and hair product manufacturer, in order to support herself and her ailing son after she was released from her servitude (Wilson 1990).

Culture of Sentiments

By defining the intentional use of sentiments and recognizing how these black female writers[1] blended sentimentalism in their literary production, we discover that this genre offered them a safe medium through which they could express both their emotions and criticism of social mores and political policies that denied basic human rights and citizenship to nineteenth-century Afro-Caribbeans and African Americans. Of course, such a quick response as this threatens to simplify what I believe to be the convoluted nature of sentimental discourse in black writing. Nevertheless Cynthia S. Hamilton reminds us that sentimentality centers on evasion. She argues effectively that both subject/object and reader conspire and collude together through the sentimental form to avoid or evade probing such disturbing issues as the nature of the slave trade, voluntary and involuntary subjection, and bodily suffering. "But whether the sentimental treatment is used in an effort to protect the self-liberated slave from a painful past or to pander to the sensibilities of middle-class readership," writes Hamilton, "the result is a facile and dangerous evasion that commodifies suffering" (Hamilton 1999, 114). Nevertheless Hamilton also recognizes that such evasions create a comfort zone, allowing writers and readers to examine these painful issues from a safe distance.

The sentimental conventions that many nineteenth-century British and American writers employs in their writing to affect their readers' sensibilities and codify moral behavior appealed to nineteenth-century Afro-Caribbean and African American writers. Sentimental discourse, they believed, would enable them to combine realism and an emotional appeal within a popular literary genre. Black writers also felt that sentimental discourse could best convey to white readers the socioeconomic oppression and political restrictions that enslaved and freed blacks experienced in the Americas.

To this end, Bruce Burgett argues that sentimentalism in the United States

> located readers' bodies as both pre-political sources of personal authenticity *and* as public sites of political contestation. The body thus served two contradictory functions within sentimentalism: it provided a surface upon which sensations were expressed for a public that could imagine itself as respecting the autonomy of everybody, and it provided a literary site for the management of those sensations through collective and potentially heteronymous means. (1998, 3–4).

Although his argument appears centered on the reader's body, Burgett's thesis is more concerned with how the body operates in "literary and political public spheres," because both the body and the body politic provide an elastic tool for questioning contradictory issues in the political and sentimental history of early America. In his introduction, he appeals to an all-encompassing definition of politics that embraces "virtually all forms of sociality, including intimate and corporeal relations," and "a name for the public space of that ideological struggle." Burgett believes that sentimentalism closes the gap between these two opposing definitions of politics "by manifesting both the forms of mediation that promise to make social relations republican and the forms of embodiment that promise to make political relations democratic" (1998, 8). Considering Burgett's argument, we begin to understand then how the black writer's use of sentimental discourse could represent a means of democratizing the slave or acknowledging the citizenship of the free black, rather than operating solely as a literary genre.

This compelling argument notwithstanding, the appropriation of this popular genre by black female writers both in the Caribbean and the United States would hopefully provide another means toward achieving their financial independence with the added caveat of imprinting their names on the literary page. This means that by unifying their stories through the language of sentiments and sentimentality, a genre that was still conversant within nineteenth-century literary circles (especially in the Americas), Afro-Caribbean and African American writers, especially black women, hoped to wear the mantle of sociability and respectability, or at the very least, familiarity, when they were soliciting their reading public. In this manner, sentimentality could award them Burgett's literary body which would confer a form of social status in literary markets, even if the use of sentiments could not guarantee them equal footing on the steps of town market halls or in residential parlors.

Sentimental discourse in the nineteenth century, then, could and did serve to break down social and (temporarily) racial barriers by claiming a common language of feeling that all humans participated in and comprehended. Afro-Caribbean and African American female writers, like their male counterparts, were engaged in reconstructing how they appeared and operated in their communities by imagining a textual body that would supplant their literal ones. By appropriating the popular genre of sentiments and sentimentality to appeal to their target audience, authors were able to enter the world of publishing and generate income through the circulation of this textual body within the marketplace. This textual body, or if you prefer, text, remedies the author's lack of social and political access because of its ability to be sociable—to circulate more freely among literate circles in ways that the woman's actual black body could not. Supplanting the human, emotive body with a narrative that employs sentimentality to depict recognizable traits of human foibles and experiences—humor, deprived (and sometimes depraved) love, ethics, pathos, celebration, rebellion, and liberation—produced human social life in a text. Consequently the circulation of Afro-Caribbean and African American women's writing and their ability to create accessible, sociable texts is crucial because such circulation was intended to promote the humanity of black women, familiarity with racial differences, and sympathy (or outrage) for the plight of black women among white American and British audiences. And it is quite possible that writing their story became one method that promised potential income for these enslaved, newly freed, and freeborn black females.

In other words, by authoring and publishing her story in the nineteenth century, an Afro-Caribbean like Mary Prince or Mary Seacole, and an African American like Harriet A. Jacobs or Harriet E. Wilson, would have transformed her visibly black body into an even more public one—written text. And in each text, she fashioned yet another body—the emotive, thinking, useful human body. This body, if not entirely deracialized, is socialized and identifiably "woman." My use of the term "woman" here is meant to highlight the social rather than biological concerns of being an unprotected woman of color in diverse nineteenth-century communities. Of course, even this new body of words, this "new" nineteenth-century text they created, is still subject to sexual and editorial threats by its very public circulation in the literary marketplace, but these women exerted better control over its movement than they did their physical bodies. For instance, Jacobs carried her manuscript with her during her tour of Europe and was able to secure an English publisher (Jacobs 1987). In this way she was able to exchange her written body for literary, commercial, and financial purposes. Through their narratives then, these early black female writers forced their readers to recognize them as active members *within*, rather than outside, their respective social structures.

Black Women's Literary Production

To examine the literary production of women, we should turn to Susan Coultrap-McQuin and her intriguing text *Doing Literary Business: American Women Writers in the Nineteenth Century*, where she argues that the careers of nineteenth-century American women writers were circumscribed by prevailing Victorian societal norms—norms constructed primarily by men. American Victorians "also encouraged competition, but warned that too much of it would destroy the rational social order. Victorians urged conformity to genteel social standards as the humane, democratic route to status and success" (1990, 7). Unfortunately Coultrap-McQuin continually stresses that writing as a career in the mid-nineteenth century was limited to "white, Protestant, and middle-class women," although she acknowledges the possibility of exceptions to her rule without listing any (1990, 21).

Notwithstanding their ambivalent interpretation of domesticity, African Americans like Harriet A. Jacobs and Harriet E. Wilson, and Afro-Caribbeans like Mary Seacole, and even Mary Prince to a lesser extent (since she orally transcribed her narrative), were likely candidates for what Coultrap-McQuin terms the "Vision of New Womanhood," even though Coultrap-McQuin's discussion is self-consciously limited to the literary production of white female writers. The "Vision of New Womanhood" promoted "aspirations for achievement within the definition of womanhood so that this 'Vision' sometimes called for blending masculine and feminine characteristics as the nineteenth century defined them, but it usually didn't go so far as to say that women and men could be the same" (Coultrap-McQuin 1990, 12). According to Coultrap-McQuin, this liberal ideal of womanhood justified Victorian women's advancement into more public social networks, like the literary marketplace—just one of the many markets wherein Seacole and Wilson, specifically, promoted themselves.

Consequently conspicuous movement outside of their proscribed racial and gender roles was problematic for "Visionary" women like Seacole and Jacobs who claimed and disclaimed various identities that facilitated (and sometimes thwarted) their attempts to circulate in the public arena. For example, Seacole in *Wonderful Adventures* portrays herself as both a fearless picaresque figure and a demure free lady of color, while Jacobs in *Incidents* describes her infirmities and the demeaning position of female slaves, but also highlights her strong will and rebellious acts against enslavement. Writing for economic survival then becomes a radical thought for nineteenth-century black women in the Caribbean and the United States, especially as few white female writers existed solely on their arts, excepting perhaps Louisa May Alcott, Lydia Maria Childs, Fanny Fern, Catharine Williams, and Harriet Beecher Stowe. Although critics like Sandra Gilbert and Susan Gubar acknowledge that these white women writers were able to establish a "female literary subculture,"[2] black women like Prince, Seacole, Jacobs and Wilson produced their texts primarily in isolation rather than within a sustained community or subculture of black writers.

When Gilbert and Gubar examine the concerns nineteenth-century white women faced as they attempted to reconcile their literary pursuits with their domestic obligations, they shed light on how women like the Brontë sisters and Emily Dickinson, to name a few, had to simultaneously fight against and dwell within the confines of the patriarchal structure of both society and the literary marketplace: "The literary woman has always faced equally degrading options when she had to define her public presence in the world. If she did not suppress her work entirely or publish it pseudonymously or anonymously, she could modestly confess her female 'limitations' and concentrate on the lesser 'subjects' reserved for ladies as becoming to their inferior powers" (1979, 64).

These lesser subjects, sewing, teaching, and domestic work, were more socially acceptable occupations than the manly pursuit of letters and sciences that required these women to either disfigure their bodies by wearing figurative or literal trousers, or by continually insisting upon their femininity and, consequently, their inadequacies as writers.

But few nineteenth-century black women, especially the four considered in this study, appear to suffer from this transgendering identity crisis that Gilbert and Gubar reveal in their research. Prince, Seacole, Jacobs, and Wilson were more concerned with demanding recognition in their communities as humans first and earning money second, than expressing anxiety about becoming social pariah by virtue of their writing.[3] Jacobs specifically writes near the end of *Incidents* that she "was impatient to go to work and earn money, that I might change the uncertain position of my children. Mr. Sands [the white father of her two children] had not kept his promise to emancipate them" (Jacobs 1990, 166). And in her preface, Wilson humbly drew attention to her pecuniary needs: "Deserted by kindred, disabled by failing health, I am forced to some experiment which shall aid me in maintaining myself and child without extinguishing this feeble life" (1990). Even Seacole solicits her friends and sympathizers to support her financially through the purchase of her narrative (1988, 26–30). So, rather than suffering anxieties about social acceptance and gender identification, the anxieties of these African Caribbean and African American women were centered on racial prejudice, basic human rights, and economic survival for themselves and their families, by any means necessary.

In my readings of Prince, Seacole, Jacobs, and Wilson, they are equally engaged in revolutionizing sentimentality as they are in writing or promoting a profit-making story. Recognizing the necessity for monetary gain for these black women is equally as important as acknowledging that this was not the only purpose for writing and publishing their stories. However, neither should this discussion suggest that Prince, Seacole, Jacobs, or Wilson expected to make writing their sole profession as did William Wells Brown, Frederick Douglass, and, later, Frances E. W. Harper.[4]

We do know that in North America during the eighteenth century, women of African descent, like Phyllis Wheatley and Sojourner Truth, were beginning to participate in polite and public discourse. Indeed,

Frances Smith Foster in her book, *Written by Herself: Literary Production by African American Women, 1746–1892*, details a comprehensive cultural history of African American women's literature from the oral slave history of "Alice" (1686) to the political tracts of activists like Maria W. Stewart and Anna Julia Cooper. Foster documents women who "testified to their personal experiences and perceptions and to those they shared with their communities . . . They used the Word [English language, religious, secular, African, and American sources] as both a tool and a weapon to correct, to create, and to confirm their vision of life as it was and as it could become" (1993, 2). Foster's study unmistakably demonstrates that an early path had been cleared for Afro-Caribbeans and African Americans to imagine themselves as innovators, contributors, and heirs to sociopolitical public discourse, through their poetry, letters, and literature.

Nineteenth-Century Literary Marketplace

Not surprisingly, the black female author, like her male counterpart, hoped to gain profit through her receipt of proceeds from sales of her narrative in the literary marketplace. Thus does her intent become two-fold because one, she expected to garner sympathy and action against the dehumanizing effect of slavery and/or the devastating effects of racism in a black woman's life, and perhaps, secondly, she hoped to make enough money to survive independently—however tenuous, such a life would be predicated on the minor sales of just one narrative. So, how viable was the literary world during this time period? Michael T. Gilmore argues that the period between 1815 and 1860 signaled "the era of the marketplace," and that "by 1850, when over ninety percent of adult whites could read and write, the United States boasted the largest literary public in history." He adds "the appearance of a mass readership meant that publishers could realistically expect to make a profit on books written by Americans" (1985, 4). Gilmore also notes the momentous conversion of American letters into commercial art: "Literature itself became an article of commerce at this time, as improvements in manufacture, distribution, and presentation helped to create a national audience for letters. The gentlemanly author who wrote for a like-minded group of equals gave way to the professional who depended for a livelihood on sales of his books to an impersonal public" (1985).

Cathy Davidson also explores this reading revolution that began in the late eighteenth century, lasting through the middle of the nineteenth century. She identifies and examines various "quiet" revolutions that impacted the Industrial Revolution: "a reading revolution that began in the latter portions of the eighteenth century and continued until the middle of the next century, a revolution not just in levels of education and literacy but in the increased access of more and more citizens to books that could be read for political and material advantage as well as for pleasure" (1986, vii).

Davidson is able to chart mid-nineteenth-century America's, "movement toward industrialization and urbanization and the democratization of the written word" (1986). In addition, she challenges other critics and readers to participate in a revolution that continuously scrutinizes and recreates modern literary and historical methodology. Although Gilmore and Davidson center their discussion on the American marketplace, obviously this movement toward a literary marketplace that moved from eighteenth-century England to nineteenth-century America, increases the American and British public's access to political, social, and entertaining reading materials.

Evidently what Gilmore and Davidson are describing is the commodification of books, and a shift from seeing literature as an expensive enterprise for both reader and publisher (available only to the elite), to experiencing literature as a more culturally accessible event. Such a movement in the literary marketplace favors healthy competition and free trade. As Gilmore puts it, "Publishing had become an industry, and the writer a producer of commodities for the literary marketplace" (1985). Nonetheless terms like "commodities " and the "marketplace" connote multiple definitions when applied to the discourse of nineteenth-century Afro-Caribbean and African American writers. Despite the appeal of the nineteenth-century literary marketplace that did favor slave narratives, memoirs, and fiction-laced autobiographies of and about Afro-Caribbean and African Americans, black female writers continually wrote within male-defined commerce. They also appropriated a proscribed literary genre with its accompanying stereotypes that, nevertheless, lent them a voice, a public ear, and a network of stylistic techniques to simultaneously reveal and cloak their selfhood and identities.[5]

Not surprisingly, their intent and purpose for such literary production was multivalent. Both Afro-Caribbeans and African Americans would need to generate a cultural and literary foundation that William Wells Brown believed must "awaken and expound the intellectual activity and comprehension of a present or approaching generation" because none had existed (1991, 140). However hyperbolic Brown's observations might have been, when we consider Foster's study that has proven the existence of such a literary precedence, Brown was engaged in rectifying a then perceived lack of intellectual property and literary production that he attributed to the horrors of slavery. If his 1855 statement was an indirect call to arms, or pens, then Mary Prince, Mary Seacole, Harriet A. Jacobs, and Harriet E. Wilson are examples of women who provided (and are still providing) the literary stimuli to the next generation—be they fugitive slaves, newly freed, or free-born—through the conception of their textual bodies, and the realization of their narratives that did and could negotiate the fluid social landscapes of the Americas in the nineteenth century.

Conclusion

Although both black and female during an intolerant age, women like Mary Prince, Mary Secole, Harriet A. Jacobs, and Harriet E. Wilson lay claim to a social life and entered into David Hume's "conversible world" of social landscapes and literary worlds where they expected their narrative bodies to inform rather than hinder their advancement in the literary marketplace. As Henry Louis Gates, Jr. points out in his discussion of the "proliferation" of black literary production, "writing became the visible sign, the commodity of exchange, the text and technology of reason" (1988, 132). Clearly through the act of telling or writing their stories, Afro-Caribbean and African American women (and men) contributed to a literary tradition, and fashioned a more stable identity for themselves that transcended the auction block.

In the presence of their "foreigness" (marked by ethnicity and gender), nineteenth-century black female writers needed to build on other identities, on other sources of stability. One of those alternative sources, as we have seen in this study, was their appropriation of sentiments to reclaim their humanity and to reveal and denounce personal, gender, and racial injustices. Through sentimentality Afro-Caribbeans like Prince and Seacole, and African Americans like Jacobs and Wilson relied in part on the emotional response they evoked from their predominately white audience to provide the leveling field between race and gender. Their insistence on such emotional, moral, or ethical responses to their highly personal yet unquestionably political narratives allows the reading public to empathize with the complicated status of black women, even if they could never truly understand it. If we turn back to Hume, we acknowledge that unity and intent became important factors in how blacks (as well as whites) told their stories. Notwithstanding what may have been their true narrative intention, the urge that these black women had to produce, to organize, and to construct their identity through literature, operates as a means of gaining them entry into the consumer culture of the Americas and allowed them to circulate their narratives in this literary marketplace. Narratives as written on or about the black body then translate into profits these women could and did attempt to manage (however tenuously) for their own social and economic survival.

Notes

1. For the purposes of this chapter, I will use the term "black" to identify nineteenth-century Afro-Caribbean and African American writers and their texts. Although I realize this is a reductive application of a broadly used signifier of race, I do so only to facilitate definitions and terms.

2. Sandra Gilbert and Susan Gubar state in their preface that "nineteenth-century literary women did have both a literature and a culture of their own—in other words, by the nineteenth century there was a rich and clearly defined female literary subculture, a community in which women consciously read and related to each other's works." See *The Madwoman in the Attic: The Women Writer and the 19th Century Literary Imagination* (New Haven, CT: Yale University. Press, 1979), xii.

3. I must not neglect to mention here that Jacobs's friendship with Amy Post put her into direct contact with the original delegates of the Seneca Falls Women's Convention in 1868, which reveals Jacobs's active pursuit of women's rights [see Dorothy Sterling's *We Are You Sister (1984)*].

4. To date, I have not uncovered evidence that Mary Prince, Mary Seacole, or Harriet E. Wilson published any major writing other than their narratives. Harriet A. Jacobs, on the other hand, did publish articles in newspapers and journals, which suggests that she may have had aspirations to a literary career.

5. Please see Carla L. Peterson's work, *"Doers of the Word": African-American Women Speakers and Writers in the North* (1830–1880) (New York: Oxford University Press, 1995). She argues that the literary production of nineteenth-century black women was designed to mask or veil their bodies in order to offer them more mobility. But in fact, such a daring entry into the world of publication placed black women at even greater risk of exposure—to potential censorship, mismanagement, or exploitation—rather than veiling or protecting them. While I am not disagreeing with Peterson altogether, I posit that through their writing, Afro-Caribbean and African American women in the nineteenth century produced a very public and commercial body that they consciously used as a saleable commodity.

Works Cited

Brown, William Wells. *The American Fugitive in Europe: Sketches of Places and People Abroad.* In *The Travels of William Wells Brown.* Edited by Paul Jefferson. Edinburgh: Edinburgh University Press, 1991.

Burgett, Bruce. *Sentimental Bodies: Sex, Gender, and Citizenship in the Early Republic.* Princeton, NJ: Princeton University Press, 1998.

Coultrap-McQuin, Susan. *Doing Literary Business: American Women Writers in the Nineteenth Century.* Chapel Hill: University of North Carolina Press, 1990.

Davidson, Cathy. *Revolution and the Word: The Rise of the Novel in America.* New York: Oxford University Press, 1986.

Foster, Frances Smith. *Written by Herself: Literary Production by African American Women,1746–1892.* Indianapolis: Indiana University Press, 1993.

Gates, Henry Louis, Jr. *The Signifying Monkey.* New York: Oxford University Press, 1988.

Gilbert, Sandra, and Susan Gubar. *The Madwoman in the Attic: The Women Writer and the 19th Century Literary Imagination.* New Haven, CT: Yale University Press, 1979.

Gilmore, Michael T. *American Romanticism and the Marketplace.* Chicago: University of Chicago Press, 1985.

Hamilton, Cynthia S. "Dislocation, Violence, and the Language of Sentiment." In *Black Imagination and the Middle Passage.* Edited by Maria Diedrich, et al. 103–116. New York: Oxford University Press, 1999.

Hume, David. *An Inquiry concerning Human Understanding.* Edited by Charles W. Hendel. New York: The Liberal Arts Press, 1955.

Jacobs, Harriet A. *Incidents in the Life of a Slave Girl, Written by Herself.* Edited by Jean Fagan Yellin. Cambridge, MA: Harvard University Presses, 1987.

Prince, Mary. *The History of Mary Prince: A West Indian Slave, Related by Herself.* Edited by Moira Ferguson. Ann Arbor: University of Michigan Press, 1993.

Seacole, Mary. *Wonderful Adventures of Mary Seacole in Many Lands.* Edited by Henry Louis Gates, Jr. New York: Schomburg, 1988.

Wilson, Harriet E. *Our Nig: The Classic African American Novels,* edited by William L. Andrews. New York: Penguin Books, 1990.

Emerson's Platonic Influence: Working toward a "Well Colored and Shaded Globe"

Elizabeth R. Schroeder

THE ANCIENT GREEKS CALLED THE WORLD ΚΌΣΜΟΣ, *COSMOS*, A concept that means both order and beauty. *Cosmos* derived from a term that meant "to weave together," to produce well-woven cloth by putting each thread in its proper place. Throughout his writings, Emerson weaves a theory of racially based aesthetics that aims to put the black body in its "proper place." There is justification for examining Emerson's concept of beauty as a major force and principle in his intellectual universe, a force that reveals the "appalling importance" he puts on "race in the Negro."[1] In his prose, Emerson explores the laws of proportionality as they adhere to the elemental relationship between power and form and how this relationship works to form a foundation of white privilege. Several passages from *Nature*, "Experience," "The Over-Soul," "Self-Reliance," "Manners," and "The Poet" explored in this chapter, expose Emerson's use and creation of a mechanism of racialist thinking that speaks to the reality that there is power in being the right form, and that there is power in declaring which form is right. This mechanism wrestles with a Platonic influence seeking to achieve perfection on the plane of real, material forms concomitantly troubled by an American landscape where white bodies and black bodies, as a result of the 1850 Fugitive Slave Law, forcibly coexist.

Emerson, as evidenced throughout the selections used for this chapter, clearly has problems dealing with raced forms. He writes from a race-based notion of aesthetics, only necessary after raced bodies are moved and grouped in the Western hemisphere, and governed by a system of idealized forms that are the pinnacle of proportionality. Order, or proportion, creates harmony and symmetry. All that is "sweet and sound" necessitates a congruence where form and power perfected are beautiful.[2] More importantly, this congruence depends, vitally, upon a proportionality that lionizes and silences the black body. Through a variety of visual and auditory metaphors employed throughout these selections, Emerson organizes "a well colored and shaded globe."[3] This is a world where forms are outlined, colored, moved, or grouped. Such a transformation of bodies helps pull beauty and power back to certain white male bodies that embody the proportion necessary for Emerson to remain at the top of this hierarchy amid the nineteenth-century American racial landscape.

With regard to his aesthetic sense, Emerson's approach echoes Plato's discourse regarding ideal forms. For Plato, human beings live in a world of sensible and intelligible things.[4] The sensible world is what surrounds humanity. It is what they see, hear, and experience. This sensible world is a world of change and uncertainty. The intelligible world, approached by the mind, is mind, is made up of the unchanging products of human reason. Anything arising from reason alone, such as abstract definitions or mathematics, makes up this intelligible world, which is the world of reality. Plato, speaking through Socrates, writes, "'There are objects which never alter, never perish, and are never deceptive, and which are not only like that in themselves, but are found in an environment which is also like that. Which class of objects, do you think, contains a higher degree of reality?' 'The class of objects which never alters is far superior in this respect.'"[5] The intelligible world, then, contains the eternal "forms" of things. The visible world is the imperfect and changing manifestation in this world of unchanging forms. What makes anything good or real is the degree to which it succeeds in reflecting its perfect appropriate form.

Plato explores these ideas in his discussion of "The Allegory of the Cave."[6] A simpler way of understanding this metaphor is understood with the idea of "chairness." For example, the "form" or "idea" of a chair is intelligible, abstract, and applies to all chairs. This Form never changes, even though chairs vary to a great degree—the Form of a chair would never change even if every chair in the world were to vanish. An individual chair is a physical, unchanging object that can easily cease to be a chair if one destroys it; the Form of a chair, or "chairness," never changes. As a physical object, a chair only makes sense in that it can be referred to the "Form" or "Idea" of chairness. All knowledge acquired about sensible objects, such as a chair, is temporary; genuine knowledge of the Forms, the "chairness," is perfectly certain forever. Even though humanity may perceive only their imperfect instances, genuine knowledge of more abstract ideas such as truth, beauty, and goodness, does exist.[7] Plato believed that the same point could be made with regard to many other abstract concepts and at times, for Emerson, conflicting concepts.

Throughout his work, Emerson invokes Plato's theory of Forms:

the structure of things as they ought to be even though nature, one of the most elemental, celebrated, and integral themes of his works, follows no such structure. Part of nature's beauty arises from its random, haphazard construction.[8] Emerson explores this in the poem "The Snow-Storm."[9] Through the use of vividly descriptive and figurative language, and employing the visual and auditory senses, Emerson depicts the ultimate beauty and power of nature.[10] The poem describes how, within just a few hours, nature can produce its own beautiful, "frolic architecture."[11] Mocking and mimicking the man-made "slow structures" that required great amounts of time and attention to detail to construct "stone by stone," nature, through "the mad wind's night-work," adorns such structures with its own snow-made "masonry."[12] Although the landscape left behind by the "north wind" appears to have been planned, it clearly had no blueprint. Its beauty and Emerson's awe erupt from the north wind's "wild work, So fanciful, so savage," and the fact that "nought cares he, For number or proportion."[13] Man cannot compete with nor control nature's will and power—ultimately he must surrender. "The farmer sighs" at the realization that his property has been overtaken, "enclosed in a tumultuous privacy of storm."[14]

While nature's productions need not depend on blueprints nor must they follow any calculated patterns,[15] human life must adhere to the strict laws of proportionality. Juxtaposed against nature's savage, wild work, Emerson writes in "Experience," "Human life is made up of two elements, power and form, and the proportion must be invariably kept if we would have it sweet and sound. Each of these elements in excess makes a mischief as hurtful as its defect."[16] Emerson has in mind a general blueprint that defines and determines the success of every human life. He explains the elemental relationship between power, form, and their absence and excess in hopes of developing an idea of the "best," and ideal, a perfect model.

"Human life is made up of two elements."[17] Very quickly, Emerson employs scientific rhetoric to describe human life. He uses the word *element:* the fundamental, essential, or irreducible constituent of an entity—the basic building blocks from which all human life, material or immaterial, is constructed. It is interesting that he chooses the word "life" instead of "experience," the title of the essay. He does this to divert readers from quickly assuming he only means social interaction. He wants to afford the sentence the connotation of materiality or physicality of human life, relating to the body as distinguished from the mind or spirit by the senses, and immateriality or social relatedness of human life manifested especially in thought and perceived by the mind.

In this passage, the first two building blocks for human life are power and form. Power means the ability or official capacity to exercise control or authority over another being—accomplished through one's body or mind. This is a process achieved through many avenues but for Emerson's purposes, one has to think of power as the physical domination he was lacking, or the mental domination in which he was rich. Given the racial climate of the late nineteenth century, one has to believe that Emerson considered, here, the domination of white bodies and black bodies, the domination of one racial form over another. Power is authoritative; the race possessing power speaks, silences, sees, and blinds. This conceptualization of power, used in tandem with the understanding of human life as material and immaterial, allows Emerson to arrive easily at his second building block: form. Emerson's focus on forms or bodies speaks to the racist mechanisms he employs while rooting white domination of blacks in various cultural structures. The structure of racism exerts power over all forms of blackness—black bodies, black movement, and black language.

In a more or less Platonic sense, one can break down these racist structures through an understanding of the ideal as the immaterial gets manifested, by variant degrees, in bodies (material forms). Emerson blends the material and immaterial reality of human life throughout this passage, demanding a strict vigilance on the part of the reader. Such semantic dance moves require multidimensional thinking, allowing for a material reading of the passage and an immaterial reading of the passage connotative of race. Power, the ideal, reflects whiteness; form, an abstract and imperfect reflection of the ideal, reflects materiality or blackness. Whiteness as the immaterial reflects Plato's cave allegory. Whiteness, as an "ideal" is the class "which never alters" and as a result "is far superior."[18] Whiteness, as power then, is eternal while blackness, as form, is understood as material of the sensible world, and as such is perishable. If blackness is the imperfect and changing manifestation in this world of whiteness—the ideal—then blackness as an imperfect reflection is perishable. Emerson, in a Platonic sense, takes whiteness in the same light as "chairness," blackness in the same light as the chair. If this is so, then blackness means an imperfect, perishable, temporal, instance of whiteness.

If one takes Emerson to be speaking of the relationship between black and white bodies, he skews the semantics of math. Proportion signifies a relationship between the give and take of elements. Sometimes a change in one quantity causes a change, or is linked to a change, in another quantity. If these changes are related through equal factors, then the quantities are said to be in direct proportion. If a change in one quantity causes a change in another quantity and the changes are inversely related then the quantities are said to be in indirect proportion. Emerson argues, without variation, that there is no room for deviation from the exercise of white power over black forms. Balance comes from the inversely proportionate relationship between white and black; any deviation from this "form" results in injury to humanity. For whiteness to mean the immaterial or power, blackness must mean the material. Balance means the black absence of power and the absence of black form—to think otherwise is to scar humanity—to skew Plato's "ideal forms."

"[A]nd the proportion must be invariably kept if we would have it sweet and sound." This portion of the passage demands balance between the immaterial and material elements.[19] Proportion is the necessary condition for humanity to have a "sweet and sound" life. Proportionality sustains power's sweetness and form's soundness. The congruity of power and form allow for the symmetry of bodily man and the harmony of immaterial man. One has to consider this in strictly racial terms. The congruity of white power and blackness must follow strict rules of proportion where an excess of either "makes a mischief as hurtful as its defect."[20] There can be no over manipulation of one form over another, nor can there be a grave disproportion between the two. Who determines this particular relationship? Emerson. Emerson choreographs this careful dance between power and form. As the representative man who is white, Emerson straddles the line between the immaterial and material. His body, as a white body, perfectly reflects immaterial whiteness and the material body. Black bodies: can they house both the materiality that defines them and the immaterial that binds them? Emerson considers this when he writes that form or power in excess makes mischief. This mischief is as hurtful as its defect. Power's defect would be the lack or excess of power; form's defect would be the lack or excess of form—thus having too much power is the same as having not enough, or too much form is the same as having none at all. Either results in disproportionality. The defect of power is hurtful because it skews the balance of human life. Imbalance thwarts man's harmony and symmetry. Exercising power outside the permissible boundaries of one's form or outside one's power is a destructive force. Frederick Douglass or Sojourner Truth are examples of forms exercising powers outside permissible boundaries. They directly challenge Emerson's unique proportionality.

Another challenge to Emerson's delicate proportion between white and black bodies arrived with the Fugitive Slave Law in 1850. This law does something vital to bodies that changes a body's relationship to space and most importantly, for Emerson, changes the proportion between black and white bodies. Prior to the law, a body's slave status could be derived from jurisdictions or geographical locations. After the law, slave status was more directly tied to the body regardless of jurisdictions or geography. The vigilance of enforcement changes—it afflicts the white body as well as the black. The Fugitive Slave Law calls upon whites, like Emerson, to be socially active. White vision now has tremendous power over and responsibility toward the black body. The black presence is no longer ambiguously absent. The Fugitive Slave Law made black bodies visible. Concomitantly it pulled white bodies into the process and criminalized them. The inactive social activist became criminal. Emerson writes, "I have lived all my life without suffering any known inconvenience from American Slavery. I never saw it; I never heard the whip; I never felt the check on my free speech and action, until, the other day, when Mr. Webster, by his personal influence, brought the Fugitive Slave Law on the country."[21] The Fugitive Slave Law made Emerson's inaction a crime. It turned individual action into social action. Individual action is no longer an act of the individual will. Likewise, whiteness is no longer immaterial; it is tied to the material black body. This law breaks down the binary of the ME and the NOT ME. Emerson begins *Nature* with a very simple taxonomy, fully inflected by race, where he distinguishes all "that is separate from us, all which Philosophy distinguishes as the NOT ME, that is, both nature and art, all other men and my own body, must be ranked under this name, NATURE."[22]

It is interesting that Emerson describes his inexperience with American slavery through visual, auditory, and then tactile imagery. He never "saw it," he never "heard the whip," nor had he "felt the check on my free speech and action."[23] In this manner, the Fugitive Slave Law complicates Emerson's understanding of the body under slavery. He understands slavery's tyranny on physical forms: the black body saw slavery, heard the whip, and felt the check on its free speech and action. The Fugitive Slave Law, like Sojourner Truth and Frederick Douglas, creates a space for deviation from the exercise of white power over black forms. Emerson believes this deviation causes physical harm over his own body for he now sees, hears, and feels slavery's influence. In Emerson's opinion, black bodies no longer function as they should or stand where they belong—invisible and outside the margins. The Fugitive Slave Law interpolates the white body to action and the black body into vision. Emerson, like the farmer from "The Snow-Storm," cannot compete with nor control the visible black body. He must "sigh" at the realization of the Fugitive Slave Law's skewing of power and form's proportion. He has no choice but to resign himself to the Fugitive Slave Law and remain with his white brethren "enclosed, In a tumultuous privacy or storm" of the coexistence of black and white bodies.[24]

As a result of the Fugitive Slave Law, Emerson must rework the relationship between two forms or "bodies" in an effort to entrench Plato's ideal forms where whiteness serves as the ideal, thereby leaving him at the top of the hierarchy. As long as black bodies occupy powerless spaces, as long as their power is proportionate to their form, then the scales do not tip. Prior to the Fugitive Slave Law, in the event that black bodies did obtain some power, Emerson could deauthenticate black acquisition of power in two ways. Emerson could write this acquisition of power as an imbalance relegating it to "mischief."[25] The power of the black body is reduced to shenanigans, playfulness, devilry, game, and rascality. Or Emerson could find justification in Plato and simply discard black power as the imperfect reflection of white power. Emerson, in an effort to rectify this split, could draw on his previous work to reclaim the power of whiteness. By returning to the examination of "Experience," and continuing on to an examination of passages from *Nature*, "Manners," "The Over-Soul," and "Self-Reliance," one can see the foundation from which Emerson could remedy the imbalance left in the wake Mr. Webster's law.

He begins this project with a quote from "Experience": all that is "sweet and sound" necessitates congruence where form and power perfected are beautiful.[26] The passage also illustrates Emerson's ability to make and recognize ideal forms through metaphors of vision and hearing. Beauty, or the harmony and symmetry between power and form, is perceived through the senses. The eye recognizes symmetry; the ear recognizes harmony. That which is sweet results from taste; that which is sound by the ear. Thus, sensual stimuli and the pleasure they yield announce proportion between power and form—or beauty. Emerson writes in *Nature* that beauty needs no explanation; it exists for the sole purpose of being appreciated as a sensory pleasure.[27] The simple observation of nature and its elements is pure delight.[28] The distinction between sweetness and soundness suggests Emerson's sense of pleasure in having power and the sense of utility involved in the form. He writes later in "Manners," "The love of beauty is mainly the love of measure or proportion."[29] Keeping aesthetic balance creates harmony and symmetry—all that is sweet and sound. Form perfected is beautiful in its utility. Power perfected works beautifully for Emerson and for this he does not apologize.

Emerson uses his vision to employ an aesthetic racial mechanism that speaks to proportion when judging the beautiful, good, ugly, or bad. Beauty and pleasure erupts from this aesthetic stance. Proportion exists only when black power is soured, the inverse of sweet, and black form is silenced, the inverse of sound. Proportion exists, as well, when black forms are soured, rendered undesirable, and black forms are silenced, having no voice. Such congruence vitally depends on a proportionality that lionizes and silences the black form. This lionization and silence was experienced in numerous ways.

In the chapter on "Beauty" in *Nature*, Emerson's Platonist understanding of forms comes into focus. Emerson, in *Nature*, engages in a discussion of "Beauty" and aesthetics where, through a variety of tactics, he arrives at an intersection of aesthetics and race. After invoking the Greek *cosmos*, Emerson explains this intersection through two mechanisms of vision: the "laws of light," and the artistic mastery of the human eye. Emerson writes, "so light is the first of painters. There is no object so foul that intense light will not make beautiful."[30] Here, he speaks to a race-based understanding of aesthetics. This aesthetic complex is understood and explained through a variety of tactics. Through this racialized understanding of aesthetics Emerson is able to explain how the world, material and immaterial, is ordered "into a well colored and shaded globe."

Emerson's first tactic toward an understanding of his race-based notion of aesthetics in this selection begins with his pointing out that the Greeks called the world *cosmos*, a concept that means both order and beauty. Thus Emerson's world is both ordered and (therefore) beautiful. What he means by this is that the world is organized or "constituted" by a hierarchy from which humanity derives aesthetic pleasures. Most importantly, to the intersection of aesthetics and race, these pleasures arise "from outline, color, motion, and grouping." One is easily tempted to compound these words with the word "body," yielding: body outlines, color of bodies, movement of bodies, grouping of bodies. Delight and Beauty necessitates the outlining of bodies and color(ing) of bodies.

Emerson's second tactic for understanding a racialized conception of aesthetics develops in his statement that "[aesthetic pleasure] seems partly owing to the eye itself. The eye is the best of artists." It is only through the eye that humanity comes to these pleasures. The eye, then, becomes a fluid, malleable, plastic lens through which man can exercise his will over nature. Thus the eye can determine race-based decisions of aesthetics. The best of artists, the eye, when viewing "mean and unaffecting" objects, can or cannot make them beautiful—it is a matter of choice. Thus the "aesthetic human eye" chooses to integrate "every mass of objects, of what character soever, into a well colored and shaded globe," precisely because it serves man's will. No object or body is free from man's outlining, coloring, moving, or grouping gaze. This speaks to Emerson's sense of ideal forms and the eye's ability both to make and recognize them. Everyone and everything is made open to the eye—what Laura Mulvey has termed the gaze.[31] The gaze totalizes and constructs a "we" that exists in opposition to otherness. This gaze establishes a conscious framing mechanism employed throughout history—from Plato to Emerson—of raced bodies. Emerson's "well colored and shaded" cosmos, then, is a reflection of his conscious choice to understand his world in terms of a beauty and order in which he, a white male, represents the ideal.

A third tactic Emerson employs to reflect a racially inflected category of aesthetics is his use of light. Light is understood as a part of nature. In *Nature*, Emerson aims to teach his readers that man can have mastery over nature or control it by his will. Light, consequently, becomes an emblem for man's exercise of his human will. Emerson's third tactic, light, when used with his second tactic, the eye, produces *cosmos:* "The eye is the best of artists. By the mutual action of its structure and of the laws of light, perspective is produced, which integrates every mass of objects . . . into a well colored and shaded globe."[32] The mutual action of the eye, human will, the laws of light, and laws of nature, have the power to determine how humanity sees its universe. Surely, if there is no "object so foul that intense light will not make beautiful," this light could make the black body beautiful, but as a vehicle of man's will it does not. From this understanding of perspective, it becomes important to flesh out who is allowed to "see." As a vehicle of man's will, the eye/I? working with light, is infused with power. This gaze sets up Emerson's me and not me binary. Thus the specular dominance of the eye of power is not available to all. To see means to outline, to color, to move, and to group bodies according to an aestheticized notion of race. Light's normalizing function constructs a radically different "other" that confirms a virtuous white male group of gazers.

For Emerson, these three tactics, *cosmos*, the eye, and light, reflect a racialized understanding of aesthetics that he seeks to understand in his struggle as a material body in order to achieve perfection on the plane of real, material forms. From this understanding Emerson can organize a "well colored and shaded globe" where he has the power to see. Emerson uses these tactics throughout his prose to establish a theoretical and aesthetic template or mythology to read forms within nineteenth-century America. This template positions him as the pinnacle or the ideal and allows him to transcend the materiality of his human form. In this form he moves toward that which is beautiful, the immaterial realm, where no one can surmount him and where no one can subject him to the Fugitive Slave Law. In this immaterial realm where he is beautiful and his form, ideal, his power is uncontestable.

Gained through perception by the senses, beauty flows from the material world to the immaterial world. The same works for man, "within man is the soul of the whole; the wise silence; the universal beauty, to which every part and particle is equally related; the eternal ONE."[33] The universe is fluid and man, through the gift of the intellect, has been given the tools for mastery over the universe. The epitome of this continuity and oneness is symbolized in Emerson's concept of the "over-soul," the shared soul, the unity and circular connection of God, humanity, and nature. In *Nature*, Emerson describes his experience as he becomes a "transparent eyeball" through which the "currents of the universal being circulate."[34] In the midst of the woods he is able to truly be at one with nature in the rawest sense: "I am nothing. I see all." Abandoning temporarily, his form, he gains awareness of his connection to the ideal—to the universe.[35] Emerson's experience as the transparent eyeball is an assertion of infinite existence as an ideal form. Only through the eyeball does Emerson transcend his bodily form, that which separates him from perfectly reflecting whiteness. Transparency serves as a precursor to transcendence.

Emerson further explores the soul and the striving for the immaterial in "Self-Reliance." Emerson strives for the immaterial—a thing proceeding from the same space from which life proceeds. In this essay, Emerson apprehends the immaterial not by the senses but through the soul, "Time and space are but physiological colors which the eye makes, but the soul is light: where it is, is day; where it was is night."[36] Plato, too, put great importance in light in order to know that the visible realm, the material, was deficient and the intelligible, immaterial realm was bountiful. He writes, "Even if a person's eyes are capable of sight, and he's trying to use it, and what he's trying to look at is coloured, the sight will see nothing and the colours will remain unseen, surely, unless there is also present an extra third thing which is made specifically for this purpose. . . . It's what we call light."[37] For both Emerson and Plato, then, the sensible world must rely on the intelligible world. Without light or the soul, the body, equipped only by the senses, is incapable of perception or transcendence. Light illuminates; it aids in the process of transcendence. When souls are directed toward things that are lit up by the sun, then they see clearly. Plato continues, "the eye's ability to see has been bestowed upon it and channeled into it, as it were, by the sun. . . . The sun is the child of goodness I was talking about, then. . . . It is a counterpart to its father, goodness. As goodness stands in the intelligible realm to intelligence and the things we know, so in the visible realm the sun stands to sight and the things we see."[38] A relationship between the sensible world and the intelligible world, between the senses, the sun, and the intellect, works toward such transcendence. Important to Emerson is the link Plato makes from this collaboration between these worlds to goodness through birthing metaphors. The senses need the sun, the child of goodness, to "see." Plato provides the link between the intelligible and sensible world through the sun. Sun, the child of goodness, straddles the two worlds. The Sun birthed from the intelligible world performs in the material world to humanity's benefit. Emerson, then, employs a birthing metaphor of goodness to truth and beauty. In "The Poet," he writes of the universe's three children, born at one time, which reappear under different names in every system of thought, and forms a trinity of truth, goodness, and beauty. These tools enable him to transcend his earthly, material body, and pass into the immaterial realm where no one can surmount or analyze him—where his form is ideal and his power is absolute. He elaborates on this process in "Manners." He writes, "A beautiful form is better than a beautiful face; a beautiful behavior is better than a beautiful form; it gives a higher pleasure than statues of pictures; it is the finest of fine arts."[39] This passage dissects transcendence through a hierarchy of beauty, goodness, and truth. He begins with the body, "beautiful face," surpassed by a "beautiful form"; then he moves from form perfected to "beautiful behavior" or goodness; goodness "gives a higher pleasure" and "is the finest of fine arts." Goodness, only achieved after beauty and truth, and understood as the degree to which it succeeds in reflecting its perfect and therefore proportionate form, becomes the passkey to transcendence. Emerson's "beautiful form," exhibiting beautiful behavior, transcends using the trinity of truth, goodness, and beauty. He passes out of darkness into light. He celebrates this victory in a poem in "Manners" where his white body serves as evidence that in both heaven and earth, in form and shape, he is beautiful and therefore he straddles, like Plato's Sun, the line between heaven and earth. As a perfect reflection of whiteness, Emerson shall be first in might. "A power more strong," treads on forms and shapes "compact and beautiful." As a perfect reflection, as the first in beauty, he shall be first in power—"for 't is the eternal law." Emerson, as a perfect form, transcends slightly ahead of "fresh perfection"—a perfection fated to excel "us," the white male. The steps of the white male, encouraged by fate, tread slightly ahead of perfection. This gait illustrates "A power". . . . "born of us—" the white male. Insurmountable, born into privilege, and fulfilling the prophecy of eternal law, Emerson, with truth, beauty, and goodness as his accoutrements, transcends the material world into the immaterial world. "For 't is the eternal law," Plato's unchanging, unswerving law, "That first in beauty shall be first in might."[40] Maneuvering truth, beauty, and goodness to the advantage of white privilege enables Emerson to surmount his material, perishable, body. Most importantly, he surpasses the black body with all its earthly carnal implications, into perfect whiteness—an action ordained by eternal law and, with the advent of 1850 Fugitive Slave Law, societal law.

Put forcibly, as a result of the Fugitive Slave Law and contact with black bodies, Emerson argues that the white body exists as the perfect ideal form. If this is true then the black form is a mere reflection, or as Frantz Fanon testifies in *Black Skin, White Masks*, "the black man is a black man; that is, as the result of a series of aberrations of affect, he is rooted at the core of a universe from which he must be extracted."[41] Emerson extracts the black man through a conceptualization of Plato's ideal forms of whiteness. The black body is incapable of reflecting truth, goodness, and beauty like Emerson's white body. The black body is an aberration. Emerson locks the black body into subordination with the white body through this imaginary. The black man is a departure from what is right, true, and correct and seals Emerson "in his whiteness."[42] The black man, as a result, is "sealed in his blackness."[43] Fanon, growing up in Martinique amid descendants of African slaves experiencing the realities of racism and white colonization, echoes this when he writes, "However painful it may be for me to accept this conclusion, I am obliged to state it: For the black man there is only one destiny. And it is white."[44] Emerson provides the ideal of whiteness by comparing it to blackness. He uses blackness as the imperfect reflection of whiteness to entrench white privilege. Ironically, in order to impose whiteness as the ideal, Emerson mentions the black body. Frantz Fanon, in an effort to redeem the black body, utilizes a similar methodology, but not by choice. The work of Fanon, particularly *Black Skin, White Masks*, constitutes one of the few attempts to activate psychoanalysis in the examination and indictment of the relation between colonizer and the colonized.[45] Fanon does not try to say blackness is the ideal—his project is not one of imposition like Emerson. Where Emerson mentions the black body to seal in the power of whiteness, Fanon must refer to whiteness in order to write about the black body. It is the conjuncture between the two bodies that engenders a vicious circle of neurosis circulating around the question of identity. This conjuncture of raced bodies engenders questions concerning identity for Emerson as well. Emerson and Fanon have vastly different projects, but both of their projects bring into focus the utter complexities of contact between raced bodies, where whiteness is the reigning ideal.

Emerson saw the complexities of human life, the riches of nature, the immense wealth of the mind, and he saw the supreme value of a system of racially based aesthetics as a force to elevate him to a height beyond the material world. His greatest interest was in man, and man's superiorities.[46] And nature fascinated him only through its relation to the elevation of man and man's mind beyond the sensible world. Emerson constructs a paradigm in which he can conceptualize himself as the perfect reflection of Plato's ideal forms. Careful interpretation of numerous passages from his prose and poetry indicates Emerson's maneuvering truth, beauty, and goodness toward a transcendence of the material, sensible world—the chaotic, blank darkness to the *cosmos* of the immaterial, intelligible world. He sanctions this move by order of "eternal law."[47] These maneuvers are motivated by "race in the Negro" and its "appalling importance."[48] With the 1850 Fugitive Slave Law, Emerson's material world saw a remapping. He could no longer deny the visibility of black bodies with which he came in contact. The law forced the breakdown of his "me, not me" binary. This necessitated a reworking of Emerson's universe—material and immaterial—and the extraction of the black body from vision. What resulted was a rigorously structured human dynamic quite opposite of nature's arbitrary, indiscriminate construction. Emerson constructed human life through the rubrics of proportion and form that echoed Plato's ideal forms—where there was no room for deviation from the exercise of white power over black forms. Blackness came to mean an imperfect, perishable, instance of the ideal. Whiteness, as this ideal, became eternal, unchanging, and therefore, powerful. It becomes impossible for the black body to exist absolutely in a world where the white body is the absolute. Over a hundred years later, Frantz Fanon, exploring the psychological repercussions of this identity-rape, comments, "The Negro is comparison. . . . that is, he is constantly preoccupied with self-evaluation and with the ego-ideal. Whenever he comes into contact with someone else, the question of value, of merit arises."[49] Emerson seals his white identity in this securely marginalized black identity. The black body, the Other, corroborates Emerson in his search for self-validation as the perfect reflection and embodiment of the ideal. "Race in the Negro," indeed, "is of appalling importance";[50] for it serves as a vehicle for Emerson's existence as a child of goodness, an offspring existing on the borderlands of Plato's material and immaterial worlds.

Notes

1. Ralph Waldo Emerson, "Race," *English Traits*, in *The Essential Writings of Ralph Waldo Emerson*, ed. Brooks Atkinson (New York: The Modern Library, 2000), 491.

2. Ralph Waldo Emerson, "Experience," *Essays: Second Series*, in *The Essential Writings of Ralph Waldo Emerson*, ed. Brooks Atkinson (New York: The Modern Library, 2000), 316.

3. Ralph Waldo Emerson, *The Fugitive Slave Law*, in *The Essential Writings of Ralph Waldo Emerson*, ed. Brooks Atkinson (New York: The Modern Library, 2000), 9.

4. Plato, *Republic*, trans. Robin Waterfield (Oxford: Oxford University Press, 1992), 254.

5. Ibid., 334.

6. The allegory of the cave is supposed to explain the ability of humankind to think and speak without any awareness of Plato's theory of Forms. In the allegory, Plato tells the parable of prisoners chained in a cave, unable to turn their heads. All they can see is the wall of the cave. Behind them burns a fire. Between the fire and the prisoners there is a suspended walkway along which puppeteers can walk. The puppeteers behind the prisoners hold up puppets that cast shadows on the wall of the cave. The prisoners are unable to see these puppets, the real objects that pass behind them. What the prisoners see and hear are shadows and echoes cast by objects that they do not see. Such prisoners would mistake appearance for reality. They would think the things they see on the wall (the shadows) were real; they would know nothing of the real causes of the shadows. Plato's point: the general terms of our language are not "names" of the physical objects that we can see. They are actually names of things that we cannot see, things that we can only grasp with the mind. S. Marc Cohen, "Allegory of the Cave," 2006, http://faculty.washington.edu/smcohen/320/cave.html.

7. Jacob Howland, *The Republic: The Odyssey of Philosophy* (New York: Twayne Publishers, 1993), 132–49.

8. Sara Sugarman, "Universal Beauty, Natural Sovereignty, and the 'Oversoul': The Central Themes of the Works of Ralph Waldo Emerson," http://www.farmingdale.edu/CampusPages/ArtSciences/AcademicDepartments/EnglishHumanities/sugarman.html.

9. Ralph Waldo Emerson, "The Snow-Storm," *Poems*, in *The Essential Writings of Ralph Waldo Emerson*, ed. Brooks Atkinson (New York: The Modern Library, 2000), 692.

10. Sugarman.

11. Emerson, "The Snow-Storm," line 28.

12. Ibid., lines 26–27.

13. Ibid., lines 15–17.

14. Ibid., lines 8–9.

15. Sugarman.

16. Emerson, "Experience," 316.

17. Ibid.

18. Plato, 334.

19. Emerson, "Experience," 316.

20. Emerson, "Experience," 316.

21. Emerson, *The Fugitive Slave Law*, 780.

22. Ralph Waldo Emerson, *Nature*, in *The Essential Writings of Ralph Waldo Emerson*, ed. Brooks Atkinson (New York: The Modern Library, 2000), 3–4.

23. Emerson, *The Fugitive Slave Law*, 780.

24. Emerson, "The Snow-Storm," lines 7–9.

25. Emerson, "Experience," 316.

26. Ibid.

27. Emerson, *Nature*, 9.
28. Ibid.
29. Ralph Waldo Emerson, "Manners," *English Traits*, in *The Essential Writings of Ralph Waldo Emerson*, ed. Brooks Atkinson (New York: The Modern Library, 2000), 351.
30. Ibid.
31. Laura Mulvey, "Visual Pleasure and Narrative Cinema," *Screen* 16, no. 3 (Autumn 1975): 6–18.
32. *Emerson*, "Experience," 316.
33. Ralph Waldo Emerson, "The Over-Soul," *Essays: First Series*, in *The Essential Writings of Ralph Waldo Emerson*, ed. Brooks Atkinson (New York: The Modern Library, 2000), 237.
34. Emerson, *Nature*, 6.
35. Ibid.
36. Ibid.
37. Plato, 234.
38. Ibid., 235.
39. Emerson, "Manners," 356.
40. Ibid., 355.
41. Frantz Fanon, *Black Skin, White Masks*, trans. Charles Lam Markmann (New York: Grove Press, Inc., 1967), 10.
42. Ibid., 11.
43. Ibid.
44. Ibid., 12.
45. Mary Ann Doane, *Femmes Fatales: Feminism, Film Theory, Psychoanalysis* (New York: Routledge Press, 1991), 217.
46. Percy W. Brown, "Emerson's Philosophy of Aesthetics," *The Journal of Aesthetics and Art Criticism* 15, no. 3 (March 1957): 353.
47. Emerson, "Manners," 355.
48. Emerson, "Race," 491.
49. Fanon, 211.
50. Emerson, "Race," 491.

Works Cited

Brown, Percy W. "Emerson's Philosophy of Aesthetics." *The Journal of Aesthetics and Art Criticism* 15, no. 3. (March 1957): 350–54.

Cohen, S. Marc. "Allegory of the Cave." 2006. http://faculty.washington.edu/smcohen/320/cave.html.

Doane, Mary Ann. *Femme Fatales: Feminism, Film Theory, Psychoanalysis*. New York: Routlege Press, 1991.

Emerson, Ralph Waldo. "Experience." *Essays: Second Series*. In *The Essential Writings of Ralph Waldo Emerson*. Edited by Brooks Atkinson, 307–326 and 469–617. New York: The Modern Library, 2000.

———. *The Fugitive Slave Law*, 779–792.

———. "Manners." *English Traits*, 341–359.

———. *Nature*, 3–39.

———. "The Over-Soul." *Essays: First Series*, 236–251.

———. "Race." *English Traits*, 489–503.

———. "Self-Reliance." *Essays: First Series*, 132–53.

———. "The Snow-Storm." *Poems*, 692.

———. "The Poet." *Essays: Second Series*. In *Emerson's Prose and Poetry*. Edited by Joel Porte and Saundra Morris, 183–98. New York: W. W. Norton & Company, 2001.

Fanon, Frantz. *Black Skin, White Masks*. Translated by Charles Lam Markmann. New York: Grove Press, 1967.

Gilman, Sander L. "Black Bodies, White Bodies: Toward an Iconography of Female Sexuality in Late-Nineteenth Century Art, Medicine, and Literature." In *Race Writing and Difference*. Edited by Henry Louis Gates, Jr., 223–61. Chicago: University of Chicago Press, 1987.

Howland, Jacob. *The Republic: The Odyssey of Philosophy*. New York: Twayne Publishers, 1993.

Mulvey, Laura. "Visual Pleasure and Narrative Cinema." *Screen* , 16 no. 3 (Autumn 1975): 6–18.

Plato. *Republic*. Translated by Robin Waterfield. New York: The Modern Library, 2000.

Sugarman, Sara. "Universal Beauty, Natural Sovereignty, and the 'Over-Soul': Central Themes of the Works of Ralph Waldo Emerson." http://www.farmingdale.edu/CampusPages/ArtSciencs/AcademicDepartments/EnglishHUmanities/Sugarman.html.

The Bodies of Black Folk: From Kant and Hegel to DuBois and Baldwin

David Farrell Krell

> "There will never, ever, be an end to racism. And things are not getting better; they are going the other way."
>
> —Dennis Rodman, interview in *Streetwise*

THE *BODIES* OF BLACK FOLK? THE TITLE IS AN IMPERTINENCE. IT ought to be a matter of the *souls* of black folk—precisely those souls that for entire epochs of European history have been denied *spirit* and *intelligence.* Yet have not these peoples also been denied their bodies, their multifarious bodies—bodies of the Earth and the world, bodies of nature, culture, and history? Have they not been denied their erotic and intelligent bodies, their free bodies?

This chapter consists of four parts. The first part, taking W.E.B. DuBois's sojourn in Germany as its inspiration, raises the question of studying abroad, particularly in Europe, for African Americans today. Such study was very important to the intellectual and artistic development of African American philosophers and writers during the past century, but today it is challenged by other pressing educational priorities and by other discourses. The second part turns briefly to Kant's "physical geography" for a sampler of European wisdom touching the black African. The longer third part turns to Hegel's *Lectures on the Philosophy of History* and *Encyclopedia of Philosophical Sciences* for his general—and generally bleak—account of black Africa. The fourth part turns to a strange passage on Africa and the Africans in Hegel's "Philosophy of Nature"—where I see something like the *bodies* of black folk entering on the scene in a way that disturbs the Hegelian system as such in its entirety, if one can say such a thing.

Viewed as a whole, this chapter is marked by a tension between its theoretical and practical aims, between the *topic* of "race in the academy" and the agenda of "a philosophy of political action" as a process of "black liberation." It seems as though I am both encouraging European study for African Americans—at a time when discourses of "multiculturalism" are bashing Europe—and also engaging in some Europe bashing of my own by reporting on some of the most outrageous and reprehensible aspects of the Western intellectual tradition. It is almost as though I were mustering the worst that Europe has to offer Africa and the African Americans of the New World precisely in order to insist that, even in the face of the worst—in the face of the bigotry, racism, and colonialism concealed beneath the philosopher's mantle—European study remains an essential part of the education of black folk in our time.

1. The Very Best Thing about America's Urban Universities

The very best thing about America's urban universities is that they are only minutes away from international airports and hence only hours away from the rest of the world. From Chicago's O'Hare Airport, for example, a student can be in Mexico City after only three hours, in Paris after seven, in Berlin after eight, in Athens after eleven, in Nairobi after fourteen. Why foreign travel and study, especially for America's minorities? And why, among all possible places, Europe in particular? Why the continent of colonialisms? If only because foreign study provides a way to get some distance on one's "American demons," as David Levering Lewis says.[1] He refers to DuBois's two years in Johann Sebastian Bach's Eisenach and Bismarck's Berlin: "He seemed to grow lighter, almost playful, and more accessible with each week."[2] Why? DuBois himself, on the first page of the first chapter of *The Souls of Black Folk*, announces his problem, the apparently permanent and ubiquitous problem of being a problem—permanent and ubiquitous, he says, "save perhaps in babyhood and in Europe."[3] Elsewhere, DuBois refers to the change in his outlook on life during those two years of study in Germany, awakening at twenty-five years of age to "something of the possible beauty and elegance of life."[4]

So much about DuBois's sojourn in Germany remains to be studied. One would have wanted to ask him about his favorite scenes and lines in Goethe's *Faust*, and, in the context of the bodies of black folk, especially about his favorite pages in *Elective Affinities*. The affinity for Goethe endured throughout DuBois's life. Further, one would like to study *The Souls of Black Folk* against the backdrop of Hegel's *Phenomenology of Spirit*, not merely because of the *Phenomenology's* famous dialectic of "lordship and bondage" but also because of the doubling and the dawning of self-consciousness in both DuBois and Hegel. For both thinkers, self-awareness is the gift of a redoubled sight, with the vision of the one filtered and refined by the vision of the other. Yet I suspect that Hegel's *Phenomenology of Spirit* is most important for DuBois because of what Hegel calls the agitated blood and the liquid flow of desirous life, of *Leben* and *Begierde*, the desire of one consciousness to possess another consciousness—to possess it in the flesh, in the body—and because of what DuBois, in a frightening phrase, calls "the red stain of bastardy."[5] More on this later.

Toward the end of his stay, with his long walking tour through central Europe, DuBois gathers materials for his first paper at Wilberforce University, "The Art and Art Galleries of Modern Europe."[6] Perhaps we today are too desperate to give beauty and elegance a chance, but there are also more "practical" reasons for study in Europe. A young African American man said to me at the end of a foreign-study period in Greece sponsored by DePaul University that he had never felt such freedom before in his life. I asked him what sort of freedom he meant. He said, "I feel as though I can do anything, be everything; nobody has had an eye on me here." Lewis writes: "DuBois felt exceptionally free, more liberated in these years than he would ever feel again."[7] DuBois himself remarks that to the African American, "even more than to the white, is the contact with European culture of inestimable value in giving him a broad view of men and affairs."[8] For DuBois, in Germany, the veil of race had become almost diaphanous. Perhaps in proximity to Weissenfels, the home of Novalis, it had indeed become the veil of Saïs, a veil of natural beauty, intimacy, intensity, and infinite promise, rather than a hindrance and an abomination.

To be sure, Europe is not and has never been a continent of innocents. The children of Lübeck will still stare, the mutual hatred of the Poles and Germans will, incredibly, still display equal amounts of the anti-Semitism that so distressed DuBois.[9] Indeed, these days, the children are likely to be skinheads and sport razor blades. No, not a continent of innocents. Yet if DuBois felt an elective affinity for Goethe and Hegel, who can say whether German culture today has lost its power to assist in liberating the African American, and who can say how much or how little the things that DuBois discovered in Germany are still among the best weapons against the self-doubt that flourishes on American shores? DuBois wrote in his journal: "I have finally proved to my entire satisfaction that my race forms but slight impediment between me and kindred souls. . . . I am here free from most of those iron bands that bound me at home."[10] When he returned stateside in June 1894, DuBois observed that for two years he had been dealing with people who were "not white folks, but folks"; he noted that the Statue of Liberty looked toward France and Germany, whereas she showed her nether parts, suitably draped, to America. Yes, DuBois returned to reality, to the American reality—but he was not the same man he was when he left. Nor do I mean to elevate study in Europe over study in Africa, Latin America, or Asia. I merely wish to speak on behalf of the remote view, the view from farther off, and to argue that in my own experience foreign study has been a powerful influence on African American students, as formative today as it was a century ago for DuBois. Nowadays, foreign study may be considered a luxury, condemned as elitism or flight from the sordid reality of the neighborhoods, a slap in the face of solidarity. DuBois himself suffered from this accusation. The white educators who had granted him the Slater Foundation Fellowship for foreign study began to worry about what they, too, considered an elitism. An American black with a PhD in economics from the University of Berlin? They brought him home just in time to prevent it. James Baldwin, between Harlem and Paris, also suffered from this accusation. So did Ralph Ellison in Rome and Richard Wright in Paris. Yet one is so grateful for what these men were able to think and write, and one knows that Paris, Rome, and Berlin were inestimably important for their living and writing. We have to avoid slipping into the jargon of antielitism; we have to expand the opportunities for foreign study for minorities; and we have to fight for the money that will make such expansion possible, especially at a time when so many Americans are of the view that affirmative action has done its work. I am not certain where foreign study fits into the agenda, and it is not for me to say. However, let us not forget DuBois, Wright, Ellison, and Baldwin (whom I will discuss in part 4), along with dozens of artists, writers, musicians, and thinkers I have not mentioned here, when we think about the education of African Americans.

I suspect, to repeat, that European study does not today stand near the top of educational priorities for African Americans. Today more than ever, we seem to be focusing on the basics, on a greater democratization of fundamental opportunities. European study smacks of the finishing school. It betrays an ostensible lack of solidarity (even if the word was originally Polish) with those who have more pressing and crushing educational needs than sojourns on the Continent. I have no answer to this objection, but I want to put the question: Is study in Europe as vital for young African Americans today as it has been for the past century? Where does it fit on the agenda and on the scale of priorities? My fear is that as it slips downward on any such scale, we come closer to viewing foreign study precisely in the way white educators in the past viewed it for DuBois. That would certainly be ironic, and it might be a tragic mistake, both for the academy in general and for black American scholars in particular.

2. Kant; Or, What All Königsberg Knows about Africa

Earlier I mentioned "the red stain of bastardy" in *The Souls of Black Folk*, thinking of it in the context of one of the books DuBois studied in Germany, namely, Hegel's *Phenomenology of Spirit.* In the present chapter, I am thinking of both these works, and of the "red stain," in terms of the psychodynamics and twisted erotisms of racism.[11] Such a *pulsional* or *libidinal* account of racism, focusing on the underlying drives that fuel bigotry and race hatred, may be no more than the weary white liberal's fascination with the perverse—scratching at an old sore rather than helping to formulate new agendas for a new time. Yet it seems to me that the kinds of study that were being pursued a generation ago by humanistic psychologists and anthropologists—I recall articles by Ashley Montagu back in the 1960s on the wretched and wrenching erotics of racism that struck me as decisively insightful—stopped too soon. For who today *understands* the veil of which DuBois speaks, "the Veil of Race"?[12] It is invoked by him in the phrases "darkly as through a veil,"[13] "beyond the Veil,"[14] "the awful shadow of the Veil,"[15] "the Black World beyond the Veil,"[16] and "straitly foreordained to walk within the Veil . . . , a veil so thick, that they shall not even think of breaking through."[17] Who is familiar with all the folds and pleats of the veil? Who understands, above all, our desire to *lift* the veil?[18]

Does the Veil of race belong to nature or to culture? Are we free to raise it or lower it at will? Perhaps the German philosophers and writers of the Enlightenment and the Romantic eras have something to teach us in this regard—DuBois certainly thought they did.

Let me turn briefly to the second volume of Kant's *Physical Geography* (1802) and its account of Africa and the "true Negro."[19] What is worth repeating from this text? What sorts of nuggets of empirical wisdom should I extract from this text? Shall I repeat Kant's opening observation that Negroes are "*born white*, except for their genitals and a black ring around the navel" (§2.1)? Kant does not cite his sources for the most part, so it is difficult to learn where most of his empirical gems have been discovered.[20] To be sure, one must praise the relative enlightenment of Kant, who does not accept the pious account of the Negro's descent from the biblical race of Ham, an account that interprets blackness as evidence of Divine retribution (§3). Kant knows about the sun and hot climates. He also knows, and relates, that the skin of peoples in equatorial climates is thick, so that when you chastise them it is best to use split bamboo rather than a whip, in order to enable the blood to escape, thus avoiding hematomas and infection (§2.8). What nuggets or semiprecious stones of empirical wisdom shall

I retain—about the eyes, legs, and sexual parts of the Negro, about their smell, their customs, their ability to run but disinclination to do so, their fearfulness and lassitude, their childlike and passionate natures? Or is it best to let these dubious treasures lie concealed on the philosopher's library shelves, where no one—especially not the philosopher—will read or translate them? By hiding them from ourselves, we can ostensibly still insist that Kant, unlike the rest of us, is transcendentally enlightened, even if, like the rest of us, he is empirically benighted. All we need do is separate the transcendental wheat from the empirical chaff. So, let us try, and in two cases. Both are pronouncements from §4, "The human being all over the world, with regard to his other innate properties":

> In hot countries human beings mature earlier but do not reach the perfection of the temperate zones. Humanity in its grandest perfection is in the race of the whites [*in der Race der Weißen*]. The yellow Indians [*sic*] already have less talent. The Negroes are much lower, and at the bottom stand a segment of the [native] American tribes [*ein Theil der amerikanischen Völkerschaften*].

> The dweller in the temperate expanses of the Earth, above all, those that lie toward the middle of these expanses, is more beautiful of body, more industrious, with a better sense of humor [*scherzhafter*], more moderate in his passions, more reasonable [*verständiger*], than any other species of man in the world. Therefore, these peoples throughout time have taught the others and have compelled them by means of their weapons. The Romans, the Greeks, the ancient Nordic tribes, Ghengis Khan, the Turks, Tamerlane, and the Europeans after Columbus's discoveries astonished all southerly lands by means of their artifices [*Künste*] and their weapons [*Waffen*].

How shall we separate the empirical from the transcendental, the empirically misinformed from the transcendentally cretinous? Worse, how shall we separate the arts and artifices from the guns, the sense of humor from the spirit of conquest? How shall we isolate the teaching, *belehren*, from the compulsion, *bezwingen?* Here one may try and try, and still be proved a dunce or a villain. And so one decides, in a fit of mercy, to scrap Kant's physical geography and all its empirical embarrassments but retain his crystalline architectonic of lucid epistemology and pristine morality. To be sure, the entire architectonic is tenuously held together by Kant's intricate account of aesthetic and teleological judgment. And, if Robert Bernasconi is right, if teleological judgment proves to be embroiled in the special teleology of racial distinction, hierarchy, and segregation, then the Kantian architectonic as a whole—with its central pillar of a morality of respect for the individual human being—will tremble and tumble. We would scarcely recognize philosophy after such a tumble, inasmuch as, both on the Continent and in Anglo-American circles, Kant is king. After all, the kingdom of ends is his, and his, the universal peace; the enlightened community adheres to him, and the moral law is at the beck and call of his Critical works and their epigones. Yet something of Kant's helter-skelter physical geography, akin to his eccentric anthropology, shows how white the moral law and even the tribunal of pure reason can be. The physical geography can help us to understand why Kantian philosophers today, the philosophers who are always right and always righteous, are ever ready to sit in judgment over those of an inferior cognitive talent and a baser moral nature. Perhaps what we can learn from Kant on the Negro, and on questions of race in general, is that intuitions *with* concepts are blinding, and that concepts *without* intuitions are what Kant, like the rest of us, is transcendentally good at, whether he is doing physical geography, Critical epistemology, or, pardon the euphemism, "moral" philosophy. Kant's community of self-proclaimed rational agents is, to repeat, the dominant philosophical community. It claims universal, a priori authority, and it still has big sticks and heavy guns, especially in the English-speaking academic and philosophical world.

However, I want to revert now to DuBois's fascination with Europe and European education—even though Kant's *Physical Geography* would have struck him as the abomination and absurdity that it is. For, in spite of all the colonialism and racism, which, as he knew, are as European as *Apfelstrudel*, Europe and classical education are closely tied in DuBois's thinking. And his thinking is *always* a thinking about education.

Perhaps my opening remarks on European study for African Americans are less tangential than they might at first seem. DuBois's debate with Booker T. Washington certainly has to do with the contrast of classical education to industrial and agricultural training, for example. DuBois's worry is that the strategy elaborated by Washington will prevent African Americans from developing their best intellectual talents. It is in the first place a worry about the rampant commercialism and materialism of the republic, and the threatening submission of the black American to the almighty dollar: "And so thoroughly did he learn the speech and thought of triumphant commercialism, and the ideals of material prosperity, that the picture of a lone black boy poring over a French grammar amid the weeds and dirt of a neglected home soon seemed to him the acme of absurdities." He adds laconically, "One wonders what Socrates and St. Francis of Assisi would say to this."[21] Later he worries, "What if the Negro people be wooed from a strife for righteousness, from a love of knowing, to regard dollars as the be-all and end-all of life?"[22] He lists "higher education of Negro youth" as the third bone of contention between Washington and himself, after political power (suffrage) and insistence on civil rights[23]; yet so many of the narratives that lace *The Souls of Black Folk* are narratives of dogged country schoolteachers and shy but determined pupils, all the Josies and Joneses of Tennessee and Georgia. The higher training and the "ambition of our brighter minds"—these are always DuBois's prime passion. And if the Rhine seems far from the dark vale of the Mississippi, it is principally the Veil of race—not physical geography—that makes it so.

Perhaps one does have to concede that there are moments in *Souls* when DuBois's ideal of classical education—which seems to be modeled on and made for students "in New England and in Europe"[24]—has to grate on the nerves of those for whom *multiculturalism* means the end of a certain Greek and German intellectual hegemony. DuBois writes:

> The riddle of existence is the college curriculum that was laid before the Pharaohs, that was taught in the groves by Plato, that formed the *trivium* and *quadrivium*, and is to-day laid before the freedmen's sons by Atlanta University. And this course of study will not change; its methods will grow more deft and effectual, its content richer by toil of scholar and sight of seer; but the true college will ever have one goal,—not to earn meat, but to know the end and aim of that life which meat nourishes.[25]

In the same vein, consider the peroration of "Of the Training of Black Men," which looks as much toward Europe as it does toward Tennessee or Ohio, and much more toward Europe than toward Georgia, in order to seek for black American scholars and the African American leadership a place beyond the Veil:

> I sit with Shakespeare and he winces not. Across the color line I move arm in arm with Balzac and Dumas, where smiling men and welcoming women glide in gilded halls. From out the caves of evening that swing between the strong-limbed earth and the tracery of the stars, I summon Aristotle and Aurelius and what soul I will, and they come all graciously with no scorn nor condescension. So, wed with Truth, I dwell above the Veil. Is this the life you grudge us, 0 knightly America? Is this the life you long to change into the dull red hideousness of Georgia? Are you so afraid lest peering from this high Pisgah, between Philistine and Amalekite, we sight the Promised Land?[26]

However, it would be unfair—and inaccurate—to depict DuBois's as the usual sort of academic and cultural conservatism that the discourses of multiculturalism wish to attack. For DuBois comes down on the side of a radical democracy of talent. He prefers the risk of *extending* educational opportunities to the worse risk of *limiting* them: "And to seek to make the blacksmith a scholar is almost as silly as the more modern scheme of making the scholar a blacksmith; almost, but not quite." When it comes to that "fine adjustment between real life and the growing knowledge of life, an adjustment which forms the secret of civilization," DuBois is concerned to let as many hands as possible work the adjustment."[27] What he opposes is setting the sights of education too low. The passion of his opposition comes through in the apparent flippancy of the following remark near the end of "Of the Wings of Atlanta": Having asked whether blacks should be taught trades or the liberal arts, DuBois replies, "Neither and both: teach the workers to work and the thinkers to think; make carpenters of carpenters, and philosophers of philosophers, and fops of fools."[28]

Nor are such questions of training and education far removed from more emotional and more volatile kinds of questions—questions of inheritance and guilt and self-loathing, questions for all Königsberg. For DuBois, higher education is the only possible way to confront the nagging self-doubt of a race subjugated by both European weapons and European talk about rings around the navel: "So here we stand among thoughts of human unity, even through conquest and slavery; the inferiority of black men, even if forced by fraud; a shriek in the night for the freedom of men who themselves are not yet sure of their right to demand it. This is the tangle of thought and afterthought wherein we are called to solve the problem of training men for life."[29]

Training human beings for life, not merely for jobs: It is a matter of afterthoughts and tangles, no doubt bound up with "The After-Thought" that closes *The Souls of Black Folk*, with its desperate plea to "turn the tangle straight."[30] The tangle of education with matters that can only be called kinky—the skein in which a psychodynamics and erotics of racism have to get tangled up—is a tangle that DuBois never tries to avoid: "Such curious kinks of the human mind [such as color prejudice] exist and must be reckoned with soberly."[31] What, after all, is the purpose of education, even and especially an education in transcendental philosophy, if not to help us confront the things that frighten us most terribly?

The "red stain of bastardy" that so affrights DuBois is not so easily understood, not even after the best Critical cognitive and moral education, even though his indignation in the face of that stain can be palpably felt throughout *The Souls of Black Folk*. Yet the indignation, and the corresponding invocation of a mythic innocence for the continent of Africa, marks certain folds or pleats in the Veil that are far from uniform and univocal. "The red stain of bastardy, which two centuries of systematic legal defilement of Negro women had stamped upon his race, meant not only the loss of ancient African chastity, but also the hereditary weight of a mass of corruption from white adulterers, threatening almost the obliteration of the Negro home."[32] Hereditary guilt, inherited from white adulterers by their mixed children, their "reds," as they are sometimes called; a "mass of corruption" implied by the "legal defilement" (the oxymoron that can go so many ways!) of Negro women by the adulterous fathers of the American black . . . and brown and copper and gold. . . . So many folds, so many overlappings, so many complications. Especially if one inherits not only the violated chastity of the maternal victim but also the male violator's viciousness—*if* such things can be inherited at all. Perhaps black infants, at least in America, are born with a faint—a faint but forever spreading—*white* ring about the navel and the genitals?

The complications of inheritance emerge once again in the chapter "Of the Dawn of Freedom." Here the historical account of Reconstruction in the South is suddenly interrupted by a different kind of text—a text that introduces autobiography, albeit veiled autobiography, in the figures of a white great-grandfather and a maternal mulatto woman:

> Thus it is doubly difficult to write of this period calmly, so intense was the feeling, so mighty the human passions that swayed and blinded men. Amid it all, two figures ever stand to typify that day to coming ages,—the one, a gray-haired gentleman, whose fathers had quit themselves like men, whose sons lay in nameless graves; who bowed to the evil of slavery because its abolition threatened untold ill to all; who stood at last, in the evening of life, a blighted, ruined form, with hate in his eyes; —and the other, a form hovering dark and mother-like, her awful face black with the mists of centuries, had aforetime quailed at that white master's command, had bent in love over the cradles of his sons and daughters, and closed in death the sunken eyes of his wife,—aye, too, at his behest had laid herself low to his lust, and borne a tawny man-child to the world, only to see her dark boy's limbs scattered to the winds by midnight marauders riding after "cursed Niggers." These were the saddest sights of that woful [*sic*] day; and no man clasped the hands of these two passing figures of the present-past; but, hating, they went to their long home, and, hating, their children's children live today.[33]

Spared the ignominy of an adulterous ancestor only because the master's wife dies before the child is conceived of a mulatto servant, nothing can yet spare the child such redoubled hatred and the lust in the eyes, unless it be the more horrific hatred and the more twisted lust of marauders: In this veiled autobiography, the first child, the dark one, is torn limb from limb, after which that child's tawny siblings, "hating," live on, passing as in a forever present-past, through their children's children. No matter how much one may affirm the conservation of races and dream of the chastity of entire continents, the world conspires to mix, to stain the black with the red.[34] The result is an attack on the Negro home, the black family, an attack so insidious because it assaults both from within and without: The victimized Negro woman bears male children sired by her white victimizer, and even though she assuredly also bears female children by that same victimizer, there seems to be a special guilt that stains the bloodline of the male, turning his rage into self-loathing. "The wrong which your gentlemen have done against helpless black women in defiance of your own laws is written on the foreheads of two millions of mulattoes, and written in ineffaceable blood."[35] Herman Melville uses the same figure to identify the irredeemable guilt and the ultimate demise of the Christian deity: "To trail the genealogies of these high mortal miseries, carries us at last among the sourceless primogenitures of the gods; so that . . . we must needs give in to this: that the gods themselves are not for ever glad. The ineffaceable, sad birthmark in the brow of man is but the stamp of sorrow in the signers."[36] If the "sourceless primogenitures" themselves are marked by the stamp of sorrow, what hope have those tawny children, as much ruddy gold as black, who are circumscribed before birth by the white ring and branded by the iron of lust and hatred, themselves the bearers of the most transcendent sorrow?

3. Kettle Logics over Africa: Hegel's *Lectures on the Philosophy of History*

DuBois's affinity for Hegel rather than Kant, especially for Hegel's *Phenomenology of Spirit*, has often been noted yet perhaps not always been well understood.[37] The dialectic of "lordship and bondage" must have seemed to him a promissory note for the United States, Hegel's declared "land of the future."[38] However, I will not deal with the fertile topic of a DuBoisian and Hegelian phenomenology; here I am merely clearing a way through Hegel's less propitious texts. This way ought to lead us back to a phenomenology that Hegel and DuBois would share, namely, a phenomenology of the science and history of the experience of consciousness, which is an experience of the doubling of self-consciousness, life, and desire. Hegel wants to be as empirically informed and conceptually adept as Kant, and for the most part he succeeds. Yet Hegel insists that spirit put its nose into every aspect of nature and history, and it is difficult for him to distill pure essences from the ferment of materials he himself loves to gather and mix. I will save for later Hegel's best mix with regard to black Africa and the golden Africans; for the moment, I am occupied by his famous—or notorious—remarks on Africa in his *Lectures on the Philosophy of History*.

For Hegel, geography is raw material for historical spirit. In his view, the perfect integration of mountains, river valleys, and maritime coasts is reserved for Europe; Asia, with its wild river valleys and its proximity to the sea, remains transitional; Africa, which is waterless highland prairie or steppe, remains undeveloped and is devoid of history. Africa—genuine Africa, which is sub-Saharan and below the Nile—remains closed off from the rest of the world, "veiled in the black color of night," deprived of the daylight of self-aware, self-conscious history.[39] Africa veiled, says Hegel. Africa veiled in the Veil of race and Kantian physical geography. Hegel calls Africa the land of gold and the land of children, and though he may be being insulting here, and may wish to be insulting, I want to spend some time with his images. He speaks of Africa as *das in sich gedrungene Goldland, das Kinderland*, "the land of gold, compact in itself, and the land of children."[40] What about this redoubled compactness—of the land, of the land's mineral deposits, and of the land's inhabitants? *Gedrungen* means compact, concise, terse, squat, stocky, thickset, stumpy—perhaps preparing for and preforming the bone structure of the Negro, which Kant and Hegel describe as ostensibly broad and heavy. (In Hegel's system, geology always prepares the way for the vegetable and animal kingdoms, as geography prepares the way for history.) Yet compact gold is essentially pure, serving as the universal, solar standard of value, so that *gedrungen* reminds us of Hegel's other favorite past participle for Africa, namely, *gediegen:* solid, pure, unmixed, native, sterling, genuine, true, upright, thorough, showing good craftsmanship and sound knowledge—from *gedeihen*, to flourish, thrive, burgeon. This second favorite past participle comes from Hegel's "Philosophy of Nature," to which I will turn in a moment.[41] Yet these almost homologous words, *gedrungen* and *gediegen*, have become for me a kind of refrain about Hegel's relation to black Africa. They express a riddle or conundrum that threatens—or promises—to undo the Hegelian system, perhaps in order to give life back to it.

The genuine character of Africa is "difficult to grasp," says Hegel, writing the very words that Hölderlin had used to define the difficulty of grasping the god: *schwer zu fassen*.[42] Africa and the African, like the god, are difficult to grasp, because when one confronts them one must dispense with the category of the general or universal, *die Allgemeinheit.* It is as though the Hegelian system must respond to—or capitulate before—the inadequacy of its most recalcitrant object: If Africa is dark and of the night, the rational system that wants to seize it must first of all conform to it, extinguishing its lights, abandoning the God and the Law that Africans are putatively incapable of intuiting. It is as though the system must mimic the faltering of the object that eludes its grasp. Here the colonialism of the grasp (that is, of what Hegel calls the *Besitzaufnahme* or *Besitzergreifung* of and by the concept) ought to feel compelled to surrender to—or at least to tremble and hesitate before—the mystery of what it nevertheless without hesitation characterizes as inferior and inadequate. Once again Hegel uses the word *gedrungen*—compact, terse, thickset, dense as gold—to describe the failure of this people to reach the universal, a failure that for essential reasons threatens to infect the system as such. Hegel writes, "To this distinction of himself as individual and as essentially universal the African—in his undifferentiated, compact unity—has not yet come."[43] The African is like the female sex in the "Philosophy of Nature," that is to say, residing close to the unity that the male craves but cannot achieve—so close that the dialectical power of differentiation has no space in which to unfold and achieve itself. Like the female of all humankind, the African is the undeveloped unity of nature—he or she is entirely natural. As the male desires the female, so the philosopher craves the dark continent and its compact inhabitants. Moreover, the philosopher desires them precisely in their undeveloped state, in their naturalness, which is the way spirit originally expressed itself, the way spirit originally *developed.* Nevertheless, the African does not come to know a higher self, whether that self be Europe or a self-conscious Africa, which would in effect be Europe. Soon Hegel will assert that the African not only does "not yet" possess the power to distinguish but also forever will lack such power. "The Negro represents [*darstellt*] . . . the natural human being in all his untamed nature [*Wildheit*] and abandon [*Unbändigkeit*]; if one wants to conceptualize him correctly, one must abstract from all reverence and ethicality, from all that is called feeling: in his character there is not a single intimation of the human [*es ist nichts an das Menschliche Anklingende in diesem Charakter zu finden*]."[44] The African, entirely natural as he or she is, exhibits what is most natural (*natürlich*) about nature, which is something entirely unnatural to spirit, such that in the end the spirit that spawned nature will have to burn her with Phoenix-fire. Such unnatural naturalness is the bane of spirit and the boondoggle of the system.

When the white European is most natural, he is a man of feeling, though never a merely or even predominantly sensuous man; for his part, the African is so utterly sensuous that he or she has no feeling whatsoever and therefore has no humanity at all. If this seems confusing, the confusion is—naturally—spirit's. The fact that there is nothing human, or *humane*, about the African is not submitted to the ultimate test—ultimate, at least, for Hegel's philosophy of nature: Hegel does not consider whether the red stain of *miscegenation* is possible, even though prior to him Kant had known of mulattoes and indeed had been fascinated by the genetics of quadroons and octaroons. In any case, and quite beyond the ultimate *natural* test, the Negro seems to Hegel an inhumane human. The inhuman(e)ity of the black is demonstrated by the fact that among the world's religions only Islam has been able to penetrate the continent of Africa. This is because Islam represents a primal religion of power, that is, recognition of a superior power by an inferior one. Such power recognition is associated with *magic*, and from the beginning Africa is identified as a land of shamans and wizards: Herodotus's *Histories* tells of "dwarfs" or men "of the same small stature, and all black," from Libya, who kidnapped a group of Nasamonian explorers (book 11, chap. 33). The village of these Libyans, whose compact physical stature (according to Herodotus's account) perhaps gives Hegel his word *gedrungen* (squat, stocky), could be reached only by leaving the desert, crossing through miles of swamp and fording rivers of crocodiles. Africans are still to this day wizards and magicians, for they believe that the human being alone—Hegel here specifically refers to him as *der Mensch*—is capable of steering the forces of nature. Such a human being has no "spiritual reverence" for God, and he or she knows no "kingdom of right." Such inhuman(e) human beings do, of course, have a sense of their dependence on the powers of nature, for otherwise they would not practice magic on the elements. Furthermore, such people represent the power of magic to themselves in terms of the fetish, a word that Hegel derives from the Portuguese word for magic, *feitiço*.[45] That they wield the fetish is not what shocks Hegel, however. What shocks him is the fact that whenever the fetish fails them, these people punish it and destroy it, creating a new fetish for themselves. What these inhuman(e) humans lack is a "relation of dependence" with respect to their gods. Africans are inhuman and inhumane in their treatment of the divine. It is almost as though the benighted and compact black, who will never advance to self-consciousness and history, has anticipated the next two centuries of European history, having achieved a freedom and radical independence with respect to traditional gods, a freedom that one might have supposed possible only for an enlightened philosopher of spirit. Whereas the African tosses away his or her outworn, ineffectual fetishes, the European remains on his or her knees: "Have mercy on us, 0 Lord!" To repeat, the religion of the genuine African, of the wizard of the fetish, manifests "no relation of dependence [*kein Verhältnis der Abhängigkeit*]."[46] The least dependent of peoples are thus destined (at least according to Hegel's kettle logic) to be utterly dependent on Europe.[47] Yet Hegel does not pause to consider the anomaly produced by his own kettle logic: The essence of a spiritual people is freedom, but these people, who are not human or even humane, much less spiritual, are insufficiently dependent, and that is why they will never be free, so that Europe will have to teach them how to become dependent, in spite of the fact that they are incorrigible. Europe will teach them by itself learning the lesson of slavery—learning the lesson *from them*, from the incorrigible, unteachable, inhuman human beings.

A second inadequacy of the African is his fear of the dead and his subsequent cult of the spirits, by which he hopes to fend off their life-threatening forces. The problem with this is that the Negro continues to believe he has power over the dead; he fails to acknowledge his proper dependence on forces outside his control. "In this way the substantial remains always within the power of the subject [*in der Gewalt des Subjekts*]."[48] In other words, the problem with the inhuman(e) Negro is that he elevates human nature beyond nature, that he takes his arbitrary will to be superior to the natural—which is of course precisely what the philosopher of spirit, who has learned the lesson of (Kantian) sublimity, will later be required to do. Because this inhuman(e) human has esteemed the human as supreme, he has "no self-respect [*keine Achtung vor sich selber*]."[49] To have self-respect, a human being must, according to Hegel, acknowledge some "higher essence" or some "higher creature [*eines höheren Wesens*]"; only if he subjects himself to a higher power will the subject, the subjected subject, be free. If faith is believing what you know ain't so, freedom is the chance to snap on your own handcuffs. A people who does not know such happy subjection must be taught it—even if, as we shall see, such a people is incorrigible.

The Negro, who, according to Hegel, is contemptuous of humanity because he takes humanity to be the supreme entity, practices the worst imaginable forms of tyranny, the most base form being cannibalism. Because of such unbridled tyranny—and this is the ultimate premise of Hegel's kettle logic—the Continent will have to be tyrannized; because of cannibalism, the savage will have to be cooked and eaten by the European spirit. The secret of cannibalism is raw sensuality. Because the Negro sees human flesh as purely sensuous—in spite of those ghosts that haunt him in the flesh—he, "the sensuous Negro," can eat human flesh. It is as though, to repeat, the Negro represents the sensuous human being as such in Hegel's system,[50] the human being who is so tyrannized by his passions that he cannot think, so that the Negro is more widespread in the world than we might have thought. Which leads Hegel to the most serious inadequacy of the Negro: the institution of slavery.

When African Negroes are brought by the Europeans to the New World, the land of the future, in order to be sold into slavery, the result is only—or almost always only—an improvement in the condition of their slavery. The slavery that permeates their own land is absolute slavery, and what the Europeans contribute to the welfare of these people may be called—although Hegel does not say so—relative slavery. Because the Negro regards himself as essentially valueless, and he does so insofar as he regards the human (that is, himself, presuming he is human) as supreme, each African has a better chance in the land of relative slavery. In the New World, the Negro has at least a chance to learn about freedom and perhaps the opportunity to yearn for it for himself.

The African Negro, the cannibal, is also a polygamist. He desires to produce as many children as he can, so that he can sell them into slavery. His total lack of respect for human life accounts for his astonishing bravery (*Tapferkeit*), which is further supported by "the monstrous strength of his body [*die große, von ungeheurer Körperstärke unterstützte Tapferkeit der Neger.*]"[51] The monstrous strength of these compact black or golden bodies, however, does not prevent their being "mowed down" by the thousands by European rifles. Because the Negro is independent, or at least nondependent on something superior to it, or him, he "allows himself to be shot down by the thousands [*sich zu Tausenden niederschießen lassen*]."[52] His contempt for life causes him to put his own life and his own monstrously strong body—his compact and flourishing body—at risk. "For," as Hegel explains, "life has worth only when it has something worthy as its goal."[53] Because the African's own life, like that of his slaves and his children, has no value, because the Negro is unworthy, the European alone can and must put a value on it. How many the European armies kill, in order to rescue the remainder in a value-producing slave trade, is no doubt what DuBois would call a nice calculation. In order to make that calculation, Hegel will have to return to the question of slavery, which the European has learned from the unenlightened Negroes, and which the European will in turn teach the incorrigible Negroes—at least those who have not let themselves be mowed down by European rifles. He will also have to return to the question of Negro bravery, the astonishing mettle of blacks, the courage of these mere children.

In the meantime, Hegel has not finished his account of the tyranny of the Africans. The sensuous rawness of the African deprives him of every societal band, every form of constitution. His social order consists of capricious subjects with an absolute lord at the top. To be sure, the king has a council, which he must consult and which can depose the lord. In Dahomey, the council sends the king parrot eggs as a sign of their discontent, at which point the king retreats to his tent in order to allow his wives to strangle him. For his part, Hegel loves these quaint travelers' and missionaries' stories: What a picaresque and dashing Mungo-Park sort of rhetoric they weave into the plaincloth narrative of spirit's otherwise ultimately quite predictable kettle logic. Indeed, Africa is the true land of the Amazons, except that the black Penthesilea squashes her own son with mortar and pestle, smearing herself with his blood.[54] The black Amazons are in fact Furies: We always knew that the compact, undeveloped, highly unified black or gold body was close to woman and to the sensuous life, but we had no idea she would turn out to be so savage.

When Hegel reverts to the bravery of the blacks, it is to weigh their fanaticism against their "general meekness [*sonstigen Sanftmütigkeit*]."[55] Kings must subject their own tribes to a bloodbath in order to rouse them to arms against an enemy and in order to secure power.[56] "The tribes are tranquil for long stretches of time, but suddenly they begin to ferment, and then they are completely outside themselves."[57] Once aroused, these people are incredibly destructive, inasmuch as theirs is "more a physical than a spiritual fanaticism."[58] When kings die, thousands are slaughtered. Such slaughter, reminiscent perhaps of the thousands who *let themselves* be mowed down by the Europeans, prompts Hegel to return to the question of slavery. The principal weakness of the Negro character is its "unbridled behavior" or "unboundedness" (*Unbändigkeit*). Such unbounded arbitrariness means that the African will never develop, will never achieve culture or formation (*Bildung*). The only essential connection the black African can have with the European is therefore the ultimate binding, to wit, slavery. The blacks themselves see nothing inappropriate in the institution of slavery—so much insight they do have; to that extent they are eminently corrigible—and they hate the English precisely because they have done more than the other European nations to *restrict* the slave trade. Chiefs consider it a prerogative to sell their captives, or even their own subjects, into slavery. In this way, slavery (European slavery, Hegel clearly means, although he writes merely "slavery," thus leading the reader to believe that he may mean African slavery) is eminently educational: "To this extent slavery has aroused a heightened sense of humanity [*mehr Menschliches*] among the Negroes."[59] Hegel does not say so but one might surmise that Negroes sold into slavery in the New World, the Negroes of the future Middle Passage, as it were, are precisely those slaves who will bear the torch of freedom back to the Africa of the Old World. For a people who lack even a hint of humanity in their character, only slavery will offer a bit "more" of what they lack and never will possess fully. So much for *Amistad.*

However, Hegel's next sentence leads us to conclude that we were wrong to suppose that it is *European* slavery that makes the inhuman Negro more humane. He writes, "The teaching that we can draw from this condition of slavery among the Negroes, the teaching that constitutes the interesting part of all this for us, is the one that we come to know from the idea that the state of nature [*der Naturzustand*] is itself the state of absolute and thoroughgoing injustice [*absoluten und durchgängigen Unrechts ist*]."[60] Indeed, there is something educational about the inherent slavishness of this self-enslaved nondependent people, this incorrigible and uneducable, this utterly and unnaturally natural, people. The state of nature bears traces of its slavish naturalness even in Europe: Slavery perdures in Greece and Rome, serfdom throughout medieval Europe, and indentured servitude into modernity. Slavery therefore (*therefore?* yes, *therefore,* at least for a kettle logic) somehow becomes "a moment of education [*ein Moment der Erziehung*]," at least for Europe, which has history and a future.[61] Education to what? To recognition of the fact that slavery is "injustice in and for itself," inasmuch as the essence of humanity is freedom—but a freedom for which humankind must first "grow ripe."[62] The *gradual* elimination of slavery is therefore more fitting than its abrupt abolition. The people who betray no movement and no development must be moved and developed to the point where the slavery that inheres in them, and which infects the history of Europe itself, is gently and patiently purged.

At this point in *Lectures on the Philosophy of History,* says Hegel, "we shall abandon Africa, never to refer to it again in what follows."[63] Of course, Hegel does return to the questions of Africa and slavery elsewhere, in the "Anthropology" of his *Encyclopedia of Philosophical Sciences.*[64] In the addendum to §393, Hegel takes up the Kantian question as to whether the various races of humankind devolve from a single set of parents. Actually, he refuses to engage the question, because he knows that others—whom he allows to remain nameless—have used it to deprive certain races of their claim to humanity, or to insist on the spiritual or intellectual superiority of certain races over others, or even to insist on the right of certain races to "dominate some others as though they were animals."[65] Hegel counters: "We can draw no conclusions from matters of descent with regard to the human being's rightful claim—or lack of it—to freedom and dominion. Human beings are rational in themselves. In such rationality lies the possibility of equal rights for all humans—the falsehood of a crass distinction into enfranchised and disenfranchised [*berechtigte und rechtlose*] genuses of humans."[66]

Hegel concedes the fact that there are different races, but he attributes this to the influences of the sundry parts of the Earth—in short, to geography. He now reiterates some of the basic premises of his geography. Even though the New World is precisely that—new—its indigenous peoples are destined to perish; for in the New World it is still the *Old* World that is to "reconfigure itself."[67] The Old World itself consists of three parts: Africa, Asia, and Europe proper. Africa is a quantum or mass that abides in "solid unity [*gediegene Einheit*]," shut off from the coast, isolated on the high steppes of the continental shelf, whereas the Mediterranean binds the northernmost segments of the continent to Asia and to Europe. Hegel claims that this division of the Earth, and subdivision of the Old World, "is not contingent, but necessary."[68] To that subdivision of the Old World corresponds the apportionment of humankind into three principal races: the Caucasian, Ethiopian, and Mongolian. The main distinguishing marks of these three races derive from the "formation of the skull and the face."[69] The angle formed by the intersection of horizontal and vertical lines, from ear to ear across the bottom of the nose and from brow to chin, is the main distinguishing mark—not only among the races but between the human race and all animal species: With animals the angle is quite acute. Protruding cheekbones and the slope of the forehead are also germane to racial classification and hierarchization. For Caucasians, the angle formed by the intersecting horizontal and vertical lines is "almost or completely" a right angle. (The most perfect angle—surprise!—is exhibited by Italians and Georgian Russians.) The African angle is not discussed, and Hegel draws no explicit consequences from his account, which, nevertheless, does not bode well for the black: "Negroes have a more narrow skull than the Mongolians and Caucasians, their brows are arched yet humped [*bucklig*], their jaws are slung, their teeth crooked, the lower jawbone extending quite far, their skin color more or less black, their hair woolly and black."[70] Nor does Hegel hesitate to offer a sketch of the *spiritual* distinguishing marks of the races, even though any such marks must surely militate against the initial claim that there is but one race, and that one—the human—inherently rational and therefore fundamentally free. The Africans, it seems, can be free only as children:

> *Negroes* are to be conceived of as a nation of children, children who do not emerge from their disinterested and uninterested ingenuousness. They are

sold, and they let themselves be sold [*Sie werden verkauft und lassen sicch verkaufen*], without any sort of reflection as to whether this is right or not. Their religion has something childlike about it. Whatever they feel concerning more elevated matters they do not retain; it passes fleetingly, in one ear and out the other. They transpose this elevated sensation onto the first pretty stone they see, making it their fetish; they discard the fetish whenever it has failed to help them. In a calm state they are of a pleasing disposition and harmless; but when a sudden rage overtakes them they commit the most frightful atrocities. The capacity for culture [*Bildung*] cannot be denied them: . . . here and there have they embraced Christianity with immense gratitude, and have spoken in the most touching way of their freedom, achieved through Christianity after a long spiritual servitude[*Geistesknechtschaft*]. . . . Yet they show no inner drive [*inneren Trieb*] to civilization. The most horrid despotism dominates their homeland; they do not come to feel the personality of the human being—for their spirit is quite asleep, remains submerged in itself, makes no progress, and thus corresponds to the compact, undifferentiated mass of the African land.[71]

The notion of "spiritual servitude" and the correspondence of slumbering spirit and compact landscape ought to give us pause. For the essence of spirit is freedom, a freedom that the dark continent of Peter Pan-like perpetual childhood will never achieve. These people *let themselves* be sold into slavery or *let themselves* be mowed down, and such *lassen*, such *Gelassenheit*, is an affront to freedom, inasmuch as it mimics and mocks freedom. Likewise, the notion of an "inner drive" to formation and culture, the drive (is it of spirit? not yet? always already?) that Negroes lack, ought to give us infinite pause. And precisely *how* geography can determine the (un)spiritual character of a people who are members of the one race, the human, remains mysterious in Hegel's system. *In itself*, the human race is free; *in Africa*, it is not. And even when forcefully removed from Africa to the New World, the land of the future, the race is not free. Except, of course, insofar as it submits in a touching and childlike way to the Christian faith. No racism here, perhaps, but a geographism as restrictive and constricting as any racism. No racism here, perhaps, but a religionism as self-righteous and as bigoted as any racism.

Yet do not such geographism and religionism—all the kettle logics that resound over Hegel's Africa—shake the system? DuBois probably had an inkling that they do. "Of the Sons of Master and Man," in *The Souls of Black Folk*, begins as follows:

The world-old phenomenon of the contact of diverse races of men is to have new exemplification during the new century. Indeed, the characteristic of our age is the contact of European civilization with the world's unde-

> veloped peoples. Whatever we may say of the results of such contact in the past, it certainly forms a chapter in human action not pleasant to look back upon. War, murder, slavery, extermination, and debauchery,—this has again and again been the result of carrying civilization and the blessed gospel to the isles of the sea and the heathen without the law. Nor does it altogether satisfy the conscience of the modern world to be told complacently that all this has been right and proper, the fated triumph of strength over weakness, of righteousness over evil, of superiors over inferiors. It would certainly be soothing if one could readily believe all this; and yet there are too many ugly facts for everything to be thus easily explained away. We feel and know that there are many delicate differences in race psychology, numberless changes that our crude social measurements are not yet able to follow minutely, which explain much of history and social development. At the same time, too, we know that these considerations have never adequately explained or excused the triumph of brute force and cunning over weakness and innocence.[72]

What, then, about this compact and solid (*gediegen, gedrungen*) land, scorched by the sun? What about this land, so arid, barren, chaste, and innocent, and yet also so productive of compact bodies? If it is New World slavery that educates the Negro, at least to the degree that it arouses something *menschlich* in him, in what would that arousal consist? Perhaps it convinces the forcefully transplanted African of the necessity of subjection, submission, and dependence as the very secret of freedom? Perhaps New World slavery is the only institution that can convince the incorrigible African that his or her arbitrary will is insufficient for freedom? Perhaps the African in turn teaches the European that the natural and the state of nature are inherently unjust? Slavery is the essence of injustice—but it is the only way incorrigible blacks and whites will learn that nature herself is unjust, and that even though she cannot be abolished, she certainly must be overcome.

What about the nature of this unjust "nature" that is the African state of nature? And what about the compact gold of the Negro, the thriving bodies of black folk?

4. The Bodies of Black Folk: From Hegel's "Philosophy of Nature" to Baldwin's *The Fire Next Time*

Kant knows black bodies before Hegel. His *Physical Geography* refers to the "black color, smoked, as it were, also the black, woolly hair, the broad face, flat nose, protruding lips . . . and the large, heavy bones [*plumpe und große Knochen*]." And he knows the difference between true Negroes and African Americans: "In America there are no national blacks [*Nationalschwarzer*], the color of the face is copper, the hair is smooth" (§1). Copper, gold, red, and smooth blacks: The Harlem Renaissance comes to Königsberg.

At first, Hegel, for his part, seems not at all interested in the bodies of black folk. He is interested in their continent, in their geography and geology, as it were. And yet.

Allow me to take you to a strange moment in Hegel's *Encyclopedia of the Philosophical Sciences*, part 2, "Philosophy of Nature." It is a moment at which something unexpected rises to disturb Hegel's otherwise sober discussion of the possibility of Earth's history. In the addendum to §339, Hegel discusses the question as to whether the Earth, viewed as a sidereal body, has a history. His reply is equivocal. Insofar as history is history of the universal, nature has "no history."[73] The Earth provides the "ground and soil" for life and for history, but it itself has none. Or, better, the Earth can be said to "have had" a history, as long as we concede that such a history ended long ago, that the process of the Earth's development remains extrinsic to it. Hegel writes, in a manner that is distinctly odd, that history "at an earlier time fell into the Earth, but now it has come to rest."[74] The unhistorical or prehistoric Earth exhibits "the movements and the dreams of sleepers," sleepers reminiscent of Walt Whitman's great poem:

> The sleepers are very beautiful as they lie unclothed,
> They flow hand in hand over the whole earth from east to
> west as they lie unclothed,
> The Asiatic and African are hand in hand, the European and
> The American are hand in hand,
> Learn'd and unlearn'd are hand in hand, and male and female
> are hand in hand . . .
> The call of the slave is one with the master's call, and the
> master salutes the slave.[75]

Indeed, the Earth represents all those who are lost in slumber—oh! the somnolence of the planet on which we drift! In this same addendum, however, Hegel rejects the notion of Chaos, that is, of an era of sheer contingency in Earth history. No, "nature essentially has intellect," Hegel insists; she springs from Jupiter's head like an armed Minerva.[76] True, the various parts of nature, for example, the parts of the Earth, her continents, may "at first" seem to be "accidental" or "contingent [*zufällig*]"; yet all the parts of the Earth—the New World and the Old, and the Old with its three continents (Africa, Asia, and Europe)—are not contingent but necessary: They are "essential distinctions." Of the essential distinction of Africa, Hegel now writes: " . . . Africa, the compact metal, the lunar, motionless in the heat, where the human being in itself grows musty [*wo der Mensch in sich selbst verdumpft*]—the mute spirit that does not enter consciousness."[77]

The identification of Africa as lunar and as dense metal is not entirely unexpected, and yet its consequences are not as predictable as one might have thought, first, because the lunar is *silver*,[78] whereas the continent of Africa is compact *gold*, hence more closely related to the sun, which shines with merciless heat, the light of the sun being responsible (as every enlightened philosopher knows) for the African's smoked skin and woolly hair.[79] (Compact gold is no doubt something more than the white world's "Goldilocks," from which DuBois recoils: Of his firstborn, DuBois laments, "Why was his hair tinted with gold? An evil omen was golden hair in my life."[80] Compact gold is not Goldilocks but is pure, dense ebon.) However, in any case, one should not think that the moon is inferior to the sun in Hegel's system. True, the moon does not turn on its own axis but has the Earth as its axis, as it has the sun for its source of light. Yet the moon is more like planet Earth than the sun is, and inasmuch as the *planetary* is central to Hegel's cosmology, the importance of the moon waxes with that of the Earth. Indeed, even the sun "serves" the Earth, perhaps in its capacity as feminine (in German, *die Sonne*), whereas the moon is king—or at least "regent"—perhaps insofar as it is masculine (*der Mond*).[81]

Yet a certain bleakness, a certain blanched pallor, also characterizes the motionless moon. To repeat, the lunar is dependent on the sun for its light, even if its power to direct the tides and stir the blood has long been attested. The waterless surface of the moon—which, unlike a comet, has no water vapor and no atmosphere—is simultaneously frozen and ashen. The moon is congealed and brittle: Its being-for-self is a keeping-to-itself, impenetrable and indifferent.[82] The moon is thirsty: "The moon is the waterless crystal that seeks to integrate itself with our seas, trying to quench its paralyzing thirst and therefore inducing the ebb and flood of the tides."[83] A certain impotence marks the parched moon, even if he (or it) is a celestial power. For the moon looks to the past, embodying as he (or it) does the sidereal character of Earth as such, which has the principle of its process, its history, behind it. Hegel's earliest (1805–1806) formulations of these points (so mysterious in their heavily logicized wording!) is as follows:

> The lunar expresses being-*for-self* in its truth, which is that it has its being-in-itself outside itself, comporting itself to such being in a negative way, yet nevertheless relating itself to it. Or, it is only the becoming of the in-itself. In terms of rotation on an axis, it is likewise outside itself, having its midpoint in another—having its immediate or abstract *in-itself* outside itself. Thus it turns about itself,[84] but it is the tranquilized, existent sort of

> rotation, not the kind that dissolves in the restlessness of the vortex.—It is therefore the perfect sphere. . . . The sun is the essence, but not the real concept. True, the sun is the mother of the Earth, but the moon is her regent, the earthly nature of Earth. The moon is as much regent as the sun and the cometary sphere; for precisely the universal and abstract is *inorganic nature*, the universal element, whereas the subject, individuality, is the being *in-and-for-itself* of the same.—The sun is tranquil, the cometary [sphere] is pure movement. The lunar is being *in-itself*, the inner, so much so, that . . . the moon looks the way the Earth must have looked when it first came to be.[85]

Whether the moon is a regent who fulfills the obligations of the king during the nightly interregnum of time and earth history, or, as the later text says, a kind of guardian or companion (*Trabant*) of the Earth, it is repeatedly associated also with the for-itself of subjectivity. Why would Hegel associate lunar Africa and the Africans with the very subjectivity he is otherwise avid to deny them? Even if it is a subjectivity or being-for-self that hangs on the past, it is nonetheless an achieved subjectivity; even if it is earthly, it is nonetheless of the Earth—and hence central to the Hegelian cosmos.

Yet Hegel also refers to Africa as compact metal. Why metal? Because metals, such as gold, silver, and mercury, "show themselves to be the most compact, most autochthonous among the bodies of the Earth."[86] However, why would Hegel associate the least autonomous of continents with the most autochthonous of bodies? Metals dwell on the very verge of crystallization; a protorationality tickles their frictionless surfaces and runs straight through their depths; a sound emanates from them when they are struck, a pure, deep tone, a chime—perhaps a kind of sorrow song. Metals flourish under the blazing moon—they seem to grow like legumes planted beneath the ascendant moon. Metals are like plants that have thrived, *gediegen*, plants that have already burgeoned in the light of the sun and which, now compact, *gedrungen*, drink from the cool silver goblet of the night.

And yet, as lunar as they may be, Africa and the African seem to enjoy some privilege when it comes to the "ideal process" of sunlight,[87] the sunlight that turns chemicals into life's breath and elements into flesh, the sunlight that sets the blood to boiling. Gold, copper, silver, mercury, iron, and molten lead—such are the compact and elemental bodies of these sun-drenched peoples of Africa. They are themselves *earths*, which is an old word for *ore*, in German, *Erz*. They are earthen people, the people of Earth, Earthmen and Earthwomen, glazed earthenware. They are compact and dense. Yet their agitated blood confounds all logics. The policemen who frisked the young James Baldwin in an empty lot in Harlem, leaving the ten-year-old boy flat on his back, were so avid in their search that they seemed to him in retrospect to have been spelunkers, miners hot for the lode and the shaft, hungry for compact metal, so much so that the boy had to wonder what on Earth those hands were groping for.[88]

Who understands the Veil, all its folds, the lift?

No doubt, it has to do with the miasma of culture, with the very worst that our history has to offer us. Yet it also has to do with sidereal Earth, and with the way sidereal Earth challenges all notions of history, necessity, and logic. It has to do with what we heard DuBois call "the caves of evening that swing between the strong-limbed earth and the tracery of the stars." It has to do with God. For there is a reference to *compact metal* I have so far failed to make, a reference not to Hegel but to his contemporary, Novalis, whom I have mentioned above as a thinker of the Veil. Novalis says in one of his last notes, "God is of infinitely compact metal—the most corporeal and most massive of all essences."[89] It—the Veil of sidereal Earth—has to do with the divine order of nature and with the upheavals of such order. And the divinity of the order of nature has to do with skin. F.W.J. Schelling, in his never-completed masterpiece *The Ages of the World*, suggests why it is that human beings love to wear gold next to their skin: It is because gold exudes a healing oil or balsam—indeed, because gold itself is a kind of second skin. We may take it that Schelling is referring to red gold, or even black gold, as the reference to oil suggests, rather than white gold.[90] In a letter to his nephew James, published as "My Dungeon Shook," Baldwin writes of the upheavals that are occurring in the divine order of nature:

> Try to imagine how you would feel if you woke up one morning to find the sun shining and all the stars aflame. You would be frightened because it is out of the order of nature. Any upheaval in the universe is terrifying because it so profoundly attacks one's sense of one's own reality. Well, the black man has functioned in the white man's world as a fixed star, as an immovable pillar: and as he moves out of his place, heaven and earth are shaken to their foundations. . . . [B]y a terrible law, a terrible paradox, those innocents who believed that your imprisonment made them safe are losing their grasp of reality. But these men are your brothers—your lost, younger brothers.[91]

It—the Veil, the Veil of the compact and flourishing golden body—also has to do with the Earthpeople as sensual human beings. Baldwin now reminds us of what D. H. Lawrence earlier in the century had to say about the pernicious anemia of Western white culture. Unlike Hegel, however, Baldwin says nothing of the tyranny of the sensuous. He writes, instead, of bread:

> To be sensual, I think, is to respect and rejoice in the force of life, of life itself, and to be present in all that one does, from the effort of loving to the breaking of bread. It will be a great day for America, incidentally, when we begin to eat bread again, instead of the blasphemous and tasteless foam rubber that we have substituted for it. And I am not being frivolous now, either. Something very sinister happens to the people of a country when they begin to distrust their own reactions as deeply as they do here, and become as joyless as they have become. It is this individual uncertainty on the part of white American men and women, this inability to renew themselves at the fountain of their own lives, that makes the discussion, let alone elucidation, of any conundrum—that is, any reality—so supremely difficult. The person who distrusts himself has no touchstone for reality for this touchstone can be only oneself. . . . Therefore, whatever white people do not know about Negroes reveals, precisely and inexorably, what they do not know about themselves.[92]

It—the Veil—therefore ultimately has to do with what this compact and courageous human being, this sensuous human being of the New World who has also tarried on all the continents of the Old, can teach Hegel about the thing Hegel cares about most, which is freedom—and the limits of spiritual freedom. Baldwin writes:

> Freedom is hard to bear. It can be objected that I am speaking of political freedom in spiritual terms, but the political institutions of any nation are always menaced and are ultimately controlled by the spiritual state of that nation. We are controlled here by our confusion, far more than we know, and the American dream has therefore become something much more closely resembling a nightmare, on the private, domestic, and international levels. Privately, we cannot stand our lives and dare not examine them; domestically, we take no responsibility for (and no pride in) what goes on in our country; and, internationally, for many millions of people, we are an unmitigated disaster.[93]

Hard words in 1962 for the American Dream. Does anything in our experience of the past thirty-five years enable us to consider them too harsh or in any way obsolete? In certain passages of *The Fire Next Time*, such as those passages on freedom, Baldwin writes for the era or age that embraces Hegel, DuBois, and ourselves in the hope that we are not incorrigible. In other passages, he—the sensuous man, the fetishist of the pen, the writer who acknowledges no higher power on whom human beings could ever depend—seems to write for the race of woman and man, for the people of Earth, the mortals, whose life is ineluctably tragic:

> Life is tragic simply because the earth turns and the sun inexorably rises and sets, and one day, for each of us, the sun will go down for the last, last

> time. Perhaps the whole root of our trouble, the human trouble, is that we will sacrifice all the beauty of our lives, will imprison ourselves in totems, taboos, crosses, blood sacrifices, steeples, mosques, races, armies, flags, nations, in order to deny the *fact* of death, which is the only fact we have. It seems to me that one ought to rejoice in the fact of death—ought to decide, indeed, to *earn* one's death by confronting with passion the conundrum of life. One is responsible to life: It is the small beacon in that terrifying darkness from which we come and to which we shall return. One must negotiate this passage as nobly as possible, for the sake of those who are coming after us. But white Americans do not believe in death, and this is why the darkness of my skin so intimidates them.[94]

Finally, the Veil is about the nature of the tragedy, the American tragedy, which is as much a tale of love and murder as it is of race. Baldwin's words remind us of the death of DuBois's firstborn child, a death that causes its father to cry, "0 Death! Is not this my life hard enough,—is not that dull land that stretches its sneering web about me cold enough,—is not all the world beyond these four little walls pitiless enough, but that thou must needs enter here,—thou, 0 Death?"[95] That death alone should lift the Veil of the color line as it lowers the mortal Veil forever: That is the irony of a tragedy that is being played out every day on the Earth, and not only on American shores. Finally, to revert once more to Baldwin, and with these compact words of his to close, it is about the inevitable, precipitous reversal that all tyranny suffers—reversal being the thing that captivated Hegel early on, spurring his phenomenology, driving his science of the appearances of consciousness. Baldwin writes:

> The racial tensions that menace Americans today have little to do with real antipathy—on the contrary, indeed—and are involved only symbolically with color. These tensions are rooted in the very same depths as those from which love springs, or murder. The white man's unadmitted—and apparently, to him, unspeakable—private fears and longings are projected onto the Negro. The only way he can be released from the Negro's tyrannical power over him is to consent, in effect, to become black himself, to become a part of that suffering and dancing country that he now watches wistfully from the heights of his lonely power and, armed with spiritual traveller's checks, visits surreptitiously after dark.[96]

Notes

This chapter was first read at the conference "The Academy and Race: Toward a Philosophy of Political Action," organized by Kevin Thomas Miles at Villanova University in March 1996; a version entitled "Die Körper der schwarzen Völker: Über Kant und Hegel zu Du Bois und Baldwin" was presented at the conference "Black Liberation in the Americas," organized by the Collegium on African-American Research, at the Westfälische Wilhelms-Universität Münster on 20 March 1999. My thanks to the following colleagues for their generous responses: Edwin Moses, Nahum Chandler, Ronald A.T. Judy, Lee Baker, Robert Bernasconi, and Lucius Outlaw. For their hospitality, I thank Walter Brogan and, once again, Kevin Miles and Lucius and Frieda Outlaw.

1. David Levering Lewis, *W.E.B. DuBois: Biography of a Race, 1868–1919* (New York: Henry Holt, 1993), 129.
2. Ibid.
3. W.E.B. DuBois, *The Souls of Black Folk* (New York: Library of America, 1990), 363.
4. Lewis, *W.E.B. DuBois,* 129.
5. DuBois, *The Souls of Black Folk,* 368.
6. Lewis, *W.E.B. Dubois,* 138.
7. Ibid., 132.
8. Ibid.
9. Ibid., 141.
10. Ibid., 145.
11. I have related such psychodynamics and eroticisms to chauvinism, militarism, and nationalism in "National Eroticism," in *Ethics and Responsibility in the Phenomenological Tradition,* the Ninth Annual Symposium of the Simon Silverman Phenomenology Center, Duquesne University (Pittsburgh, Pennsylvania, 1992), 33–56.
12. DuBois, *The Souls of Black Folk,* 417–18.
13. Ibid., 368.
14. Ibid., 405.
15. Ibid., 407.
16. Ibid., 418.
17. Ibid., 424–25.
18. See Michael Naas, "Vivre à l'ombre: W.E.B. DuBois et le voile de la race," unpublished manuscript. I myself cannot help but hear in DuBois's Veil a concealed reference to Schiller's "Saïs" and Novalis's *Apprentices at Saïs.*
19. I cite Immanuel Kant from Eckhard Henscheid, *Der Neger (Negerl)*(Frankfurt am Main: Fischer, 1986). Hereafter, this volume will be cited parenthetically by section and paragraph only. I should note at the outset that the revelations made by Robert Bernasconi concerning the relationship of Kantian teleological judgment (as developed in the pre-Critical writings) to the phenomenon of race came as a shock to me. As a result of those revelations, I ought to have recast altogether part 2 of this essay. Yet Bernasconi's discovery is so potent and so disturbing that I believe it will take years to assimilate it. In what follows, I ignore the texts on teleology from the 1770s, concentrating instead on the final formulation of Kant's "physical geography."
20. Once again, Bernasconi shows the way: His archival work—inspired in part by Michel Foucault but marked by a style all his own—has uncovered the essential sources for the later *Physical Geography* in the pre-Critical texts on teleology of the 1770s.
21. DuBois, *The Souls of Black Folk,* 393.
22. Ibid., 419.
23. Ibid., 398.
24. Ibid., 433.
25. Ibid., 420.
26. Ibid., 438.

27. Ibid., 421.
28. Ibid., 423.
29. Ibid., 425.
30. Ibid., 547.
31. Ibid., 425.
32. Ibid., 368.
33. Ibid., 383.
34. I am not yet prepared to comment on DuBois's text "The Conservation of Races" (1897), which I have not studied with sufficient care; it is clear to me, however, that I am touching on this much debated article and that the force of my own engagement will have to take me to it.
35. DuBois, *The Souls of Black Folk*, 436.
36. Herman Melville, *Moby-Dick* (Boston: Houghton Mifflin/Riverside Press, 1956), chap. 106, 356.
37. Did DuBois really "borrow more or less intact" from Hegel's *Phenomenology of Spirit* "notions of distinct, hierarchical racial attributes"? (Lewis, *W.E.B. DuBois*, 139). I doubt whether such "notions" are there, although one will have better—and worse—luck with Hegel's *Lectures on the Philosophy of History*. See Georg Wilhelm Friedrich Hegel, *Vorlesungen über die Philosophie der Geschichte*, vol. 12 of *Werke*, ed. Eva Moldenhauer, Karl Markus Michel, and Helmut Reinicke (Frankfurt am Main: Suhrkamp, 1969–71), 114. Hereafter, this work is cited parenthetically as *PG*. I reserve for another time the more fruitful and more challenging topic of DuBois and Hegel's *Phenomenology of Spirit*.
38. PG, 114.
39. Ibid., 120.
40. Ibid.
41. See also the typical uses of *Gediegenheit* in Hegel's early philosophy of nature: in one case, the "undisclosed purity" of the sun in photosynthesis, in the other, the "sound" quality of the well-established leaves of a plant. Hegel's text, based on his lectures at Jena, is reprinted as the *Jenaer Systementwürfe III: Naturphilosophie und Philosophie des Geistes*, ed. Rolf-Peter Horstmann (Hamburg: F. Meiner Verlag, "Philosophische Bibliothek Bd. 333," 1987). The references to *Gediegenheit* to which I am referring appear on pages 121 and 128.
42. PG, 121–22.
43. PG, 122.
44. Ibid.
45. PG, 123. Jacques Derrida has read Hegel on Africa in terms of the "fetish" in the Freudian psychoanalytic sense: The result is a remarkable deconstruction of Hegel's ethnocentrism, colonialism, and racism. See Derrida, *Glas* (Paris: Galilée, 1974), 232A–236A; see the English translation by John P. Leavey, Jr., and Richard Rand (Lincoln: University of Nebraska Press, 1986), 206A–211A. My own account of "Kettle Logics over Africa" is indebted to Derrida. See, for example, *De la grammatologie* (Paris: Minuit, 1967), 375; and the translation by Gayatri Chakravorty Spivak (Baltimore, MD: Johns Hopkins University Press, 1974), 265. See also *Glas*, 224A.
46. PG, 123.
47. Kettle logic is what our unconscious practices, according to Freud, when we return to a neighbor a kettle that we inadvertently damaged while it was in our possession. In our haste to muster every conceivable argument in our defense, we remonstrate with our neighbor thus: "Look, it isn't really damaged at all, and anyway, it was like that when you gave it to me, and besides, never borrowed a kettle from you in the first place!"

48. PG, 124.
49. Ibid.
50. See Georg Wilhelm Friedrich Hegel, *Enzyklopädie der philosophischen Wissenschaften im Grundrisse* (1830), vols. 8–10 of *Werke*, ed. Eva Moldenhauer, Karl Markus Michel, and Helmut Reinicke (Frankfurt am Main: Suhrkamp, 1969–71), 9:431, §350. Hereafter, this work is cited parenthetically as EPS.
51. PG, 125.
52. Ibid.
53. PG, 126.
54. PG, 127.
55. PG, 127.
56. Ibid., 128.
57. Ibid., 127.
58. Ibid.
59. PG, 128–29.
60. Ibid., 129.
61. Ibid.
62. Ibid.
63. Ibid.
64. It is irritating that the *Register* to the twenty-volume Suhrkamp edition of this work does not contain this or most other references to Africa and the Negro; see page 20 of the *Register*, which does not record either the references in 9:351, 375 (on "der südliche Mensch"), 476, and 504, or 10:57–63. The omissions make research on this topic even more difficult than it otherwise would be—although one hates to accuse editors and indexers of suppression, or repression, even when it comes to such a fraught topic.
65. EPS, 10:57.
66. Ibid., 10:57–58.
67. Ibid., 10:58.
68. Ibid.
69. Ibid., 10:59
70. Ibid.
71. Ibid., 10:59–60.
72. DuBois, *The Souls of Black Folk*, 475.
73. EPS, 9:345.
74. EPS, 9:347.
75. From the eighth stanza of "The Sleepers," in Walt Whitman, *Leaves of Grass*, ed. Sculley Bradley and Harold W. Blodgett (New York: Norton, 1973), 432–33.
76. EPS, 9:349.
77. EPS, 9:351.
78. Ibid., 9:132.
79. Ibid., 9:476. See Hegel's cosmology or celestial mechanics, esp. §§279–80; compare the early formulation of these issues in the 1805–06 lectures, in *Jenaer Systementwürfe III*, 28–29.
80. DuBois, *The Souls of Black Folk*, 507.
81. EPS, 9:131–32. See also Hegel, *Jenaer Systementwürfe III*, 29.
82. EPS, 9:128.
83. Ibid.
84. Compare what Hegel elsewhere calls "lunar return [*Lunarische Zurückkehren*]," which he associates with the liver in the human body (*Jenaer Systementwürfe III*, 145).
85. *Hegel, Jenaer Systementwürfe III*, 29.

86. EPS, 9:132.
87. Ibid., 9:477.
88. James Baldwin, *The Fire Next Time* (New York: Dell, 1962), 32.
89. "Gott ist von unendlich gediegenen Metall—das Körperlichste und Schwerste aller Wesen." See Novalis, *Werke, Tagebücher und Briefe Friedrich von Hardenbergs*, in 3 vols., vol. 2, *Das philosophisch-theoretische Werk*, ed. Hans-Joachim Mähl (Munich: Carl Hanser Verlag, 1978), 820.
90. F.W.J. Schelling, *Die Weltalter Fragmente in den Urfassungen von 1811 und 1813*, ed. Manfred Schröter (Munich: Biederstein Verlag and Leibniz Verlag, 1946), 32–33.
91. Baldwin, *The Fire Next Time*, 20–21.
92. Ibid., 62–63.
93. Ibid., 120.
94. Ibid., 123–24.
95. DuBois, *The Souls of Black Folk*, 509.
96. Baldwin, *The Fire Next Time*, 129.

II

Mutual Relations: Race, Gender, Formations

The Sentimental Slave Body in Frederick Douglass's *The Heroic Slave*

Therese M. Rizzo

ANALYSES OF FREDERICK DOUGLASS'S WORK AS AN AUTHOR, RHETORICIAN, and orator often exclude his provocative fictional novella, *The Heroic Slave* (1853).[1] Critical engagement with this text is focused mainly on its abolitionist function or its connection to other nineteenth-century tales of maritime insurgency and slave rebellions.[2] Finding a context for this very singular story has proven difficult because Douglass's body of work does not contain many comparative pieces to this fictional text, nor does the handful of extant early African American fiction give critics a plethora of analogous work. *The Heroic Slave* is a pioneer text as it represents a moment when African American authors were beginning to experiment beyond genres deemed acceptable for their work, namely autobiographical slave narratives. With this text, Douglass merges the slave narrative (a genre that enabled African Americans to access the world of publishing but also kept them limited to one specific niche), with that of the white dominated world of fiction. *The Heroic Slave* proves to be a fascinating mix between both of these literary spheres and it enables Douglass to carve out a space for himself as fiction author.

The Heroic Slave is based on the true-to-life story of Madison Washington, a runaway slave from Virginia who led a revolt aboard a slave-trading ship, *The Creole*, in 1841. At the time of the rebellion, *The Creole*'s story received attention in the press, and there is evidence to show that Douglass was quite interested in this occurrence.[3] But Douglass did not choose to write *The Heroic Slave* as a factual account of the slave revolt aboard *The Creole*. Rather, he decides to take the historical persona of Madison Washington and create a fictionalized narrative detailing Washington's flight to freedom. Merging a historical event with a fictional narrative allows Douglass to redefine the concept of African American masculinity through *his* portrayal of Madison Washington. Douglass's fictionalized account of Washington's escape to freedom is quite remarkable and unlike many other slave tales, so, to that end, this text does not purport to be a typical portrayal of a slave's search for freedom.[4] Instead Douglass uses the story to examine how white standards of masculinity have dehumanized black men. The omnipresent white gaze upon the black male body marks it as a vulnerable site, and Douglass describes the very real physical and sexual violence implied and exacted by that gaze. By depicting Washington's journey to physical and mental inviolability, Douglass reveals the true peril of the black body as it is used to signify white superiority, desire, angst, and control.

The relationship Douglass develops between Madison Washington and the novel's white male lead character, Mr. Listwell, creates a complex space wherein a black man explores the limitations of his personal agency under the constant surveillance of the white male gaze. Even though Mr. Listwell wields a seemingly benevolent gaze, Douglass uses this character to interpose narratives of white masculinity, which historically sought to establish racial superiority based upon a desperate need to believe in black male inferiority. Douglass's text investigates what current critics see as nineteenth-century America's positioning of dominant narratives on masculinity—namely that white masculinity could only define itself in contradiction to what it saw as its opposites, femininity and black masculinity. Because the black male is a threat to the established binary created by white prejudice, he must constantly be made to renounce his masculinity through a number of forced acts including submission, violence, and surveillance. When he is not an active recipient of violence, the black male becomes subjugated to white tyranny by being made to remain a passive observer to that violence. The dehumanizing and psychical effects of this forced submission to acts of violence manifest themselves in narratives where submission implies not only an inability to fight against one's oppressors; it abdicates one's male standing.

In *The Heroic Slave*, Douglass confronts the effects of violence and submission exacted by white male brutality and the objectification of the white gaze. Instead of forbidding acts of submission by black men attempting to protect themselves, he redefines what submission means for black masculinity. To do this, he positions *The Heroic Slave* inside of a precarious relationship to the most popular literature of the day: the Sentimental novel. The Sentimental novel hit its peak in the 1850s[5] with such best-sellers as Susan Warner and Harriet Beecher Stowe and, as Stowe showed, the abolitionist foray into this genre proved just as successful. An investigation into the connection between *The Heroic Slave* and Sentimentalism reveals that Douglass's text embodies many of the qualities associated with Sentimentalism. Most importantly, Douglass's intense focus on the vulnerable black male body mirrors the Sentimental focus on the body of the white heroine. As P. Gabrielle Forman asserts, "sentiment and sympathy are affectionally bound; that is, they fall within the realm of visionary feminism and sentimental abolition."[6] Confirming *The Heroic Slave*'s connection to Sentimentalism allows us to understand how Douglass navigates the terribly divisive issue of black male submission to authority figures within the institution of slavery.

Sentimental heroines are marked by the way that they seem to willingly submit to others when confronted with obstacles of power—most often the aggression and control displayed by incompetent male guardians and lascivious or corrupt male suitors. In order to navigate around these controlling men, many Sentimental heroines utilize acts of temporary submission to protect and promote self-interests while placating the source of authority. These acts of situational submission do not affirm an innate belief in submitting to the will of others; they suggest that protecting one's self sometimes calls for appeasing or deceiving patriarchal sources of power.

Using this model of situational submission allows me to align *The Heroic Slave* and its protagonist with a Sentimental character study of an atypical individual who must finesse arduous situations involving overwhelming sources of hegemonic power. Washington employs situational submission to effect personal change and ensure his physical well-being, and Douglass's use of this Sentimental technique modifies earlier versions by focusing on issues of physical action in real and metaphorically liminal spaces. Acts of submission enable Douglass's hero to physically protect himself by not physically fighting back against white violence and tyranny. Douglass's use of the Sentimental form and, most importantly, situational submission deliberately thwarts white expectations of black masculinity.

To illustrate how Douglass uses white literary conventions to create a prototype for black masculinity, this chapter focuses on Listwell's insatiable desire to watch Washington, and on his construction of the black male body. I also investigate Washington's performative space in the novella as he narrates his escape from slavery in the very uneasy domestic space of the Listwell home. I argue that Douglass uses Washington as a canvas for representations of the black masculine. Douglass's heroic slave emerges as a new model of manhood through the physical and emotional demands placed upon him by a black masculine version of bodily tribulations. Here, he navigates his desire for personal freedom, fear of cowardly behavior, and impulses toward physical violence as retribution against others. As both Douglass and his heroic slave enter into the wilds of white literary discourse, the vulnerable black body is continually tested in its relationship to the white gaze and the dominant cultural narratives surrounding that body.

Douglass Creates a Hero—or— How to Write Black Fiction

Before Douglass could examine white constructions of black masculinity, he had to first insinuate himself into a hostile literary marketplace. The history of the African American novel is fraught with many of the same tensions surrounding black Americans access to political, social, and cultural institutions. Nineteenth-century black authors were pigeonholed into biographical, slave narrative genres because their writing was considered inherently didactic or mimetic rather than imaginative or fictive. William L. Andrews argues that "by the early nineteenth century black narrators realized that to assume the privileged status of author in the literary discourse of white America, they would have to write self-authorizing, that is, self-authenticating, narratives."[7] Because narratives had to have a one-to-one correspondence to the lived experiences of the author, black texts authenticated through personal experience and vouched for by a credible white intermediary became antithetical to fiction narratives.

Enter Frederick Douglass, an exslave who made a name for himself as a rhetorician, editor, newspaperman, and orator. *Despite* these many accomplishments, Douglass was just as limited in his access to fiction. As a skilled writer in many different methods of composition, Douglass was aware of himself as a craftsman and sought to refine his authorial mechanisms. Andrews maintains that "the more Douglass learned to stage-manage his voice and adopt personae in his speeches and writing, the more white reviewers complain about his 'thinking more of his speech than of the end for which he professes to make it.' "[8] White anxiety projected toward a black author attempting to further his craft is not surprising when we consider that most white audiences only wanted to hear stories or speeches that allowed them a voyeuristic look inside the otherwise obscure world of the enslaved.[9] If a black author moved outside the already established modes of address for African Americans, then he or she would be creating something not directly for white consumption nor regulated by dominant literary restrictions.

Because Douglass and other African American writers were limited in their access to wider literary forms, it becomes even more imperative to examine the genres that they did have access to when they began to write fiction. *The Heroic Slave* "show[s] much more evidence . . . of a negotiation between the world of fact and fiction and a greater self-consciousness about what and how the fictive may be expressed."[10] Sentimental forms, combined with the slave narrative genre he had already found so much success with, gave Douglass access to established narratives that portrayed protagonists maneuvering around patriarchal figures who controlled their physical safety.[11] Douglass would most likely have been aware of Susan Warner's novels, and Robert S. Levine points out that Douglass approved of Harriet Beecher Stowe's attempts to "create in the (white) reader a sympathetic identification with the plight of the slave."[12] Warner and Stowe's Sentimental heroines show readers that it is possible to endure and even manipulate seemingly over-whelming obstacles. The Sentimental novel celebrated women who could and did thwart patriarchal control without open or hostile rebellion. The key to their safety is always knowing when to allay an oppressor through an act of temporary submission to win a bigger emotional or physical battle.[13]

Knowing that Sentimentalism offers an already established and extremely popular narrative form that allows for subtle, yet important, victories over seemingly formidable oppression, it does not seem unusual that Douglass would have seen the opportunity to utilize Sentimental forms for his story. Foreman's concept of "sentimental abolition" helps to explain how Douglass explores the concept of black masculinity while utilizing Sentimental forms. Foreman asserts, "Sentimental abolition coincides with, and borrows from, the power of extended domestic spheres . . . it stresses the affectional over the authoritative, or, in other words, emphasizes that the heart is the only true site of change and redemption."[14] Specifically for Douglass "sentimental abolition allows him to explore emotive arenas in order to energize political protest."[15] Foreman's notion of "emotive arenas" illustrates how Douglass accesses narrative spaces otherwise inaccessible to African American authors. Sentimental abolition, and the emotive arenas it allows, enables Douglass, in Foreman's estimation, "to recognize that only the white male gaze and ear have the actual power to confirm his slave protagonist Madison Washington's subjectivity."[16] I would also add that Douglass uses the white male gaze and its narratives of patriarchal dominance as a natural binary to his burgeoning vision of black masculinity.

Because Douglass is navigating an unwelcoming literary culture as well as a traditionally white, female genre, it is no surprise, then, that he chooses to open his story with an invocation of his authorial agency within America's national and literary discourses. *The Heroic Slave* tells the story of an extraordinary runaway slave, Madison Washington, who must escape from his Virginia plantation before he later leads a slave rebellion on a slave ship. Although the story mainly turns on the tale of Washington's emotional and physical perils in his search for freedom, Douglass begins the narrative by staking a claim for his narrative voice equal to that of any white author. He also argues that his hero deserves a place in American history, and presumably, literature. To force Washington into a national landscape, Douglass constructs his hero as, what I term, a cultural mulatto. That is, Washington can claim a paternal line that descends from white American patriots and a maternal lineage that emanates from American soil itself. Douglass, then, becomes the only author who can construct such a thoroughly American hero.

Douglass begins his tale in a grandiose fashion by situating the importance of place as a synecdoche for familial lineage: "The State of Virginia is famous in American annals for the multitudinous array of her statesmen and heroes. She has been dignified by some the mother of statesmen. History has not been sparing in recording their names, or in blazoning their deeds."[17] Despite the importance of Virginia as a breeding ground for American democracy, Douglass as quickly asserts that "not all the great ones of the Old Dominion have, by the fact of their birth-place, escaped underserved obscurity."[18] To reinscribe that neglected history, Douglass identifies Washington as a lost patriot: "By some strange neglect, *one* of the truest, manliest, and bravest of her children,—one who, . . . will, I think command the pen of genius to set his merits forth, hold now no higher place in the records of that grand old Commonwealth than is held by a horse or an ox."[19] Under this system of descent, Douglass can claim that his black hero should be held in familial and historical relation to other Virginia statesmen such as Patrick Henry and Thomas Jefferson.[20] He also carves out a space for his narrative by pointing out that Virginia has not failed to produce more than just white statesmen, but that that there are no records or white narratives capable of measuring the achievements of *all* Virginia's proud sons. By unambiguously declaring that only the "pen of genius" can account for that which has been forgotten—African American contributions—Douglass creates a space for the black author as a narrator of this country's forgotten history and as a willing source of communal memory.

Douglass's move to secure Washington's equal place in history does more than simply suggest that a black man should be seen as an equal statesman. By explicitly naming Washington's familial connection to white men through a mythic paternity, both his hero and his text occupy a mixed heritage, which allows access to dominant white literary discourses and creates what Russ Castronovo calls a "hybrid articulation."[21] After all, as Virginia's forgotten son, Washington has never received the rightful inheritance that would guarantee him a spot within the "annals" of history and literature. Krista Walter argues that "Douglass supplants the slave's stigmatized racial identity with a glorified nationalistic identity, giving his Northern white readers a ready means of identifying or sympathizing with a black man."[22]

But I would counter that both Washington's mixed American ancestry and Douglass's personal investment in the telling of this tale are meant to claim a national inheritance denied to African Americans. Douglass's deliberate representation of interconnected black and white families, which so closely echoes Sentimentalism's emphasis on the family, is not unconsciously done in an era obsessed with racial purity and the myth of the mulatto. Foreman similarly argues that "Douglass's genealogical revisions also illuminate his, and abolitionism's, complicated relation both to the feminized, and to the erotically fraternal."[23] By merging the image of the maternal South with the hardy statesman produced by her patriotic fecundity, Douglass hints at the kind of deliberately inflammatory, yet artfully coded, work of fiction that will follow. His intentional conception of a textual and familial relationship to white culture suggests a conscious act of literary miscegenation. From the first pages of this story, Douglass means his reader to see Madison Washington as a man who must navigate between a multitude of contradictory and perilous landscapes.

The Constraints Imposed on Black Masculinity

Establishing his entrance into the American landscape is a battle that Douglass faces in the first lines of his text; however, proving that his hero is indeed a man amongst men and, more specifically, a black man worthy of hero status becomes the larger work of this novel. In a text like *The Heroic Slave*, we must always remain aware of the conscious ideological shift Douglass is attempting by narrating a construct of black masculinity. The idea that a black man could be considered a man in anything more than biological function was an on-going debate in nineteenth-century America. Black men had to first establish their right to claim masculinity before they could be seen as rightful participants in narratives surrounding masculinity. Much of David Walker's 1829 *Appeal to the Coloured Citizens of the World*, for example, is concerned with convincing readers that black men must be seen as men and accorded universal male suffrage: "All persons who are acquainted with history . . . and who can dispense with prejudice long enough to admit that we are *men*, notwithstanding our *improminent noses* and *wooly heads*, and believe that we feel for our fathers, mothers, wives and children, as well as the whites do for theirs."[24] Walker seeks to reverse arguments found in white narratives claiming that stereotypical racial differences make black men essentially different from white men.

According to historian Edward E. Baptist, representations of Southern white masculinity were dependant upon their configurations of the black male as an effeminized Other to support notions of white masculinity. Baptist claims that "the denial of black manhood was central to white manhood, American nationalism, and class relations."[25] Moreover, "concepts of white manliness that structured households, animated political conflict and consensus, and authorized violence depended on the disempowerment of blackness."[26] Because most white men were allowed to act as patriarchs within their own homes, citizens within the republic, and jailers or rapists within slave communities,[27] white masculinity seemed to imply "privileges" forever out of reach for black men. Stereotypes about white men perpetuated the idea that "the man of action was unencumbered by sentiment and totally focused on advancement, the quintessential individualist and the self-styled ruthless competitor. He was the rugged individual succeeding in the world of commercial capitalism."[28] If masculinity narratives were wrapped up with the idea of personal success, then enslaved black men were already at a major disadvantage, as their labor could produce no personal advancement or security. James Horton and Lois E. Horton point out most white narratives on masculinity included "combinations of characteristics, values, and actions" with "self-assertion and aggression as key elements."[29] Being able to wield power and aggression was all the more potent, as Baptist argues, because of the binary white men depended upon: "[T]he everyday presence of males without rights allowed those with rights to congratulate themselves and to believe that their own manly commitment to republican freedom justified the difference."[30]

The struggle for the male slave attempting to obtain his freedom under this system of hyperanxious white patriarchy became both a physical and ideological battle. The slave had to carve out some sort of psychical space wherein he could see himself as more than just the object of white male projections. But, at the same time, he could not let the overseer or the master intuit any traces of his conception of self outside of their representations of him. Considering that physical or mental resistance was always interpreted as a threat to the core identity of white masculinity, the slave must always navigate, as Baptist posits, "a pathway between submission and death."[31] But the pull to physical rebellion against slave masters and overseers or running away from the plantation was not easily forsaken. David Walker, for example, uses shame as a method to spur slaves toward rebellion: "The man who would not fight under our Lord and Master Jesus Christ, in the glorious and heavenly cause of freedom and of God—to be delivered from the most wretched, abject and servile slavery—ought to be kept with all of his children or family, in slavery, or in chains, to be butchered by his *cruel enemies.*"[32] Horton and Horton point to the way that ideas like Walker's were internalized by slaves: "Among the slaves, men who refused to submit to the master's authority were accorded respect. Those who submitted too easily to the master's authority lost respect."[33] But Douglass recognizes in *The Heroic Slave* that open rebellion was not always possible, so acts of submission allow him to navigate his hero between physically arduous encounters.

Sloughing off the limitations imposed by white culture onto the black masculine took more than just a speculative shift in consciousness; there were very tangible physical threats against black men underpinning narratives of white violence. White violence against African Americans extended to the black male body, namely in its vulnerability to physical and sexual assault. Bernier observes that in *The Heroic Slave* "the black male body becomes a complex and highly politicized sign which, when packaged for consumption according to the dictates of white abolitionist imperatives, must conform to dominant codes of white American masculinity."[34] And the ways in which we "package" the black male body, according to Bernier "render [it] easily accessible and acceptable, according to both visual and textual dictates, for assimilation by the white male reader."[35] The black male body acted as a complicated site for white desire, and Patricia Hill Collins reminds us that slave bodies "and all that was contained in those bodies (labor, sexuality, and reproduction) were objectified and turned into commodities that were traded in the marketplace."[36] The dehumanization process inherent in positioning bodies as a commodity that can be broken down, catalogued, and contained for value leaves the individual as a series of bodily fragments.

It is the fiction attached to those bodies—and their parts—that Collins sees as most destructive to black male identity: "Because black men did hard manual labor, justifying the harsh conditions forced upon them required objectifying their bodies as big, strong, and stupid."[37] For Collins, this stereotype is a double bind because "[m]en allegedly possessed the wildness attributed to blacks as a race, but they carried the additional characteristic of being prone to violence. This combination of violence and sexuality made black men inherently unsuitable for work until they were trained by white men and placed under their discipline and control."[38] Owing to the belief that black men were both hypersexed and overly violent, their bodies were marked as simultaneously titillating and fearful—both expressions of furtive sexuality. Under white patriarchal control, the black male body becomes a site for the projection of white fears and desires that need to be contained and diverted into acceptable modes of representation, i.e., the laborer or the reproductive stud.

The white male gaze that causes the fracture of black male identity is not just fraught with the envy of the signifier to the signified but that of the voyeuristic lover to the object of its desire. Christopher Looby discusses a brilliant example of white male desire in radical abolitionist Thomas Wentworth Higginson who was an enthusiastic proponent for black male access to the armed forces. Higginson eventually left his other duties behind to lead the first regiment of ex-slaves in the Civil War. But his interest in the black soldiers also hid a thinly veiled sexual desire. Higginson's desire to lose himself inside of their black bodies[39] reveals a consumption fantasy akin to rape and a longing for and belief in the objectivity of the black male body. Foreman sees a similar rape fantasy play out in Stowe's *Uncle Tom's Cabin* as "Tom is rendered powerless, and the gazing power is put back in the master's hands."[40] Douglass also evinces fear due to a similar inability to protect himself. Maurice O. Wallace notes that Douglass's *Narrative* "reveals his own sexual vulnerability by a scopophobic worry betraying the spectragraphic surrogacy of the black woman's body for Douglass's frightful fantasies of male rape."[41] It would seem, then, that nineteenth-century desire for the black male body turned on violence as much as it did on projected longing for that body.

The cultural narratives surrounding masculinities that emerged in the nineteenth century tell the story of white anxieties and the need to render the black male body into an object that could be safely contained. Jackson points out that so many of the problematic "contradictions and anxieties"[42] layered within dominant representations of the black masculine do not reveal how black men think about themselves but how "[b]lack corporeal inscriptions are infused iterations of whiteness ideology embodied as black corporeal objects, but complicated by the irregularities subsumed in a profound matrix of desire and control."[43] Jackson's observation reminds us that it would be almost impossible for an early African American author to completely divorce himself from the burden of objectifying constructions placed upon him by dominant white narratives. Even accounts of black masculinity created by abolitionists for the sake of black emancipation exploited the pain and vulnerabilities of the black body.[44] It behooves us, then, to find the many places that *The Heroic Slave* attempts to define black masculinity through the narrative voice of a black man trying to escape from the dominant white gaze.

From the beginning of the novel, Douglass makes it clear that

Washington's autonomy is threatened by the institution of slavery and his masculinity is called into question by the ever-present threat of violence and violation stemming from the white male gaze. *The Heroic Slave* opens with the introduction of a white northerner, Mr. Listwell, who is traveling through Virginia and stumbles upon Washington in a stolen moment in a secluded wood. Washington is deciding whether to run away when Listwell comes to overhear his musings on the subject. We are aware that Listwell, who "stealthily drew near the solitary speaker,"[46] is not a welcome participant in Washington's heartfelt soliloquy. As "our traveller [*sic*] gazed upon him"[47] we find out that, "Madison was of manly form. Tall, symmetrical, round, and strong. In his movements he seemed to combine, with the strength of a lion, a lion's elasticity."[48] Listwell's vision of Madison becomes even more erotic as he gazes upon Washington's beautiful body: "His torn sleeves disclosed arms like polished iron. His face was 'black, but comely.' His eye, lit with emotion, kept guard under a brow as dark and as glossy as the raven's wing. His whole appearance betokened Herculean strength; yet there was nothing savage or forbidding in his aspect."[49] This highly impassioned and arousing characterization vacillates between descriptions of Washington's "manly form" and his idealized racial characteristics. We are meant to understand that Washington is an excellent specimen of the masculine form, but also that his "Herculean strength" would not be used in "savage" violence, presumably against the intruding white man who is watching him. The biblical description of Washington as "black, but comely,"[50] loosely quoted from the "Song of Solomon," also seems another method to placate the fears of the white male by rendering Washington's body knowable.

Despite the physical attributes that mark the slave's body as strong but gentle, Listwell manifests fear and more than a little desire as he watches the slave and "almost trembled at the thought of his dangerous intrusion."[51] But Listwell is unable to leave his hiding place for a safer location when he realizes that he had "long desired to sound the mysterious depths of the thoughts and feelings of a slave."[52] Listwell's deep desire to understand the inner lives of slaves reveals the fact that a slave was in many ways a curiosity for those not involved in the everyday lives of these people. Moreover, Listwell's secret longing to enter into the inner life of a "slave" displays a violation fantasy and makes the object of his desire appear almost as a caricature of a man. His curiosity, desire, and fear also show that he sees the slave as an Other—or something that he cannot penetrate with his understanding of humanity—and as an object that can be divined with further study. Through Listwell's eyes, both Washington's body and his soul are presented as objects for consumption. He is a figure who is meant to manifest the epitome of masculine strength and beauty but is also dehumanized by his potential for exploitation.

Although Listwell's pernicious white gaze is portrayed as inevitably benevolent by his resolution to become an abolitionist,[53] Washington's private moment has been usurped by and interpreted through the very lens of masculinity that the novel seems to interrogate. Therefore, this surveillance affirms that the black male slave body, even as it struggles to conceptualize freedom, is never liberated from the inimical white gaze, no matter if it is friend or foe who is watching. bell hooks succinctly notes that, "Thriving on sadomasochist bonds, cultures of domination make desire for that which is despised take on the appearance of care, of love."[54] But no matter how benevolent the gaze may be or the extent to which it manifests an "appearance of care," the strictures of white authority implied by constant surveillance seem to be an inescapable reality.

Finding the Heroic in *The Heroic Slave*

In many ways, Douglass never finds a way to completely subvert the voyeuristic white gaze until Washington literally leaves the confines of American soil at the end of the novel. But while he is still under the geographical auspices of the institution of slavery, Washington's only means to subvert the hegemony of the white gaze is through the use of trickery and narrative inversion. We begin to see Douglass's intentional reconfiguration of the black body and its position inside of white domesticity and the narratives surrounding that space when Washington unexpectedly chooses Listwell's home as a stopping-place on his journey to Canada. Washington enters an officially coded scene of domestic bliss, one that mirrors Douglass's position as a black author entering into the seemingly hyperdomestic landscape of Sentimentalism. As the narrator sets the scene of Washington's unexpected disruption of this domestic space, the area is coded in the idyllic images of nineteenth-century hearth and home: "Mr. and Mrs. Listwell sat together by the fireside of their own happy home, in the State of Ohio. The children were all gone to bed. A single lamp burnt brightly on the centre-table. All was still and comfortable within; but the night was cold and dark."[55] This description of the fortified home, impervious to the threats of the outside world, clearly reifies the image of the nineteenth-century home as a true sanctuary in the storm. Placing the Listwells at the epicenter of the home also affords them the distinction of being the rightful inhabitants of such a perfectly correct space. This deliberate coding, then, should make Washington's appearance all the more unsettling.

Although Washington does temporarily disrupt the home and its occupants, once he is recognized, Listwell greets the slave with an over-whelming welcome. But Washington is not a family friend, and he grows understandably suspicious of Listwell's advances. Washington's unease reminds his host that these welcoming addresses are being offered toward a slave—a figure who should not benefit from the safety and comfort of domesticity. Washington is understandably "disconcerted and disquieted"[56] by someone who seems to recognize him but of whom he has no recollection. As Listwell assures Washington that he has "seen your face" and that he "*know*[s] *all*,"[57] the runaway slave is confronted with the reality of the white gaze and its ability to know him—to know his body—without him having the slightest idea of its surveillance.

Because the slave understands the code of white domesticity that does not invite the black body into its confines, Washington's uneasy entrance into this middle-class domestic space must be seen as a troubled negotiation of his entrance into the domesticity implicit in Sentimentalism. Although Washington might be offered the sanctuary and safety of the home as its quasilegitimate guest, he does not completely emerge unscathed by his entrance into domesticity. Washington is made into a spectacle—a storyteller of titillating tales for the pleasure of the white family's curiosity. As DeLombard points out, "The eyewitness testimony of former slaves enabled Northern audiences to observe vicariously events at which they were not present, specifically the beating, whipping, rape, and murder of black bodies in the South."[58] Washington is forced to perform in front of the family, and, through this, Douglass further perverts the traditional domestic scene of familial bliss by staging an around-the-fireside storytelling scene that allows Washington to recount the horrors of slavery in the most idyllic of settings. Sitting around the fire after eating, Washington finishes a lengthy recounting of his movements over the last five years when Listwell implores, "If it does not weary you too much, do tell us something of your journeyings—we are deeply interested in everything which can throw light on the hardships of persons escaping from slavery."[59] Listwell sounds like a child eager to hear stories of far away, exotic places and events. Of course, this would-be travel narrative is mitigated by the fact that Washington is not a tourist—i.e., he has not gone out to search for fortune or adventure but to escape the horrors of slavery. Therefore, Listwell's eager pining to hear all about the "hardships of persons escaping from slavery" is more than just a little grotesque considering the implicitly titillating nature of the adventure story he is requesting. Listwell's enthusiasm reveals his inability to envision the slave as anything other than a creature made to satisfy his whims.

But Douglass and his hero are not caricatured fools who will perform for Listwell's enjoyment. Instead, Washington narrates a story of complex situational submission that ends up subverting the very nature of a heroic adventure story. As if he is aware that his body is made into a spectacle of blackness for this family, Washington's story does not portray dauntless acts of brave adventurers or the scintillating details of heroic deeds that the family, and the reader, expects from this scene. As Washington sits in the drawing room relating his tale to a rapt audience, we experience a synthesis of spheres—the sanctuary of domesticity with the cruel journey taken by the runaway slave—and Washington's mere presence changes the way these spaces become assigned meaning.

As Listwell pushes the runaway slave to relate the details of his journey, Washington's recollections mark one of the most pivotal moments in this text. In a most painful incident where he is forced to watch another slave attacked for helping him, Washington must choose between protecting his physical body or playing the stereotypical hero who fights for others at all costs. While hiding in the woods as he travels to the North, Washington befriends another slave, a tree-cutter who has been working in and around the woods where he was resting. Washington entrusts the last of his money to the slave because he deems him trustworthy and asks the tree-cutter to go into town and buy some supplies. As Washington waits for the slave's return, he decides to switch his hiding place to another tree, and, when he sees the good Samaritan on the horizon, he realizes that the tree-cutter is being trailed by "*fourteen men*, with something like guns in their hands"[60] looking for the source of the tree-cutter's money. Given that Washington moved from his original hiding place, the innocent tree-cutter cannot find him to prove that the money is not stolen and so must face the wrath of the collected white men: "After searching about the woods silently for a time, the whole company gathered around the old man; one charged him with lying, and called him an old villain; said if he did not instantly tell where he got it, they would take the shirt from his old back, and give him thirty-nine lashes."[61]

Because of Washington's actions, the tree-cutter is going to be beaten, and, if Washington does not act in the innocent slave's defense, he will disappoint the expectations of readers anticipating the daring hero to fight his way out of peril. However, this is no Romantic action story; if Washington strays from his hiding place, then he risks more than just a hero's temporary setback—he will either be killed for standing up to fourteen white men or be returned to his Virginia plantation as a runaway slave. Faced with the reality of a very difficult choice, Washington delivers his decision in a simple, straight-forward manner: "Of course I did not present myself; but hugged my hiding-place securely. If discovered and attacked, I resolved to sell my life as dearly as possible."[62] Washington's use of the word "sell" is ironic in its multiple meanings to barter or sell goods, to give something away, or to give up a person to his enemies (*OED*). If Washington plays the typical hero and gives himself away then he would be "selling" himself back into slavery by betraying himself to his enemies.

Not helping his fellow slave, when ostensibly it is Washington's fault that the tree-cutter came under scrutiny, is a defining moment in this text. Douglass risks losing part of his audience—namely readers who subscribe to valorized notions of white masculinity and its supposed ability to safeguard the defenseless. In this moment, Washington could easily be accused of becoming a very *unheroic* hero. But Douglass codes Washington's choice to remain hidden in a way that allows astute readers to see that Washington cannot lay claim to some pointlessly chivalrous notion of white masculinity. As a vulnerable black runaway slave traveling without friends or guidance, he does not have the privilege of playing some romantic hero who can save the day. Instead, Washington must submit to the indignity of watching the innocent tree-cutter slave, who sought only to help him, beaten by the barbarous men below. The pain of witnessing white violence becomes the price for protecting his body: "They now took hold of him, and began to strip him; while others went to get sticks with which to beat him. I felt, at the moment, like rushing out in the midst of them; but considering that the old man would be whipped the more for having aided a fugitive slave, and that, perhaps, in the *melée* he might be killed outright, I disobeyed this impulse."[63] As Washington quells his strong instinct to help, he does not look away from the violence he feels responsible for: "They tied him to a tree, and began to whip him. My own flesh crept at every blow, and I seem to hear the old man's piteous cries even now. They laid thirty-nine lashes on his bare back, and were going to repeat that number, when one of the company besought his comrades to desist."[64] Although Washington does not join the "melee," he does participate in this moment through his first-hand knowledge of the shared physicality of black bodies subjected to white violence.

This, then, is a crucial moment in the formation of Washington's situational submission. Although Washington's impulse is to help the man who was more than willing to help him, he must curb his desire by rationalizing how his assistance could harm the tree-cutter more than it might help. Maggie Sale asserts that "Douglass's Washington rejects the Andrew Jackson model of masculine aggression and acquisition in favor of a different masculine model that incorporates moral restraint and respect for other peoples."[65] In this form of masculinity, being able to vicariously suffer another's pain—by understanding the pain of white violence—marks a different kind of bravery. Therefore, Douglass is testing his readers in this moment. Because this episode has been coded in the trappings of an adventure tale, it might be difficult for some readers to accept Washington's decision and still call him heroic.

Washington cannot give in to his impulse to help the slave, so he substitutes physical empathy for heroic action.[66] He admits that his "flesh crept at every blow," and he "hear[s] the old man's piteous cries even now."[67] The constraints of slavery do not allow Washington to act as a traditional hero; instead, Douglass uses Washington's body as an empathetic vehicle that can be metaphorically substituted for treecutter's body. Washington becomes almost Christ-like in his ability to bear other's pain. In turn, Douglass becomes the authorial vehicle by which that pain is released in narrative form. Jeannine DeLombard argues that in his *Narrative* Douglass "marshals the visual power of the injured black body to convey the brutality of the South's peculiar institution,"[68] and I would suggest that visual power works in much the same way in *The Heroic Slave*. Indeed, DeLombard's position that the *Narrative*'s "editorial apparatus implies that to be a Southern slave is not only to be denied physical autonomy, forced to perform backbreaking labor, and subjected to arbitrary violence, but it is also to be a silent witness to such physical suffering"[69] echoes Washington's position as the witness to violence he cannot alleviate or revenge. Douglass makes it clear that the pain of witnessing indiscriminate white violence takes a kind of courage unknown to traditional white masculinity.

Through this model of masculine submission, *The Heroic Slave* presents an image of resistant black masculinity that does not conform to white standards. Douglass accepts the heightened vulnerability surrounding the black body and allows his hero to remain a black masculine exemplary while still protecting his body and manipulating the white male gaze. And in this way, Washington becomes a trickster who understands the burden and dehumanizing effects of the white gaze but who will not be stymied by its insatiable desire to consume him. By allowing his hero safety during key acts of situational submission, Douglass indicates that notions of black masculinity are not dependant on actions deemed valid and acceptable by white standards. Through a complicated performance where the black male body is expected to satiate the demands of whiteness, Washington thwarts the expectations of his white patron, Listwell, and the readers who want to vicariously experience his degradation and humiliation. By not allowing himself to be defeated by witnessing violence or his inability to revenge that violence, Washington becomes a man and a character outside of white understanding and beyond the effects of white surveillance.

Notes

1. Douglass first published *The Heroic Slave* in 1853 in *Autographs for Freedom*, a gift-book consisting of works by famed abolitionists with a frontispiece dedicated to a featured selection by Harriet Beecher Stowe. There is some evidence to suggest that Douglass might have imagined his novella as a response to Stowe's overwhelming success with *Uncle Tom's Cabin* (1852). Robert S. Levine suggests that there are "significant parallels between the two works: both make use of temperance themes; both idealize the family; and both temper their portrayals of black violence." Levine, "An Analysis of Reception," 83.

2. See Herman Beavers's "The Blind Leading the Blind: The Racial Gaze as Plot Dilemma in 'Benito Cereno' and 'The Heroic Slave.'"

3. For a detailed analysis of *The Creole* revolt see *The Creole Mutiny* by George Hendrick and Willene Hendrick or "The Creole Affair" by Edward D. Jervey and C. Harold Huber. For an analysis of the fictionalized accounts surrounding the Creole revolt see Celeste-Marie Bernier's "'Arms Like Polished Iron': The Black Slave Body in Narratives of a Slave Ship Revolt." Bernier's article spends time "contextualizing" the historical material available on the revolt and the "subsequent adaptations produced by Douglass, Brown, Child and Hopkins." Bernier, "Arms Like Polished Iron," 92.

4. In "A Comparative Exploration of Narrative Ambiguities in Frederick Douglass's Two Versions of the Heroic Slave," Bernier notes that Douglass's 1863 version is changed to look like a slave narrative in comparison with his first version, which did not purport to be an authentic slave narrative. Bernier, "Comparative Exploration," 71.

5. The American novel, specifically the Sentimental novel, reached new heights in the 1850s. Warner's first novel, *The Wide, Wide World* (1850) and her second novel, *Queechy* (1852), were both record-breaking best-sellers. Stowe's *Uncle Tom's Cabin* broke Warner's records with her best-selling abolitionist novel. These novels established a genre that continued to sell amazingly well throughout the nineteenth century. As Marion Wilson Starling points out, the Sentimental model was well known after Warner's initial success, and it did not "take long to ascertain the ingredients of the Susan Warner success motif." Starling, *The Slave Narrative*, 300.

6. Foreman, "Sentimental Abolition," 196.

7. Andrews, "The Novelization of Voice," 23.

8. Ibid., 24.

9. Andrews, "The Novelization of Voice," 23–26. Refer to this essay for information on what white culture demanded from black authors.

10. Ibid., 25.

11. To support the idea that Douglass's text embodies Sentimental tropes, Celeste-

Marie Bernier points out that a comparative analysis of Douglass's 1853 and 1863 versions of *The Heroic Slave* reveals that Douglass's 1853 version, the text under discussion in this chapter, has much more of a connection to Sentimentalism. Bernier, "A Comparative Exploration," 78. Bernier's observation is understandable since *The Heroic Slave*'s first version was written during the height of the Sentimental novel.

12. Levine, "An Analysis of Reception," 74.

13. In my work on Susan Warner's second novel, *Queechy* (1852), I have argued that many Sentimental heroines lacked the financial, political, and/or physical resources needed to adequately protect themselves from the patriarchal establishment, so they had to develop ways to ensure their continued safety and prosperity. This often meant handing over some measure of their personal prerogative to the fathers, husbands, brothers, or sons who represented a particular form of patriarchal control in their lives. For example, when *Queechy*'s heroine tries to silence a disruptive cousin, Fleda does not engage in a confrontation with the man but, instead, chooses silence and tears as her weapons: "Fleda cried excessively; and Charlton, now alone with her, felt as if he had not a particle of self-respect left to stand upon. One such agony would do her more harm than whole weeks of labour and weariness" (Warner, *Queechy*, I:358). Later, the narrator tells us that the disruptive cousin "passed the night in unmitigated vexation with himself. But his repentance could not have been very genuine, since his most painful thought was, what Fleda must think of him!" (Ibid.). By avoiding a verbal confrontation, Fleda looks as if she submits to her cousin's will and can thereby use her submission and her tears to make a larger statement. In this kind of uncertain situation, it might seem easier for a woman to yield to a man's will rather than engage in an argument that could end in physical violence or her enforced isolation from a larger community. It is difficult, however, for modern day readers to accept the concession of an argument as something other than an assimilationist act. But what we must understand is that the heroine concedes certain victories so that she can manipulate the situation for her benefit once she feels that she has gained the advantage in a conflict. It is through this combination of concession and manipulation that the heroine can gain the upper hand over her opponent—an opponent, we must remember, who she must continue to live with, serve, and, ostensibly, appear to or actually love.

14. Foreman, "Sentimental Abolition," 192.

15. Ibid.

16. Ibid.

17. Douglass, *The Heroic Slave*, 25.

18. Ibid.

19. Ibid.

20. Ibid.

21. Castronovo, "Ambivalence, Diaspora," 252.

22. Walter, "Trappings of Nationalism," 237.

23. Foreman, "Sentimental Abolition," 192.

24. Walker, *Appeal*, 4–5.

25. Baptist, "Absent Subject," 137.

26. Ibid.

27. Ibid.

28. Horton and Horton, "Violence, Protest, and Identity," 383.

29. Ibid., 382.

30. Baptist, "Absent Subject," 137.

31. Ibid., 145.

32. Walker, *Appeal*, 12.

33. Horton and Horton, "Violence, Protest, and Identity," 384.
34. Bernier, "Comparative Exploration," 75.
35. Ibid.
36. Collins, *Black Sexual Politics*, 55.
37. Ibid., 56.
38. Ibid., 56.
39. Looby, "As Thoroughly Black," 85.
40. Foreman, "This Promiscuous Housekeeping," 66.
41. Wallace, "Constructing the Black Masculine," 86.
42. Jackson, "Scripting the Black Masculine," 12.
43. Ibid.
44. DeLombard points out, "the tension inherent in the abolitionist tendency to simultaneously represent and exploit the slave's pained black body subtly inheres in the juridical metaphor upon which the antislavery movement drew in order to respond to the juridical exclusion of African Americans from the body politic." DeLombard, "Eye-Witness," 249. Fionnghuala Sweeney concurs with the idea that the "victimization of male slaves" often occurred in white abolitionist narratives and included an element of overt feminization of black men. Sweeney, "Domestic Institutions," 65.
46. Douglass, *The Heroic Slave*, 26.
47. Ibid., 28.
48. Ibid.
49. Ibid.
50. The quotation is taken from The Book of the Song of Solomon chapter 1, verse 5. From the King James version, the original passage reads: "I am black, but comely, O ye daughters of Jerusalem, as the tents of Kedar, as the curtains of Solomon. Look not upon me, because I am black, because the sun hath looked upon me: my mother's children were angry with me; they made me the keeper of the vineyards; but mine own vineyard have I not kept."
51. Douglass, *The Heroic Slave*, 28.
52. Ibid.
53. Ibid., 30.
54. hooks, *We Real Cool*, xii.
55. Douglass, *The Heroic Slave*, 31.
56. Ibid., 33.
57. Ibid.
58. DeLombard, "Eye-Witness," 251.
59. Douglass, *The Heroic Slave*, 39.
60. Ibid., 42.
61. Ibid.
62. Ibid.
63. Ibid., 43.
64. Ibid., 43.
65. Sale, "Critiques from Within," 703.
66. Critics who have read scenes of violence witnessed and renarrated by Douglass in his autobiographies have come to see that violence as "establish[ing] an image of powers as the central criterion and reference point within Douglass's world. Power becomes the one thing he can never forget, the commodity that will be negotiated, recirculated, and exchanged in all of his later works." Giles, "Narrative Reversals," 785. However, Washington's rationalization is not motivated by cowardice or fear. In fact, Douglass makes it clear that the pain of witnessing indiscriminate white violence

takes a kind of courage unknown to the traditional white masculinity. Jeffrey Steele points out that Douglass "model[s]" his "reader's response" by creating characters that "articulate[e] the *personal* expense of slavery. Through an act of identification with such anguish, his readers begin to *feel* the agony of bondage." Steele, "Politics of Mourning," 101. And not only does the reader feel pain, Evan Carton argues that "at its most sublime, feeling is the vehicle by which one may discover and exercise a will beyond and against one's natural, self-serving inclinations." Carton, "What Feels an American?," 28. Feeling another's pain and being able to identify with and humanize that suffering individual creates an intimate exchange between Washington, the tree-cutter, and, hopefully, the reader.

67. Douglass, *The Heroic Slave*, 43.

68. DeLombard, "Eye-Witness," 245.

69. Ibid., 257.

Works Cited

Andrews, William L. "The Novelization of Voice in Early African American Narrative." *PMLA* 105 (January 1990): 23–34.

Baptist, Edward E. "The Absent Subject: African American Masculinity and Forced Migration to the Antebellum Plantation Frontier." In *Southern Manhood: Perspectives on Masculinity in the Old South*, Edited by Craig Thompson Friend and Lorri Glover. Athens: University of Georgia Press, 2004.

Beavers, Herman. "The Blind Leading the Blind: The Racial Gaze as Plot Dilemma in 'Benito Cereno' and 'The Heroic Slave.'" In *Criticism and the Color Line*. Edited by Henry B. Wonham. New Brunswick, NJ: Rutgers University Press, 1996.

Bernier, Celeste-Marie. "A Comparative Exploration of Narrative Ambiguities in Frederick Douglass' Two Versions of *The Heroic Slave* (1853, 1863?)." *Slavery & Abolition* 22 (August 2001): 69–86.

———. "'Arms Like Polished Iron': The Black Slave Body in Narratives of a Slave Ship Revolt." *Slavery & Abolition* 23 (August 2002): 89–106.

Carton, Evan. "What Feels an American? Evident Selves and Alienable Emotions in the New Man's World." In *Boys Don't Cry?* Edited by Milette Shamir and Jennifer Travis. New York: Columbia University Press, 2002.

Castronovo, Russ. "'As to Nation, I belong to None': Ambivalence, Diaspora, and Frederick Douglass." *American Transcendental Quarterly* 9 (September 1995): 245–60.

Collins, Patricia Hill. *Black Sexual Politics: African Americans, Gender, and the New Racism*. New York: Routledge, 2004.

DeLombard, Jeannine. "'Eye-Witness to the Cruelty': Southern Violence and Northern Testimony in Frederick Douglass's 1845 *Narrative*." *American Literature* 73 (2001): 245–75.

Douglass, Frederick. *The Heroic Slave*. In *Three Classic African-American Novels*. Edited by William L. Andrews. New York: Penguin Group, 1990.

Foreman, P. Gabrielle. "Sentimental Abolition in Douglass's Decade: Revision, Erotic Conversion, and the Politics of Witnessing in 'The Heroic Slave' and *My Bondage and My Freedom*." In *Criticism and the Color Line*. Edited by Henry B. Wonham. New Brunswick, NJ: Rutgers University Press, 1996.

———. "'This Promiscuous Housekeeping': Death, Transgression, and Homoeroticism in Uncle Tom's Cabin." *Representations* 43 (1993): 51–72.

Giles, Paul. "Narrative Reversals and Power Exchanges: Frederick Douglass and British Culture." *American Literature* 73 (2001): 779–810.

Hendrick, George, and Willene Hendrick. *The Creole Mutiny: A Tale of Revolt Aboard a Slave Ship*. Chicago: Ivan R. Dee, 2003.

hooks, bell. *We Real Cool: Black Men and Masculinity*. New York: Routledge, 2004.

Horton, James Oliver, and Lois E. Horton. "Violence, Protest, and Identity: Black Manhood in Antebellum America." In *A Question of Manhood*. Edited by Darlene Clark Hine and Earnestine Jenkins. Indianapolis: Indiana University Press, 1999.

Jackson, Robert L. *Scripting the Black Masculine Body: Identity, Discourse, and Racial Politics in Popular Media*. Albany: State University of New York Press, 2006.

Jervey, Edward D., and C. Harold Huber. "The Creole Affair." *The Journal of Negro History* 65 (Summer 1980): 196–211.

Levine, Robert S. "Uncle Tom's Cabin in Frederick Douglass' Paper: An Analysis of Reception." *American Literature* 64 (March 1992): 71–93.

Looby, Christopher. "'As Thoroughly Black as the Most Faithful Philanthropist Could Desire': Erotics of Race in Higginson's *Army in a Black Regiment*." In *Race and the Subject of Masculinities*. Edited by Harry Stecopoulos and Michael Uebel. Durham, NC: Duke University Press, 1997.

Sale, Maggie. "Critiques from Within: Antebellum Projects of Resistance." *American Literature* 64 (December 1992): 695–718.

Sterling, Marion Wilson. *The Slave Narrative: Its Place in American History*. Boston: G.K. Hall and Co., 1981.

Steele, Jeffrey. "The Politics of Mourning: Cultural Grief-Work from Frederick Douglass to Fanny Fern." In *Criticism and the Color Line*. Edited by Henry B. Wonham. New Brunswick, NJ: Rutgers University Press, 1996.

Sweeney, Fionnghuala. "Domestic Institutions: Transatlantic Gender Politics and Economic Power in Frederick Douglass' Variant *Narratives*." *Slavery & Abolition* 23 (December 2002): 59–72.

Walker, David. *Appeal to the Coloured Citizens of the World*. Canada: HarperCollins, 1995.

Wallace, Maurice O. *Constructing the Black Masculine: Identity and Ideality in African American Men's Literature and Culture, 1775–1995*. Durham, NC: Duke University Press, 2002.

Walter, Krista. "Trappings of Nationalism in Frederick Douglass's *The Heroic Slave*." *African American Review* 34 (Summer 2000): 233–47.

Warner, Susan. *Queechy*. 2 Vols. New York: George P. Putnam, 1852.

Writing Realism, Policing Consciousness: Howells and the Black Body

Henry B. Wonham

> "a man has as many social selves as there are individuals who recognize him and carry an image of him in their mind."
> —William James, *The Principles of Psychology*

WILLIAM JAMES'S FAMOUS CHARACTERIZATION OF SELFHOOD AS A composite of the images carried around by others has the unsettling effect of taking responsibility for consciousness away from the subject, of locating the constituents of the self in *other* minds. The images one projects materially through dress and bodily gesture combine to form a "stream of selves," which may or may not possess "the attribute of continuity."[1] Whether or not these selves cohere to produce a "kind of unity" is really beside the point, according to James, for in either case what matters is the material and fragmentary nature of what one means by "a 'Me.'"[2] The clothes, in other words, literally make the man.

Anticipating William's trenchant critique of the "'pure' Self," Henry James's world-weary Madame Merle describes the Jamesian position on consciousness in a classic passage from *The Portrait of a Lady* (1881):

> What shall we call our "self"? Where does it begin? Where does it end? It overflows into everything that belongs to us—and then it flows back again. I know a large part of myself is in the clothes I choose to wear. I've a great respect for *things!* One's self—for other people—is one's expression of one's self; and one's house, one's furniture, one's garments, the books one reads, the company one keeps—these things are all expressive.[3]

Isabel Archer, Henry James's version of the ebullient, naive "American girl," rejects Madame Merle's theory of the material self with characteristically stubborn idealism, insisting "nothing that belongs to me is any measure of me. . . . Certainly the clothes which, as you say,

I choose to wear, don't express me." Although "fond of metaphysics," Isabel is "unable to accompany her friend into this bold analysis of the human personality"—an analysis which, whatever he may think of the sinister Madame Merle, James's super-fine narrator joins her in performing throughout the novel.[4]

William Dean Howells was not famous, like his closest literary friend, Mark Twain, for donning eccentric apparel, but he understood very well the psychological import of Madame Merle's discourse on the clothing of personality. In the same issue that contained his glowing review of William James's *The Principles of Psychology*, *Harper's Monthly* also published the first installment of Howells's novel *An Imperative Duty*, in which Dr. Olney, a nerve specialist, returns after several years in Europe to his native Boston. The narrator records Olney's impressions of the city's African American citizens:

> Olney fancied that Boston did not characterize their manner, as it does that of almost every other sort of aliens. . . . Their barbaric taste in color, when it flamed out in a crimson necktie or a scarlet jersey, or when it subdued itself to a sable that left no gleam of white about them but a point or rim of shirt collar, was invariably delightful to him. . . . [T]hey had that air of being clothed through and through, as to the immortal spirit as well as the perishable body, by their cloth gaiters, their light trousers, their neatly buttoned cutaway coats, their harmonious scarfs, and their silk hats.[5]

As Olney's reflections on the relation between African American dress and personality imply, Howells occasionally conceived of the self in Jamesian terms as an unstable, ongoing process in which multiple "characters" constantly vie for ascendancy. Basil March speculates in *A Hazard of New Fortunes* that the self is not a finite entity capable of change or development but that "there's the making of several characters in us; we *are* each several characters, and sometimes this character has the lead in us, and sometimes that."[6] Olney's reflections on African American style emerge from a related insight, his sense that personality is a matter entirely of dress, that one's self can be worn and changed like a crimson necktie or a scarlet jersey. Sounding very much like Madame Merle herself, he theorizes that black fashion has profound psychological and even spiritual significance, for the dandies he observes possess an air of being "clothed" inside and out, "as to the immortal spirit as well as the perishable body."

Yet as the Dean's critics have always taken pains to point out—usually by way of unflattering comparison with the James brothers—Howells was decidedly squeamish about representing the self in Jamesian terms as a form of process.[7] Unable to regulate their appetites and ambitions, Bartley Hubbard in *A Modern Instance* and Angus

Beaton in *A Hazard of New Fortunes* exemplify the moral dangers that ensue when the self in Howells's fiction becomes unhinged from its stable center; but Howells can entertain the image of a free-floating consciousness only long enough to explain that its movements take place beyond the pale of realistic literary representation. Thus, after hinting at the morally dubious nature of Bartley's attraction for Marcia, he places the sources of Bartley's passion beyond his own representational reach, securing them in those "fastnesses" of the mind "which psychology has not yet explored."[8] Later in the novel he repeats this gesture by refusing to track Marcia's "inner" reaction to the news of Bartley's death: "Marcia had been widowed so long before that this event could make no outward change in her. What inner change, if any, it wrought is one of those facts which fiction must seek in vain to disclose."[9]

This refusal to imagine mental processes that might destabilize the self is one of the most characteristic tendencies in Howells's representation of the human mind.[10] He often explicitly questions the foundations of personality, implying in Beaton's case, for example, that the self is no more than a succession of moods, but this dangerous assertion is almost always treated as "one of those facts which fiction must seek in vain to disclose." For all his interest in Jamesian psychology, Howells is unable, like Isabel Archer, to pursue the implications of Madame Merle's "bold analysis of the human personality." He refuses, as Anthony Hilfer has argued, "to track a consciousness" that cannot be "relevantly structured in purely ethical terms."[11]

The reasons for Howells's retreat from psychological representation were both ethical and aesthetic. Having suffered repeated episodes of nervous collapse, he was intimately aware of the emotional cost associated with the experience of a free-floating consciousness, the sense of terror that awaits the self which has lost its bearings. As a boy he warded off neurotic fits of homesickness and depression by burying himself in books, deploying literature as a form of emotional "self-defense" against unconscious fears.[12] "Borrowing strength from literature," as John W. Crowley puts it, Howells plunged into a therapeutic course in reading "so as to leave [himself] no chance for the horrors that beset [him]."[13]

When he turned to professional authorship, Howells continued to regard literature—or, more precisely, literary realism—as a means of preserving the always suspect integrity of the self by delimiting the free play of consciousness. Writing became a way of channeling anxieties about the self outward, where they could be objectively observed and controlled. In *Years of My Youth* he describes the neurotic fears that plagued him as an adolescent, explaining that "in self-defense I learnt to practice a psychological juggle; I came to deal with my own state of mind as another would deal with it, and to combat my fears as if they were alien."[14] Fashioning his aesthetic values in response to this notion of writing as therapeutic objectification, Howells came to "dislike personality and consciousness, and to hate any work in which [he found] present anything of the author besides his genius."[15] In order to promote the psychological well-being of his readers and himself, the writer must "be constantly in the position of an outsider studying carefully his effects."[16] He must learn to juggle conscious and unconscious material, maintaining "self-possession and self-control" by treating suppressed anxieties "as if they were alien."

The word "alien" in this context is intriguing, for it recalls Olney's observation that blacks are unlike "every other sort of aliens" in Boston. Indeed, it is precisely because African Americans exist for Howells at the outer limit of alienation, at the farthest remove from the familiar, that Olney can theorize so boldly and with such apparent objectivity about what he considers the artificial nature of black personality. His observation that African Americans appear "clothed through and through, as to the immortal spirit as well as the perishable body" causes the nerve specialist no anxiety about his own fragile sense of identity—which is very much at issue in the novel—because blacks are perfectly "alien" to his conception of self. Describing what he sees as he passes through black neighborhoods in Boston, Olney can entertain an image of unstable identity—of the Jamesian socially constructed self that "overflows into everything"—because the black selves in question do not threaten to transgress the unstable margins of *his* personality.

Throughout his fiction, Howells indulges versions of Olney's insight—the idea that there is no clear core of identity—but this threatening possibility rarely produces an alternative image of selfhood. Instead, Howells customarily takes refuge in the alleged limitations of his medium or proclaims ignorance of what takes place in the "fastnesses" of mental life, conveniently allowing writerly objectivity to function as a shield against self-knowledge. But what if the character into whom one channels dangerous knowledge about the self is so utterly "alien" as to remove any threat to the writer's own sense of coherent identity? Describing Rhoda Aldgate's frantic walk through Boston after the revelation of her black ancestry in *An Imperative Duty*, Howells delves impressively into mental fastnesses that are usually closed to him:

> She seemed to be walking swiftly, flying forward; but the ground was uneven: it rose before her, and then suddenly fell. She felt her heart beat in

> the middle of her throat. Her head felt light, like the blowball of a dandelion. She wished to laugh. There seemed to be two selves of her, one that had lived before that awful knowledge, and one that had lived as long since, and again a third that knew and pitied them both. She wondered at the same time if this were what people meant by saying one's brain was turned.[17]

Here there is none of Howells's usual reluctance about tracing the mental processes of a fractured identity. Rhoda's dizzy impressions of Boston's black neighborhoods, like Olney's paradoxical speculations on black selfhood and attire, suggest that Howells's meditation on the self can at times approach Jamesian depths. He *can* take seriously the idea of a personality that is "clothed through and through"; he *can* represent a fragmented, discontinuous self. Howells's infrequent but charged representation of blackness is one of several literary strategies that make this region of the mind, or this image of the self, accessible to his imagination. The African American persona or presence in his work functions as what Toni Morrison calls an "enabler," a "projection of the not me," mirroring forth an image that Howells cannot approach directly.[18]

Howells's complicated representation of blackness developed as a result of his strikingly personal engagement with the issue of race in America.[19] Yet in making the black body a vehicle for the exploration of his own anxieties, he echoed a familiar motif in the long tradition of white representations of African American experience.[20] That motif involves the cancellation of black subjectivity and the assumption—widespread in antebellum literature—that blacks lacked the capacity to suffer acute anxiety. James Kirke Paulding's collection of *Letters from the South* (1817), for example, contains a typical early representation of African American slaves who are distracted from their suffering on the auction block by the sound of a nearby banjo: "At that irresistible signal, the light-hearted slaves, the very prototypes of children in their joys, their sorrows, their forgetfulness of the past, their indifference to the future, listened, dried their tears, and soon they were dancing."[21] Their simplemindedness, as Paulding represents it, frees the slaves from extended misery, for members of their "gay, harmless, unthinking race" seem incapable of entertaining either lasting or contradictory emotions. Later writers like Mark Twain and Charles W. Chesnutt would learn to deploy the stereotype of the depthless African American for ironic purposes, yet their inversion of expectations depended upon, and perhaps did little to dislodge, the pervasiveness of the type, which Paulding acknowledged in bluntly asserting that "the idea of connecting feeling or sentiment with a slave actually makes us laugh."[22]

George Tucker's 1824 novel, *The Valley of Shenandoah*, deploys a telling version of this paradigm in its depiction of the emotional dynamics of a slave auction. The true sufferers, it turns out, are the whites: "One not accustomed to this spectacle, is extremely shocked to see beings, of the same species with himself, setup for sale to the highest bidder, like horses or cattle; and even to those who have been accustomed to it, it is disagreeable, from their sympathy with the humbled and anxious slave."[23] It might seem that, byway of "sympathy," whites share the slave's degradation in this episode, but Tucker elsewhere explains that the apparently "anxious slave" is really quite content. His anxiety is experienced solely by whites in the audience, who erroneously identify with a creature incapable of subjective emotion. Tucker explains that "The error of this subject proceeds from a white man's supposing himself in the situation of the slave, without recollecting that these people were born slaves, and that there is as much difference between their feelings respecting their condition, and those of a white man, as is the privation of sight to one who is born blind, and one who has become so."[24]

Tucker's metaphor of blindness is well chosen, for it not only dismisses the parallel between white and black "feelings" about slavery but altogether cancels black subjectivity. The anxiety whites experience at the auction block is white anxiety, projected onto unfeeling brutes in a paradoxical act of displacement—paradoxical because it serves so many ideological interests. The African American's "unreflecting gaiety," as Paulding characterizes it, obviously served antebellum Southern interests by rationalizing a paternalistic system in which the master class could pretend to bear the psychic burden of slavery. Yet the same characterization of blacks as depthless creatures lay behind much early abolitionist literature, which tended to locate the principal evil of chattel slavery in the system's degradation of white values. From either point of view, the early representation of blackness in much American writing hinged on an assumed lack or blankness, available for inscription by the white writer, a blankness capable of reflecting an image of white subjectivity.

The denial of personality to blacks in American fiction persisted long after the antebellum period, when the ideological purposes of this sort of disfranchisement were at least clear. Henry James evokes an image of the purported blankness or "vacancy" of African Americans in *The American Scene*, where blacks are denied "any claim to a 'personality'" on the grounds that "they obviously, they notoriously, didn't care for themselves."[25] Kenneth Warren comments that, in James's view, "the African Americans on the scene are not candidates for subjectivity in their own right but problems to be overcome or solved."[26] Their vacancy is a problem for the narrator, yet it is also an opportunity to debate the value of subjectivity in a book that counts heavily on the redeeming power of its narrator's subjective vision. The representation of African American blankness, as in Tucker's novel, tells more about the observer than about the observed, and indeed the episode eventually reaffirms the voyeur's sense of his own powers. The scene concludes with James's assertion that he possesses enough subjectivity to compensate for the perceived African American lack. Blacks might experience hunger or thirst, physical manifestations of their degradation, but the anxiety associated with their experience, like the anxiety of the slave on the auction block, can only be felt by the narrator, who observes from "a cushioned and kitchened Pullman" car.

Howells's own representation of blackness belongs to this tradition of psychological effacement. Olney enforces a benign but uncompromising uniformity on the members of Boston's African American community when he comments that "all alike seemed shining with good-nature and good will, and the desire of peace on earth," and most African American characters in Howells's fiction appear equally devoid of individualizing traits.[27] The central black character in the short story "Mrs. Johnson," for example, possesses a "ragged gayety" that echoes Paulding's "unreflecting gaiety" in that it is more a negation of other traits than a trait in itself.[28] Moreover, African American suffering is somehow unreal to Howells, even when it is historically documented. Reviewing Sarah Bradford's biography of Harriet Tubman for his *Editor's Study* column in 1886, he observes that Tubman's story "affects us like a tale 'Of old, unhappy, far-off things, / And battles long ago,' and nothing within the date of actual history."[29] As a forceful, heroic, dynamic African American personality, Tubman constitutes an anomaly for Howells, who concedes that "it is only now and then, when some dark shadow of our shameful past appears, that we can believe there was ever a tragic element in our prosperity."

Tubman is a dark shadow who complicates "our prosperity" by insisting on the tragic element in African American experience. Howells's fictional representation of blacks generally resists this element by defining black emotion as inauthentic. The narrator of "Police Report," for example, speculates that "it will be long before . . . the prejudices and passions when painted black will seem otherwise than funny."[30] Similarly, Basil March comments in *An Open Eyed Conspiracy* on the ludicrous artificiality of blacks who drop their native dialect in order to imitate white mannerisms and emotional expressions.[31] When Howells encountered Paul Laurence Dunbar's poetry in 1896, he scrambled to rationalize the undeniable presence of emotion in poetry by an African American by identifying Dunbar's literary achievement as evidence of "white thinking and white feeling in a black man." "I have sometimes fancied," he admitted in his review of Dunbar's *Majors and Minors*, "that perhaps the negroes *thought* black, and *felt* black; that they were racially so utterly alien and distinct from ourselves that there never could be common intellectual and emotional ground between us, and that whatever eternity might do to reconcile us, the end of time would find us as far asunder as ever. But this little book has given me pause in my speculation."[32] Dunbar's achievement constituted an important but anomalous human event in Howells's view of African American character. Blacks in his fiction and critical prose generally either adopt "white thinking and white feeling," as ludicrous as that seems to Basil March, or they simply do not feel in any profound and individual way at all, remaining instead, as they appear to both Olney and Howells, "utterly alien," "dark shadows of our shameful past."

The point to be emphasized is not that Howells was or was not a racist, but that his quite traditional effacement of African American subjectivity served important psychological purposes. Much as Tucker sees white anxiety inscribed on the blank faces of unreflective slaves, Howells often projects his own psychological dilemmas onto the "dark shadows" of his fiction. Lacking authentic personality themselves, African Americans become shorthand symbols for mental and spiritual states that Howells has difficulty representing in experiential terms. This complicated dynamic of emotional displacement is at work when Isabel March draws an ambiguous metaphysical link between black bodies and white souls in *A Hazard of New Fortunes*, implying that her "angelic" janitor embodies a spiritual condition whites can only hope to attain in the afterlife: "We shall all be black in heaven," she asserts, "that is black-souled."[33] The janitor's foreshortened individuality, what Paulding would call his "unreflective gaiety," is perfectly stereotypical, yet for both Howells and Isabel this lack of individuation transforms the black body into a powerful symbol of psychological possibilities crucial to the novel.

In Isabel's view, to be black is to lack personality, to be a soul without the delineations of character. Olney implies the same thing when he comments on the gaudy clothing of the African American dandies, clothing that creates the effect of personality where in fact there is none. Both comments draw heavily upon a traditional stereotype, and both go some way toward explaining Howells's more personal uses of the fictional black body, which—when it appears at all in his writing—is constantly at risk of fading into spiritual obscurity. Olney observes this tendency in *An Imperative Duty* when he describes a black minister with "no discernible features," who appeared "like a wavering blur against the wall," "entirely black," "a thick, soft shadow" dressed in "absolute sable."[34] This very invisibility, the seeming unreality of the black body, is what makes Howells's obscurely drawn African Americans such serviceable emblems of the mind in crisis. As a "wavering blur" the minister embodies the condition of undifferentiated identity into which Rhoda Aldgate suddenly finds herself sinking as she relaxes her control over the movements of consciousness. Her whiteness, heretofore presumed inviolate, dissipates against an all-consuming black background as she herself becomes no more than a wavering shadow against the wall, her mind free-floating "like the blowball of a dandelion." Consciousness, "the nice, whitened truth of the shirtfront," as Howells describes it elsewhere, fades into a blur when confronted with "the black truth" of the unconscious mind.[35] Race becomes a metaphor for psychology, a vehicle for dramatizing the eruption into consciousness of psychic states that ought to remain beyond the realist's representational grasp.

Understood this way, Rhoda's mixed ancestry appears to be the metaphorical embodiment of a waking dream, the unexpected collision of conscious and unconscious thoughts in a mind that has lost the power of differentiation. That power is almost identical to what Howells means by "the critical faculty," which is "vividly and constantly alert" during the process of literary invention but "wholly absent" in dreams.[36] Literature served Howells as an effective means of emotional "self-defense" against unconscious fears precisely because writing, as he understood it, involved acute discrimination between conscious and unconscious material. Yet for all his desire to fashion an aesthetic position that served his emotional needs, Howells's fiction constantly tests the limits of consciousness by entertaining images of the human mind in crisis during those dream-like moments when the realist's "critical faculty" is dormant or impaired. William C. Fischer has argued that "reverie" offered Howells one effective device "for giving the impression of turbulent mental processes at the accessible edge of consciousness";[37] blackness afforded him another. Whenever the black body appears in Howells's fiction, there is a marked dreaminess or unreality about it, as if the representation offered a strategy for outflanking his own psychological scruples, a vehicle for introducing unconscious material that weighed heavily on Howells's own sense of identity but that he regarded as antithetical to the therapeutic purposes of his aesthetic.

Moreover, while he repeatedly asserts the immorality of "reverie" as a state of mind, Howells's representation of blackness affords him certain liberties. There is nothing immoral about the African American dreamer, for in Howells's evolutionary view blacks naturally embody a condition of psychological confusion that adult whites can approach only through dissipation and relapse. Bartley's dreaminess in *A Modern Instance*, his susceptibility to unconscious drives, for instance, is the unmistakable symptom of a moral collapse that takes place in a zone Howells refuses to examine as he marks off the "fastnesses" of mental life that are closed to literary realism. Rhoda's dreaminess in *An Imperative Duty*, on the other hand, signals an equally traumatic dissolution of the self, but one that Howells can approach boldly because its racial terms help unlock his anxiety about penetrating the self's defenses. He encounters Rhoda's crisis of identity much as Olney does, in a mood that "sought and could have won no justification from his moral sense, which indeed it simply submerged and blotted out for a time." Rhoda's drop of black blood, the "remote taint of her servile and savage origin," seems to authorize—for both Olney and Howells—a suspension of the moral and critical faculties that inform the realist's representation of the world.[38]

Writing of American literature generally, but in language that is especially relevant to Howells, Toni Morrison describes her increasing realization that the pervasive Africanist presence in American writing functions as a convex mirror for the white literary imagination, reflecting a distorted but revealing picture of the self. The subjective "fears and desires" that Howells generally polices so effectively become part of "an extraordinary meditation on the self" when his attention turns to what Morrison calls the "choked representation of an Africanist presence": "In minstrelsy, a layer of blackness applied to a white face released it from law. Just as entertainers, through or by association with blackface, could render permissible topics that otherwise would have been taboo, so American writers were able to employ an imagined Africanist persona to articulate and imaginatively act out the forbidden in American culture."[39] Whether Howells's aesthetic program marked off areas that were forbidden to American culture generally or to himself alone is a question that falls beyond the scope of this essay. More to the point is Morrison's notion, reconsidered in the context of Howells's literary career, that a "layer of blackness" applied to the background of his fictive world rendered these psychic areas "permissible" to his imagination.

Versions of the argument between Isabel Archer and Madame Merle over the nature of the self were hotly contested in a variety of cultural venues at the end of the nineteenth century. Andrew Hedbrooke took Madame Merle's side in an article entitled "Individual Continuity," published in the *Atlantic* in 1886:

> No doubt there are lives that do go on with apparently unbroken coherence—tranquil, native, or village lives, whose sun always rises over the same horizon, and whose radii of interests, from year to year, go out to the same unchanged circumference. Here the constantly overlapping continuity of the neighborhood existence helps to keep a man's own thread of personality unbroken. But when we once cut loose from geography, make friends and break with friends . . . then how far backward over our days can the uninterrupted "I" be said to extend? In truth, this whole matter of the individual identity—the I-ness of the I—is thick with difficult questions.[40]

At the time these lines were written, William James was already directing most of his energy toward answering such questions in an effort to place conceptual limits on "the I-ness of the I." Jackson Lears points out that the voluminous self-help literature of the day offered a variety of remedies intended to reconnect the "thread of personality" that modern urban life seemed inevitably to sever. Confronting the awesome possibility that there might be no clear core of self, many of the success manuals of the age recommended empowerment of the will as a means of achieving a version of Emersonian "Self-reliance" in the modern world. In the absence of an organic "I-ness" around which to organize subjectivity, a coherent self might at least be constructed through obedience to an authoritative will.

Howells was himself thoroughly engaged in "this whole matter of the individual identity," and indeed his propagandizing efforts on behalf of literary realism might be read as a defensive stand against the fragmentation of personality, a condition he and others associated with modernity. Describing the therapeutic advantages of a realist aesthetic, he argues in "Criticism and Fiction" that the wrong kind of books—"novels that merely . . . coddle our sensibilities or pamper our gross appetite for the marvelous"—pose a real danger for the self, which is always at risk of relapsing into a barbarian condition of undifferentiated identity. Such novels, he explains, are literally "innutricious, and clog the soul with unwholesome vapors of all kinds. No doubt they too help to weaken the moral fibre, and make their readers indifferent to 'plodding perseverance and plain industry' and to 'matter-of-fact poverty and commonplace distress.'"[41]

Realist fiction, on the other hand, instead of further dissipating the self, concentrates its authority by engaging the critical faculties in a healthy appreciation of commonplace poverty and distress. Whereas romance threatens the authority of the conscious self by obscuring its vision of reality, confusing conscious sensation with unconscious fantasy, realism performs psychic therapy by driving a wedge between light and darkness, foreground and background. The "innutricious" vapors that emerge unpredictably to beset the romantic imagination are swept away, deemed unreal, by an aesthetic project that explicitly proposes to reconnect the thread of modern personality by ministering to the embattled self.

Reflecting on his childhood struggle to achieve a coherent sense of identity, Howells reveals himself to be a Jamesian at heart, for he conceives of Andrew Hedbrooke's elusive "Individual continuity" as something constructed by careful labor. A coherent self-image is the work of a lifetime and the result of studious objectification:

> Through the whole time when a boy is becoming a man his autobiography can scarcely be kept from becoming the record of his family and his world. He finds himself so constantly reflected in the personality of those about him, so blent with it, that any attempt to study himself as a separate personality is impossible. His environment has become his life, and his hope of a recognizable self-portrait must lie in his frank acceptance of the condition that he can make himself truly seen chiefly in what he remembers to have seen of his environment.[42]

Unlike the African Americans Olney passes in the street, on whose faces neither time nor Boston leaves an impression, the boy's "environment has become his life." His separate personality—the "I-ness of the I" or what one means by "a 'Me' "—is so "blent" with other impressions as to be utterly indistinguishable. And yet there is the "hope" of piecing together a recognizable self-portrait, a hope identified with the ethic and aesthetic of literary realism, which takes as its project the construction of a usable self out of fragmentary images. The realist's perspective is, by Howells's definition, discriminating and constructive; it separates out those impressions necessary to a coherent self-portrait and coerces them into a sense of unity. Howells was aware that this continuity is manufactured, achieved only through effort; indeed, he repeatedly insists in "Criticism and Fiction" that realism performs much-needed cultural work, unlike romance and melodrama. Those forms of "impossible fiction" appeal like sweets or shiny stones to the primitive sensibility of the "boy of thirteen" or the "barbarian of any age," both of whom represent for Howells a condition of psychological chaos.[43] The savages, barbarians, and children who appear with surprising frequency in his critical prose offer an image of the mind prior to the sorting out of individual identity that becomes possible through the realist's power of objectification, his ability to project unwanted aspects of the self outward and to treat his fears "as if they were alien."

If the barbarian appetite for "impossible fiction" represents one threat to the realist's conception of self, another lies at the opposite extreme of "sophistication." Echoing Emerson's call in "The American Scholar" for a literature that embraces "the common . . . the familiar . . . the low," Howells writes in "Criticism and Fiction" that "the mass of common men have been afraid to apply their own simplicity, naturalness, and honesty to the appreciation of the beautiful. They have always cast about for the instruction of someone who professed to know better, and who browbeat wholesome common-sense into the self distrust that ends in sophistication."[44] Whereas a barbarian sensibility threatens to compromise the self by pursuing gratification of a too "simple sort," sophistication represents a parallel danger by inspiring distrust in the natural, honest vision around which the realist attempts to organize the fragmentary constituents of selfhood.[45] Emotional stability and a coherent sense of identity are the products of "common-sense," which expresses itself in an artistic vision that caters neither to primitive appetites nor to the equally distorting excesses of over-refinement. The perspective of the realist, whether it surveys the contemporary scene or dwells on memories of childhood, makes a healthy individuality possible by mediating the cultural extremes of barbarism and sophistication.

Given realism's important therapeutic purposes, it is easy to understand why Howells placed certain mental processes beyond the representational horizon of his fiction. The unconscious mind, which comes into play for Howells when consciousness loses its equilibrium, is a distinctly fascinating but unwelcome guest within an aesthetic program that intends to nourish consciousness by clearing the mind of unhealthy vapors. Howells's most characteristic gesture in dealing with the mind thus involves a sudden start and stop. Unconscious thoughts typically encroach upon the fragile dominion of the self in moments of moral weakness or emotional crisis, when Howells seems resigned to demonstrate "what a shaky thing the human mind is at its best."[46] But instead of pursuing the course of this encroachment, Howells retreats behind the self-imposed limitations of his medium with a statement like "the swiftness of these mental processes no words can suggest; we can portray life, not living."[47]

This formulation neatly explains the logic of the start and stop gesture. Howells can portray the mind as a static object, what he calls "life," and—as long as his objectivity is secure—he can even accept that the mind is a "shaky thing." He cannot portray the mind as Jamesian process, as "living," because such a representation violates the ethical and aesthetic imperatives of his art. To portray "living" would be to dismiss the self as a fiction. Howells was at least as convinced as the James brothers that the self is an artificial construct, and his work registers, more than theirs, the painful effort required to preserve its authority over mental life. Unlike the Jameses, however, Howells ultimately conceived of literature as a form of constructive therapy whose highest function and aspiration was creative resistance to knowledge of the self's vulnerability. Thus, for all his interest in psychology and psychological fiction, his fascination with dreams and the unconscious, Howells characteristically backs away from literary representation of mental events, often echoing in spirit the words of Silas Lapham: "I don't suppose it was meant we should know what was in each other's minds. It would take a man out of his own hands. As long as he's in his own hands, there's some hopes of his doing something with himself; but if a fellow has been found out—even if he hasn't been found out to be so very bad—it's pretty much all up with him. No, sir, I don't want to know people through and through."[48]

If Howells's notion of literature as therapy for consciousness makes him look like a member of the Victorian thought police, vigilantly guarding against insurgent ideas that might diminish the authority of the self, it should be pointed out that he expended almost as much effort attempting to get around his self-imposed aesthetic limitations as he did erecting them. His move from the polite literary community of Boston to New York might be read as part of this effort to extend his imaginative horizons, and indeed New York has an uncanny liberating effect on Isabel and Basil March when they arrive there from Boston at the beginning of *A Hazard of New Fortunes*.[49] The move is fraught with psychological consequences, for unlike Boston, where firmly established social relations cause personal identity to stand out in high relief, New York operates for the Marches as a kind of "solvent" that "reduces all men to a common level, that touches everybody with its potent magic and brings to the surface the deeply underlying nobody."[50] After "the intense identification of their Boston life," this loss of individuality strikes Isabel as "a relief," though she "had her misgivings, and questioned whether it were not too relaxing to the moral fibre."[51] In response to this sentiment, Basil strikes a characteristically Howellsian pose: "March refused to explore his conscience; he allowed that it might be so; but he said he liked now and then to feel his personality in that state of solution."[52]

This intriguing exchange is full of the ambivalence Howells always expresses about the authority of the self and the desirability of its dominion over mental life. He seems tempted to agree with Isabel that the loss of individuality constitutes a relief from the artificial posturing of Boston social life. His narrator goes so far as to say that the effect of New York "for consciousness, for egotism, is admirable" and "doubtless finally wholesome."[53] Yet in identifying this challenge to the self as "wholesome," Howells is aware that he has undermined the entire project of a therapeutic realism, and so he retreats behind Isabel's "misgivings," offering the disreputable Beaton as the novel's only example of what might be called a free-floating consciousness, a personality unsupported by "moral fibre." The moral consequences of Beaton's freedom are never in doubt: he is "selfish and mean, weak-willed, narrow-minded, and hard-hearted."[54] His lack of center creates a vacuum, so that "the man who had no control over himself liked logically to feel his control over some one else."[55] Unattractive as Beaton is, however, he is the novel's principal figure of the artist, and his frank refusal to perform a charade of personal identity is distinctly appealing to Howells—so much so that he must invoke the all-too-familiar limitations of literary representation to ensure that the fastnesses of Beaton's consciousness remain closed.[56] Howells's narrator might as well be describing the poverty of his own representational project when he writes that Kendricks, the earnest young correspondent for *Every Other Week*, "could not have penetrated to that aesthetic and moral complexity which formed the consciousness of a nature like Beaton, and was chiefly a torment to itself."[57] Beaton's mind inhabits a region that is inaccessible to the realist's vocabulary, a region that "can only be very clumsily interpreted in language."[58] His perverse lack of "common-sense" is yet another of "those facts which"—despite their immense appeal to Howells's imagination—"fiction must seek in vain to disclose."

March's own ambivalence about the self's authority is even more pronounced than his wife's. He admits to the pleasurable sensation that accompanies the loss of individuality but allows with Mrs. March that too much relaxation might be dangerous. Under the circumstances, his abrupt refusal "to explore his conscience" appears to be a caricature of Howells's refusal to explore mental processes that involve the self in "aesthetic and moral complexity." An unmistakable pattern emerges: Kendricks cannot see into the morbid emptiness of Beaton's nature; March refuses to examine the depths of his own ambivalence about the self; Isabel is beset by misgiving about the pleasant impersonality of life in New York; Howells cannot, or will not, track consciousness beyond the self-imposed limitations of his realistic aesthetic.

Yet if Howells refuses to allow the Marches to experience the loss of control over consciousness as a perfect "relief," he does permit Isabel at least one moment of unqualified insanity. "How could I have lost my head so completely?" she asks Basil after almost renting an apartment that meets none of her requirements for cost and comfort.[59] Her sudden abandonment of common sense, that all-important faculty in Howells's fiction, is provoked by the literally enchanting presence of "one of those colored men who soften the trade of janitor in many of the smaller apartment-houses in New York by the sweetness of their race." Both the house, with its "dark mahogany trim, of sufficiently ugly design," and the "angelic" black janitor offer a repudiation of whiteness and individuality—a repudiation that Isabel finds inexplicably appealing.[60] The house, once a luxurious home, is now "cut up into five or six dwellings," an image of the fragmentation March associates with New York and about which Isabel elsewhere expresses an ambivalent blend of "relief" and trepidation.[61] Yet her "misgivings" are nowhere evident in Isabel's irresistible attraction to this man and his house, with its gloomy halls, numerous partitions, and small, shadowy rooms that "must darkle in perpetual twilight."[62] When the janitor informs her that the building has neither an elevator nor steam heat, she responds incoherently: "We'll take it, Basil, if it's like the rest."[63] Basil clarifies her enthusiasm:

> "If it's like him, you mean."
> "I don't wonder they wanted to own them," she hurriedly philosophized. "If I had such a creature, nothing but death should part us, and I should no more think of giving him his *freedom*—"[64]

As Basil implies, the black janitor and the dismembered old house are closely linked in Isabel's imagination. Together they compose a sable background, a figure for the "underlying nobody" into which consciousness inevitably finds itself sinking in New York. Basil warns, " 'The next time a colored janitor opens the door to us, I'll tell him the apartment doesn't suit at the threshold. It's the only way to manage you, Isabel.' 'It's true,' " she admits, " 'I *am* in love with the whole race.' "[65] Assuming the role Howells usually reserves for his narrator, March compliments himself for reining in Isabel's nonsensical enthusiasm: "If it hadn't been for my strength of character, you'd have taken an unfurnished flat without heat and with no elevator, when you had just sworn me to steam heat, an elevator, furniture, and eight hundred."[66]

The importance of this episode, which occupies two of *Hazard*'s five hundred pages, should not be overemphasized. Yet as a telling exception to the rule by which Howells generally represents consciousness, it possesses an unexpected centrality to the novel's major themes. This "choked representation" of blackness is an important part of Howells's ongoing meditation on the self, an attempt to describe his powerful affinity for an aspect of consciousness he cannot approach directly. Whereas Beaton's egotism illustrates the moral predicament into which excessive "sophistication" must inevitably lead the self, Isabel's janitor occupies the other end of Howells's evolutionary scale, where identity is equally threatened by the downward pull of a barbarian state. The difference is that whereas Beaton's *immoral* excesses are constantly filtered through the narrator's critical and ethical sensibility, the janitor's *amoral* blackness enables Howells to entertain a serious challenge to the self without engaging in his usual censure. The janitor is a figure for what Howells elsewhere calls the "merely natural man," an amoral creature who, although entirely human, exists prior to individuation.[67] In this potent image of blackness, "choked" and effaced though it is, Howells finds it possible to celebrate the demise of self without his characteristic defensive stand behind the inadequacy of language.

In fact, the janitor is a figure who seems deliberately conceived as a way to overcome the limitations Howells repeatedly imposes on his art. When the Marches find their way to his building by perfect accident, Isabel exclaims, "Well, I do believe it is a sign," and indeed the entire episode represents a departure from what William Fischer has appropriately called Howells's "nonsymbolic aesthetic."[68] Abandoning his usual reluctance to employ what Fischer calls "figurative images for representing the invisible noumena of subjective truths," Howells here invests the black body with rich symbolic content. The African American persona, "serviceable to the last," as Morrison puts it, enters the novel as a way of "both talking about and of policing" the self, enabling the author to carry his meditation on consciousness beyond the narrowly circumscribed limits of his aesthetics.[69]

The role of blackness as an enabling background against which to test images of consciousness and selfhood is even more pronounced in *An Imperative Duty*. Late in that novel Olney compares the "blond presence" of his old friend Mrs. Atherton with what might be described as the black absence represented by Rhoda Aldgate.[70] In contrast to the "large and handsome" "sumptuousness" of Mrs. Atherton, in whom Olney feels "the tameness of the Northern type," Rhoda's beauty is more elusive. Howells uses a familiar gesture to describe its inaccessible charm: "It was the elder world, the beauty of antiquity, which appealed to him in the lustre and sparkle of this girl; and the remote taint of her servile and savage origin gave her a kind of fascination which refuses to let itself be put into words."[71] This refusal should cause no surprise, for Howells clearly understands Rhoda's blackness, her barbarian origin, as the source of Olney's sexual fascination. We therefore expect him to close down the meditation on her beauty before it yields to the pressure of unconscious material. But because the object of Olney's developing passion is a black woman, she seems susceptible to a level of figurative imagery Howells is otherwise reluctant to employ. Having invoked the limitation of words as a shielding device, he nevertheless immediately strains to overcome that limitation, representing Rhoda's sexuality in vividly symbolic imagery:

> it was like the grace of a limp, the occult, indefinable lovableness of a deformity, but transcending these by its allurement in infinite degree, and going for the reason of its effect deep into the mysterious places of being where the spirit and the animal meet and part in us. When Olney followed some turn of her head, some movement of her person, a wave of the profoundest passion surged up in his heart, and he knew that he loved her with all his life, which he could make his death if it were a question of that. The mood was of his emotional nature alone; it sought and could have won no justification from his moral sense, which indeed it simply submerged and blotted out for the time.[72]

Howells comes perilously close in this passage to condoning a doubly taboo sexual fascination. Not only does he appear to approve Olney's convenient blotting out of conscience, but he seems equally untroubled by the prospect of miscegenation. This uncommonly risky territory is made available by Rhoda's body, which functions as an emblem of unconscious desires that Howells can represent only through her form. If we imagine what he would have to say about Beaton or Bartley Hubbard in Olney's emotional state, with conscience intentionally "submerged" in order to indulge illicit sexual desires, it is easy to recognize the passage above as a glaring exception to his customary treatment of mental life. Because the object of Olney's fascination is black, Howells is able to describe the nerve specialist's emotional state with a license he rarely permits himself. Her blackness unlocks the fastnesses of Olney's mind, opening to view, as if by reflection, that region of *his* mental life where "the spirit and the animal meet and part in us."

If Howells's image of Rhoda's savage charm is indeed a means of representing the site of Olney's illicit desires, as I am suggesting, then we are back to the peculiar emotional dynamics of George Tucker's auction block. The whites who gather to observe the auction see their anxiety in the face of the slave. Their emotional response to the slave's degradation, although motivated by "sympathy," is entirely unreciprocated, for the slave's unreflective nature insulates him from emotional experience. Lacking authentic subjectivity, the black body becomes a place to record white anxiety about the human tragedy of slavery.

Howells was not, like Tucker, an apologist for white supremacism, and his views about race were undeniably progressive in the context of Jim Crow America. His representation of blackness, however, was motivated by an impulse to explore what Howells himself might call "white thinking and white feeling." Unable, like Basil March, to imagine black subjectivity as anything but a parody and an imitation of whiteness, Howells makes the fictional black body a vehicle for representing emotional and psychological states that his fully individualized white characters can entertain only at the price of severe moral censure. Like Tucker's slave, and like the "dark and abiding presence" that haunts so much American literature, Howells's black body is the site of a reflexive meditation on the self.[73] Having marked off large territories of mental and emotional life as inaccessible, he deploys blackness as a symbolic rebuke to the self-imposed limits of his realist aesthetic.

Notes

I would like to thank John W. Crowley for nursing this chapter through its troubled infancy. Without his insight and example it would never have survived.

1. William James, *The Principles of Psychology*, 2 vols. (New York: Henry Holt, 1890) 1:135.
2. Ibid., 1:103.
3. Henry James, *The Portrait of a Lady* (1881; reprint, Boston: Houghton Mifflin, 1963), 172.
4. Ibid., 173.
5. William Dean Howells, *An Imperative Duty*, ed. David J. Nordloh et al. (1891; reprint, Bloomington: Indiana University Press, 1970), 6–7.
6. William Dean Howells, *A Hazard of New Fortunes*, ed. David J. Nordloh et al. (1890; reprint, Bloomington: Indiana University Press, 1976), 485–86.
7. See, for example, Thomas Galt Peyser, "Those Other Selves: Consciousness in the 1890 Publications of Howells and the James Brothers," *American Literary Realism* 25 (Fall 1992): 20–37; John W. Crowley, "Howellsian Realism: A Psychological Juggle," *Studies in the Literary Imagination* 16 (Fall 1983): 45–55; Andrew Delbanco, "Howells and the Suppression of Knowledge," *The Southern Review* 19 (1983): 765–84; Anthony Hilfer, *The Ethics of Intensity in American Fiction* (Austin: University of Texas Press, 1981).
8. William Dean Howells, *A Modern Instance* (1882; reprint, New York: Library of America, 1982), 208.
9. Ibid., 586.
10. Hilfer writes that "*A Modern Instance* presents a giant STOP sign to life's most vital forces. It seems to proclaim that 'Consciousness will be ethical or it will be nothing at all'" (68).
11. Ibid., 68.
12. William Dean Howells, *Years of My Youth and Three Essays*, ed. David J. Nordloh (Bloomington: Indiana University Press, 1975), 81.
13. Crowley, "Howellsian Realism," 48; Howells, *Years of My Youth*, 71.
14. Howells, *Years of My Youth*, 81.
15. *Selected Letters of William Dean Howells*, vol. 1, ed. George Arms et al. (Boston: Twayne,1979),177.

16. *Interviews with William Dean Howells*, ed. Ulrich Halfmann (Arlington: *American Literary Realism*, University of Texas at Arlington,1973), 22.

17. Howells, *An Imperative Duty*, 60.

18. Toni Morrison, *Playing in the Dark: Whiteness and the Literary Imagination* (Cambridge, MA: Harvard University Press, 1992), 51, 38.

19. See Edwin Cady, *The Road to Realism*, 2 vols. (Syracuse, NY: Syracuse University Press, 1956), 1:11–60.

20. Morrison's *Playing in the Dark* is largely responsible for rejuvenating critical interest in white representations of African American character and experience, though, as Morrison acknowledges, her pathbreaking study belongs to a long-standing critical tradition. Some important prior contributions to that tradition include Sterling A. Brown, *The Negro in American Fiction* (1937; reprint, New York., Atheneum, 1969); Hugh M. Gloster, *Negro Voices in American Fiction* (New York: Russell and Russell, 1948); Seymour L. Gross and John Edward Hardy, eds., *Images of the Negro in American Literature* (Chicago: University of Chicago Press, 1966); Nancy M. Tischler, *Black Masks: Negro Characters in Modern Southern Fiction* (University Park: Pennsylvania State University Press, 1969); Catherine Juanita Starke, *Black Portraiture in American Fiction* (New York: Basic Books, 1971); and Jean Fagan Yellin, *The Intricate Knot: Black Figures in American Literature*, 1776–1863 (New York: New York University Press, 1972). Important recent works that pursue the complex process of African American representation in American literature include Eric Lott, *Love and Theft: Black Face Minstrelsy and the American Working Class* (New York: Oxford University Press, 1993); Eric Sundquist, *To Wake the Nations: Race in the Making of American Literature* (Cambridge, MA: Harvard University Press, 1993); Kenneth W. Warren, *Black and White Strangers: Race and American Literary Realism* (Chicago: University of Chicago Press, 1993); and Shelley Fisher Fishkin, *Was Huck Black: Mark Twain and African-American Voices* (New York: Oxford University Press, 1993).

21. James Kirke Paulding, *Letters from the South, Written during an Excursion in the Summer of 1816*, 2 vols. (New York, 1817) 1:58; discussed in Yellin, *The Intricate Knot*, 32–48.

22. Paulding, *Letters from the South*, 1:127.

23. George Tucker, *The Valley of the Shenandoah: Or, Memoirs of the Graysons*, 2 vols. (New York, 1824), 2:207; discussed in Yellin, *The Intricate Knot*, 19–31.

24. Tucker, *The Valley of the Shenandoah*, 1:64.

25. Henry James, *The American Scene* (1907; reprint, Bloomington: Indiana University Press, 1968), 398.

26. Warren, *Black and White Strangers*, 115.

27. Howells, *An Inperative Duty*, 7.

28. William Dean Howells, "Mrs. Johnson," in *Suburban Sketches* (New York: Hurd and Houghton, 1871), 20.

29. William Dean Howells, *Editor's Study*, ed. James W. Simpson (Troy, NY: Whitston, 1983), 41.

30. William Dean Howells, "Police Report," *Atlantic Monthly* (January 1882): 11.

31. William Dean Howells, *An Open-Eyed Conspiracy: An Idyl of Saratoga* (New York: Harper, 1897), 104–5.

32. William Dean Howells, "Paul Laurence Dunbar Announced," in *W D. Howells as Critic*, ed. Edwin H. Cady (New York: Routledge and Kegan Paul, 1973), 251. For an excellent discussion of Howells's critical writing on African American authors, see William Andrews, "William Dean Howells and Charles W. Chesnutt: Criticism and Race Fiction in the Age of Booker T. Washington," *American Literature* 48 (fall 1976): 327–39. Elsa Nettels also provides useful insight into Howells's relationships with

black writers and his representation of African American character in *Language, Race, and Social Class in Howells's America* (Lexington: University of Kentucky Press, 1988), especially chaps. 5 and 6.

33. Howells, *A Hazard of New Fortunes*, 48.

34. Howells, *An Imperative Duty*, 63.

35. Howells, *Selected Letters*, 5:77–78.

36. William Dean Howells, *Impressions and Experiences* (New York: Harper, 1896), 112–13; quoted in Crowley, "Howellsian Realism," 52.

37. William C. Fischer, Jr., "William Dean Howells: Reverie and the Nonsymbolic Aesthetic," *Nineteenth-Century Fiction* 25 (June 1970): 2.

38. Howells, *An Imperative Duty*, 89–90.

39. Morrison, *Playing in the Dark*, 17, 66.

40. Andrew Hedbrooke, "Individual Continuity," *Atlantic Monthly*, August 1886, 263–67; quoted in T. J. Jackson Lears, *No Place of Grace: Anti-Modernism and the Transformation of American Culture 1880–1920* (New York: Pantheon, 1981), 36.

41. William Dean Howells, *Criticism and Fiction and Other Essays*, ed. Clara Kirk and Rudolph Kirk (New York: New York University Press,1959), 47.

42. Howells, *Years of My Youth*, 57.

43. Howells, *Criticism and Fiction*, 53.

44. Ralph Waldo Emerson, *Selected Writings of Emerson*, ed. Donald McQuade (New York: Modern Library,1981), 61; Howells, *Criticism and Fiction*, 12.

45. Ibid., 53.

46. Howells, *A Hazard of New Fortunes*, 181.

47. Howells, *An Imperative Duty*, 54.

48. William Dean Howells, *The Rise of Silas Lapham*, ed. David J. Nordloh et al. (1885; reprint, Bloomington: Indiana University Press,1971), 80.

49. Amy Kaplan has brilliantly discussed the symbolic consequences of this move in *The Social Construction of American Realism* (Chicago: University of Chicago Press, 1988), 44–64.

50. Howells, *A Hazard of New Fortunes*, 243.

51. Ibid., 297.

52. Ibid.

53. Ibid., 243–44.

54. Ibid., 476.

55. Ibid., 466.

56. According to John W. Crowley, Howells betrayed his conflicted identification with Beaton by clothing the reprobate artist in a conspicuous fur-lined overcoat that resembles one Howells owned but felt intensely guilty about wearing. Crowley, personal correspondence with the author, 26 May 1994.

57. Howells, *A Hazard of New Fortunes*, 394.

58. Ibid., 467.

59. Ibid., 47.

60. Ibid., 46.

61. Ibid.

62. Ibid., 47.

63. Ibid., 46.

64. Ibid.

65. Ibid., 48.

66. Ibid., 47.

67. Howells, *Impressions*, 101; quoted in Crowley "Howellsian Realism," 50–51.

68. Howells, *A Hazard of New Fortunes*, 46; Fischer, "William Dean Howells, 15.

69. Morrison, *Playing in the Dark*, 28.
70. Howells, *An Imperative Duty*, 89.
71. Ibid., 89–90.
72. Ibid., 90.
73. Morrison, *Playing in the Dark*, 33.

Genealogical Ambiguity and Racial Identity: Adoption and Passing in Kate Chopin's "Desiree's Baby" and Jessie Redmon Fauset's "The Sleeper Wakes"

Marina Fedosik

DESPITE POPULAR IMAGININGS OF AMERICAN NATIONAL IDENTITY AS a free choice akin to that of love and marriage, identity formation and recognition in America have been largely controlled by biological scripts and relations of descent.[1] Blood, "a signifier not only of class, but also of bodily, sexual, racial, and cultural difference," according to Betsy Erkkila, has long served in America both as "a means of affirming political community, kinship, citizenship, and the union" and as "the grounds for exclusion, expulsion, negation, and extermination."[2] An analysis of breaches in protected and protective blood lines in American kinship shows that genealogy—alongside and often more so than visual difference or nonbiological kinship relations (such as marriage and adoption)—has played a major role in racialized social stratification of bodies in segregated America. This chapter focuses on Kate Chopin's "Desiree's Baby" and Jessie Redmon Fauset's "The Sleeper Wakes"—passing narratives that feature adoptees and explore the process of racial identity construction in the absence of both bodily markers of race and known genealogy. Through scenarios of ambiguous or unknown descent these stories examine possibilities of interracial kinship formation in American society at the turn of the twentieth century. Both Chopin and Fauset represent passing and adoption as challenges to genealogical certainty in the process of establishing familial ties across the color line. Passing, which depends on concealed ancestry, and adoption, which (in these stories) precludes the knowledge of descent, make conspicuous the significance of (un)known genealogy for racial identity formation and access to socially empowering group memberships.

Stories of passers in "Desiree's Baby" and "The Sleeper Wakes" tell us of racially mixed persons seeking inclusion in the national body and access to socioeconomic privilege through admission into white family structures. Both Desiree, the protagonist of "Desiree's Baby" and Amy, Jessie Fauset's heroine, are denied membership in a white family because of their supposed blackness.[3] Their white husbands choose to terminate marriages on the basis of their wives' "impure" racial identities. The cost of being identified as black is not the same for Desiree and Amy because of the differences in their upbringing and self-identification. But despite plot variations, both stories expose the impregnability of boundaries that prevent the black body from entering socially empowering white domesticity.[4] By focusing on interactions of race, class, and gender in familial context, these passing narratives show how racist public discourses regulate the formation of kinships to assure the reproduction of segregation and inequality.

The plot of "Desiree's Baby" is built around the social ban on legally acknowledged kinship of black and white persons and on reproduction of racially mixed identities. Desiree, a white woman adopted by a wealthy Southern family, is accused of having a drop of black blood after she gives birth to a mulatto child. Crushed by the sudden revelation and her husband Armand Aubigny's rejection, Desiree takes her child and walks away into bayou. The whiteness of Aubigny's bloodline seems to be restored until the ending of the story reveals that it is in fact Armand who is partially black. By the ironic reversal of passing at the end of the story, Chopin not only critiques the unquestionability of patriarchy, which puts a white man in charge of the social rank and racial identity of a woman, but also demonstrates the significance of genealogies for American identity formation.

Desiree is disempowered by the lack of genealogical knowledge. It seems estrangement from biological kinship ties that support essentialist scripts of identity should give her the freedom to "experiment with multiple subject positions, and to cross social and economic boundaries that exclude and oppress."[5] But the status of an adopted child hardly promises Desiree fluidity of identity; instead, she is enslaved by her past or, rather, by the absence of her past. Passing and adoption may offer more room for the invention of self, but each of these situations threatens to destabilize identity by making it vulnerable to unexpected discoveries. The obscurity of Desiree's origins leaves her open to Armand Aubigny's accusations. Although Desiree points out that her skin is even whiter than his, it takes only Armand's word and a letter from Madame Valmonde (whose silence on the subject confirms doubts about her adoptive daughter's race) for the verdict to be accepted, even by Desiree herself.

The whiteness of Desiree's body does not hold up against the blackness of her child's. Her race is determined by the skin color of her son and, more importantly, by her husband Armand, a white male with a known family tree. His own racial background is not even questioned. In the passing narrative shaped by the gender politics of the post-Reconstruction era, it is often the woman's body—a vessel containing potentially destructive proof of a contaminated bloodline—that has to be feared, blamed, destroyed, or put out of sight in case of its failure to maintain unambiguous lineage—even if the culprit is a male passer.[6] In her study of "black baby" stories written before and at the time of Harlem Renaissance, which "recount the downfall of women found guilty of miscegenation or passing," Laura Dawkins demonstrates that the narrative conflict created by the birth of a black baby to all-but-white parents is predominantly resolved through death of either the child or the mother.[7] Armand, empowered by his social position, gender status, and seemingly impeccable racial pedigree, can pass his blackness onto Desiree, who is unable to prove the purity of her bloodline.

It is common to assume that Armand does not know of his blackness until the end of the story, which makes him an unintentional passer. I, however, would like to read the passing of Armand Aubigny as intentional.[8] Such a reading allows for highlighting collaborations of race and gender politics applied to maintain white patriarchal social order through the institution of family.

We do not know for certain if Armand had read the letter from his mother revealing that he was black before he married Desiree. But he could have had enough clues to his blackness growing up. He lived with his mother in Paris for eight years and probably remembered enough of her to suspect his true origin. The fact that he and his father returned to Louisiana only after his mother's death suggests an attempt to hide a dark genealogical secret. Knowledge of his race could explain Armand's cruelty to slaves and a sudden change in his attitude after the birth of the baby. For Armand, as for any passer, the act of childbirth has specific importance. The body of a child, as an extension of the body of the passing parent, may confirm their parent's whiteness or expose their hybridity, "contaminate" the body of their family, and bring their exclusion from the privileged white kinship. A white-looking baby could "redeem" Armand from blackness and be a living proof of his lawful belonging to the white race. But as the days pass by and the baby turns darker and darker, Aubigny goes back to his old ways and "the very spirit of Satan seem[s] suddenly to take hold of him in his dealings with slaves."[9] Apparently he is frustrated by the failure to reproduce whiteness and secure his white racial identity.

If we assume that Armand knows he is black, then his sudden passion for Desiree is explicable. He falls in love when he sees her at the gate where she was found eighteen years earlier, but "[t]he wonder was that he had not loved her before; for he had known her since his father brought him home from Paris" (1607). Desiree standing at the gate again reminds Armand of her origin, and he suddenly realizes what she could do for him. He grasps a possibility for himself to produce an heir and secure access to his wealth, which is available to him as long as he is passing successfully. Armand knows that marriage to a white woman with known genealogy may jeopardize his social status, but if he marries a girl with no past, the blackness of their child could be blamed on her. So when the birth of the baby, the ultimate test for Armand's whiteness, reveals blackness of one of the parents, he confers the status of the tragic mulatta on his wife to whitewash himself.

Armand has to annul kinship ties to his wife and son because he chooses not to admit blood relationship to a colored person. Margaret D. Bauer has convincingly shown that for Armand the revelation of his black heritage would be "devastating" in the Louisiana of his time where even the free colored people were considered second-class citizens.[10] Having a "keen understanding of the precarious position he was in as heir to his father's estate"[11] and aware of other perils of being black in Lousiana in the middle of the nineteenth century, Armand can save his white male identity only by accusing his wife of racial impurity. But even though Armand has enough clout to preserve his body and protect his social position threatened by revelation, there is a price to pay. To stay "white" he has to renounce his wife and progeny thus forsaking the right to reproduce. Armand's survival as a white male and his access to privilege depend on interrupted genealogy and truncated kinship. He cannot afford to accept blackness as part of his identity and/or to sustain familial ties with a "black" woman and a child.

Armand's story is exemplary of how a racist society denies mulattoes the possibility of fully embracing and recognizing the complexity of their racial identification and family lineage as it also curtails one's freedom in creating a family. Through marginalizing and erasing racially mixed genealogies, segregated American society suppressed reproduction of identities that blurred the classifying criteria of race. Nonacknowledgement of white genealogies of mulattoes in segregated America robbed them of part of their kinship and excluded them from socially empowering white family structures. The racial identity of mulattoes was commonly reduced to its black component. Passing, which promised a light-skinned biracial person an enhanced social mobility in a racist environment, nonetheless confined his/her to a rigid choice of white over black racial identification, and necessitated the rejection of black ancestry. In the case of discovery, the passer was likely to lose familial ties created on the other side of the color line. The outing of the passer or the death of the mulatto/a character before they can enter a relationship leading to legally acknowledged reproduction is common in the literature of passing.[12] And even if such a relationship has been established, the survival of the passing mulatto/a, and the preservation of the established kinship often depends on successful reproduction of whiteness in the body of their child. The right to procreate is granted to a mulatto/a on condition that their progeny do not disturb the racial status quo.[13]

Under the laws of the slaveholding American South, both Desiree, a woman with an ambiguous bloodline, and Armand, a mulatto, are denied the possibility to sustain their kinship, but ultimately Desiree is victimized by Armand's scheme more than he is by its failure. Desiree's adoptive status means that she cannot claim either black or white identity because she does not know enough of her past to affiliate herself with either. She was brought up as white, but knowing that even the return to her adoptive family would not guarantee the preservation of her white identity, she crumbles under "a quick conception of all that this accusation [being black] meant for her" (1609). Passing narratives often end in a return of passing protagonists to their roots, but there is no possibility of a "racial homecoming" for Desiree. Desiree is stripped of her identity and, as a consequence, of familial ties to both her adoptive parents and her husband. There is no known genealogy, and the lack of options allows Desiree but an "atavistic" return to nothing, to "reeds and willows that grew thick along the banks of the deep, sluggish bayou."[14] Upholding the uncertainty, Chopin does not explicitly pronounce her character's death; she simply removes Desiree from the stage into the symbolic realm of nothingness. An adopted foundling, Desiree comes out of nowhere and returns to nowhere.

In the short story "The Sleeper Wakes," written by Jessie Redmon Fauset almost three decades after Chopin's "Desiree's Baby," the destiny of Amy, a passing adoptee, unfolds in a different way. Both Chopin and Fauset portray light-skinned female protagonists with uncertain racial background who live in a segregationist patriarchal society. Amy and Desiree are teetering on the color line as they try to come to terms with their racial identities in the absence of genealogical knowledge. But whereas Chopin portrays Desiree as a tragic mulatta victimized by white patriarchy, whose passing condition is transferred onto her by her husband, Fauset grants her protagonist more freedom in racial self-identification as well as in breaking and (re)creating familial and communal ties. Unknown genealogy, which annihilates Desiree, becomes a source of strength and hope for Amy.

Such difference in portrayals of racially ambiguous female characters may be attributed to the race affiliations that shaped Chopin's and Fauset's perspectives as well as to sociocultural climates of the time periods in which the stories were written.

Several scholars noticed different approaches of white American and African American authors to representations of biracial characters and situations of crossing the blood lines. M. Giulia Fabi, for example, points out that "[a]lthough scholars have often taken for granted and overestimated their similarity, white-authored representations of the tragic mulatto and African American representation of miscegenation and passing constitute profoundly different literary traditions."[15] Fabi notices that in contrast to "tragic mulatto/a" narratives authored by nineteenth-century white authors, pre–Harlem Renaissance African American fiction rarely represents passing as a tragic condition. Even if passing results in the demise of the mulatto/a, it rarely happens because of some innate tragic flaw of character, but due to the system of racial discrimination. Teresa C. Zackodnik considers the "tragic mulatta" of the post–Civil War American literature "a creation of white female abolitionists" and observes that as "a sensationalized figure of ruined womanhood"[16] it did not go beyond giving the pleasure of sentimentalist identification to the readers. In contrast, African American women authors between 1840s and 1950s used the mulatta character for political purposes, namely to "invoke and manage both American and British abolitionist empathy"[17] and, in the context of sympathetic identification, to criticize racist social practices. Laura Dawkins, in her analysis of representations of miscegenation, observes that whereas white authors and some Harlem Renaissance writers who internalized racist ideology read racial mixing as destructive for both black and white races, there were examples of seeing the mulatto/a as a sign of hope for peaceful coexistsence or unification of races.[18]

The differences in the treatment of the passing figure by black and white writers can be explained by different issues the authors are exploring through the trope of passing and the readership they address. For a white author and audience the body of the passer, outwardly unmarked but harboring blackness in its blood, was likely to represent the anxiety of white America over uncertainty of racial division and the desire to unmask and reinscribe blackness. For African Americans, however, the passer was a more positive figure because s/he embodied the freedom to cross the color line and the possibility of claiming equality based on the universality of human nature.

Amy, the protagonist of Jessie Fauset's "The Sleeper Wakes," manages to achieve a universalistic, "raceless" state of consciousness after she tries to live both as a black and a white woman. She is able to develop such perspective, to a large extent, because of her uncertain genealogy. At the age of five Amy is adopted by the Boldins, a middle-class black family. There is surprisingly little information in the story about Amy's life before adoption, and she has no recollection of birth parents. Until the age of five she lived with a "tall, proud, white woman," who used to read her fairy tales about palaces and beautiful princesses.[19] There is no indication that the "tall, proud, white woman" was her mother, so she cannot be a reliable clue to Amy's race and class. And yet, the fact that Amy lived with her and was treated as a daughter may account for Amy's preadoption self-identification as white and privileged. We learn that Amy "had almost no dealings with colored people and she knew absolutely none of the class to which Mrs. Boldin belonged" (2). She, however, demonstrates awareness of racial difference and identifies herself as white. When the white woman takes her to meet her new family, Amy asks "Am I going to be colored now?" (2). Amy's question suggests her unconscious understanding of racial categories as constructed and dependent not necessarily on an individual's skin color, but rather on kinship ties, shared domesticity, and proximity to black or white bodies.

Her adoption experience leaves Amy with a complex entanglement of racial and class (self)identifications, often unconscious, that determine her actions. She is growing up in a lower middle-class black family, but is living in a romantic dream fueled by memories of the fairy tales read to her by the white woman and by movies.[20] Since she is adopted, "she [is] always living in some sort of story" dreaming of romantic love and a luxurious life, probably compensating for a change in her environment (2). Although Amy acquiesces to her being colored, her vicarious living through heroines of fairy tales and movies and her own white face in the mirror support her (at least partial) self-identification as white. Conveniently the mystery of her birth could justify any racial affiliation. Amy grows up sheltered from racism and does not manifest awareness of the incongruities of her racial identity. She is surprisingly unselfconscious when perceived as white by a saleswoman in a department store and as black by people who know her family. Such fluid racial (self)identification nurtures Amy's awareness of the arbitrariness and social nature of racial categories. She, however, learns the value of being white when she realizes that exciting lives of her favorite movie stars happen to white women and in places different from where her adoptive family lives.

When Amy decides to run away from home, she is not planning to pass and disassociate herself from her black adoptive relatives. It is clear that she does not want to sever ties to her family because when she is dreaming of her wonderful future, it is not only of clothes, men, and infinite possibilities for entertainment, but also about money for her adoptive parents and college for her adoptive brother. But she feels that to fulfill her romantic dreams she "must get out in the world" (5), and inevitably her desires can be satisfied only if her white body is removed from the black bodies of her adoptive kin and their familial connection is silenced. Amy internalizes the segregationist ideology by which society operates and, having options, chooses to live in New York as a white woman.

Staging the upcoming sentimental awakening of her heroine, Fauset emphasizes Amy's emotional aloofness and "unfired" nature (5). She attributes Amy's not feeling "pangs of separation" from her adoptive family or remorse for running away to her adoption experience "when as a tiny child she was taken from that so different home and left at Mrs. Boldin's" (5). Amy is not cruel or disrespectful, but "cold" and "fastidious," unable to feel deeply for others (5). Because she does not feel attached to the Boldins or possess a racial consciousness, Amy easily accepts her white patron Zora's assumptions about her being an illegitimate child of a wealthy white family and passes. She does not yet "grasp at all the infamy of exploitation of self," mainly because of her indifference and an absence of racial discrimination experience (7). Amy's desire for upward mobility and her lack of self-reflection make possible her marriage to Stuart Wynne, a wealthy retired broker and a racist. This marriage, or rather its dissolution after Amy's confession of her passing, becomes an enlightening experience for Amy, who is provoked into developing a sense of racial identity and into an understanding of socio-political mechanisms that determine access to social privilege.

Although Amy is not happy about her husband's racism, she does not experience it directly because she does not think of herself as black. Amy's decision to identify herself as colored is a sentimental gesture provoked by the empathy she feels toward a black valet abused by Wynne. "[B]oth surprised and frightened" by the sympathy she feels towards the valet, especially as she "had held so aloof from other people's interests all these years," Amy decides that her reaction is prompted by her being colored. She says, "I *feel* it inside of me. I must be or I couldn't care so about Stephen" (23). Amy compares Stephen to her adoptive brother Cornelius of whom "she would think almost maternally" (11) and experiences her sympathy for Stephen as a familial, consanguine feeling. Living in a society that limits the exchange of sympathy between white and black people, Amy naively racializes and essentializes her feelings. She is able to come to terms with the sentiment that she deems publicly impossible for a white woman only by privatizing and familializing it and later by reimagining her racial subject position.

Witnessing the hard-heartedness of her own husband and her white patron Zora, Amy comes to a conclusion that her own "persistently kind and unexacting" nature is probably due to "some racial distinction woven in with the stuff of which she was formed" (22). Amy conceives of racial difference not in terms of corporeality, but personality. The whiteness of her skin, and lack of sociopolitical, insight allow Amy to disengage racial distinctions from the bodily difference and divide people into two "racial" groups on the basis of their inner qualities:

> There were two divisions of people in the world—on the one hand insatiable desire for power; keenness, mentality; a vast and cruel pride. On the other there was ambition, it is true, but modified, a certain humble sweetness, too much inclination to trust, an unthinking, unswerving loyalty. All the advantages in the world accrued to the first division. But without bitterness she chose the second. (22–23)

Since she is placing her racial identification in a sentimental context, Amy cannot grasp the meaning of race as a socially constructed category that regulates access to socially mobile and empowering identities. Even after separation, she believes that Wynne's feelings for her can redeem their marriage. Only a full understanding of the discrepancy between her romantic expectations and the reality of her marriage gives her courage to reject Wynne and establish herself as a self-reliant professional with a strong sense of identity.

When Amy marries Wynne, he gives her access to the upper-class lifestyle. She knows she does not love him, but she has been waiting for a Prince Charming all her life to save her from a dreary existence, and Wynne fulfills her expectations. Well-prepared by her childhood fantasies for the role of a middle-class married woman, Amy accepts her husband's patronizing; she is content to be "like a well-cared for, sleek, house-pet, delicately nurtured, velvety, content to let her days pass by" (11). Although she has a vague suspicion that she "is driving a bargain," Amy feels that her beauty entitles her to all the benefits her marriage brings. She is taking Wynne's feelings for granted and does not understand their union as a social contract. When after their divorce Wynne claims that she "sold" herself in marriage because she did not love him then, Amy is surprised and hurt by the inconvenient truth. Amy's romantic fantasies are broken as she suddenly understands the transactional nature of marriage and its investment in social inequalities. Although she is ready to reunite with her ex-husband after their divorce, her hopes of reinstatement as a wife are frustrated by Wynne, who offers her no more than concubinage. Amy is offended by the suggestion of her licentiousness and helplessness, when Wynne predicts that she is "bound to fall to some white man" (20), because she will not receive alimony and cannot hope for the same class status living as a colored person. When Amy realizes that Wynne dares to offer her an illicit sexual relationship because he immediately downgraded her (in line with the racist beliefs of the time) from a respectable middle-class wife to an immoral and impure colored woman, she begins to see that their conflict as "actuated by something more than mere sex antagonism, there [is] *race* antagonism there—two elements clashing" (22).

By asking Amy to become his lover, Wynne clearly communicates that, being a colored woman, Amy does not have the right or hope to be his kin. She still can maintain a relationship with a white man and live on his money, but she cannot inherit his wealth or bear his name or his legitimate children. After the divorce, Amy loses social status granted to a white woman in marriage; the doors of an upper-class domestic space are shut in her face. And it does not matter that Amy looks white; her (invented!) genealogy defines the color of her skin and limits her access to socioeconomic privilege implied in kinship with a rich white man. But Amy does not grasp at first that by proclaiming her blackness she endangers not only her social status but also her body, which is immediately commodified and recast as open to sexual advances of a white man. Her beauty does not inspire love in Wynne anymore—only lust and contempt are left. Amy understands that to her ex-husband she has become just another body on an auction block.

Such development of events, although surprising to Amy, proves to be logical given the sociocultural context of her marriage. In the post-Reconstruction period, one of the main functions of the American family, as an institution vital to the maintenance of social hierarchies, was reproduction of racial difference and white patriarchy. Miscegenation taboos, which prohibited establishing familial ties across the color line, controlled sexuality and reproductive desire of black and white men and women and served as an additional barrier to social mobility of African Americans. Although the abolition of slavery removed a legal divide between black and white Americans, it strengthened vicarious segregation mechanisms that regulated reproduction of white and black identities. Unreliability of visible race markers in a society with a history of interracial sexual liaisons caused a heightened awareness of genealogies. The "one-drop rule" applied to separate black and white bodies was based on genealogical criterion "concerned with origins and lineages of reproduction" rather than on "identifying and securing difference on and/or in the body itself."[21] The fact that Fauset's and Chopin's heroines' attempts for membership in the white domesticity fail as soon as their racial purity is questioned reveals that in a patriarchal racialized society the segregationist politics of racism notably relies on the genealogical criterion for regulating access to social privilege. However, ancestry or progeny cannot always be a reliable indicator of one's race. Using adoption as a plot element, Chopin and Fauset provide a compelling example of the arbitrariness of the genealogical criterion and its investment in racist ideology.

In "The Sleeper Wakes," adoption emphasizes the opportunistic character of racial identities in a segregated society and subverts both biological and genealogical criteria of racial identification. In the absence of genealogical knowledge, Amy's blackness can be proved neither by visible signs nor by known blood relatives. Amy's racial identity is constructed through reverse logic. She is not placed with a black family because she is proven to be black; she is invented as black because she has been placed with a black family. Wynne believes Amy's confession only when she reasons with him saying that if she were white she would have never been removed from a white family to be put next to the black bodies of her adoptive parents. The representation of both biological and genealogical criteria as irrelevant may suggest that when biology and genealogy fall short, racialization happens by association, based on proximity of bodies.[22] Amy is read as white among the whites, whereas in the black community, being one of the Boldins, she is automatically perceived as a mulatta. Social institutions may have labeled her "colored" just to be on the safe side and to prevent her possibly black blood from mixing with white bloodlines. Amy's ambiguous genealogy equates her with the disadvantaged social group and bodes downward mobility.

Unlike Chopin, Fauset does not subject her character to childbirth, which could provide an (albeit unreliable) clue to her past. Instead, Fauset allows her protagonist to exercise free will in choosing her identity if only to the extent possible in a racist environment. As a statement of her independence and disregard for the externals, Amy decides not to reconstruct her genealogy and confirm her race, but idealistically decides to be a "citizen of the world" (25). She reinstates kinship ties with her adoptive black family, but does not want a race consciousness, black or white. She cannot completely reject the advantages of her white skin color in a racist society. Her immediate plans are centered around her own dressmaking business, with rich white women as primary clientele. She may even need to pass again for the sake of her career, but she does not want to confirm her whiteness because "there would always be people urging her to keep up the silliness of racial prestige" (25).

Amy's decision to forfeit the knowledge of her ancestry defies political struggle against inequality in favor of sentimental identification. Following a convention of nineteenth-century adoption narratives, described by Marianne Novy, "[t]urning away from a rich but cold world" Amy "chooses the group that is more oppressed, whether because of class or poverty . . . or race/ethnicity" and represents "heritage with spiritual value as preferable to heritage with material value."[23] Amy's choice to be colored is not portrayed by Fauset as political, just as her revolt against her husband's cruelty was a sentimental gesture rather than conscious political resistance. Even though she is planning to *some day* "work and help *with* [emphasis mine] colored people," her desire to work for the betterment of black community is vague.[24] She feels the affinity with African Americans because they are "the only ones who have really cared for and wanted" her and offered her the ties of kinship, which to her, an adoptee, are extremely important (24). By accepting the black part of her identity Amy chooses to be a member of a family. Her coming home, contingent upon recognition of blackness as part of her identity, promises her an acceptance into the domestic sphere, which was denied to her by Wynne on the basis of her race. The fact that her adoptive kinship with the Boldins is based on affection and not on consanguinity emphasizes the voluntarism of her self-identification as black, and although for Amy her racial homecoming is not an intended political declaration, it is a form of resistance. The reinstatement of familial ties, which she had to sever having become a part of the white world, affirms her right to be a part of a family.

Thus, although Amy's kinship with Wynne does not survive due to her ambiguous descent, she is not portrayed as a victim of genealogical confusion and white patriarchy. Fauset offers an alternative to the classic tragic mulatta story in which, according to Susan Gillman, "the conventions of the search for origins and the revelation of kinship result in fearful exposure, with identity destroyed rather than affirmed."[25] Although ultimately adoptive status and whiteness of skin do not offer Amy infinite possibilities to experiment with her subject position, they give her relative freedom of self-identification and movement between black and white communities. Unlike Desiree, she survives the reversal of her racial identity and rejection by her white husband. Her experience on both sides of the color line gives her strength to stand up against the power of patriarchy and establish herself as an independent professional. Whereas Chopin shows the depth of despair of a disempowered woman in a racialized patriarchal society, Fauset offers a model for resisting paternalistic assignments of racial and social status. Still, Amy has to face social consequences of her choice. Her kinship in the end is restricted to her black family and her reproductive possibilities remain unclear, even though she is not destroyed socially or physically by the implications of her racial identification. Fauset's withholding from her protagonist the experience of childbirth, although it could be read as supportive of Amy's feminist individualism and independence, may as well signal the usual fate of a biracial character—truncated reproduction of a mixed/ambiguous identity.

Domestic fiction concerned with family dynamics and kinship structures became a prominent genre for exploring sociopolitical implications of interracial relations in the post-Reconstruction era. For the emancipated black population the legal right to kinship, voluntary reproduction, and ownership of children was synonymous with social empowerment and successful participation in the body politic of the nation. The history of exclusions of black Americans from full citizenship is the history of preventing them from establishing and maintaining kinship structures. Slavery, which turned the black body into a commodity, precluded African Americans from building families modeled on the example of white domesticity by forbidding slaves to marry and by freely breaking up mother/child bonds. The abolition of slavery meant for a large number of freed African Americans not only personal mobility but also the ability to (re)create family ties destroyed by decades of bondage. It is, however, important to remember that the emancipatory power of domesticity depended on belonging to the privileged race and social class and was widely unavailable to the black population. Even middle-class African American families did not have the power to escape segregation and social stigma of race. The politics of segregation limited kinship and reproductive choices of black (and white) Americans to members of their racial group. Domestic arrangements controlled by the taboo of miscegenation helped to keep African Americans disenfranchised and safely contained, ideologically, in their own imaginary community and, territorially, in racially homogenous domestic spaces.

The black patriarchal desire and black female aspirations to empowering domesticity incessantly frustrated by the politics of racial discrimination, made passing a lucrative possibility to those who could cross the color line due to the whiteness of their skin as they claimed their privilege on a higher level as a member of a white family. Numerous stories of passing, unexpected genealogical discoveries, and disastrous reemergence of black blood in white families reflect the anxiety over miscegenation in the post-Reconstruction national imagination. Racial mingling with newly freed slaves, and the possibility for a black body to enter the realm of white domesticity, exacerbated this angst. Traditionally the passing narrative unmasks the arbitrariness of racial identity and its importance as a tool, which controls access to empowering social positions. The analysis of the combination of passing and adoption themes in Kate Chopin's "Desiree's Baby" and Jessie Fauset's "The Sleeper Wakes" reveals the importance of the genealogical criterion in racial identity formation and draws attention to the role of family in maintaining racial segregation. These stories of familial in/exclusions of passers with ambiguous genealogy exemplify how in a racialized, segregationist post-Reconstruction society, kinship politics developed to confine black and white bodies to separate domestic spaces and to assure the reproduction of racial difference and social inequality through the institution of family.

Notes

1. Werner Sollors, *Beyond Ethnicity: Consent and Descent in American Culture* (New York: Oxford University Press, 1986), 151.

2. Betsy Erkkila, *Mixed Bloods and Other Crosses: Rethinking American Literature from the Revolution to the Culture Wars* (Philadelphia: University of Pennsylvania Press, 2005), 7.

3. Although Desiree's adoptive mother summons Desiree back "home to Valmonde" (1610), we cannot be sure that Desiree is fully accepted even as a member of her adoptive family. She remains "nameless" until her marriage, and it is unclear if her adoptive father supports Madame Valmonde's decision to take her back.

4. Domesticity, although often understood as a private "woman's sphere," has been examined by several scholars as a site of political empowerment for both men and women (Kaplan, "Manifest Domesticity," 1998; Tate, *Domestic Allegories* 1992). In the post-Reconstruction era, newly freed African Americans were simultaneously encouraged to emulate white domesticity and barred from participating in it as equals.

5. Elaine K. Ginsberg, "Introduction: The Politics of Passing," in *Passing and the Fictions of Identity* (Durham: Duke University Press, 1996), 16.

6. Although the trope of a child's body as evidence is not limited to narratives with female passing protagonists, male passers are usually represented as having more control over their reproduction and its consequences. White racial identities of male passing characters in, for instance, *The Autobiography of an Ex-Colored Man* by James Weldon Johnson, *The House Behind the Cedars* by Charles Chesnutt, and *Black No More* by George Schuyler, are threatened by childbirth, but the passing men are portrayed as successful manipulators of the color line rather than its victims. The narratives may briefly mention their success in reproducing whiteness without dwelling on their fears, anticipation, and the actual scene of childbirth, or show male passers empowered by their assumed racial and gender status to accuse their wives of the racial transgression.

7. Laura Dawkins, "Black Babies, White Hysteria: the Dark Child in African-American Literature of the Harlem Renaissance," in *The American Child: a Cultural*

Studies Reader, ed. Caroline E. Levander and Carol J. Singley (New Brunswick, NJ: Rutgers University Press, 2003), 169–70.

8. Having come to this conclusion independently, I later discovered a similar reading in Margaret Bauer, "Armand Aubigny, Still Passing After All These Years: The Narrative Voice and Historical Context of *Desiree's Baby*," in *Critical Essays on Kate Chopin*, ed. Alice Hall Petry (New York: Hall, 1996).

9. Kate Chopin, "Desiree's Baby," in *The Norton Anthology of American Literature*, ed. Nina Baym. 6th shorter ed. (New York: Norton, 2003), 1609.

10. Margaret Bauer, "Armand Aubigny, Still Passing after All These Years: The Narrative Voice and Historical Context of *Desiree's Baby*," in *Critical Essays on Kate Chopin*, ed. Alice Hall Petry. (New York: Hall, 1996), 165.

11. Ibid., 167.

12. E.g., Charles Chesnutt's *A* House *Behind the Cedars.*

13. Gertrude, Clare, and Irene's conversation in Nella Larsen's *Passing* (168) provides a compelling example of such double standard. The complicity of Gertrude's white family in her passing shows the relativity of the color line which can be readjusted privately as long as it does not threaten to upset the dominant public discourse of racial segregation. The fact that Gertrude is still threatened by the possible visible blackness of her children indicates the limits of her white family's acceptance and shows the importance of secrecy that veils mixed genealogies, which subvert the established color hierarchy.

14. Chopin, "Desiree's Baby," 1609.

15. Julia M. Fabi, *Passing and the Rise of the African American Novel* (Chicago: University of Illinois Press, 2001), 3.

16. Teresa C. Zachodnik, *The Mulatta and the Politics of Race* (Jackson: University Press of Mississippi, 2004), xi.

17. Ibid.

18. Dawkins, "Black Babies."

19. Jessie Redmon Fauset, "The Sleeper Wakes," in *The Sleeper Wakes: Harlem Renaissance Stories by Women*, ed. Marcy Knopf (New Brunswick, NJ: Rutgers University Press, 1993), 2.

20. Deborah McDowell addresses Fauset's portrayal of the fairy tale as a tool for socializing women into their traditional gender roles in "The Neglected Dimensions of Jessie Redmon Fauset," *Afro-Americans in New York Life and History* 5, no. 2 (1981): 33–49.

21. Richard Dyer, *White* (New York: Routledge, 1997), 20.

22. Passing, a successful concealment of blackness, depends on inserting the white body of the passer into the white background, where it cannot stand out. In literature, outings of passers often happen when they can be seen next to their black relatives' bodies.

23. Marianne Novy, *Reading Adoption: Family and Difference in Fiction and Drama* (Ann Arbor: University of Michigan Press, 2005), 145.

24. Fauset, "The Sleeper Wakes," 24.

25. Susan Gillman, "The Mulatto, Tragic or Triumphant?" 229.

Works Cited

Bauer, Margaret. "Armand Aubigny, Still Passing after All These Years: The Narrative Voice and Historical Context of *Desiree's Baby*." In *Critical Essays on Kate Chopin*. Edited by Alice Hall Petry. New York: Hall, 1996.

Chopin, Kate. "Desiree's Baby." In *The Norton Anthology of American Literature*. Edited by Nina Baym. 6th shorter ed. New York: Norton, 2003.

Dawkins, Laura. "Black Babies, White Hysteria: The Dark Child in African-American Literature of the Harlem Renaissance." In *The American Child: a Cultural Studies Reader*. Edited by Caroline E. Levander and Carol J. Singley. New Brunswick, NJ: Rutgers University Press, 2003.

Erkkila, Betsy. *Mixed Bloods and Other Crosses: Rethinking American Literature from the Revolution to the Culture Wars*. Philadelphia: University of Pennsylvania Press, 2005.

Fabi, Julia M. *Passing and the Rise of the African American Novel*. Chicago: University of Illinois Press, 2001.

Fauset, Jessie Redmon. "The Sleeper Wakes." In *The Sleeper Wakes: Harlem Renaissance Stories by Women*. Edited by Marcy Knopf. New Brunswick, NJ: Rutgers University Press, 1993. First published in *The Crisis* (August–October 1920).

Gillman, Susan. "The Mulatto, Tragic or Triumphant? The Nineteenth-Century American Race Melodrama." *The Culture of Sentiment*, ed. Shirley Samuels. N.Y.: Oxford University Press, 1992, p. 221–43.

Ginsberg, Elaine K. *Passing and the Fictions of Identity*. Durham, NC: Duke University Press, 1996.

Kaplan, Amy. "Manifest Domesticity," *American Literature* 70 (1998): 581–606.

Larsen, Nella. *Passing*. In *Quicksand and Passing*. Edited by Deborah E. McDowell. American Women Writers Series. New Brunswick, NJ: Rutgers University Press, 1986.

Novy, Marianne. *Reading Adoption: Family and Difference in Fiction and Drama*. Ann Arbor: University of Michigan Press, 2005.

Sollors, Werner. *Neither Black nor White Yet Both: Thematic Explorations of Interracial Literature*. New York: Oxford University Press, 1997.

———. *Beyond Ethnicity: Consent and Descent in American Culture*. New York: Oxford University Press, 1986.

Tate, Claudia. *Domestic Allegories of Political Desire: The Black Heroine's Text at the Turn of the Century*. New York: Oxford University Press, 1992.

Zackodnik, Teresa C. *The Mulatta and the Politics of Race*. Jackson: University Press of Mississippi, 2004.

III

Body/Language: Visions and Revisions

The Body against Itself in Faulkner's Phenomenology of Race

Laura Doyle

CIVIL WAR WITHIN THE BODY OF THE NATION: A LIVING ENTITY under siege from itself yet constituting itself in the process. The history of Anglo-America unfolds through just such violent internal rupture: Parliament against King, British America against Britain, South against North.[1] Meanwhile, the bodies that together form the postbellum nation's body in the United States, be they native American, immigrant, or exslave, likewise suffer betrayal from within—exiled physically from home and past yet haunted by them in memory. Often these bodies literally trek north- or westward, against themselves and out of community, feeling the pull of return and reunion in the movement of departure.

In *Light in August*, William Faulkner dramatizes this tragic movement of a body—national and human—founded on its own splitting, its failed flight from itself, the novel enacting in its narrative form the folded-over and captive relation of the body to itself.[2] Many critics have noted the looping structure of *Light in August*, especially the way we learn of Joanna Burden's death, meet Joe Christmas, and then loop back to learn about their histories. Here I will emphasize the novel's fundamental loop*hole* or slippage of self-coherence that mirrors the ontological rupture of the racialized body in the South, which itself reiterates the traumatic crossing of liberty and slavery in the nation's body.

Light in August exposes race as the phantom that both promises and withdraws the body's unity—and the nation's. The novel reveals, on the one hand, how race in the United States disciplines bodily self-relation and choreographs from within a fateful plot for the body's movements; yet on the other hand, Faulkner's text exposes race as an empty category, undefinable and unverifiable, projected onto the "coloured" or "white" body from outside. A tyrannical phantom, race in *Light in August* lurks between the categories of real and imagined, history and nature, black and white, thus inhabiting what Merleau-Ponty theorizes as the body's chiasm.

Understanding this ghostly, doubled body by way of both Merleau-Ponty's phenomenological vocabulary and W.E.B. DuBois's discussion of the black American's "double-consciousness," and focusing on how the processes of social projection and interpellation take up and exploit this doubleness, this chapter reads Faulkner's novel as a guide to our ongoing entanglement in the snarled legacies of violence, the body, and the South. Ultimately I will suggest that Faulkner anchors these legacies in the reader. He captures, not necessarily consciously, the defensive turn in the (national) body's self-relation, witnessed again in the implicated acts of writing and reading.

A Slip of the Gun

Light in August opens with Lena Grove's reflections on the strange motions of time as lived by human consciousness. Because Lena anticipates the arrival of the wagon on which she expects to hitch a ride, "*it will be*," she thinks, "*as if I were riding for half a mile before I even got into the wagon, before the wagon even got to where I was waiting, and that when the wagon is empty of me again it will go on for a half mile with me still in it.*"[3] Lena goes on to correlate this pregnant and doubled experience of time with her own state of pregnancy and her task of tracking down the child's father, Lucas Burch. She imagines that there will be a triumphant moment of convergence of past, present, and future when she and Burch meet: "He will hear the wagon but he won't know. So there will be one within his hearing before his seeing. And then he will see me and he will be excited. And so there will be two within his seeing before his remembering."[4] And then, she implies, there will be union and closure.

But this is exactly what the novel never allows. The man Lena first approaches thinking she has found Lucas Burch turns out to be Byron Bunch, and when Lucas Burch finally sees Lena, she has already given birth (and holds the baby in her arms); he quickly escapes out the window. The novel's whole narrative, in fact, arcs along a looping structure with just such an escape hatch or window, by way of which a body disappears and then reappears in the polis, in a nation's social script, as other to itself.

The central loophole moment in *Light in August* is the so-called murder scene, which is of course also the culmination of Joe Christmas's racially fated life.[5] We approach this scene three times, but three times the key event is eclipsed. We enter first with Lena as she arrives in the town of Jefferson, sees the smoke of Joanna Burden's burning house, and hears of her death. Then we turn back abruptly in chapter

5 to the night before the event, and we approach it again. We follow Joe's actions up until the following night when he walks toward Joanna's house, thinking, "*Something is going to happen to me.*"[6] Yet for the reader, this "something" has already happened; we have already lived through it in our knowing—like Lena riding in the wagon before it arrives.

After a chapter break and narrative cut, we loop back dramatically to Joe as a five-year-old boy and, in the next six chapters, live through events of his earlier life; in chapter 12, we arrive again at the scene of the crime. Now we come closer. We are in Joanna's bedroom; Joe has entered with razor in hand but has set it down to light the lamp. We hear her ask him to pray once more and listen to him say no three times; we watch him as he watches her pull out the revolver and shoot: "he was watching when the cocked shadow of the hammer flicked away."[7] We almost arrive at closure, bringing the long past to its endpoint. Yet as the gun's hammer flicks and misses, so the present slips, the text slips, and we find ourselves in the moment *after* the murder scene at the opening of the next chapter. We are "standing in the middle of the road" with Joe, who is holding the revolver that a moment before was aimed at him.[8] We have arrived again at the climax but again we miss the essential moment. It has slipped from the fiction's grasp.

The present-tense moment that the death scene should represent thus operates instead as the slippage point at the center of the novel, signaling many other gaps or textual loopholes, especially the "missing piece" in our knowledge about the racial identity of Joe Christmas.[9] The gap in Joe's identity is itself a function of two other offstage scenes of violence—the deaths of his mother and his father, both of them killed, in effect, by Joe's grandfather, Doc Hines. These murders leave untraceable Joe's race. And, of course, this missing piece functions as the blank moment on the screen onto which others project a racial lineage. The novel is a circle that returns repeatedly to these points of slippage; in particular, the narrative elides Joe's violent point of origin within such missing moments, while also unfolding from exactly this elision.

In this way and in others, Faulkner reveals how the anticipatory interval of being-in-time, epitomized in Lena's "body-waiting-for-wagon," can get snagged by, or taken up by, a social order that uses this span of time as a point of coercive entry into the body's self-relation. In other words, Faulkner shows how an existential lag, inherent to the doubled body, leaves an opening in being that social signs, and nations, urgently enter, splitting the body into two terms or poles, opposed and ranked: white over black, man over woman, sign over body.

To clarify Faulkner's rendering of this colonized lag in bodily being requires, itself, a brief cut or lag, a move in this essay away from the novel so as to reenter it again by way of the world that surrounds and exceeds it.

The Inside Called Out

One of the primary things a body knows is itself, quite sensorially. Toni Morrison's rendering in *The Bluest Eye* of Claudia's fondness for each of her scars, her intimacy with her scabs, delights in exactly this: the body's small acts of self-touching. In Merleau-Ponty's phenomenological description, "The body . . . is not itself a thing, an interstitial matter, a connective tissue, but a *sensible for itself*."[10] Or again, "Our body is a being of two leaves, from one side a thing among things and otherwise what sees and touches them."[11] Thus "when one of my hands touches the other, the world of each opens upon the other because the operation is reversible at will," and this is so "because they . . . are the hands of the same body."[12] Within the "circle of the touched and the touching," neither the sameness of the one body nor the difference of the two parts but rather both of these together open up a world—literally a span of time and space—within this circle.[13] Our dimensionality in time and space is given forth by this bodily morphology. Each body is in this sense two bodies, or "two leaves"—or a kind of double helix where two opposite sides of one ribbon touch and describe a circle of time and space, a here and now, an entry into worldness.

Or, rather, in the case of the animate human body, *almost* touch, *almost* close into a circle, and this almostness is equally essential to the possibility of worldness. The slippage moment is the hyphen in self-touching. Merleau-Ponty is right, I think, when he emphasizes that there is always a difference or noncoincidence (*écart*) at the heart of this meeting between a body and itself. He describes it this way: "If my left hand is touching my right hand, and if I should suddenly wish to apprehend with my right hand the work of my left hand as it touches, this reflection of the body upon itself always miscarries at the last moment: the moment I feel my left hand with my right hand, I correspondingly cease touching my right hand with my left hand."[14] At the moment when the body verges on closure with itself, closure of the "circle of the touched and the touching," there is what he calls a "brief torsion," for "Never does the perception grasp the body in the act of perceiving."[15]

Yet in this torsion, which he also compares to a chiasmus or inverted parallelism of self with self, there is both decentering *and* possibility: "[T]his incessant escaping . . . this hiatus between my right hand touching and my right hand touched . . . is not an ontological void, a non-being." Instead, "if these experiences never overlap, if they slip away at the very moment they are about to rejoin, if there is always a 'shift,' a 'spread' between them, this is precisely because my hands are two parts of the same body, because it moves itself in the world, because I hear myself from both within and without."[16] In short, the chiasm of the body entails an existential condition in which "I am from the start outside myself and open to the world."[17] I am not so much a corporeal as an intercorporeal phenomenon, even for myself.

Yet for Joe Christmas, as for all marginalized or marked persons, this meeting of the self as something already-in-the-world, this coming to the self "from without" as well as within, leaves him vulnerable to the world's denigration of him and his body: in his case, the world first enters and takes up his body with the sign "nigger bastard" and so taints and makes violent this self-relation. With this vulnerability in mind, we can add an ontological accent to W.E.B. DuBois's seminal remarks on the black American's "double-consciousness, this sense of always looking at one's self through the eyes of others," which issues in "two souls, two thoughts, two unreconciled strivings . . . in one dark body."[18] Fictionalizing and corporealizing what DuBois so starkly names, Faulkner traces in this novel how the chiasmatic or folded-over processes of embodiment can dovetail destructively with the political interests of the human community. More precisely, they dovetail with the process of what Marxist theorist Louis Althusser calls "interpellation." Borrowing from the use of the term in government, whereby the proceedings of a government chamber are interrupted so that a minister can be questioned, Althusser develops the idea of interpellation as a kind of societal calling out by which the self becomes a social subject, for this self is called to occupy or answer to a certain position in the social order. For Althusser, this hailing of the self into social subjectivity is instantaneous: in fact, one is always already called out, so that one identifies one's position within the ideological order with one's *self*.[19]

I am emphasizing that one's identification of self with a social designation works as successfully as it does because of the way the calling intrudes into and usurps the chiasmatic bodily self-relation. Because the hands are sensible as well as sentient, and because the two touch but never quite meet, corporeal self-relation is a circle with a loophole, and that loophole is the outsideness of oneself that belongs to the world: interpellation enters *here*.

Light in August specifically dramatizes this interpellating interruption when the five-year-old orphan Joe gorges himself on toothpaste. Extending the observations of Philip Weinstein about interpellation in this scene, I suggest that this process takes root precisely in the chiasmatic opening in Joe and in turn entangles all the other characters in the novel.[20] In the well-known passage, Joe discovers a tube of sweet toothpaste in the dietitian's room, and it becomes his secret indulgence to sneak into her room and eat from it. One day the dietitian enters unexpectedly with one of the young interns and Joe quickly hides behind a curtain. Despite the dietitian's protestations and her urgent concern about being caught, she and the intern begin to make love. Joe is of course ignorant of the meaning of their moans and whispers, preoccupied instead with being caught himself. Cornered, he keeps eating toothpaste against the warnings of both his stomach and his sense of danger. The experience draws him deeply inside, into a heightened bodily self-relation: "He was not hearing anything at all now. Very likely he would not have heard a gunshot beyond the curtain. He seemed to be turned in upon himself, watching himself sweating, watching himself smear another worm of paste into his mouth which his stomach did not want. . . . Motionless now, utterly contemplative, he seemed to stoop above himself like a chemist in his laboratory, waiting." Joe feels the vomit rise and, apprehending his "caughtness" in this moment of self-involvement, he "watch[es] with astonished fatalism for what was about to happen to him." This watching pause is the anticipatory pause inherent to the ontological condition in which one belongs both to oneself and to a world, in particular a world that directs its mode of surveillance and discipline toward that condition. When Joe vomits, when his insides are expelled into the outside, he is discovered and named by the dietitian: " '[Y]ou little rat! Spying on me! You little nigger bastard!"[21]

This is the moment that will stay with Joe Christmas all his life, in the shed with the black girl, in his first sex with the waitress, in his relation to Joanna Burden, provoking him to repulsion and violence: it is the moment that, as the narrator says at the opening of this chapter, "memory believes before knowing remembers." The phrase captures the process by which the interpellated self is felt as *the* self, the self-relating self. The moment in which Joe "turn[s] in upon" himself gets dramatically and bewilderingly colonized, taken up into a Southern script. Thus, long before and long after conscious knowing directs his idea of himself, Joe "believes" in the sign "nigger bastard." His very intimacy with his body has been woven into that sign. In the dietitian's naming of him, his body is brought in by being cast out.

And it is no coincidence—in fact, it is crucial—that from the dietitian's side, this is a moment of *sexual* transgression, that she, too, is concerned about being caught by authorities. The creation of this scene suggests Faulkner's grasp of the complex social drama he represents. The order that calls out Joe through the dietitian as a "nigger bastard" has already called out the dietitian by way of a set of corollary terms—something like "white woman subject to sexual policing." The face-off between the dietitian and Joe indicates the interdependence of sexual and racial ideologies: one order depends on and "calls out" the other.[22] In fact, the order into which Joe is now being interpellated has already so fully taken up the dietitian that, from within it, she projects onto him a will to capture and expose her that in turn leads *her* to participate crucially in society's interpellation of him. She becomes paranoid about him. (For weeks after this scene "she could seem to look nowhere and be nowhere without finding the child watching her," and even at night "always against her eyelids or upon her retinae was that still grave, inescapable parchment coloured face watching her.")[23] She concludes that she must cast him out to save herself, and indeed the logic of the South's racial patriarchy tells her that she can stake her salvation on his ruin. Tipping off the matron about Joe's supposed lineage, she makes sure he gets sent away; and so he lives the rest of his childhood with Mr. McEachern, who further inducts him into the discipline of knowing himself through his dissociation from himself.

Catechism/Chiasm

When Joe is adopted by McEachern, he moves fully into a condition of reified embodiment, into the place where ontological slippage within the body becomes fully organized as mastery over or containment of the body's volatile doubleness. In this experience, the promise latent in the "span" of space and time within the body—the pause within which one realizes that anything might happen next, precisely because a "next" *is* manifest in this pause—is deployed for defensive rather than self-creating purposes by means of a tyrannical self-relation, a reification of the fold in being. This reified embodiment is what we witness in the scenes in which McEachern beats eight-year-old Joe because he won't learn his Presbyterian catechism.

When McEachern asks Joe three times "exactly on the dot of the hour" at 8:00 a.m., 9:00 a.m., and 10:00 a.m. on a Sunday morning, "Do you know it now?" "the boy" "did not look up," "did not move"; he sits "rocklike," only answering "No." Likewise, when McEachern leads him out to the stable to whip him, "the boy" follows him "erect," "rigidfaced." Joe is resisting but in order to do so, he is also giving up animate motion and gesture, substituting "rocklike" solidity for the interiority that would leave him vulnerable to the outside: "When the strap fell he did not flinch, no quiver passed over his face. He was looking straight ahead, with a rapt, calm expression like a monk in a picture."[24] No quiver, no flinch—no span, no opening, no slippage; in short, no registering of a bodily self-relation. And yet the irony is that this very rigidity betrays an extraordinary self-relation in the form of bodily self-control. This twist is further implied by the fact that Joe's rigidity mirrors McEachern's. Sharing "a very kinship of stubbornness,"[25] McEachern and Joe both act mechanically and impassively throughout the whipping scenes: "McEachern began to strike methodically, with slow and deliberate force, still without heat or anger. It would have been hard to say which face was the more rapt, more calm, more convinced."[26] Joe's bodily behavior has thus mirrored the catechism's mechanisms of enforcement; he has been a match for it, not succumbing, and yet ironically entering its self-reifying discipline nonetheless.[27] It fixes him for the second time, as the dietitian did the first: now the terms of gender take him up, for "twenty years later memory is still to believe *On this day I became a man*."[28] So by age eight, Joe Christmas is both "nigger bastard" and "man," his very body sutured into the world by these names.

The narrative itself mirrors this discipline and this suturing. It unflinchingly tells the story of interpellation at the site of the body. During the whipping scene as in the earlier orphanage scene, Joe loses his name and becomes "the boy" for the narrator and the reader. In similar moments throughout the novel, the narrator frequently acknowledges the limits of his access to his characters' interiors (particularly Joe's and Joanna's), such as in his remark that "*It would have been hard to say* which face was the more rapt, more calm, more convinced" or when he describes Joe standing ready to be whipped "with pride and *perhaps* despair."[29] In this scene, we want to know if Joe feels despair; we perhaps want to know that he feels *something*, even despair. Here, though, as in many other scenes describing Joe, the narrator can only say "perhaps"; "he," too, is left outside this reified condition of being; it has no opening, even for him. Faulkner has created characters that give him limited access, and that opacity is exactly their drama, a tale of bodies turned against their own chiasmatic openness to others.

In his adulthood Joe repeatedly revives the joined signs of race and man as prompts to violence, as both the point of alienation from himself and a way of experiencing himself in the world—of coming to himself from outside himself: "Sometimes he would remember how he had once tricked or teased white men into calling him a negro in order to fight them, to beat them or be beaten; now [in the North] he fought the negro who called him white."[30] Joe seeks out the experience of beating or being beaten, with race giving him the prompt for these moments. It is his way into the world.

Yet his compulsion to enter the world through violence reaches a crisis, tellingly, via his sexual relations with women in the North. The narrator tells us that when he goes North, crossing the nation's effaced but operative dividing line, and finds out that there are "white women who would take a man with black skin" he goes wild, becomes sick, and "stayed sick for two years."[31] This snag in the primal interpellative segregation of white woman and black man, founded on a vigilant Southern logic of racial purity, leaves Joe ontologically disoriented—nauseated and sick. His point of identity—the trauma of his supposed mixed-blood birth, his very bodily self-relation—has been defined within this either/or position of black and white, and so to be released from that opposition is to be utterly unanchored.

Faulkner Called Out

Faulkner thus acutely narrates the interpellative and violent appropriation of Joe's self-relation. At the same time, his novel betrays its own entanglement in these processes, despite Faulkner's later revisions that make Joe's race uncertain.[32] For the novel sometimes makes seductive the colonization of the body through the sign of race; it expresses a kind of investment in race that reminds us of the author's own visceral and historical embeddedness in race, as in the lyricized rhetoric of "white blood" and "black blood," of "white being" and "black being" that runs through several key scenes, including Joe's walk through Freedman's Town. Yet just as Joe remains inscrutable in the whipping scenes, so *Faulkner as author of the novel* remains unreadable in any conclusive way here. This point, which I'll return to in the conclusion, suggests that art shares ground with, even as it contends for ground against, the culture's calling-out of its subjects. Joe's "rigidfaced" reification of his body veils his investments; so, too, ambiguous narration veils Faulkner's. The conventions of fiction, like the scripts of catechism, submerge the impulses of the author while also channeling them and drawing readers into their current.

The narration of Joe's race feelings reveals the complexity of this submersion, as in the following passage describing a phase in Joe's wandering years when he lives with a black woman in the North:

> He *now lived* as man and wife with a woman who resembled an ebony carving. At night he would lie in bed beside her, sleepless, beginning to breathe

deep and hard. He would do it deliberately, feeling, even watching, his white chest arch deeper and deeper within his ribcage, trying to breathe into himself the dark odor, the dark and inscrutable thinking and being of negroes, each suspiration trying to expel from himself the white blood and the white thinking and being. And all the while his nostrils at the odor which he was trying to make his own would whiten and tauten, his whole being writhe and strain with physical outrage and spiritual denial.[33]

The first thing to note about this passage is that all of it is rendered as Joe's perception as he seeks a racial essence for himself; it is this perception that mediates the author's relation to the essentializing of race. It is apparently Joe himself who imagines the demons that harass him as white being and negro being, and he tries here to turn away from the one and wholly embrace the other. Of course his new strategy to become black will fail too because the whole event is a social fantasy he cannot escape; even in trying to become the "other" race now, he continues to move within the binary of race. The strange and unlocated "now" that opens this passage reinforces this entrapment, perhaps thus hinting at the narrator's ironic witnessing. For "now" marks this phase as an expression of Joe's desire to live in a frieze moment, to transcend the drama of race by finally achieving the fantasy of oneness and racial essence at its heart. But of course, instead, he moves round and round the same circle of himself: "He thought it was loneliness he was trying to escape and not himself. But the street ran on: catlike, one place was the same as another to him. But in none of them could he be quiet."[34] Caught in this incessant drama of escape *from himself*, he is placeless and yet restless, stuck but in constant motion: "He might have seen himself as in numberless avatars, in silence, doomed with motion, driven by the courage of flagged and spurred despair."[35] And this is the basic motion he repeats. The slip of the hinge, the crossing of the span at the heart of being, is caught, for Joe, in an eternal repetition. Time cannot unfold; it is emptied of future and past because it is overdetermined by the social scripts that have normalized the One, the Same, the "always" of race.

So we might say that the narrator simply narrates here, exposing implicitly how the fantasy of purification fails for Joe and deeming him defeated by the already written narrative of race and heredity. Particularly in light of both the missing evidence of Joe's "real" blood lineage and the placing of these desires within Joe's consciousness, this account of Faulkner's story makes sense. Yet it may not be complete. For the narrative's rendering of the fantasy may well serve at the same time to "call out" readers into a racist romance, by echoing racial stereotypes in its emphasis on a dark odor of negro being, by borrowing racial science's ideology of unmixable bloods, and, most tellingly, by emulating in its prose rhythms this insistent syntax of reified being.

In other words, the description of Joe's visceral struggle with race becomes the danger of a racist reader's visceral response to the familiar, essentializing details of race thinking, especially given the history of race in the United States that U.S. readers share with Joe. In the above passage we are faced, like Joe, with a seemingly inexorable binary choice between white and black. The response to this impossible choice no doubt depends on the reader, and yet certainly Faulkner, by omission, allows entry to the reader who accepts race as biological, inexorable, and hierarchical. If we call to mind Faulkner's contemporary white audience, this seduction by the sign of race is all too easy to imagine, and this is a risk with which Faulkner was apparently willing to play. It is only in the novel's larger logic, which quietly leaves a gap where Joe's race should be, that this seeming inexorability is exposed as a projection that follows from prior processes of visceral interpellation.

The novel may, in fact, at once expose and indulge in the fantasy of race-as-fate. It may equivocate; it may even be *about* such equivocations. It may imply that reading fiction, like writing it, feeds on these habitual equivocations. With this implication, Faulkner's novel makes a triple turn, as I'll suggest at the close of this chapter. Yet, first, we must approach this convoluted possibility through the enigmatic figures of Joanna Burden and Gail Hightower.

Joanna Burden: The Ghost of a Prayer

Joanna Burden potentially disrupts and realigns the bodily semiotics of Joe's life, that is, his ontological entry through the signs "nigger bastard" and "man." She helpfully de-races and unmans him. She is the one who pauses over the fact that neither Joe nor anyone else knows who his father was and therefore no one knows Joe's race. He is not necessarily a "nigger." Through Joanna, Faulkner reminds the reader of this uncertainty that is nowhere else reiterated. And because Joanna makes love to Joe with "manlike" gestures, she confuses his sense of who is the man and who the woman in their relationship.[36] At first, in other words, but only at first, Joanna is a counterinterpellating force, to which Joe is drawn. But it may be that he is drawn most deeply to her as a challenge to his fateful ability to reproject his reified self-relation onto others, as her mirroring name suggests. It may be that there is no Joanna at all. As with the matter of race, Faulkner's narrator hints at this hidden loophole in his portrait of Joanna but meanwhile tells the story as if it were hers as much as Joe's.

As readers have noted, Joe's first encounter with Joanna Burden unfolds as a return to birth, to earth, and to mother, which might be read as his longing for a scene of primary self-relation.[37] Waiting for night outside her house on the day he arrives in Jeffferson, he "lay in the copse, on his belly on the dark earth. . . . His arms were crossed, his forehead rested upon them, in his nostrils the damp rich odor of the dark and fecund earth."[38] Folded into himself with crossed arms, his body cradled in a dark curved shape, he returns in gesture to a holding position, a supporting embrace. When he finally enters the house through the window, "he seemed to flow into the dark kitchen: a shadow returning without a sound and without locomotion to the all-mother of obscurity and darkness."[39] Joe is moving backward to a point of origin—even perhaps seeking a new beginning, one that acknowledges a maternal origin or self-origin—or so we might think if we didn't already know better, for Faulkner has already put his loopholed narration between us and Joe's past, put himself between us and Joe, forestalling the hope that self-relation might finally be lived peaceably with other-relation. Nonetheless, by invoking a window from his youth, the narrator at the same time encourages our sense that in this present-tense moment Joe is moving backward: "Perhaps he thought of that other window which he had used to use."[40] This is the window of his bedroom at McEachern's, out of which he first escaped, but now he is climbing back into rather than out of it, as if he were climbing back into himself, to touch himself.

The novel characterizes the sexual relationship that then develops between Joe and Joanna, a single woman living alone in the house, as unfolding in three phases: from a gender-troubling phase wherein Joanna makes love like a man; to a second phase in which she becomes sexually wild and voracious, presumably like a woman; to the final reactionary one in which she invites him to pray for redemption with her. Wishing, apparently, for a child, she also tells him she is pregnant in this last phase, although this announcement, again apparently, turns out to be a fabrication.

Apparently is all one can conclude because we never enter Joanna's consciousness directly throughout these phases. Although the three phases are rendered as if defined by Joanna's perverse, archetypal sexual transformations, the text just hints that, after all, "Joanna" in all her phases is most profoundly the projection of Joe. Readers have noted the descriptions of Joanna's weird sexuality: the "untearful and unselfpitying and almost manlike yielding of the surrender,"[41] or the "spiritual privacy so long intact that its own instinct for preservation had immolated it, its physical phase the strength and fortitude of a man."[42] Yet little attention has been paid to the casting of these descriptions. Many of them are written from within Joe's perception and they often begin with an "as though": "Even after a year it was as though he entered by stealth to despoil her virginity each time anew. It was as though each turn of the dark saw him faced again with the necessity to despoil again that which he had already despoiled—or never had and never would."[43] We might understand these as accounts of the despoliation of Joanna, but both the "as though" phrasing and the content of the descriptions—such as the compulsively repeated "despoiling"—allow us to understand all of this as Joe's originary trauma played out upon a Joanna whose own motives we never glimpse.

Faulkner's use of sentence fragments reinforces this ambiguity of attribution. In the passage describing her "almost manlike yielding," we begin within Joe's memory of Joanna's sexual responses; the two sentences that follow seem at first to stand as neutral narrational descriptions of Joanna, but on closer look, the lack of direct reference to Joanna or even to a "her" and the lack of subject-verb beginnings make these sentences hover unattached, lingering *perhaps* within Joe's perceptions, and potentially even resonating with Joe's past as much as Joanna's: "Sometimes he thought of it that way, remembering the hard, untearful and unselfpitying and almost manlike yielding of that surrender. A spiritual privacy so long intact that its own instinct for preservation had immolated it, its physical phase the strength and fortitude of a man. A dual personality."[44] Such descriptions recall the eight-year-old Joe facing McEachern even as they purport to describe Joanna Burden.

Readers tend to see Joe and Joanna's relationship as a strange symbiosis of two persons whose interdependent histories bring them together to a fatal denouement.[45] But something else emerges when we recall that we know Joanna only through Joe and never experience her from within herself, except in a dialogue that does not square well with Joe's perceptions of her. In this novel about projection onto an absence (the attaching of "nigger" to an elusive threat), Joanna emerges as another ghost figure. More than a doppelg'nger, she is like Beloved in Toni Morrison's novel, one who catalyzes the archaic complexes of others and whose own existence is unworldly.

There is, however, a strange break in this phantasm: that dialogue in which Joanna shares her history with Joe. After a summer-long hiatus in their first frenzied sexual phase, one day Joe finds Joanna sitting on his cot when he enters his cabin. He "stopped in midstride, in complete astonishment."[46] This encounter is something his interpellated body could not have foretold. A true event in his life, perhaps the first, it constitutes a twist in the social drama, a cut or break: something happens.

And now Joanna enters the narrative proper, as a voice beyond Joe's projection. For fifteen pages we hear the story of Joanna's life and ancestors, their settling in Jefferson, the killing of her brother. And although Faulkner's narrator tells the first two-thirds of her story, Joanna tells the last third in a long monologue. This passage fulfills the reader's desire to move out of Joe's consciousness exactly by his entering another's world. In this moment unmediated by Joe, Joanna appears calmly thoughtful. Joe and Joanna ask each other genuine, unfated questions, including Joe's yearning-filled "when do men that have different blood in them stop hating one another?"[47] For the first time, Joe *expresses* dissatisfaction and pain. In a life and a novel that seem to move in a muffled slow-motion world where emotion and reflection fall flat, this scene feels like an awakening, a moment that opens up other possible futures. The conversation ends, moreover, with the admission that has been pressing for voice all along: when Joe tells Joanna he knows nothing of his parents "Except that one of them was part nigger," she asks, "How do you know that?" and he answers, "I don't know it."[48]

In short, this dialogue has a structure of hope rather than despair because time now holds surprise—even if it does so via the telling of how history and ancestry repeat themselves, because it is the telling and the hearing that surprise. Perhaps we have a force to match the pull of interpellation, a force derived from the voice speaking of and from its body, which then turns, listening, toward another's speaking body.[49] Perhaps we have finally met a Southern storytelling that narrates race as *aporia* rather than alibi.

Yet no, it's not so after all. Instead, the next chapter announces: "In this way the second phase began. It was as though he had fallen into a sewer."[50] The momentary purging of racial-sexual myth from the ontological gap, the decolonization of the chiasm by this admission of the unknowability of race and gender as features of the lived body, is not sustained by Joe or the narrative or, apparently, Joanna. The conversation between Joe and Joanna gets named instead as "an act of capitulation" and before long, Joe finds himself again thinking, "*This is not my life. I don't belong here.*"[51] Thus, although now they certainly speak to each other from and about the body, they do so desperately, madly, particularly Joanna: "she insisted on a place for concealing notes, letters";[52] "she had an avidity for the forbidden wordsymbols, an insatiable appetite for the sound of them on his tongue and on her own";[53] and she gives orders ("for a whole week she forced him to climb into a *window* to come to her.")[54]

As usual, the window gives it away.[55] In this novel the window is the threshold crossed by trespassing, as a break-in or break-away. The window, like the one Lena Grove climbs through to meet her fate as an unwed mother, signifies, suggest, a kind of Foucaultian escape into captivity—a captured escape, we might say, wherein the will to be forced, the will to be called out even into subjugation, is already written into the script, the catechism. So the window is the escape hatch that betrays; it is the apparent view into the outside that is actually a reflection of the looker, who is in turn the vehicle of a projection arranged by the social world from "behind" the looker.

We know the projectionary reaction has set in when Joanna becomes so "wild" amidst the "throes of nymphomania" that she breathlessly calls Joe "Negro! Negro! Negro!"[56] The text encourages us to see Joanna as living out her own overdetermined body ("the abject fury of the New England glacier exposed suddenly to the fire of the New England Biblical hell" as well as "actual despair at frustrate and irrevocable years");[57] yet it also deviously continues to confuse her with Joe at a syntactical level. In the following passage, the "dual personality" becomes "two creatures" that sound ever more like the two warring parts of Joe, especially given the absence of clear pronoun reference:

> Perhaps he realised he could not escape. Anyway, he stayed, watching the two creatures that struggled in the one body like two moongleamed shapes struggling drowning in alternate throes upon the surface of a black thick pool beneath the last moon. Now it would be that still, cold, contained figure of the first phase who, even though lost and damned, remained somehow impervious and impregnable; then it would be the other, the second one, who in furious denial of that impregnability strove to drown in the black abyss of its own creating that physical purity which had been preserved too long now even to be lost. Now and then they would come to the black surface, locked like sisters; the black waters would drain away.[58]

These three phases—ostensibly Joanna's—could equally describe Joe's movement from a "cold contained" child into a fighting, "furious" man, and then, finally, into one "locked" in battle with himself. The language here also resonates with earlier descriptions of Joe's struggle with himself in darkness, as in the Freedman town scene. But much more explicit is the closing line of this paragraph: "She would stare at him then with the wild, despairing face of a stranger; *looking at her then he paraphrased himself:* 'She wants to pray, but she don't know how to do that either.'"[59] In describing Joanna, the passage tells us, Joe describes himself; and his sense of this figure as a stranger accords well with his alienated self-relation. The dynamic of projection is fully laid bare as this phase nears its end. First we learn that "[s]he was in his mind so constantly that it was almost as if he were looking at her" so that "[h]e began now to be afraid."[60] The narrator then sums up the drama: "Thus he put his belief, his fear of what she might do, into his own mind by believing that he had put it into hers."[61]

Prayer, we learn, is crucial to this dynamic of projection, and it might be understood as its inscape. In Emmanuel Levinas's definition, prayer rests on the assumption of the unknowability of an other, and it understands implicitly that "the responses are heard only in the demands. . . . [T]he epiphany comes, in the Saying, from the one who receives the revelation."[62] Prayer is an "'extradition' of the self to the neighbor." It names "an order to which I am subjected before hearing it or that I hear in my own saying."[63] It is no wonder, then, that Joe resists prayer: he might hear himself and his desires in a way that, in the saying, would recognize his immersion in "the order to which he is subjected" and that he wishes to leave unnamed. It would be a giving over of himself to himself as himself. He wants only to murder this wish.

And so, in keeping with the regressive unfolding of his relationship with Joanna, Joe lives out the final night of their relationship, the night of Joanna's death, as his own crisis in the Southern Garden of Gethsemane.[64] He refuses to pray while praying nonetheless, in Levinas's sense. Ironically, Joe recalls his refusal to join Joanna in prayer as he lies "on the fecund earth" outside her house, this time in "the ruined garden"[65] while he hears the "clock in the courthouse two miles away strike ten and then eleven" until finally, an hour later, he "hear[s] the last stroke of the far clock cease and die away."[66] Throughout this interval, he feels himself as "the volitionless servant of the fatality in which he believed he did not believe"[67]—"believed he did not believe," and yet perhaps does believe, because perhaps his refusal to pray is his form of prayer, as in the barn with McEachern. The biblical echoes in his thinking suggest as much: "The dark was filled with the voices, myriad, out of all time that he had known, as though all the past was a flat pattern. And going on: tomorrow night, all the tomorrows, to be a part of the flat pattern, going on. He thought of that with quiet astonishment: going on, myriad, familiar, since all that had ever been was the same as all that was to be, since tomorrow to-be and had-been would be the same. Then it was time."[68] Joe could almost say, "My God! My God! Why hast thou forsaken me?" Thinking, reflecting on himself, he is thus praying by default. And it is as if the text hears his prayer without his uttering it: the passage registers his unspoken address to the order to which he is subjected. Such moments threaten indeed to reveal to him his condition, which is why murder seems the only solution. Only in Gail Hightower do we witness a praying that admits its discoveries to itself, and, in turn, we glimpse our own attitude of prayer toward the text, the Book, enabling us to ask it, now, our own questions.

Gail Hightower: The Return of Interpellation

Before we even know who "he" is, we learn that "[f]rom his study window he can see the street."[69] The penultimate chapter of the novel similarly stations him here: "Now the copper light of afternoon fades; now the street beyond the low maples and the low signboard is prepared and empty, framed by the study window like a stage."[70] The "street" in this novel is a stage and on it is played the drama of bodies in public, of bodies that perform and project their chiasmatic crises of interpellation. This is the same "street" that Joe runs on for twenty years, including once more on the day he is finally castrated and killed.

But Gail Hightower only watches the street. He has withdrawn, he thinks, from the stage of the world ever since the traumatic exposure of his phantasmic relation to his wife, to the ministry, and to the Civil War. But this distance from the drama is itself a delusion, for there remains a gap that connects him to its unfolding: "The house, the brown, unpainted, unobtrusive bungalow is small too and by bushing crepe myrtle and syringa and althea almost hidden save for *that gap through which from the study window he watches the street.*"[71] Insofar as he maintains even an onlooker's attachment to the street through the window, and especially insofar as he continues, at dusk, to make the street a stage for his peculiarly reified projections, he leaves himself vulnerable to a living reenactment.

The narrative, furthermore, hints at Hightower's underlying similarity to the Joes who live in the street of the world. Like Joe Christmas, Hightower is split from himself; he is two, a "dual personality": "His face is at once gaunt and flabby; it is as though there were two faces, one imposed upon the other, looking out from beneath the pale, bald skull surrounded by a fringe of gray hair, from behind the twin motionless glare of his spectacles."[72] Byron Bunch observes that it was "as though the whole man were fleeing away from the nose which holds invincibly to something yet of pride and courage above the sluttishness of vanquishment like a forgotten flag above a ruined fortress."[73] Also like Joe, Hightower watches himself from the outside, watches himself acting, as if on a stage with invisible directors: "He seems to watch himself among faces . . . as though he watched himself in his own pulpit, from the rear of the church, or as though he were a fish in a bowl."[74]

Yet unlike Joe, Hightower comes to understand the dynamics of interpellation and projection that ramify and strain this splitness. After musing on himself as a fish in a bowl, he thinks: "And more than that: the faces seem to be mirrors in which he watches himself. He knows them all; he can read his doings in them. He seems to see reflected in them a figure antic as a showman."[75] Hightower names the process of projection and comes to see each person as a "showman" in this spectacle of mutual unconscious mirroring. In fact, in the last passage about him he recounts his whole earlier life as a gorgeous drama of projection. We review through his memory the conditions under which his body enters and is taken up by the social drama, especially of the Civil War. An only child—born late to middle-aged parents in the wake of the War, lonely, mesmerized by the black servant Cinthy's fantastic stories of his grandfather's violence and especially that of the grandfather's violent death on horseback—he spends hours in the attic fingering "the folds" of his father's winter war coat both because of the "evocation of his dead mother's hands which lingered among the folds" and because the coat "had assumed the properties of those phantoms who loomed heroic and tremendous,"[76] especially his grandfather. By the time he is a young seminarian, he has fused his religious calling with a phantasmic historical one, and he dreams of announcing to his elders at the seminary: "Listen. God must call me to Jefferson because my life died there, was shot from the saddle of a galloping horse in a Jefferson street one night twenty years before it was ever born."[77]

Hightower's obsession with this scene of his grandfather's death reflects the ransoming of bodies by both a past of which they are "innocent" and by a larger social body divided against itself: the grandfather's death is, after all, a tableau from the Civil War, the legacy of a social body at war with itself, which Hightower introjects. This is the historicity and tragedy of interpellation, wherein the body joins a national history in which the chiasmatic self-relation is massively organized into a series of social alterities, where self-relation is irretrievably entangled with a hostile other-relation.

Hightower's "sin" is that he was utterly seduced by the drama, eagerly projecting his own image into the tragic spectacle of a warring social world. As he later realizes, his relation to both his wife and his congregation is impelled by his will to projection, or the mutuality of projection and corporeally lived interpellation. In the case of his wife, when he first meets her, "he did not see her at all because of the face which he had already created in his mind."[78] Likewise, he thinks later, in his ministry, "I served it by using it to forward my own desire. I came here where faces full of bafflement and hunger and eagerness waited for me, waiting to believe; I did not see them. Where hands were raised for what they believed that I would bring them: I did not see them."[79] Hightower offers an elegant description of the ironic mutuality of interpellation and projection: "I *served* [the ministry] *by using it* to forward my own desire." He further recognizes the chain of projections and interpellations—the desire to be called out—that moves the social world: "where faces full of . . . eagerness waited for me, waiting to believe." The community is in a posture of imminence, of suspension, of waiting at an opening they want closed and filled.

Although Hightower realizes all of this, he cannot let go of his attachment to these dramas altogether. He sits at his window each evening anticipating the "interval of silence and waiting."[80] His experience in these moments offers a perfect narrative of the chiasmatic moment with its unresolved anticipations: "He leans forward. Already he can feel the two instants about to touch: the one which is the sum of his life, which renews itself between each dark and dusk, and the suspended instant out of which the *soon* will presently begin."[81] This is the left hand about to cross over from touching to touched, the moment of imminence, when being both is and is known—when the horses gallop, the hooves kick, and the sword is drawn in battle, when heroism is expectant and the South is poised for triumph. But in the next instant he reflects that when he was younger and "his net was still too fine for waiting, at this moment he would trick himself and believe that he heard them before he knew that it was time," and then he considers the possibility that "[p]erhaps that is all I ever did, have ever done."[82] Finally he arrives at the admission that in indulging his phantasmic relation to reality not only was he the "instrument" of his wife's "despair and death" but he is also "in turn the instrument of someone outside [him]self."[83]

In his self-consciousness but also in his seduction by the drama of closure and triumph, Hightower emerges as a reader-figure. His position at the window makes him a kind of witness to the point of entry into the social order, a listener at the loophole that is after all a trap. From this angle, he seeks to preserve the "interval" moment, just before "the gun crashes"—the moment of imagining and anticipating, fantasy and suspension. And we readers do the same.

For is not "the interval of silence and waiting" the state that art recreates endlessly, indulgently, holding out its promise of closure but extending suspension in a fantasy? Hightower, we should recall, hoped that in the ministry he would discover "his future, his life, intact and on all sides complete and inviolable, like a classic and serene vase."[84] Paradoxically, like the figures on that Grecian urn, like the horse's hooves in Hightower's fantasy, art holds the moment of motion in suspension: the motion is thus both frozen in time and freed from *telos*. As Faulkner reflects, "The aim of every artist is to arrest motion, which is life, by artificial means, and hold it fixed so that a hundred years later, when a stranger looks at it, it moves again since it is life."[85] Yet in doing so, art betrays history, or life, even as it represents it. On the other hand, and equally equivocally, art participates in a history even as it claims to transcend it.

As readers, we seem to seek out this fence-sitting, in-between condition, this suspension between outside and inside, history and essence, beauty and tragedy, truth and fiction. Perhaps, above all, we want, through art, to keep open that span across which fantasy can spread itself. This is the heroism and the delusion of art. Yet this desire for the suspended, transcendent moment cannot escape the present's claim on us, as Hightower learns once more, nor the other's claim on us in the present.

Faulkner's text tells us all of this even as it holds out for our seduction the fantasy of oneness, of essence, of race. It tells us we have made up our history even as it naturalizes and mystifies the history it makes up. It tells us we are readers, interpreters, makers, even as it writes us into its inherited script. Thus, I see Faulkner's method somewhat differently than does Jean-Paul Sartre, who early appreciated the phenomenological quality of Faulkner's narrative technique. Using the term "suspension" to indicate the "arrested motion in time" that Faulkner renders, Sartre concludes: "In Faulkner, there is never any progression, nothing which can come from the future"; instead, "his preoccupation [is] with the past."[86] On the contrary, Faulkner reveals not only that the past's embeddedness in the body creates a story in the future but also that the body's volatile if coerced intercorporeality, its orientation from outside itself and its involuntary immersion in a world of motion, unsettles it, pivots it again and again toward the future. Thus Lena's pregnancy and the birth that once more compels Hightower into the street form the chiasmatic magnet of futureness toward which history draws.

Perhaps the scene of Joe's castration best illustrates the triple turn of Faulkner's text. After Percy Grimm slashes his genitals, Joe "looked up at [the men] with peaceful and unfathomable and unbearable eyes. Then his face, body, all seemed to collapse, to fall in upon itself."[87] We witness here the collapse of the chiasm, the collapse of the body into itself, which—after a long life in which this self-relation has been thoroughly reified—comes as a kind of relief. The rhetoric of this scene, including the "pent black blood" that now rushes out from Joe in a "black blast," serves to remystify the body-as-race. Yet the chapter ends with this release of blood as the thing that the circle of men will never forget. It becomes a memory that enters and leaves exposed the chiasmatic ontology of those who witness it. As the narrator says, "They are not to lose it, in whatever peaceful valleys, beside whatever placid and reassuring streams of old age, in the mirroring faces of whatever children they will contemplate old disasters and newer hopes. It will be there, musing quiet, steadfast, not fading and not particularly threatful, but of itself alone serene, of itself alone triumphant."[88] This uncloseable moment, in other words, will span generations; it will be imprinted on the bodies and in the eyes of the children, who themselves embody the uncontrollable, historical extension of ourselves into others and the future. Call it the return of interpellation. Call it prayer, enmeshed in the tragic sublime of the body that provokes and escapes our names for it. These men and their children are snagged by this moment in which their own violence looks back at them; to this extent they are forced to live in the same ceaselessly opened gap that has held Joe captive.

And so, too, perhaps, are we held in suspense, caught in this distended history of Joe and a nation. We are the third term, the third turn, the ghostly witnesses in this ongoing spectacle of bodies, race, and violence in the South. Will we be dragged from our chairs by the study window? Or, looking expectantly through it, are we readers the guardians of suspense and another future?

Notes

1. For discussion of the racial discourse of the "Norman Yoke" that rhetorically shaped the internal rupture of the English Revolution, see Christopher Hill, *Puritanism and Revolution* (New York: Schocken Books, 1964), 50–122. For discussion of this rhetoric as it informs English and U.S. identities, see Leon Poliakov, *The Aryan Myth: A History of Racist and Nationalist Ideas in Europe*, trans. Edmund Howard (London: Chatto Heinemann, 1974); Ivan Hannaford, *Race: The History of an Idea in the West* (Baltimore: Johns Hopkins University Press, 1996); Reginald Horsman, *Race and Manifest Destiny: The Origins of American Anglo-Saxonism* (Cambridge, MA: Harvard University Press, 1981); and Laura Doyle, *Bordering on the Body: The Racial Matrix of Modern Fiction and Culture* (New York: Oxford University Press, 1994).

2. My discussion of this novel resonates with Eric J. Sundquist's emphasis on "the trauma of the house divided," but my racial interpretation is more phenomenological and more interested in the mutuality of individual and national bodies (*Faulkner: The House Divided* [Baltimore: Johns Hopkins University Press, 1983], 95).

3. William Faulkner, *Light in August* (1932; reprint, New York: Vintage Books, 1990), 8.

4. Ibid., 9.

5. "So-called" because, as John N. Duvall has argued, Joe's intention to murder Joanna is uncertain (he sets down the razor after entering her bedroom), and it is apparently in self-defense that he finally kills her, since she tries to shoot him first. While, of course, Joanna is killed in this scene, her death may not technically be murder, or at least not in the first degree. In this light, Duvall points out, the readiness of critics to refer to Joe as murderer is disturbing, perhaps a reflection of overdetermined racist assumptions ("Faulkner's Critics and Women: The Voice of the Community") in *Faulkner and Women*, ed. Doreen Fowler and Ann J. Abadie (Jackson: University of Mississippi Press, 1986), 41–57.

6. Faulkner, *Light in August*, 118.

7. Ibid., 283.

8. Ibid.

9. For a related and provocative discussion of this missing moment of Joanna's death, see Duvall, "Faulkner's Critics and Women," 50–54; and for a different approach to the centrality of our not knowing Joe Christmas's race, see Donald M. Kartiganer, "'What I Chose To Be': Freud, Faulkner, and the Abandonment of Design," in *Faulkner and Psychology*, ed. Kartiganer (Jackson: University of Mississippi Press, 1991), 288–314.

10. Maurice Merleau-Ponty, *The Visible and the Invisible*, trans. Alphonso Lingis (Evanston, IL: Northwestern University Press, 1968), 135. Further references to this source will appear as VI.

11. Ibid., 137.

12. Ibid., 141.

13. Ibid., 143.

14. Ibid., 9.

15. Ibid., 7, 9.

16. Ibid., 148.

17. Merleau-Ponty, *Phenomenology of Perception*, trans. Colin Smith (1962; reprint, London: Routledge & Kegan Paul, 1986), 456.

18. W.E.B. DuBois, *The Souls of Black Folk* (1903; reprint, New York: Signet, 1995), 45.

19. Louis Althusser, "*Lenin and Philosophy*" *and Other Essays*, trans. Ben Brewster (London: New Left Books, 1971), 162–64.

20. See Philip Weinstein, *What Else but Love? The Ordeal of Race in Faulkner and Morrison* (New York: Columbia University Press, 1996), 170. Similarly Kartiganer speaks of Joe as a character "spoken by a pre-existing binary system of race—and of sexuality" ("'What I Chose to Be,'" in *Faulkner and Psychology*, ed. Kartiganer, 307). In *House Divided*, Eric Sundquist also remarks on Faulkner's understanding of race as a projection (68).

21. Faulkner, *Light in August*, 122.

22. I undertake a full discussion of this interdependence in the context of a system of racial patriarchy in *Bordering on the Body* (10–34).

23. Faulkner, *Light in August*, 123.

24. Ibid., 149.

25. Ibid., 148.

26. Ibid., 149–50.

27. For discussion of Joe's "education" in terms of Foucaultian discipline, see Philip Weinstein, *Faulkner's Subject: A Cosmos No One Owns* (New York: Cambridge University Press, 1992), 103–4.

28. Faulkner, *Light in August*, 146.

29. Ibid., 150, 149, my emphasis.

30. Ibid., 225.
31. Ibid.
32. On these revisions, see Regina K. Fadiman, *Faulkner's "Light in August": A Description and Interpretation of the Revisions* (Charlottesville: University of Virginia Press, 1975). Critics vary widely in their views on Faulkner's degree of investment in racial essentialism; see, for example, Judith Bryan Wittenberg, "Race in *Light in August:* Wordsymbols and Obverse Reflections," in *The Cambridge Companion to William Faulkner*, ed. Philip Weinstein (New York: Cambridge University Press, 1995), 146–67; the essays in *Faulkner and Race*, ed. Doreen Fowler and Ann J. Abadie (Jackson: University of Mississippi Press, 1987), especially James Snead, "*Light in August* and the Rhetorics of Racial Division," 152–67; Doreen Fowler, "Joe Christmas and 'Womanshenegro' " in *Faulkner and Women*, ed. Fowler and Abadie, 144–61; Deborah Clarke, "Gender, Race and Language in *Light in August*," *American Literature* 61 (October 1989): 398–413; Sundquist, *House Divided*, especially 76; and Erskine Peters, *William Faulkner: The Yoknapatawpha World and Black Being* (Darby, PA: Norwood Editions, 1983).
33. Faulkner, *Light in August*, 225–26; my emphasis.
34. Ibid., 226.
35. Ibid.
36. For a range of discussions of this point, see Robert Dale Parker, "Sex and Gender, Feminine and Masculine: Faulkner and the Polymorphous Exchange of Cultural Binaries," in *Faulkner and Gender*, ed. Donald M. Kartiganer and Ann J. Abadie (Jackson: University of Mississippi Press, 1996), 73–96; Wittenberg, "Race in *Light in August*," in *Cambridge Companion*, 146–67; and Ralph Watkins, " 'It Was Like I Was the Woman and She Was the Man': Boundaries, Portals, and Pollution in *Light in August*," *Southern Literary Journal* 26 (Spring 1994): 11–24.
37. Critics have long interpreted Joe's struggles as his internal conflict between masculine and feminine, or as a fear of the feminine. Cleanth Brooks first offered such a reading in *William Faulkner: The Yoknapatawpha Country* (New Haven, CT: Yale University Press, 1963), 66–69, 127–35. For other more recent and more feminist discussions of Joe's relation to the feminine and the maternal, see Philip Weinstein, *What Else But Love?*, 156–83, and *Faulkner's Subject*, 12–41; and Doreen Fowler, " 'You Can't Beat a Woman': Preodipal Mother in *Light in August*," *Faulkner Journal* 10 (Spring 1995): 55–64.
38. Faulkner, *Light in August*, 228–29.
39. Ibid., 230
40. Ibid.
41. Ibid., 234.
42. Ibid.
43. Ibid.
44. Ibid.
45. While critics such as Weinstein place Joanna among the portraits of women as "nonsubjective others" (*Faulkner's Subject*, 13), and others speak of a mirroring dynamic between Joe and Joanna (Sundquist, *House Divided*, 81–85; Wittenberg, "Race in *Light in August*," in *Cambridge Companion*, ed. Weinstein, 155–56), it seems to me that Faulkner leaves open the more radical possibility that this affair, as it is rendered, is wholly Joe's projection.
46. Ibid., 240.
47. Ibid., 249.
48. Ibid., 254.
49. On listening in Faulkner's fiction, see Weinstein, *Faulkner's Subject*, 23; and

David M. Wyatt, "Faulkner and the Burdens of the Past," in *Faulkner: New Perspectives*, ed. Richard H. Brodhead (Englewood Cliffs, NJ: Prentice-Hall, 1983), 103. This moment constitutes an exception to the pattern Weinstein finds, wherein women listen but have no listeners for their stories.

50. Faulkner, *Light in August*, 256.
51. Ibid., 258.
52. Ibid., 259.
53. Ibid., 258.
54. Ibid., 259; my emphasis.
55. For other discussions of windows or doors in Faulkner, see Ralph Watkins, "It Was Like I Was the Woman"; Virginia V. James Hlavsa, *Faulkner and the Thoroughly Modern Novel* (Charlottesville: University of Virginia Press, 1991), 117–22; and Kenzaburo Ohashi, "*Light in August:* The Spell of the 'Window' and the Tragedy of the 'Earth,'" trans. Ikuko Fujihira, in *Faulkner Studies in Japan*, ed. Thomas L. McHaney (Athens: University of Georgia Press, 1985), 116–47.
56. Faulkner, *Light in August*, 260.
57. Ibid., 258.
58. Ibid., 260–61.
59. Ibid., 261; my emphasis.
60. Ibid., 269.
61. Ibid., 270.
62. Emmanuel Levinas, "Truth of Disclosure and Truth of Testimony," in *Basic Philosophical Writings*, ed. Adriaan T. Peperzak, Simon Critchley, and Robert Bernasconi (Bloomington: Indiana University Press, 1996), 106. Further references to this source will appear as BPW.
63. Ibid., 106.
64. For a thorough reading of *Light in August* as based on biblical texts, especially the gospels of John, see Hlavsa, *Faulkner and the Thoroughly Modern Novel*, 61–208.
65. Faulkner, *Light in August*, 280.
66. Ibid.
67. Ibid.
68. Ibid., 281.
69. Ibid., 57.
70. Ibid., 466.
71. Ibid., 57; my emphasis.
72. Ibid., 89.
73. Ibid., 363.
74. Ibid., 488.
75. Ibid.
76. Ibid., 469.
77. Ibid.
78. Ibid., 479.
79. Ibid., 487.
80. Ibid., 466.
81. Ibid., 486.
82. Ibid.
83. Ibid., 491.
84. Ibid., 478.
85. Faulkner, quoted in Jean Stein, "William Faulkner: An Interview," in *Three Decades of Faulkner Criticism*, ed. Frederick J. Hoffman and Olga W. Vickery (East Lansing: Michigan State University Press, 1960), 80.

86. Jean Paul Sartre, "Time in Faulkner: *The Sound and the Fury*," in *Three Decades of Faulkner Criticism*, ed. Hoffman and Vickery, 227–28. For other discussions of Faulkner's representation of history, see John Sykes, *The Romance of Innocence and the Myth of History: Faulkner's Religious Critique of Southern Culture* (Macon, GA: Mercer University Press, 1989); Michel Gresset, "Faulkner's War with Wars," in *Faulkner and History*, ed. Javier Coy and Michel Gresset (Salamanca, Spain: Salamanca University Press, 1986), 13–28; and Wyatt, "Faulkner and the Burdens of the Past," in *Faulkner: New Perspectives*, ed. Brodhead.

87. Faulkner, *Light in August*, 464–65.

88. Ibid.

Policing the Racial Divide: The Body, The Nation, and the Emmett Till Murder

Carol E. Henderson

> Emmett Till's dead body reminded us that the bad old days are never farther away than the thickness of skin, dark skin that some pale-skinned people claim the prerogative to strip away, burn or cut or shoot full of holes. It is not an accident that the hacked, dead face of Emmett Till looks inhuman. The point of killing and mutilating him, inflicting the agony of his last moments, was to prove he was not human.
>
> —John Edgar Wideman, "The Killing of Black Boys"

IN AUGUST OF 1955, MONEY, MISSISSIPPI, BECAME THE FOCAL POINT OF one of the most gruesome crimes ever committed on American soil. It is a murder that continues to haunt the African American literary imaginary, refashioning itself in ways that affect the very manner in which we view the American body politic, and more specifically, the African American male presence in that politic. Given society's incessant preoccupation with the black male body—be it on the basketball court, the big screen, or in the jurisdictional "big house"—a reassessment of the Till murder is timely. As John Edgar Wideman cogently argues in his article "The Killing of Black Boys," the bodies of black men are once again being used to justify "increasingly brutal policing of the racial divide." A generation of young black men dying in the street supports this fact. Jobless, addicted, undereducated, and hopeless, these men become the physical proof of white supremacy. Their bodies "point backward, the way Emmett Till's battered corpse points backward, history and prophecy at once: This is the way things have always been, will always be, the way they're supposed to be."[1] Thus Till's death stands at a significant juncture in African American cultural history, transfiguring past, present, and future critical approaches to the disfigured and wounded black body.

Till's body also serves as a precursor to one of the most intense social and political periods following the post-Emancipation era. This period, known as the volatile 1960s, found African Americans "standing at the crossroads" of America's polarized society, contemplating new and revised ways to achieve economic and social equality. According to one scholar, "the battle cries of black activists, writers, musicians, and other blues people of the 1940s and 50s"[2] sounded the alarm for political and governmental change. Their Call, reinterpreted by a new generation of thinkers and doers during the 1960s, erupted into "bloodshed and cataclysmic upheavals that not only sounded the death knell for centuries of segregation in the United States but also sent shock waves through out the country and around the world."[3] But it was in the 1950s that the murmurs of this Call were heard. As Rayfield Mooty, the second cousin of Emmett Till states in an interview:

> Historians will talk about the good and the bad [of the Civil Rights Movement], but they don't want to deal with the ugly. . . . The ugliness of racism is not a White man telling a Black woman to give him her bus seat—bad as that is—but the confident home-invasion, kidnapping and murder of a fourteen-year old Black youth and the exoneration by jury of the youth's apparent killers.[4]

It is in this explosive social climate that I reexamine the cultural precepts affecting the African American body politic as shifts in the aesthetics of black culture and black intellectualism presupposes a response to American racism that not only recoups but also reaffirms the integrity of black humanity vis-à-vis the marked and tortured body.

Although many readers may be familiar with the grisly details of the Till case, the retelling of these facts is as compulsory an act as the rhetorical unearthing of the injustices contained therein. It is in the telling that these stories become "mooring places," ghostly touchstones for cultural remembrances and the performance of community rites. I carry out this ritual here: Fourteen-year-old Emmett Till, an African American Chicago native, was in Mississippi visiting relatives for the summer. On August 28, in the wee hours of the morning, Till is kidnapped at gunpoint from his relatives' cabin by two Caucasian men—twenty-four-year-old Roy Bryant, and his then thirty-six-year-old half brother J. W. Milam. Till's *alleged* crime: he had whistled at Carolyn Bryant, Roy Bryant's wife, during a recent visit to the Bryant's Grocery and Meat Market earlier that week. Mose Wright, the sixty-four-year-old grandfather of Till's cousin Curtis Jones, pleads for Till's life. He explains to the men that Till is from up North and did not understand how things worked between blacks and whites in the South. Wright suggests whipping the boy in an effort to spare his life.

Ignoring Wright, the men drag Emmett outside and threaten Wright's life on the way out the door. He is told that if he makes any trouble, he would not live to see his sixty-fifth birthday. When the boy did not return the next day, Till's cousin phones the sheriff and reports him missing. Milam and Bryant are arrested and charged with kidnapping. Three days later, Till's naked and decomposing body is found in the Tallahatchie River by a white teenager who happened to be fishing in the area. Till had been brutally beaten. His right eye had been gouged out; the left eye was detached and dangling from its socket. His tongue, eight times its normal side, was protruding from his mouth. One of his ears was missing. His forehead had been crushed on one side (suggesting extreme torture), and the bridge of what used to be his nose was barely recognizable. All but two of Till's teeth were missing. There was also evidence that he had been shot in the head. In an effort to prevent the body from being discovered, his murderers had tied a 100-pound cotton gin fan to his neck with barbed wire. After the discovery of Till's body, Milam and Bryant are subsequently charged with his murder.[5] Five prominent Delta attorneys agree to represent Milam and Bryant after the men's trial becomes a regional battle cry for preserving the Southern way of life. On September 19, Milam and Bryant go on trial for the murder of Emmett Till. The trial lasts five days. The jury, all white and all male, deliberate a little more than an hour. Their verdict: not guilty. Milam and Bryant are released and subsequently acquitted of all charges.

The reaction to the Till murder and the verdict in the case is immediate and widespread. Till's death sparks national outrage in various communities across the country as civic leaders from the NAACP and other civil rights organizations condemn the South for allowing such a heinous act to occur on their soil. Protest rallies are held in cities across the country condemning the verdict. Editorials are written in major black and white dailies in the states and abroad criticizing the court proceedings and the behavior of the judge and jury.[6] For white Americans, Till's death was a wake-up call. As Kay Bonetti of the American Audio Prose Library recalls, "ordinary White people everywhere were horrified by what happened, and it did something to them. It made them recognize this as something that simply can't go on. This can't happen in this day and age, and we've got to stop it. And then it was a wake-up call for all humanity" (1995). For others, Till's case is a painful reminder of the vulnerability of *all* African Americans in this country. "Two months ago," recalls Mrs. Till, "I had a nice apartment in Chicago . . . I had a good job. I had a son. When something happened to Negroes in the South, I said: 'That's their business, not mine.' . . . Now I know how wrong I was. The murder of my son has shown me that what happens to any of us, anywhere in the world, had better be the business of us all."[7] Emmett's death signals a change in the fight against racism, and brought to the forefront of the Civil Rights struggle the cost at which many of us have gained our limited freedoms. After all, the Movement is to ensure that our *children* would have the right to life, liberty, and the pursuit of happiness despite this country's previous record on the matter. Till's death proved otherwise. It demonstrates that even our children are not immune to hateful acts of violence, racism, and bigotry.

For many, Till's murder reemphasizes the deep-seated animosity that exists between the North and the South. As is the case during slavery, the black body would once again serve as the world stage upon which the dialogue of race and gender is performed. Its players—both black and white—assume their roles as willing and unwilling participants in a production that uses America's historical narrative as its backdrop, and the changing social climate in the South as its figurative impulse. But the script remains the same. As Ruth Feldstein determines, "the two white men felt compelled to avenge what they perceived as a racial and sexual transgression."[8] Embedded in Feldstein's observations are all the mythological assumptions associated with villainizing the African American male (child) as the social predator of white women. Activist Angela Davis points out that "in the history of the United States, the fraudulent rape charge stands out as one of the most formidable artifices invented by racism. The myth of the Black rapist has been methodically conjured up whenever recurrent waves of violence and terror against the Black community have required convincing justifications."[9]

Although the Till case *does not* involve an instance of rape, the same sort of cultural psychosis that fed the fears and anxieties in this case can be directly tied to the ideological assumptions Davis points to in her work. During the Till trial rumors purported that Till tried to rape Carolyn Bryant. These allegations are unfounded and have never been proven. However these allegations—like echoes of the past—point to the cultural web of racist and sexist ideology that frames the black male body in America's body politic. Moreover, this cultural grounding has fueled troubling reinterpretations of the Till case. As Angela Davis cogently reports, cultural critics such as Susan Brownmiller have erroneously collapsed the Till case within their social critiques of other notorious *rape* cases of this century, including the Scottsboro Nine, and the Willie McGee case.[10] Brownmiller goes so far as to assert that Till's alleged wolf whistle was no small "tweet of hubba-hubba or melodious approval" but a "deliberate insult just short of physical assault." In Brownmiller's mind, Till *is* a rapist, and his alleged act of transgression was the "last reminder to Carolyn Bryant that this black boy, Till, had in mind to possess her [Bryant]."[11] Brownmiller's assessment of the Till case is troubling to say the least, but it is her personal reflections on the "question of race" (the title of a chapter in her lengthy book on rape and women) and the Till murder that merits closer scrutiny here. Besides its contentious nature, Brownmiller shapes her observations in a feminist rhetoric that sounds the alarm for all women concerning the threatening potential of little black black boys as rapists. As she concludes:

> For a period of fifteen years after the murder of Emmett Till whenever a black teen-ager whistled at me on a New York City street I smiled my nicest smile . . . to any and all who let me know from a safe distance their theoretical intent. After all . . . [w]asn't a whistle or a murmured 'May I f—k you?' an innocent compliment? And did not white women . . . have to bear the white man's burden of making amends for Southern racism? It took fifteen years for me to resolve these questions in my own mind, and to understand the insult implicit in Emmett Till's whistle, the depersonalized challenge of "I can have you" with or without the racial aspect. Today a sexual remark on the street causes within me a fleeting but murderous rage.[12]

These sorts of characterizations belie the social, cultural, and political currents of Till's murder, bringing to the forefront society's barely repressed fears of black male sexuality and masculinity. The interplay between fact and fantasy, mythmaking and mythological fulfillment, or, as is the case in the Till murder, the *perceived* threat of acting upon or acting out this racial fantasy, underscores the ways in which the black male body is fashioned as Other, sexualized and demonized. It is the *suggestion* that "little black boys grow up to be big black men" that amplifies white male (and with respect to Brownmiller, white female) anxiety in this case, particularly as it relates to the issue of miscegenation. This subtext underwrites the cultural narrative of this murder as notions of manhood become inextricably tied to the "preservation" of nation, honor, and white womanhood. Critics like Martha Hodes and Sandra Gunning have argued elsewhere that American society and civilization has traditionally been figured as the white female body, "silent, helpless, in immediate need of protection from the black beast."[13] History demonstrates that white supremacists have used this argument to justify violence against African American men. Although neither Milam nor Bryant openly confessed that they were supremacists, their ideological thinking would suggest that they were at least bedfellows with those individuals who believed in separating the races and maintaining the institutionalized belief (legally, socially, and politically) that whites were superior to blacks in every facet of American life. "As long as I live and can do anything about it, niggers are going to stay in their place," Milam told reporter William Bradford Huie. "Me and my folks fought for this country and we've got some rights."[14] In espousing this nationalist rhetoric, Milam and Bryant sought to perform their civil duty and affirm their American citizenship vis-à-vis the murder of Emmett Till. Tragically their "patriotism" is acted out upon the surface of Till's body in a manner that makes the *depth* of their convictions known.

Body of Evidence: Reclaiming the Black Flesh

> Earlier in the day the prosecution called young Till's mother, Mrs. Mamie Bradley, 33, of Chicago, to the witness stand and she stoutly maintained that the dead body sent to her was that of her son. The boy's body, bludgeoned and shot in the head, was found in the Tallahatchie River on Aug. 31, but the defense has questioned whether the body was that of Emmett.
>
> —John N. Popham, *New York Times*

One of the major controversies in the judiciary proceedings of the Till case centered on the identification of Emmett Till's body. Defense attorneys in the case argued that the corpse found in the Tallahatchie River was so badly decomposed that positive identification was impossible. Prosecuting attorneys argued however that Till's mother and his cousin's grandfather Mose Wright were able to positively identify Till's body based on certain indisputable family features, and a ring inscribed with the initials L. T.[15] Editor George E. Curry poignantly records in *Emerge Magazine* the process by which Mamie Till Bradley identified the body of her son. Curry's interview offers an interesting countertext to the legal findings in the case that suggest that the prosecution failed to prove the identity of the body.

That the trial hinged on these facts of evidence is striking. In questioning her ability to identify the remains of her son, it appears that defense attorneys had hoped to wrestle control away from Mamie Till who had, only weeks earlier, waged her own war in the media when she arranged for an open casket funeral for her son. At that time, she placed two pictures of him taken prior to his murder in the casket's lid facing his body. These symbolic gestures accomplished two things: it allowed Mrs. Till to reclaim the identity of her son as the public was able to judge for itself whether the body that lay before them belonged to that of Emmett Till. The shear brutality of this case clearly suggests intent on the murderers' part to *literally* erase the physical identity of Emmett Till. In disfiguring his face, his killers' sought to reinscribe the one surface that made him unique, that made him identifiable to his family and friends. Mrs. Till's efforts counter these attempts to efface the memory of her son as she challenges not only the social context in which his body is read, but also the philosophical tenets that render his flesh "invisible" or "bodiless" within the rhetoric of America's political and media driven consciousness. Her actions enable her to *re*invent the social meaning of the marks inscripted on his person as that which was done to him in private now became a matter of public discourse.

This latter point warrants careful consideration as the sheriff's earlier attempts to not only keep the casket sealed but to have the child's body quickly buried in Mississippi undoubtedly reveals an intention on his part to prevent public scrutiny of a key piece of evidence. A piece of evidence, I might add, that directs critical attention to the ways in which black bodies are "disposed of" in the South. As writer James Baldwin cogently concludes, "had [Till] been a 'Mississippi Boy,' his bones might yet be irrecoverable at the bottom of the river, or nourishing the earth of various and celebrated Mississippi plantations."[16] Baldwin's observations are telling, particularly as they relate to the Till case. The defense in this case spent an inordinate amount of time dismantling—by this I mean de-authenticating—the identity of Till's body. As *New York Times* reporter John Popham writes, "The defense called as witnesses Dr. L. D. Odken, Greenwood; H. D. Malone, an embalmer of Cleveland, and Sheriff H. C. Strider of Tallahatchie County. All testified that they viewed the body recovered from the river three days after the boy was kidnapped and in their opinion the body appeared to be decomposed to the extent that it would have been, had it been in the water from ten to fifteen days."[17] The irony here lies in their very gesture and the energy used to promulgate it. Emmett's body was a physical sign of what these Mississippi "experts" did not want seen. "Don't let the sun go down and that body is out of the ground," they ordered Mose Wright.[18] Crosby Smith, Mose Wright's brother-in-law, recalls that just three hours after the body was found a hole was being dug for it in a local graveyard. "They were getting ready to spill that boy into it," states Crosby, "He hadn't even been embalmed."[19] It is obvious that this strategy to suppress evidence was meant to make the case against Milam and Bryant more difficult, and the social indictment against Mississippi unwarranted. Yet, the more haunting question then becomes *if* the body found was not that of Emmett Till, then whose was it?

This is the rhetorical question Baldwin points to in his earlier statement on the murder. Baldwin's ironic interplay of terms, his references to "rivers," "plantations," and "Mississippi," his juxtaposition of the terms "Mississippi" and "Boy," his allusions to bones and bodies being buried and forgotten, all return the reader's attention to Mississippi's cultural heritage. This social history embodies both the river Mark Twain's Huck sailed down and (probably whistled down no doubt) with his ever-present "shadow" (Jim) in *Huckleberry Finn.* Jim's presence in Twain's novel is paradoxical to say the least. Jim represents both "absence" and "presence" as his adult male body is put in direct conflict with his almost infantile characterization. By joining "Mississippi" and "Boy" together in the same phrase (as it relates to the Till case), Baldwin draws attention to this literary and cultural history as he reiterates the ways in which black men are perpetually emasculated in a social dialogue that creates no distinction between the two—black men are *seen* as "boys" and black boys are *read* as possessing the same wants and desires as men within the Southern context. This characterization varies in more subtle ways in the urban setting but it is still there nonetheless. If *Huckleberry Finn* is indeed the great American classic, how does one read these ideological frameworks given the present history? This seems to be the question Baldwin is asking. And, in connecting Till's murder to these legacies, Baldwin bears witness to those nameless victims disremembered and unaccounted for "at the bottom of the river, or nourishing the earth" of someone's Mississippi plantation as Till's mutilated flesh personifies "the evidence of things not seen."[20] In the process, Baldwin signifies upon the communal history of the South as Till's body becomes another reminder of Mississippi's ugly past and its complicated social and racial relations.

Both Milam and Bryant admitted after the trial that they wanted to make an example out of Till, they wanted to "put a few people on notice" with respect to desegregation and outside attempts to change their way of life in Mississippi. As suspect J. W. Milam asserts in his interview with reporter William Bradford Huie:

> "Niggers ain't going to vote where I live. If they did, they'd control the government. They ain't going to go to school with my kids. And when a nigger even gets close to mention sex with a white woman, he's tired of livin' . . . I stood there in that shed and listened to that nigger throw that poison at me and I just made up my mind. "Chicago boy," I said, "I'm tired of 'em sending your kind down here to stir up trouble. Goddamn you, I'm going to make an example of you—just so everybody can know how me and my folks stand."[21]

That they chose to use the body as text coincides with an American history replete with images of black male bodies, lynched and otherwise. These acts of terrorism set a public stage designed to not only disempower and intimidate African American communities; these acts fashion a public discourse aimed at controlling the social and political meanings of the body itself as it simultaneously devalued the worth of African American life.

There is still much debate, however, regarding the classification of Till's murder: is it a lynching or is it not? The answer to this question is complex. I tend to agree with critic Jacqueline Goldsby who considers the Till murder a "low tech lynching" although I'm uncomfortable with her designated term.[22] I do disagree with Stephen J. Whitfield's assessment that the Till murder was not a lynching. His criteria for judging this case overlooks the social implications of the act itself, its racial meaning, its social dialogue within the historical narrative that records assaults against black male bodies. The fact that the act was committed by two individuals (and not a mob) does not negate the *intentions* of Milam and Bryant. Moreover, the fact that Emmett was not castrated does not absolve these gentlemen of the "mob mentality," a psychosis that clearly points to underlying issues directed at people of color. Interwoven into these and other discussions are the complicated cultural and social dialogues that govern class, gender, and race relations. The passage of the 14th (1868) and the 15th (1870) Amendments in the latter part of the nineteenth century had a profound effect on the ways in which white men viewed their political and social agency. Directly tied to this notion is the *translation* of social and political power into legal and economic viability. In other words, white men felt the recently emancipated African American citizenry was encroaching upon their right to everything in American society. One way to counter these anxieties was to engage in communal terrorism. Violence thus became the national "dialect"; it was the language understood—the means by which sovereignty and dominance were attained.

Public announcements of lynchings prior to their staging, as well as death certificates that claim these acts were committed by "parties unknown," each lend themselves to the creation of an intricate web of cultural subplots that, at best, seeks to *de*legitimize the African American public subject. These same factors can be said to be operating in the Till case. The legislative and social assault against Jim Crowism and legalized segregation in the 1950s heightened awareness on the part of white southerners that change was on the horizon. The favorable ruling on behalf of African American children in the 1954 *Brown vs. Board of Education* case caused many Southern segregationists to term this day "Black Monday." These social factors provided a backdrop for the Till case reminiscent of the Reconstruction era. Given this dynamic, Mrs. Till's early actions to not only arrange an open casket funeral, but to also make Till's mangled face part of the social fabric of American history should then be read as a gesture of defiance on her part to *legitimize* the public subjectivity of her son. That is, recover the social and political meanings of his body.

Having been a native of Mississippi, Mrs. Till was well aware of the possible outcome of her son's murder trial. Legal precedents in that state and others across the country illuminate the sinister way in which law was/is shaped around the absence and presence of the black body.[23] Still, Mrs. Till sought to validate her son's life and expose the corruption of the South's visible and not so visible institutions' violent racism. In introducing *her* narrative of her son's life, presenting pictures of him prior to his death, *re*contextualizing his identity as that of a son and not a villain, Emmett became more than just an abstract "thing," a disfigured "it," a monster or a sexual predator. He became a person, a three dimensional being with a past, present, and lost future. In restoring his dignity, Mrs. Till follows those actions of other historical figures that have, over time, worked to reconstitute African Americans' humanity through print and visual culture. In this way she turns a tragic incident into a triumphant achievement as Emmett's body and the individual pain he endured become the catalyst for unified efforts to end social and political apathy in the African American community and elsewhere. Mamie Till's decision to "let the whole world see" changed the very way we would come to understand the private and public discourses of the American body politic for decades to come. And Till's mangled body stands as a haunting reminder of the cost of imagining an America in the past, present, and future.

Notes

1. John Edgar Wideman, "The Killing of Black Boys" 278.
2. Patricia Liggins Hill, ed., "Cross Road Blues: African American History and Culture, 1960 to the Present," 1344.
3. Ibid.
4. Clenora Hudson-Weems, "Resurrecting Emmett Till," 75.
5. Juan Williams's *Eyes on the Prize: America's Civil Rights Years, 1954–1965* (Viking, 1987), 37–57 and George E. Curry's "The Death that Won't Die: Memories of Emmett Till 40 years later" in *Emerge* 6, no. 9 (July–August 1995): 24–32.
6. One juror told *Time* magazine, "if we hadn't stopped to drink pop, it (the deliberations) wouldn't have taken that long"(Curry 32). Other startling admissions include the facts that (1) all five defense attorneys admitted years later that they believed the prosecution had provided enough evidence to convict the two men, and (2) all the jurors believed the defendants were guilty of murder but nonetheless chose to acquit for political reasons.

7. Mrs. Till quoted in Juan Williams's *Eyes on the Prize*, 57.

8. Ruth Feldstein, *Motherhood in Black and White: Race and Sex in American Liberalism, 1930–1965*, 263.

9. Angela Davis, "The Myth of the Black Male Rapist," 173.

10. See pages 78–79 in particular for Davis' discussion of Brownmiller.

11. Susan Brownmiller, *Against Our Will: Men, Women, and Rape*, 247.

12. Ibid., 248.

13. Sandra Gunning, *Race, Rape, and Lynching: The Red Record of American Literature, 1890–1912*, 6–7; Martha Hodes, "The Sexualization of Reconstruction Politics: White Women and Black Men in the South after the Civil War," 402–17.

14. William Bradford Huie, "Shocking Story of Approved Killing in Mississippi," 50.

15. The irony of Till's fate, along with that of his father Private Louis Till (the previous owner of the ring), did not go unnoticed by this scholar. Private Till's conviction for raping two women, and murdering another remains suspect. As critics like Ruth Feldstein point out, "The guilt or innocence of Louis Till and the details surrounding his court-martial and hanging remain in dispute, particularly in light of the fact that in Europe during World War II, eighty-seven of the ninety-five soldiers hanged for rape and murder of civilians were African American" (297). Scholars like Stephen J. Whitfield, who suggest that the "guilt of the father casts a tiny but eerie shadow on a case already sufficiently weighted with evidence of the sinister bend of the human heart," (119) casts an even larger shadow on the analysis of this case. As Whitfield himself admits, "Of course, Emmett Till had never known his father, whose crimes were utterly irrelevant and immaterial to the charges against the defendants in the courtroom in the Delta in 1955" (117). Then why the interest in the father's crime? One can only speculate that the "tiny but eerie shadow" Whitfield speaks of unveils a "sinister bend of the human heart" that believes that the sins of the father are indeed the sins of the son. Yet lost in this speculative gesturing of genealogical paternalism is the pain of the mother.

16. James Baldwin, *The Evidence of Things Not Seen*, 41. Note: Baldwin's comments remind me of a recent A&E segment I saw entitled "The FBI Files." This show focused on the murders of three civil rights volunteers, James Chaney, Andrew Goodman, and Michael Schwerner. Briefly, these men (ages 21, 20, and 24 respectively) were killed by Klansmen (one of them included the deputy sheriff of Philadelphia, Mississippi) in June of 1964 as they sought to help Southern blacks register to vote. Their bodies were found two months after their disappearance on the property of one of the wealthiest men in Mississippi. Had the FBI not paid the informant $30,000, (his identity is still not revealed for fear he will be killed) their bodies might not have *ever* been found. What is striking about this case is that during the two-month search for these men, other bodies were discovered in various parts of the county, in various forms of disfigurement. It is obvious that these men died without any social or legal rights. They were Southern black men, apparently victims of the Klan, who had "disappeared" without a trace. Till's murder, although nine years prior to the FBI case, nonetheless testifies to this legacy of countless black men murdered without cause. Baldwin's analysis of the Till murder some thirty years after its occurrence returns our attention to the historicity of these bodies.

17. John H. Popham, "State Rests Case in Youth's Killing," 15. More back scene drama indicates that the sheriff, in declaring the body "unrecognizable," refused to do investigative work on the case. A special prosecutor was appointed by the state, but received no cooperation to conduct the investigation. See Juan Williams's *Eyes on the Prize* for further discussion, esp. 44–45. Another note: the sheriff's testimony at the

trial contradicted earlier statements prior to the trial wherein he verified (or at least agreed) that the body found was that of Emmett Till. His change in opinion greatly influenced (and may have lead to the shift in) the public reaction of white southerners to the case in Sumner. See "MISSISSIPPI: The Place, the Acquittal," 25; William M. Simpson, "Reflections on a Murder: The Emmett Till Case," 177–200, esp. 192.

18. "The Death that Won't Die," 30.

19. Ibid.

20. Here I'm signifying upon Baldwin's title of his 1985 book of the same name that contains his thoughts on the Atlanta child murders of 1981, and the uncanny ways in which these murders (and their underlying social issues) resonate with the Till incident.

21. Huie, "Shocking Story of Approved Killing in Mississippi," 50.

22. See "The High and Low Tech of It: The Meaning of Lynching and the Death of Emmett Till," 245.

23. For seminal studies on law and the legal shaping of the black personae see A. Leon Higginbotham's *In the Matter of Color: The Colonial Period* (Oxford University Press, 1978) and *Shades of Freedom: Racial Politics and Presumptions of the American Legal Process* (Oxford University Press 1996); Patricia L. Williams's *The Alchemy of Race and Rights* (Harvard University Press, 1991) and Derrick Bell's *Faces at the Bottom of the Well: The Permanence of Racism* (Basic Books, 1992).

Works Cited

Baldwin, James. *The Evidence of Things Not Seen.* New York: Holt, Rinehart, and Winston, 1985.

Bonetti, Kay. *An Interview with Clenora Hudson-Weems* [audiotape]. Columbia, MO: Audio Prose Library. Order #407–9. ISBN 407–9.

Brownmiller, Susan. *Against Our Will: Men, Women, and Rape.* New York: Simon and Schuster, 1975.

Curry, George E. "The Death that Won't Die: Memories of Emmett Till 40 Years Later." *Emerge*, 6, no. 9 (July–August 1995): 24–32.

Davis, Angela Y. "The Myth of the Black Male Rapist." In *Women, Race & Class.* New York: Random House, 1981.

Feldstein, Ruth. *Motherhood in Black and White: Race and Sex in American Liberalism, 1930–1965.* Ithaca, NY: Cornell University Press, 2000.

Goldsby, Jacqueline. "The High and Low Tech of It: The Meaning of Lynching and the Death of Emmett Till." *The Yale Journal of Criticism*, 9, no. 2 (1996): 245–82.

Gunning, Sandra. *Race, Rape, and Lynching: The Red Record of American Literature, 1890–1912.* New York: Oxford University Press, 1996.

Hill, Patricia Liggins, ed. "Cross Road Blues: African American History and Culture, 1960s to the Present." In *Call and Response: The Riverside Anthology of the African American Literary Tradition.* New York: Houghton Mifflin Company, 1998.

Hodes, Martha. "The Sexualization of Reconstruction Politics: White Women and Black Men in the South after the Civil War." *Journal of the History of Sexuality* 3 (1993): 402–17.

Hudson-Weems, Clenora. "Resurrecting Emmett Till: The Catalyst of the Modern Civil Rights Movement." *Journal of Black Studies* 29, no. 2 (November 1998): 179–88.

———. *Emmett Till: The Sacrificial Lamb of the Civil Rights Movement.* Troy, MI: Bedford, 1994.

Huie, William Bradford. "Shocking Story of Approved Killing in Mississippi." *Look* 24 (January 1956): 50–51.

Popham, John H. "State Rests Case in Youth Killing." *New York Times*, September 23, 1955. Section L, p. 15.

Twain, Mark. *The Adventures of Huckleberry Finn.* Berkeley: University of California Press, 2003.

Whitfield, Stephen J. *A Death in the Delta: The Story of Emmett Till.* New York: Free Press; London: Collier Macmillan, 1989.

Wideman, John Edgar. "The Killing of Black Boys." In *The Lynching of Emmett Till: A Documentary Narrative.* Edited by Christopher Metress. Charlottesville: University of Virginia Press, 2002. 278–288.

Williams, Juan. *Eyes on the Prize: America's Civil Rights Years, 1954–1965.* New York: Viking Press, 1987.

A Space beyond Beulah: Assessing the Mixed Race Body in Danzy Senna's "The Land of Beulah"

Simone C. Drake

DANZY SENNA'S SHORT STORY "THE LAND OF BEULAH" WAS PUBlished in 2000, the same year that the U.S. census added the multiracial category. The addition of the multiracial category suggested that perhaps DuBois's color line was no longer stratifying the country.[1] Prior to the census category change in 2000, the November 18, 1993 cover of *Time* magazine featured the computer-morphed image of a racially ambiguous woman above the title, "The New Face of America: How Immigrants Are Shaping the World's First Multicultural Society." The managing editor's note informs readers that while the woman does not exist, she was "selected as a symbol of the future, multiethnic face of America."[2] In response to this *Time* issue in general, and to the morphed image in particular, Senna declares facetiously, "Of course, anyone could see that women just like the computer face they had created did exist in Puerto Rico, Latin America, and Spanish Harlem. But the editors at *Time* remained unaware of this, seeming to prefer their colored folk imaginary, not real."[3] Senna's commentary not only implies that the editors are limited in their cross-cultural exposure, but it also explicitly refutes the editors' assertion that the morphed woman does not yet exist. Senna is part of a literary conversation that emerged simultaneous to political conversations around multiracial identity. Senna's critique of the morphed image and the premise of her short story call attention to how the census change is an attempt to move the nation beyond race as much as it is an attempt to satisfy people like Senna who are multiracial and do not want to choose either or.

Time employed the morphed image on the cover as the exigency for a set of articles discussing immigration and the increasingly multicultural society that immigrants are producing. All of these articles either implicitly or explicitly suggest that race would matter much differently at the dawning of the twenty-first century than it had in times past—that is, all of these articles except for the one written by the Nobel laureate Toni Morrison. In "On the Backs of Blacks," Morrison frames her analysis of immigrants and multiculturalism as "race talk."

> The explicit insertion into everyday life of racial signs and symbols that have no meaning other than pressing African Americans to the lowest level of the racial hierarchy . . . participates freely in this most enduring and efficient rite of passage into American culture: negative appraisals of the native-born black population. Only when the lesson of racial estrangement is learned is assimilation complete. Whatever the lived experience of immigrants with African Americans—pleasant, beneficial or bruising—the rhetorical experience renders blacks as noncitizens, already discredited outlaws.[4]

Morrison and Senna's response to the utopian multiculturalism inherent in *Time's* visual and narrative rhetoric suggest that we ought to be wary of arguments that immigration, migration, and the transnational flow of cultures will erase race. While the social construction of *race* certainly is an ideology worth relinquishing, the fact is that despite migratory and cultural changes, race continues to matter in the United States—and as Toni Morrison notes, race continues to matter most pervasively "on the backs of blacks."

The census change and the *Time* article are just two examples of efforts to do what I refer to as "move beyond race." These moves beyond race are moves toward what Senna refers to in an interview as "the end of blackness."[5] Racial mixture, then, ends up operating as a "cure" that eradicates DuBois's color line, and replaces it with the face of Charles Chesnutt's "future American" or Jean Toomer's "blue race."[6] These are, of course, faces that are not new to the Americas, as Senna noted, but they are faces whose existence had received minimal recognition prior to the *Time* special issue. Thus, whether it is Chesnutt's and Toomer's discourse privileging racial amalgamation, *Time* magazine's "new face of America," or the new addition to the census categories, each suggests that if we can erase race—read blackness—then we can achieve what cultural studies scholar Paul Gilroy calls "radically nonracial humanism."[7] Such democratic idealism is glaringly absent in Senna's narrative. Indeed, "The Land of Beulah" demands that we think critically about how the mixed race body is assessed in such moves beyond race. Senna ultimately suggests that U.S. racial geographies are mapped on the black body, and especially on the mixed race female body, in such a restrictive manner that until that geography is repaired, moves beyond race are futile.

Beulah Land

In "The Land of Beulah" Senna signifies on cultural and biblical conceptions of "Beulah" in order to illustrate the tenuous mapping of U.S. racial geographies and their affect on the mixed race female body. It is important to recognize the various representations of Beulah that Senna signifies on in order to appreciate fully Senna's critique of how the mixed race body is assessed in moves beyond race. "The Land of Beulah" is set in Brooklyn, New York. The protagonist of the story is simply named Jackie. She is the daughter of a jazz singer white mother and a jazz musician black father. They have been long separated. Jackie's phenotype is racially ambiguous, disallowing a comfortable space on either side of the black-white binary. As a result, the narrative is consumed by her futile attempts and desperate hopes of finessing the color line. This is particularly true after her black boyfriend, Kip, dumps her because she is not "black" enough—she "can walk away from this [race] any time" (Senna 2000, 197). After becoming "recently single, unhappy, homeless for some land she couldn't quite remember," Jackie stumbles upon Beulah, an abandoned, lovely mutt with "shiny black fur, long satiny ears, and little brown dots above her eyes" (194–95). Beulah is left tied to a street sign with an extension cord, wearing a tag engraved with the name BEULAH. Jackie takes Beulah home, feeling sorry for her because the dog's name reminds her of a black maid named Beulah on a 1950s television sitcom her grandmother used to watch.[8]

Jackie's sympathy for the dog is heightened when she later discovers a small hole between Beulah's nostrils that reminds Jackie "somehow of slavery, of shackles and deformities too deep to ever heal" (Senna 2000, 203). Although Jackie finds herself obsessed with showering Beulah with toys and attention, Jackie also finds that she cannot control her urge to beat Beulah for each puppy-like act of destruction she performs in Jackie's apartment. Despite knowing that hitting as a discipline technique was inappropriate, "she lost control: She slapped the puppy on its butt when it tore her fancy sheets, and jerked its leash too hard when they went walking" (199). Ironically Jackie declares, "that she never loved anyone more, and possibly never would" (199). The love-hate relationship Jackie develops with Beulah is predicated upon Beulah's uncanny ability to remind Jackie of how "a racialized conception of property implemented by force and ratified by law"[9] during the U.S. slave era, continues to refuse black bodies full incorporation into the nation in the post–civil rights era. This reminder is compounded when, in an effort to remedy Beulah's behavior problems, Jackie starts taking her on daily visits to a dog park.

Once Jackie begins frequenting the dog park, the multiple representations of "Beulah" are most clear. The dog that is chained and mutilated becomes a metaphor for the black body that remains oppressed—like that of the maid—even after slavery. The dog park, then, is a metaphor for the biblical "Beulah Land" in the book of Isaiah, chapter 62. Chapter 62 in its entirety refers to the "millennial kingdom" or the second coming of Christ. Christ is the bridegroom who comes and redeems his bride, bestowing upon her the "land Beulah." The promise of redemption here is repeated when John Bunyan describes the land of Beulah as a paradisiacal waiting place in *Pilgrim's Progress*, and it is repeated again in the poetry of William Blake where Beulah Land is the highest level of euphoria on earth. In these instances, the land of Beulah is a safe space where the righteous is redeemed. Jackie suggests that the dog park provides the safety inherent in the Beulah eschatology. She insists that despite everyone being strangers, "there was an intimacy to their encounters . . . the way lovers see each other before the day begins" (Senna 2000, 208). Jackie hopes that her imposed paradisiacal sense of the dog park will somehow make the park a safe space for her raced and gendered body that stratifies but never occupies a clear space on the color line. Her hopes are unfulfilled, however, when she abandons Beulah in the dog park and returns to her unhappy life of maintaining her appearance and keeping company with superficial friends. Senna utilizes Jackie's failed attempt to locate a space beyond race as a warning to those who present mixed race bodies as evidence of a "new face of America."

The Dog Park

Jackie's proclamation of intimacy makes the dog park sound like a libratory space in which she can escape the color line. That liberation is short lived due to a final representation of Beulah that fuels Jackie's violence toward the dog. As a mutt, Beulah is emblematic of Jackie. Jackie strikes out at Beulah because she sees no way of reconciling her own racial in-betweeness. As a mixed-breed dog that bears specific symbols of slavery, Jackie recognizes her own pain in Beulah's vulnerability. This recognition of what Beulah represents spurs the beatings. The beatings are also spurred by a profound realization of self-hatred that Jackie had never recognized before. "Jackie had never thought herself ill-tempered before. But that first evening, she walked into her bedroom only to find Beulah peeing on her bed . . . Jackie felt something—a clicking in her brain. She'd never felt it before. In one swift motion, she picked Beulah up by the scruff of her neck and flung her to the floor . . . Jackie kicked her sharply in the ribs . . . Jackie hungered to do more, but Beulah ran . . . (Senna 2000, 198–99). Beulah ultimately forces Jackie to recognize the intersections of her own race, gender, and sexuality that prohibit the dog park from being a redemptive Beulah Land.

Unable to stop abusing Beulah, Jackie takes her veterinarian's advice that Beulah simply needs more exercise, and begins taking her to the dog park. Although Jackie initially describes the dog park inhabitants generally as people, her narrative attention is devoted only to Nan, the haggard thirtysomething/young fortysomething doctoral candidate who has been writing her dissertation on Victorian birth control methods for ten years, and the Weather Girls, a group of single, childless white women whom Nan hates because they have not given up hope on finding a man and because they own purebred dogs. Senna's narrative leaves it unclear as to whether Jackie willfully omits the presence of men from the park or if they in fact were ever present. Either way, the park becomes an intimate feminine space that eases the lingering memories of her unpleasant break-up with Kip who envied Jackie's ability to "escape" race. The intimate feminine space of the park helps Jackie to feel safe from Kip's betrayal. After becoming acquainted with Nan and the Weather Girls Jackie concludes, "that while she could be a black girl or a white girl, depending on how she decided to fix her hair, she was always a woman."[10] Jackie registers the complex matrix of racial politics, but she seems oblivious to gender politics, and particularly to the intersections of race and gender when constructing an identity.

Jackie wants to believe that she can escape race depending on how she styles her hair, but she concedes that gender is inescapable when the Weather Girls remind her of her city friends. "Those city friends were black, while the Weather Girls at the dog park were white, but they were basically the same" (209). This statement fails to register, however, that bodies are marked by both pigmentation and sex—the two are interlocking factors that cannot be assessed separately in this case. Yes, Jackie will always be a woman, but the multiple dimensions of her identity ensure that her raced experiences are connected intricately to her gendered experiences. This connection is most visible in Jackie's relationship with Nan.

Nan's feelings of possessiveness toward Jackie highlight Jackie's failure to understand the complex dimensions of her own identity. Jackie complains that Nan tries to expand their friendship beyond the dog park, but Jackie declines because "Nan was too possessive" (210). Nan's constant stream of advice and lover-like possessiveness is symbolic of hegemony. Nan's philosophies are rooted in patriarchal and pseudoscientific epistemologies that were the force behind the Atlantic Slave Trade and European imperialism. It is suspicious then that Nan is invested in possessing Jackie. Nan's character and background reinforce such suspicion. Jackie describes Nan as sexless. Nan is completing a PhD and historically academe has been a white, male-dominated space. Furthermore, Nan's area of concentration, Victorian studies, is not coincidental. Great Britain's Victorian Era occurred during the height of the industrial revolution and British colonialism. Her research topic on Victorian birth control methods is significant because the Victorian era also marked a newfound concern with sexuality, the domestic sphere, and prostitution. This concern gave rise to the emphasis on purity and domesticity that produced the cult of true womanhood, which emerges simultaneously with the development of racial discourses that situated blackness as a sign of impurity and whiteness as its converse. Piety, purity, domesticity, and subservience—the cardinal virtues of the cult of true womanhood—served not only to define the boundaries of acceptable female behavior, but to also define black women outside of the realm of true womanhood while firmly inscribing elite and middle-class white women within this paradigm.[11] Despite pursuing a research topic that has radical implications for women and their bodies, Nan's topic also delves into an area that socially immobilized black women—black women like Beulah the domestic who, despite breaking color barriers on a sitcom that was the first nationally broadcast weekly television series starring an African American, found that such "firsts" failed to compensate for the stereotypical role imposed on her. Nan's project to challenge the cult of true womanhood, then, is limited to rejecting patriarchal gender ideologies but affirming racial ideologies that continue to marginalize black women.

Nan also invokes Charles Darwin's pseudoscientific notions of racial hierarchies.[12] Nan "schools" Jackie on Darwinian selection when she derides the Weather Girls' purebreds and assures Jackie that her and Jackie's "standard mongrels" had much better chances of surviving in the wild (209). In light of Nan's education, her advice to Jackie represents an attempt to discipline Jackie—who is Beulah—training Beulah is training Jackie. Although Nan has some admirable attributes, many of her ideologies resonate with the racial science that subordinated people of African descent. Her desire to influence Jackie's thoughts, as well as her desire to control and discipline Jackie's behavior is indicative of the power the U.S. government employs to define and control its black subjects through the interaction of legal and cultural discourse that rely on race and racial thinking for their validity.

The Wound that Cries Out

Considering the suspicious nature of Nan's presence in the narrative, it is productive to ponder why Jackie is so drawn to her and even longs for her presence. Trauma theory offers an insightful method for interpreting Jackie's relationship with Nan. It is important to note, however, that in my turn to trauma theory I am cognizant that reading racialized people as experiencing trauma can be problematic. When the text itself calls attention to this trauma, however, I believe it is fruitful and necessary to engage the discourse. This is particularly true of much mixed-race literature, as it rather consistently focuses on the psychologically damaging affects of being as scholar Werner Sollors calls it, "neither black nor white."[13] So then, Cathy Caruth's interpretation of the compulsion to repeat catastrophic events as symbolic of a "double wound" provides a framework for critical analysis of Jackie and Nan's relationship.[14]

Caruth draws on what Freud terms "traumatic neurosis"—the unwished for and yet somehow reconciling repetition of a catastrophic event—in order to articulate her argument that the *voice* that cries out when it is paradoxically released *through the wound* is more striking than the inadvertent repetition.[15] In Jackie's case, the inadvertent repetition is represented through the various Beulah tropes in the texts and how they are all reminders of a history that is riddled with the residue of slavery. Caruth draws an etymological connection between trauma and wound and makes the point that in Freud's text, "*trauma* is a wound inflicted not only upon the body but also upon the mind." This historical trauma thus extends beyond the Beulah tropes to Jackie whose mixed race body exemplifies how the repetition of trauma is inflicted upon the mind. Jackie's life as a phenotypically white woman is a source of daily trauma, which for example, is demonstrated in the context of her relationship with Kip. Their relationship becomes a source of trauma for him as well because it forces him to attend to his hypervisibility that is read against her invisibility.

Caruth argues that when the voice of the inflicted cries out the voice "bears witness to the past he has unwittingly repeated. The voice witnesses a truth that the inflictor of the wound cannot fully know" (2–3). As far as "double wounds" are concerned, Caruth explains that the first wound is not fully known until it imposes itself again through repetitive action. The second wound then proves that "trauma is not locatable in the simple violent or original event in an individual's past, but rather in the way that its very unassimilated nature—the way it was precisely *not known* in the first instance—returns to haunt the survivor later on" (4). The most compelling aspect of Caruth's double wound argument concerns the wound's relationship to "the voice of the other." As Caruth articulates it, this relationship provides a productive method for analyzing *racial wounds* in Senna's text.[16] When Caruth acknowledges the sensibleness in recognizing Clorinda's voice [the wounded] as representative of "the other within the self that retains the memory of the 'unwitting' traumatic events of one's past," she also proposes a second option. Caruth states, "But we can also read the address of the voice here . . . as the story of the way in which one's own trauma is tied up with the trauma of another, the way in which trauma may lead, therefore, to the encounter with another, through the very possibility and surprise of listening to another's wound" (8). This second option provides key insight for interpreting Jackie's relationship with Nan, as well as explaining Jackie's treatment of Beulah.

Both Beulah and Jackie represent the historical wounds of slavery. The dog's wound is represented through the hole in her nose, while Jackie's wound is represented through her racially mixed body. Jackie responds to Beulah's puppy-natured destruction of her apartment and personal belongings by throwing her, kicking her, slapping her, and jerking her leash too hard. The beatings become a ritual, something Jackie yearns for and feels exhilarated by. Prior to the first beating, Jackie notices a small, round hole between the dog's nostrils. After feeling repulsion, then horror, then pity, Jackie begins to cry, "The hole was more than she could handle" (202). The pity Jackie feels does not prohibit her from beating Beulah, but it does make her more aware of her own unhealed racial wounds, as well as her inability to remedy them.

Beulah is "the other within the self" that retains the trauma of Jackie's ancestral past. The hole in her nose that makes Jackie weep because of its reminder of slavery clearly represents the first wound, the mortal wound that must be repeated in order to be assimilated into the conscious. Jackie's racially ambiguous body represents the second wound that was unassimilated in the first instance of trauma and can only be known when it returns to haunt the survivor in the future. Thus Beulah is the wound that cries out "in the attempt to tell us of a reality or truth that is not otherwise available."[17] Jackie is so unsure of who she is and what she really wants that she fails to hear Beulah's potentially redemptive voice and instead Jackie hears only Nan's hegemonic voice. Freud notes that "suggestion"—the patient's submissiveness to the physician—helps remedy the compulsion to repeat.[18] But Jackie seeks Nan as a sort of false therapist—she hears Nan's voice instead of Beulah's—thus perpetuating the compulsion to repeat instead of accepting Beulah's "suggestion" that would help "loosen" the repression.

Caruth's "voice of the other" offers us a way of understanding both Beulah and Nan as "the story of the way in which one's own trauma is tied up with the trauma of another, the way in which trauma may lead, therefore, to the encounter with another" (1996, 8). Beulah's relationship with the trauma of slavery is rather apparent. She represents the racial wounds that persist into the present through Beulah the domestic and Jackie's own *warring ideals* surrounding her racial identity. Jackie's difficulties reconciling the racial geography of the U.S. conjure Beulah's presence. As a symbol of white supremacy, it is not as obvious how Nan possesses any trauma that is tied up with that of Jackie. A different sort of analysis offers a method for interpreting Nan's entanglement with Jackie's trauma.

Dismantling a Race House

In *The Melancholy of Race*, Anne Anlin Cheng argues that one of the United States' greatest fallacies is the premise that "all men are created equal" when American history presents such a different story. She argues that the "exclusion-yet-retention" of racialized others creates a melancholic bind for dominant White America.[19] The contradiction of the nation's founding principles—life, liberty, and the pursuit of happiness—for marginalized racial groups affect both the oppressed and the oppressor. Cheng points out that the oppressor, or dominant white identity, cannot escape these contradictions, and thus shares marginalized people's racial melancholia.

One of the reasons Cheng's work is compelling is because she emphasizes that privilege and power do not exempt white Americans from racial melancholia—it is a national melancholia that transcends the color line. By reading Nan through the lens of racial melancholia, and the guilt and denial of guilt that are entangled in the racialization process, we can understand how Jackie and Beulah's repeated-and-shared trauma is also shared with Nan. Such a reading relies on Nan's research on Victorian England, particularly birth control for its plausibility. Nan's work literally connects her with the origins of race, racial thinking, and their intersection with gender—inventions that will ultimately shape the U.S. racial formation. Cheng reminds us that power and privilege do not exempt white Americans from melancholia. Perhaps, then, we should read both Nan and Jackie as a melancholic pair that lament the impossibility of racial purity in Americans, which would account for Nan's disdain for the Weather Women and their purebred dogs. In other words, Jackie and Nan exist in the hole that is national melancholia that transcends the color line. Literally Jackie and Nan are the mutts of American history. Jackie's trauma necessarily forces her encounter with Nan. Thus neither Beulah nor Nan nor the dog park can provide Jackie with an intervention plan that allows her to be comfortable in her racially mixed body.

Jackie's inability to disavow the one-drop rule is tied to her inability to love herself. Despite her craving to beat Beulah, the language of the narrative depicts a very conflicted relationship. After beating Beulah for the first time, Jackie spends the evening showering Beulah with affection and declaring her love for the dog. Such behavior suggests that Jackie has never been loved with the depth and unconditional acceptance that she gets from Beulah. Jackie feels bad about abusing Beulah and even doodles pictures of her when she is at work. Jackie's doting, if not romantic sentiments, does not however overpower her need to also exhibit aggression: "Even as Jackie kicked and beat and cursed Beulah, she loved her. Beulah was all that mattered to Jackie. Their relationship was one of extremes. Extreme hatred, extreme love. Violence seemed just another form of intimacy. Jackie wondered if you could truly love something without sometimes despising it. Jackie raged against Beulah, while simultaneously sacrificing everything for the beast" (207). This love-hate relationship is spurred by Beulah's unmistakable parallels with Beulah the domestic. But it is also spurred by Jackie's own self-hatred. She sees Beulah as a replication of herself. At moments she loves herself and thus she loves Beulah, but she cannot maintain the self-love because she is consistently mired in a past that compromises her ability to inhabit the present fully and satisfactorily. Beulah reminds Jackie of her racial ambiguity and forces her to acknowledge the persistence of the color line. Instead of emulating the unconditional self-love that is indicative of Beulah's forgiving and happy-go-lucky personality, Jackie abandons Beulah in the park. Jackie has no knowledge base with which she can incorporate Beulah's lessons of self-love, hence her return to the beauty salons and her previously dissatisfying life.

When Jackie returns to her previous dissatisfying life, that return is reminiscent of Senna's construction of Elemeno in her first novel, *Caucasia*. The possibility, yet ultimate disappointment of Beulah Land's (the dog park) security resonates with Elemeno. Elemeno is a place, people, and language that exists only in the imagination of Birdie and Cole Lee, the two young, biracial sisters in *Caucasia*. Birdie describes Elemeno the language as having "no verb tenses, no pronouns, just words floating outside time and space without owner or direction" (6). Her sister Cole offers a racial and spatial framework for understanding Elemeno as not just a language, but also as a people and as a place.

> The Elemenos . . . could turn not just from black to white, but from brown to yellow to purple to green, and back again. She said they were a shifting people, constantly changing their form, color, pattern, in a quest for invisibility . . . their changing routine was . . . less a game of make-believe than a fight for the survival of their species. The Elemenos could turn deep green in the bushes, beige in the sand, or blank white in the snow, and their power lay precisely in their ability to disappear into any surrounding. (7)

Elemenos are shifting people similar to the folkloric shapeshifters. They employ trickster techniques for survival in a world where their species is endangered and they become chameleons, blending appropriately to different cultural landscapes. The fact that Elemenos need to constantly shift in order to elude extinction prompts Birdie to question, "the point of surviving if you had to disappear" (7). In other words, the racial geography of Elemeno the place never permits Elemenos the people to be themselves.

The parallels between the racial landscape of Elemeno and the geopolitics of race in the United States prompts Senna to explain that the title of her novel, *Caucasia*, turns "race into a place instead of a condition." Caucasia, Elemeno, and the land of Beulah become racialized places even when the sole point of their creation is safety. It is worth asking, then: Does the census category addition allow Elemenos to be themselves or does it create a false sense of security that it cannot deliver? It would seem that in spite of Senna's assertion that Caucasia turns race into a place instead of a condition, Caucasia is an inescapable condition that plagues the geography. The image *Time* morphs is evidence of this, as it seems to suggest that mixed race people are potentially the cure for this condition in this particular geography. But the fact of the matter is that we have always had this potential and that law or other cultural designs have thwarted it. The fact that the magazine does not register this—hence its assertion that she does not exist yet—reminds us that Caucasia will remain a condition that plagues the U.S. geography.

Race is geography in the places Senna imagines and critiques, which is why even in these so-called safe spaces Senna treats the mixed race body as a form of imprisonment that reflects the absurdity of racialization. Jackie's abuse of Beulah and her own self-hatred represents her frustration with the binary construction of black-white racial identities that further alienate her in a space she would like to feel comfortable in. Beulah performs a continuous and what Jackie perceives to be malicious destruction of Jackie's apartment that prohibits even the interior space of her apartment from being a safe space. Robyn Wiegman notes "To imagine ourselves outside such regimes of corporeal visibility is not only at some level unthinkable, but also intolerable to our own conception of who and what we 'are'" (4).[20] Our inability to *imagine* that which Wiegman speaks of renders Jackie unable to feel secure in her relationship with Kip, at work, or in the dog park, not because race and racialization permeates the public and private sphere, but also because of her own inability to imagine herself "outside such regimes of corporeal visibility."

This narrative, then, is about the way all Americans are entangled in the melancholic dilemma that is race. Nan's white phenotype does not move her beyond race, Kip's black phenotype does not move him beyond race, and Jackie's mixed phenotype does not move her beyond race. Senna calls attention to how geography and race remain intricately interconnected despite increases in immigration, migration, and the transnational flow of culture. These phenomena certainly do change the *face* of the United States so to speak, especially on a cultural level, but they do not erase the histories of racialization in the United States; and these changes alone cannot erase how such histories manifest in the present. Aside from disrupting a variety of utopian democratic ideals that indeed do not exist in the United States, Senna ultimately demands that scholars, the media, and citizens in general think critically about the intersection of race and gender beyond race discourse.

Although the editors at *Time* might not realize it, it is no coincidence that they morphed a woman's face. If the economic growth and increased cultural diversity of the nation is "on the backs of blacks," as Morrison asserts, then the permanence of race is inscribed on the black woman's body. How the black woman's body is assessed in moves beyond race is indeed critical to all U.S. citizens' access to the nation's democratic ideals. Put differently, women (re)produce the nation writ large, which means black women—phenotypically white or black bodies—are simultaneously the cure and the disease. For *Time*, the racially ambiguous, but nonetheless of African descent morphed woman's body is presented as a cure that grants the nation access to unraced spaces.[21] Senna, however, disrupts such utopianism in her counternarrative, which asserts that if we assess the mixed race body as an idyllic geography, we effectively render black women ungendered, because such assessments fail to consider the complex and interlocking factors of race and gender. This assertion is evidenced in Jackie's own transformation into Beulah when she begins neglecting her appearance, stops showering and changing clothes regularly, develops calluses on her hands, stops waxing her legs, and makes no effort to attend to her filthy fingernails and feet that are "as tough as hooves." Jackie not only becomes Beulah, but she becomes ungendered. In this instance, Jackie's mixed race body operates as a disease, not a cure—it is the residue of the colonial discipline that drove modernity and created a global color line.

Despite the unsavory repercussions of employing the mixed race body as a tool for accessing an idyllic geography, like literary scholar Robert Reid-Pharr, Senna believes it is fruitful "to imagine life beyond the veil."[22] Her narrative warns, however, that these imaginings must necessarily move beyond discourse entrenched in utopian democratic idealism when the reality is that the nation continues to be stratified by and subject to the color line. The lesson that "The Land of Beulah" seems to want to teach, then, is that privileging racial mixture not only fails to erase race, but in the case of the mixed-race black woman, such privileging demands that she is sacrificed ultimately to imaginations beyond the veil. Senna challenges us to instead imagine a space beyond Beulah that Toni Morrison sums up well as, "a space where race both matters and is rendered impotent"—not a utopian paradise, but a messy and complicated *home.* Such imaginings might create access to a space outside of what Morrison refers to as the "race house"—a secure space where the raced *and* gendered body is "psychically and physically safe."[23]

Notes

I am indebted to the engaged reading, thoughtful criticism, and provocative conversations offered by Jesse J. Scott as I wrote and revised this chapter, as well as the larger project portions it is extracted from.

1. In *The Souls of Black Folk* (1903) philosopher and sociologist, W.E.B. DuBois, famously declared that there is a metaphorical line that divides white America and black America, limiting black Americans' full access to citizenship.

2. "From the Managing Editor," *Time*, 18 November 1993, http://www.time.com/time/magazine/article/0,9171,979727,00.html?promoid=googlep.

3. Danzy Senna, "The Mulatto Millennium," in *Half and Half: Writers on Growing up Biracial and Bicultural*, ed. Claudine Chiawei O'Hearn (New York: Pantheon Books, 1998), 14.

4. Toni Morrison, "On the Backs of Blacks," *Time*, 18 November 1993, http://www.time.com/time/magazine/article/0,9171,979736,00.html.

5. Claudia M. Milian Arias, "An Interview with Danzy Senna," *Callaloo* 25, no. 2 (2002): 448.

6. Chesnutt and Toomer expressed similar opinions on the efficacy of racial amalgamation during the early twentieth century. In "The Future American: What the Race is Likely to Become in the Process of Time" (1898), Chesnutt presents a utopian

illusion that privileges amalgamation. Toomer presents a similar sentiment in his poem "The Blue Meridian" in 1936.

7. Paul Gilroy, *Against Race: Imagining Political Culture beyond the Color Line* (Cambridge, MA: Belknap Press of Harvard University Press, 2000), 17.

8. The ABC sitcom, *Beulah*, ran from 1950–53, starring Ethel Waters in its first two years and Louise Beavers in its final year. *Beulah* was the first nationally broadcast weekly television series starring an African American. Despite this first, Beulah took on the stereotypical mammy role, solving *her* white family's problems and keeping them happy.

9. Cheryl Harris, "Whiteness as Property," *Critical Race Theory: The Key Writings that Formed the Movement* (New York: The New Press, 1995), 276–91.

10. The fact that Jackie refers to the group of single, childless white women as the Weather Girls is ironic, as this name makes it almost unavoidable not to think of the black singing group—large black women singing about raining men. The selection of this particular name seems to suggest that the social, political, and economic climate has not changed for women across racial lines. Thus it is interesting to consider whether these women with their purebred dogs are waiting for a racially "pure" era, or are the dogs a substitute for the racial purity they can never achieve.

11. In *Black Feminist Thought: Knowledge, Consciousness, and the Politics of Empowerment*, Patricia Hill Collins argues that the mammy figure effectively stripped black women of fertility and sexuality while buttressing the ideologies of the cult of true womanhood. Hazel Carby also offers an analysis of the effects of the cult of true womanhood on black women in *Reconstructing Womanhood: The Emergence of the Afro-American Woman Novelist*.

12. Darwin connected race to biological evolution. This connection not only bolstered Enlightenment ideologies concerning race, but also paved the way for eugenics.

13. Werner Sollors, *Neither Black nor White yet Both: Thematic Explorations of Interracial Literature* (Cambridge, MA: Harvard University Press, 1997).

14. Cathy Caruth, *Unclaimed Experience: Trauma, Narrative, and History* (Baltimore: Johns Hopkins University Press, 1996).

15. In *Beyond the Pleasure Principle* Freud utilizes Tasso's romantic epic, *Gerusalemme Liberata*, as an example of traumatic neurosis. During a duel Tancred unknowingly kills his beloved, Clorinda, who is disguised in the armor of an enemy knight. After Clorinda's death, Tancred slashes at a tree when caught in a magic forest. The tree bleeds and cries out in the voice of Clorinda that Tancred has wounded her once again.

16. I am not sure who coined the term *racial wounds*, but aside from myself, J. Brooks Bouson also employs the term in *Quiet as It's Kept: Shame, Trauma, and Race in the Novels of Toni Morrison*. Bouson hopes that her scholarship will "aesthetically repair . . . deep and abiding *racial wounds*."

17. Julie Rivkin, et al., *Literary Theory*, 4.

18. Ibid., n. 174.

19. Slave narratives also dedicated much attention to demonstrating the manner in which slavery was not only inhumane for the slaves, but also how it dehumanized the slave master.

20. Robyn Wiegman, *American Anatomies: Theorizing Race and Gender*, (Durham, NC: Duke University Press, 1995), 4.

21. The racial composition of Eve was: 15 percent Anglo-Saxon, 17.5 percent Middle Eastern, 17.5 percent African, 7.5 percent Asian, 35 percent Southern European, and 7.5 percent Hispanic.

22. Robert Reid-Pharr, *Conjugal Union: The Body, the House, and the Black American* (New York: Oxford University Press, 1999), 13.
23. Toni Morrison, "Home," 9–10.

Works Cited

Arias, Claudia M. Milian. "An Interview with Danzy Senna." *Callaloo* 25, no. 2 (2002): 447–52.

Caruth, Cathy. *Unclaimed Experience: Trauma, Narrative, and History*. Baltimore: Johns Hopkins University Press, 1996.

Cheng, Anne Anlin. *The Melancholy of Race*. New York: Oxford University Press, 2001.

Chesnutt, Charles W. "The Future American: What the Race Is Likely to Become in the Process of Time." In *Charles W. Chesnutt: Essays and Speeches*. Edited by Joseph R. McElrath, Jr., Robert C. Leitz III, and Jesse S. Crisler, 121–25. Stanford, CA: Stanford University Press, 1999.

DuBois, W.E.B. *The Souls of Black Folk*. New York: Vintage Books/The Library of America, 1990.

"From the Managing Editor," *Time*. 18 November 1993. http://www.time.com/time/magazine/article/0,9171,979727,00.html?promoid = googlep.

Gilroy, Paul. *Against Race: Imagining Political Culture beyond the Color Line*. Cambridge, MA: Belknap Press of Harvard University Press, 2000.

Harris, Cheryl. "Whiteness as Property." In *Critical Race Theory: The Key Writings that Formed the Movement*. Edited by Kimberlé Crenshaw et al., 276–91. New York: The New Press, 1995.

Morrison, Toni. "Home." In *The House that Race Built: Black Americans, U.S. Terrain*. Edited by Wahneema Lubiano, 3–12. New York: Pantheon Books, 1997.

———. "On the Backs of Blacks," *Time*. 18 November 1993. http://www.time.com/time/magazine/article/0,9171,979736,00.html.

Reid-Pharr, Robert. *Conjugal Union: The Body, the House, and the Black American*. New York: Oxford University Press, 1999.

Rivkin, Julie, and Michael Ryan, eds. *Literary Theory: An Anthology*. Malden, MA: Blackwell Publishers, 1998.

Senna, Danzy. *Caucasia*. New York: Riverhead Books, 1998.

———. "The Land of Beulah." In *Giant Steps: The New Generation of African American Writers*. Edited by Kevin Young, 194–214. New York: Perennial, 2000.

———. "The Mulatto Millennium." In *Half and Half: Writers on Growing Up Biracial and Bicultural*. Edited by Claudine Chiawei O'Hearn, 12–27. New York: Pantheon Books, 1998.

Sollors, Werner. *Neither White nor Black yet Both: Thematic Exploration of Interracial Literature*. Cambridge, MA: Harvard University Press, 1997.

Toomer, Jean. "The Blue Meridian." In *The New Caravan*. Edited by Alfred Kreymborg, Lewis Mumford, and Paul Rosenfeld. New York: W. W. Norton & Company, Inc., 1936.

Wiegman, Robyn. *American Anatomies: Theorizing Race and Gender*. Durham, NC: Duke University Press, 1995.

A Phenomenology of the Black Body

Charles Johnson

A BAWDY OLD BLACK FOLKTALE CELEBRATES THE PHYSICAL SUPERIORITY of black men:

> Two white farmers sat before the stove in a general store in Alabama, arguing over who had the longest tool as an old Negro named Willis swept the front porch. They agreed to compare lengths. The man with the longest would get $25 for each additional inch. The first unzipped his fly. Six inches. The second did the same. Seven. The first turned to Willis, and said, "Let's see yours, Willis." The janitor trembled and shook his head. "Nassuh, Ah doan think Ah'd better do that, sar." The white man became angry. "I said for you to get in on this heah bet, Willis!" Afraid to say no, the janitor uncoiled his tool on the table—it took a while, friend: Willis just kept throwing it out like a fishing line. Twelve inches. Someone said, "God damn!" The two men gave Willis $125, and he raced home to show the money to his wife Maybelle. Staring skeptically at her husband, Maybelle asked. "You got alla that just for being big?" Willis whooped and went into hysterics. "Honey, that was the easiest money Ah ever made! Them white folks just better thank the Lord Ah wasn't on hard."

Laughing at the good fortune of Willis, we may lose sight of the fact that his triumph is based on cultural assumptions that lock him into the body and, to echo W.E.B. DuBois, create in his life a "double-consciousness" in need of resolution. This seeks to define the ambiguity of his situation and describe the harrowing constraints upon both Willis and his white competitors.

Our past experience as a people can often be understood through its expression in language, myths, stereotypes, symbols, and folktales like this one. As multilayered complexes, they present collectively shared and communicated meanings. But before we can talk intelligently about the "black experience" of the body, in this or any other narrative, we must first get clear on what is essential to all experience—the correlate of consciousness and its content, *noesis-noema*, or subject and object. A rule for phenomenology is that there is never an object without a corresponding subject, and that "Consciousness is always consciousness *of* something," to quote Edmund Husserl. Given the universality of these structures for consciousness, it is reasonable to say that there is neither an impenetrable "white" or "black" experience, which are mutually exclusive, but rather that there are diverse human variations upon experience, which can always be communicated imaginatively or vicariously across racial, political, and cultural lines through language in its two analytic forms: philosophy and literature. Perhaps this point is disagreeable to proponents of cultural pluralism, but it is a presupposition of the philosophy of experience—phenomenology—that is here assumed as a working methodology. The symbol of the black body, for example, if interrogated, should disclose a racial experience wrought mythically. Our folk literature simultaneously conceals and reveals our primordial racial situation, and must be carefully unpacked if we wish to wrench self-understanding from it.

Black writers, particularly novelists and poets in search of fresh ways of seeing things familiar, frequently feel the power of folk myths and stereotypes and, so moved, wrestle with uncovering their meaning. Weaving in and out of Frantz Fanon's works are thematizations of black consciousness from the vantage point of existential phenomenology, but without a turn to the body as the radix for interpreting racial experience. In his controversial essay, "The Primevil Mitosis," Eldridge Cleaver brooks the stereotype of black American physicality by now checking his own feelings (as an experiencing subject) against the myth, now rendering its terms rigidly abstract, now pursuing its more painful political implications. His conclusion: "The gulf between the Mind and Body will be seen to coincide with the gulf between the two races."[1] But *is* there such a gulf between the Mind and Body?

Cleaver assumes a basic division between the bodily and mental experiences of blacks and whites. Racism is the given, historically constituted and lying in wait for black consciousness, concealing the ethical dualism which has—over long centuries of Western cultural development—made white "good" and black "evil." Cleaver, focusing on one aspect of the phenomenon, the psychophysical, finds that blacks are stripped of a mental life, which leaves them only a bodily existence (albeit a superior one like that of our janitor Willis), and he assigns them the name, "The Supermasculine Menial." He writes: "The body is tropical, warm, hot; Fire! It is soft, pleasing to the touch, luscious to the kiss. The blood is hot. Muscles are strength."[2] Alienated from this sensuous profile of the body, whites are characterized by Cleaver as "The Omnipotent Administrator." Weakness, frailty, cowardice, effeminacy, decay, and impotence are profiles associated with the white man's situation of abstraction from the body. Here, Cleaver's concerns in *Soul on Ice* are basically political, sexual, and polemical, not philosophical. But his attempt to explain our experience of embodiment may yield more philosophically than the author knows. His division recalls Paul Ricoeur's belief that, "It is possible for man to take two divergent and non-reconcilable perspectives upon himself because within man there is a non-coincidence which is that of the *finite* and the *infinite*,"[3] or of the physical and mental, consciousness and the body. It is even more illuminating when compared to Fanon's statement that, "There are times when the black man is locked into his body."[4]

Sexuality is not truly at issue in *Soul on Ice*. That is merely the manifestation of a larger problem of consciousness and the body in the black experience. The issue at stake is how blacks experience their own bodies within a world of racial restriction. By speaking descriptively, by casting the problem in absolute and often simple terms, Cleaver offers us the occasion for a broader consideration of experience, the body, and black consciousness.

Modern philosophy in the West since Descartes has entertained the idea that man is not identical with his physical being. In a crude formulation, man is presented mythologically and often philosophically as a mixture of mind and matter, spirit and flesh, consciousness and body, carnal shell and *Ka*, and remains to himself something of a mystery. The dialectic of matter and mind, subject and object, is a thread running the length of Western intellectual history, beginning with Plato's world of flux and world of forms. The later sundering of man and the world into mental and physical substances by Descartes in *The Meditations* throws light on the issue Cleaver is trying to bring to clarity—consciousness is experienced as being identical with, yet curiously distinct from, the body. One could almost categorize Western philosophy along the lines of whether a particular approach is primarily concerned with the subject of experience, consciousness, idealism, or the soul; if it emphasizes the object, matter, materialism, the body; or if it seeks a reconciliation between the two. Maurice Merleau-Ponty offers a simple but concise formulation to correct this false dualism that underlies the division between "The Omnipotent Administrator" and "The Super-masculine Menial": "I am my body."[5] It is that which reeves the subject to a world, anchors him in history, thus individualizing him, and makes possible perception and "meaning." It is my point of reference on the universe. I, as subject, am often at "one" with it, yet my relation as a human self to my body is also that of *radical otherness*. I *am* my body while I am also *not* my body (or I experience myself as not simply reducible to my body as the empirical object of physics, chemistry, neurology). Experience without "embodied consciousness" is as unthinkable as experience with the *noesis-noema* correlate: it is the irreducible way we are in the world. I am conscious of the world through the medium of my body.

To say that the body is our anchorage in the world is to bring this discussion to a consideration of "intentionality," the structure which gives meaning to experience. Intentions are at the heart of consciousness, or the *noesis*-pole, to the extent that they determine the manner in which we perceive the world. At this instant, let us say that I am a white administrator on campus. A strapping black student with a full natural, dashiki, coal-black complexion, and dark sunglasses comes into my office with a "dip-down," rolling gait. If my hobby is painting, perhaps I look toward the colorfulness of his clothing, and see him as a future subject for my canvas. Suppose I have just read Claude McKay's *Home to Harlem*, a novel which emphasizes the natural spontaneity of blacks; in this case I see the rhythms of his walk, the musicality of his movements in contrast to my own. Or, finally, suppose I am concerned that my daughter is being bused across town to a black school—Will she encounter people like this? In each instance the same student presents these multiple profiles of himself, they *are* his appearances, and each discloses a different "meaning." We have yet to speak of *his* experience upon entering the room and what my intentionality causes to arise in his consciousness. To "intend" an object or content of consciousness is to be "informed" by it as well as to *give form* to it. The mind is in no way passive; it is a participant in each act of knowing—self and object being inseparable poles of experience. It is also possible *not* to see other "meanings" or profiles presented by the object if the perceiver is locked with the "Natural Attitude," as Husserl calls it, and has been conditioned culturally or racially to fix himself upon certain "meanings." Rollo May, for example, reports of a patient who could not see an object placed before him on a table—it remained invisible on the basis of his inability to bring it forth intentionally as a content of consciousness.[6]

But consciousness is "embodied." Our desires, too, are "embodied," and it is clearly the case that every act of intending involves, to some extent, "interest." By this I mean that acting, willing, and intending are closely related. I see the student in a certain way because I fear for my daughter while she is across town. To *per*ceive a content is to *con*ceive that content. "The theory of the body image is, implicitly, a theory of perception."[7]

My body for me is not an assemblage of organs juxtaposed in space; my possession of it is undivided, and I know where my limbs are through a *body image*, know, when I sit at my desk, how my crossed feet appear, although I cannot see them. In all perception within a figure-ground relationship, where I either bring an object forth for attention or let it remain undifferentiated in the "ground," my body is the third term: it points me to the left or right, determines up and down, allows me to know space because as "embodied consciousness" I am in space, and know time because embodiment has temporality as one of its structures.

Right and left, established by the body, are sources of the lawful and forbidden; the body is emblematic; if I am "downcast," the body gestures accordingly with a drooping posture. "The body is our general medium for having a world."[8] The blind man's stick is no longer alien to him, not a mere object, but his bodily extension; the woman with a feather in her hat keeps a safe distance between it and things that might snap it off, but without looking: she *feels* these distances. All this is understood by the term *body image*, or in the work of Fanon, *body schema*. We see that motility is basic to intentionality.

Our first phenomenological act in a thematization of the black body involves a suspension or bracketing of all sociological and scientific theories concerning race. We wish to purify a field in which the body becomes the primary focus of racial consciousness. Whether black or white, the body is still experienced as having an ambiguity, a noncoincidence of mind and matter. I *am* my body, but clearly there is magic in the fact that when I say "Spread your fingers" the digits on my hand do so. I see my hand on my desk and sometimes it is alien; perhaps I do not even recognize it as *mine* when I see it in a photograph. Stranger still, I know that I cannot see myself as others see me, white and black, as if the secret of my body and the objectivity of its "outside" belongs, not to me, but to everyone else. Furthermore, I am black. I do not see what the white other sees in my skin, but I am aware of his intentionality, and—yes—aware that I often disclose something discomfiting to him. My body gives me the world, but, as that world is given, it is one in which I can be unseen. I walk down the hallway at the university and pass a professor I know well. He glances up quickly, yet does not acknowledge that he knows me. He has seen a black, a body, that remains for him always in the background, seldom figured forth save as maid, taxi driver, or janitor. Passing, he sees me as he sees the fire extinguisher to my left, that chair outside the door. I have been seen, yet not seen, acknowledged as present to him, but in a peculiar way. I call down the hallway, "Professor Peterson!" Recognizing me, he says, "Ah, Charles," and figures me forth. He offers me his hand and, shaking it, I see perhaps what he has seen: the darkness of the black body suggests "stain" primordially. For him, and at odd moments for me, this stain of my skin gives in a sudden stroke of intentionality "darkness," "guilt," "evil," an entire galaxy of meanings. Yet, it is *I* who perceive myself as "stained," as though I were an object for myself and no longer a subject. In fact, the stain of the black body seems figuratively to darken consciousness itself, to overshadow my existence as a subject. Is it this way for him? Cleaver writes:

> The chip on the Supermasculine Menial's shoulders is the fact that he had been robbed of his mind. In an uncannily effective manner, the society in which he lives assumed in its very structure that he, minus a mind, is the embodiment of Brute Power. The bias and reflexes of the society are against the cultivation of even the functioning of his mind, and it is borne in upon him from all sides that the society is deaf, dumb, and blind to his mind.[9]

That is, incapable of the intentionality that would allow the Supermasculine Menial to disclose an interiority. We shall call this situation the "black-as-body." Quoting Fanon: "In the white world the man of color encounters difficulties in the development of his bodily schema. Consciousness of the body is solely a negating activity . . . the body is surrounded by an atmosphere of uncertainty."[10] I am aware of each of my limbs through my *body image;* similarly, I am aware of my skin surface, my epidermal encasement through my *body image*, and particularly when I am "seen." "Saying that I have a body is thus a way of saying that I can be seen as an object and that I try to be seen as a subject, that another can be my master, so that shame and shamelessness express the dialectic of the plurality of consciousness, and have a metaphysical significance."[11] Fanon warns that "though Sartre's speculations on the existence of the Other may be correct . . . their application to a black consciousness proves fallacious. That is because the white man is not only the Other, but also the master, whether real or imaginary." And again: "Jean-Paul Sartre has forgotten that the Negro suffers in his body quite differently from the white man."[12]

The experience of the black-as-body becomes, not merely a Self-Other conflict, nor simply Hegel's torturous Master-Slave dialectic, but a variation on both these conditions, intensified by the particularity of the body's appearance as black, as "stained," lacking interiority and, as Fanon writes, as being "overdetermined from without." The body as opaque and consciousness as invisible is developed in Cleaver's brief essay. And if that consciousness is not experienced by the Other as invisible, it is the repository for the offscum of racial relations—to black subjectivity is attributed the contents that white consciousness itself fears to contain or confront: bestial sexuality, uncleanliness, criminality, all the purported "dark things." In R. W.

Shufeldt's *The Negro, A Menace to Civilization* (1907) and Thomas Dixon, Jr.'s, *The Leopard's Spots*, the idea is extended to include black blood, which carries the germ of the underworld and the traits of lower orders of animals; one drop of black blood, for example, will cause a white family to revert to Negroid characteristics even after a full century; the mulatto, though possessing white blood, is depicted as dangerous because his surface "outside," not being stained, betrays the criminality and animality of his interior.[13]

The stereotype with which we began discloses the black-as-body but, as a pure literary presentation, it conceals the original situation of "embodied consciousness" made a problem for itself by "stain." Consider the concern our grandparents had with body complexion, "brightening the race" through careful marriage, the terrible importance of fair skin, curly hair, and "yellah women." They were not fools, these old folks; they knew what they experienced. And understood skin-bleaching creams and straightening combs as important because these changed their stained "outsides" upon which, in this social system, the depth of their "insides" would be gauged by others. (Indeed, critic Robert Bone has called Christianity in James Baldwin's *Go Tell it on the Mountain* a "spiritual bleaching cream.") Stain recalls defilement, guilt, sin, corpses that contaminate, menstruating women; and with them come the theological meanings of punishment, ostracism, and the need to be "cleansed." It was never so much that, "If you're light, you're alright," meant that whiteness was rightness on the basis of the lack of pigmentation alone; rather, it meant that, "Washing a Moor white over three generations," degree by painful degree, led to his social recognition by the Other as human subject, as—in some cases—his possessing a soul, as "inside."

I am walking down Broadway in Manhattan, platform shoes clicking on the hot pavement, thinking as I stroll of, say, Boolean expansions. I turn, thirsty, into a bar. The dimly-lit room, obscured by shadows, is occupied by whites. Goodbye, Boolean expansions. I am *seen.* But, as a black, seen as stained body, as physicality, basically opaque to others—a possibility that, of course, whites themselves have in a room of blacks. Their look, an intending beam focusing my way, suddenly realizes something larval in me. My world is epidermalized, "collapsed like a house of cards into the stained casement of my skin."[14] My subjectivity is turned inside out like a shirtcuff. "And so it is not I who make a meaning for myself, but it is the meaning that was already there, preexisting, waiting for me,"[15] much like a mugger at a boardwalk's end. All I am, can be to them, is as nakedly presented as the genitals of a plant since they cannot see my other profiles. Epidermalization spreads throughout the body like an odor, like an echoing sound. This feeling differs little from that of sexuality: a sudden dizziness and disorientation, an acute awareness of my outside, of its being for others, a tight swell at my temples. But it is not the pathological feeling of "inferiority" alone that Fanon speaks of when my being is stolen—it is Cleaver's perception of the black-as-body. Yet, Fanon is correct. "For not only must the black man be black; he must be black in relation to the white man."[16] Because it is from whites that the intention, the "meaning" of the black body comes. I sit at the bar, ignoring the Others; but the body is acutely aware of them, knows immediately when someone outside my peripheral vision has stood up. It is intense, as though consciousness has shifted to the skin's seen surfaces.

Our body responds totally to this abrupt epidermalization; consciousness for the subject is violently emptied of content: one, in fact, draws a "blank," though clearly for the white Other my interiority is, if not invisible, a space filled with sensuality, crime, or childlike simplicity. There are physiological reactions: the pulse and adrenalin increase, the seen skin becomes moist, as if the body is in open conspiracy with the white Other to confirm the sudden eclipse of my consciousness entirely by corporeality. I feel its sleepy awkwardness, and know myself not as subject but as slumberous, torpid matter. The Other awaits my slurring my words; my mouth, dry as ash, seems ready to realize his expectation. He awaits a signal of my "Negroness"—perhaps my brutalizing the language when I order a beer: some signal that we in our bodies are not the same. If I am the sort of "Negro" brought up to be a "credit to the race," I must forever be on guard against my body betraying me in public; I must suppress the profile that their frozen intentionality brings forth—I police my actions, and take precautions against myself so the myth of stain, evil, and physicality, like a Platonic form, does not appear in me.

Or, let us say, I sit sipping expresso with a white friend in the Village, discussing Borges, Barthelme, Baraka, basketball, the incredible Pele. I've smoked myself into a sore throat; I sip the scum-surfaced coffee merely to wet my lips, to ease my throat. Our conversation turns circuitously and comes to Walt Frazier. The Other slaps my knee soundly. He says, "Man, that cat is the most beautiful animal I've ever seen on a basketball court. I mean, he moves like—like a cheetah, or a big jungle cat." Make no mistake: this comes from him as the highest compliment. He is "hip," you see, liberal, a Left Bank intellectual—it is merely a *faux pas*. He has not reduced us to a "nothingness." The reduction is to "muscles are strength." Paradoxically, we are reduced to the body as the subject of physics—Brute Power. Yet, as with the rush of sexuality, a torpor glazes over my consciousness, a languor arises like a sleepiness in my limbs. The thickness of the world's texture is thinned. The body commonly extends itself in vehicles, buildings, machines, and clothing. "Consciousness is being toward the thing through the intermediary of the body—to move one's body is to aim at things through it; it is to allow oneself to respond to their call."[17] But the black-as-body must see such a call as dubious, even though the "White Only" signs have been torn down, because there remain strict territorial boundaries, real or imagined, when we experience the searing Sartrean "look" of the hate-stare, when the world is epidermalized. Our body in these cases comes awake, translates itself as total physicality—it, oddly enough, feels as if it is listening with its limbs to the Other as my interiority shrivels like something burned, falls into confusion, feels threatened and, if it does not make me constitute myself as hatred (unable to change the world, I emotionally change myself), it momentarily, like a misty field, hazes over.

But we have not completely answered the question raised by Cleaver. There are black modes of flight from the black-as-body situation to consider. So far we have said that in a situation structured by a color-caste system, a black's consciousness and his lived-world (*Lebenswelt*) are frequently epidermalized and thrown into confusion when others intend him as the black-as-body. Once I am so one-sidely seen, I have several options open to me on the level of consciousness. These are also stages in recent black history:

(A) I accept this being seen only from the outside, accept my human possibility of being matter *sans* mind for the Others. I craftily use this invisibility of my interior to deceive, and thus to win survival, as the folk-hero Trickster John frequently does in the "Old Marster and John" cycle. My stain is like the heavy make-up of a clown; it conceals me completely. The motto of this useful opacity is the rhyme: "Got one mind for whitefolks to see / Got another one that's really me." That is, not being acknowledged as a subject is my strength, my chance for cunning and masquerade, for guerrilla warfare: I am a spy in the Big House. I cynically play with their frozen intentions, presuppositions, and stereotypes; I shuffle and appear lazy to avoid work, or—if I am a modern—I manipulate their basic fear of me as Darkness and Brute Power to win concessions. It is what Ralph Ellison calls "Rinehartism" in his novel *Invisible Man.* In Richard Wright's "novel-of-ideas," *The Outsider*, the protagonist is Cross Damon, a black existential hero with an extensive background in Heidegger, Husserl, and French phenomenology, who is freed from his former life by a freak subway wreck in Chicago. He assumes a new identity, but needs a false birth certificate. He thinks: "He would have to present to the officials a Negro so scared and ignorant that no white man would ever dream that he was up to anything deceptive." By shuffling, head-scratching, eye-blinking, and butchering the language, Cross pulls off the grotesque deception, and the author explains:

> And as he stood there manipulating their responses, Cross knew exactly what kind of man he would pretend to be to kill suspicion if he ever got into trouble. In his role as an ignorant, frightened Negro, each white man—except those few who were free from the race bias of their group—would leap to supply him with a background and an identity; each white man would project out on him his own conception of the Negro and he could safely hide behind it. . . . He knew that deep in their hearts those two white clerks knew that no human being on earth was as dense as he made himself out to be, but they wanted, needed to believe it of Negroes and it helped them to feel racially superior. They were pretending, just as he had been pretending.[18]

(B) Perhaps I vindicate my eloquence, culture, and my charm to demonstrate to the Other that I, despite my stained skin, do indeed have an inside. "Y'know, I was just thinking about Boolean expansions," I tell the barkeeper. I self-consciously sprinkle my speech with French (my interiority is Continental, you see). Perhaps I pretend that I am not Afro-American at all, but part Indian, Jamaican, or an African—a flight from the historical experience of American antebellum slavery in which epidermalization reaches its acme.

(C) Or I am radical, and seize the situation at its root by reversing the negative meaning of the body and, therefore, the black-as-body: "It is beautiful," I say, "I am a child of the Sun." The situation of the black-as-body possessing noncognitive traits is not rejected in this most recent variation of cultural nationalism, but rather stood upon its head: the meaning still issues from the white Other. I applaud my athletic, amorous, and dancing ability, my street-wisdom and savior-faire, my "soul," the food my body eats ("Yeah," I scream at my white friend in the Village, "we're naturally superior to you at sports. Uh huhn, and we satisfy our women better *too!*"); I speak of the communal ("single-body") social life of my African ancestors before the fifteenth-century slave trade, their bodily closeness to the earth. I am Antaeus in this persuasion of the alienated black self's phenomenological pilgrimage to itself, and the whites—flesh-starved invaders, freebooters, buccaneers, seamen who bring syphilis to ancient Africa—are alienated physically from the earth. They see their lost humanity in me. They steal me to take it home. If I am a member of the early Nation of Islam and believe in its mythology of Yacub, the black scientist who created a "white beast" from the black community, I intend the whites as quasimen "grafted" from the original black-as-body until, by degrees, the Caucasian appears as a pale and pitiful abstraction from myself, ontologically removed several stages from the basic reality which I represent.

Curiously, this persuasion in which stain and the black-as-body are inverted is ahistorical; it must involve a complete reconstitution of cultural meanings with the black body as its foundation: two thousand years of color and symbolism must be recast. Hence, we see the black-as-body in this profile generating new cultural forms: African dress (body extensions), Swahili (what my body speaks), the Nation of Islam and Black Church of Christ (my interiority is black, you see), but behind such a cultural revolution, which I create, is the enigma of the black-as-body in a state of stain. I portray my body to myself as "luscious to the kiss," beautiful, "tropical," soulful, sensuous—as "Fire!" My knowledge is natural, from "Nature" (another vast body) and is called "mother-wit," a form of knowing antithetical to the lifeless thoughts in the upper recesses of the Omnipotent Administrator's brain. I intend the white body as pitifully unstained, stiff, decadent, rigid, unnatural, cerebral, and pasty like something left under my kitchen sink, away from the skin-darkening sun, for too long a time. No attempt to bridge the false dualism of the Supermasculine Menial and the Omnipotent Administrator, between the body and consciousness, is made in these variations.

It should be clear that what is described in Cleaver's "The Primevil Mitosis" is a general human possibility based upon the ability of "embodied consciousness" to be made a problem for itself within a racial caste system. As we have seen, the problem is not diminished by the customary strategies for escaping it. The black body remains an ambiguous object in our society, still susceptible to whatever meanings the white gaze assigns to it.

Postscript, 1993

This chapter, which originally appeared in the Winter 1976 issue of *Ju-Ju: Research Papers in Afro-American Studies*, was written in 1975 as my "style paper" for the PhD program in philosophy at SUNY-Stony Brook. Back then all doctoral candidates were required to submit for the faculty's approval an essay using the methods of one of the three principal schools of twentieth-century philosophy—analytic or British, American philosophy (pragmatism), or phenomenology—and since aesthetics was my field of concentration, I chose the latter. If memory serves, this was easily one of the hardest years of my life. As a graduate student living on a teaching assistantship, I was broke, but that June saw the birth of our son Malik, and the feverish writing of the first draft for *Oxherding Tale*, a novel I would publish seven years later. I remember monkishly retreating into one of the foulest apartment buildings in Port Jefferson, New York (it was all we could afford that summer) and, when I wasn't working on the novel, reading Sartre's *Being and Nothingness*, Heidegger's *Being and Time*, and Merleau-Ponty's *The Phenomenology of Perception* back-to-back in about the space of a month. Out of that context of unemployment and impoverishment and general concerns for my son, and fresh from my immersion in these seminal works of the German and French phenomenological movements, this chapter was conjured.

Looking back across eighteen years at this descriptive analysis, I realize that my hope was to examine the black male body as a cultural object and to inquire into how it has been interpreted, manipulated, and given to us, particularly in popular culture. In general, too little has changed in the social world since the essay was first published. Indeed, for a few years things got worse. In the Bush campaign's exploitation of Willie Horton to frighten voters in 1988, in the racial slur about "Gorillas in the Mist" from the policeman who beat Rodney King as he would a dangerous animal, in the television footage of black male destructiveness during the Los Angeles riot, in the rise of the white supremacy movement in the last decade, in Pat Buchanan's attack on NEA for funding a film about gay black men (and ex-Klansman David Duke's startling though brief political success), in the decimation of black communities by AIDS, in the sexual harassment charges against Clarence Thomas, who according to Anita Hill described himself as "Long Dong Silver," in the sexist "gangster" lyrics offered by Ice T and other rap artists, in the gang-banging legions of Crips and Bloods, in the relentless barrage of statistics about murder among young black men and their failure to support their families, and even in the popular novels of several black women authors during the decade of the 1980s, we find that the black male as "Negro beast"—violent, sex-obsessed, irresponsible, and stupid—still has great currency and acceptance in our culture.

However, it's important to point out that none of these cultural meanings cluster around the black *female* body. In an amazing and revolutionary feat of cultural reconstruction, contemporary black women have made dominant the profile of the female body as, first and foremost, *spiritual:* a communal-body of politically progressive, long-suffering women who are responsible, hard-working and compassionate, who support each other in all ways, protect and nurture their children and live meaningful lives without black male assistance. The black female body is, in fact, frequently offered to us as the *original* body of a humankind descended from a black Eve of Africa. Clearly, this profile owes much to both black cultural nationalism of the late 1960s (variation "C" in the essay) and to the embracing of feminism by many black women in the 1980s. Nevertheless, like the Negro Beast stereotype, the Ur-mother profile is a mythology that obscures and one-dimensionalizes our possibilities for experiencing each black person as individual, historical, and so unique that—as in the case of my son or daughter, for example—it must be said that no one like them has ever lived before or will ever live again.

Recently one of my colleagues in African American Studies said to me that black women have succeeded in culturally "defining" themselves in their own terms and not those of the racial (or gender) Other. If he's right, then we have no choice but to conclude that black males have *not* done this quite as well as their female counterparts. As my friend, a gentle and scholarly man, put it: "People don't know who we are. Even *we* aren't sure who we are.

But isn't that precisely the perennial human dilemma? That we are, after all, beings who must fashion moment by moment what meaning our lives will have, beings in *process* who are subject in a single lifetime to change, transformation, self-contradiction, and constant evolution? In phenomenological terms, one can only achieve adequateness in describing the black male body by employing what some philosophers have called "genetic phenomenology," i.e., by examining an individual as he (or she) exhibits over time a series of profiles or disclosures of being. For a life is process, not product (or pregiven meaning). It more resembles the verb, not the noun.

This, just maybe, explains the current interest of young people in the unusual life of Malcolm X. There is much for critics of culture and philosophers to discuss in Spike Lee's monumental film tribute to this slain leader. Begin with the opening scene when Malcolm Little—a drug-dealer, pimp, and thief—visits a barber shop and has lye combed into his hair, which straightens it so thin another customer says, "It looks white." Go next to Malcolm in solitary confinement at Charlestown State Prison, where he is made to live like a caged animal. Then contrast both of these scenes to Malcolm X on his knees in a temple in Mecca, his hands raised to Allah, an ancient, haunting Muslim prayer sliding from his black throat like song. Here, the black male body is the instrument of the Most High. It is a global body connected to America, Africa, and the Middle East. It is capable of surrender and strength. It is cleansed of drugs, tobacco, and alcohol. It is the temple, the repository, of two millennia of Islamic scholarship, the living vessel for a culture that achieved a remarkably high level of sophistication when Europe was struggling through its Dark Ages—indeed, the culture that preserved Aristotle and transmitted him back to the West. For the first time in motion-picture history, and perhaps in pop culture, the black male body is experienced as the embodiment of intellectual, political, and spiritual ideals.

And yet all these profiles are of *one* life. If Malcolm X had not been slain in 1965, we doubtlessly would have witnessed more, an unfolding of idea and image that, for the phenomenologist, can only suggest the open-ended character of being. If there has been some slim progress since I first published "A Phenomenology of the Black Body," it is of this sort. A gradual accumulation of profiles that expand and qualify our experience of black men: General Colin Powell coolly professional at the center of the Persian Gulf conflict, athlete Arthur Ashe, widely admired for his courage and humanitarianism, astronaut Ron McNair honored for his contributions to the nation and NASA, Seattle mayor Norm Rice laboring, day in day out, to serve an American city that still works. Any accounts we have of black males in the future must, I believe, take these men—and the meanings their lives embody—into consideration.

Notes

1. Eldridge Cleaver, *Soul on Ice* (New York: Dell, 1968), 174.
2. Ibid., 169.
3. Cited in Don Ihde, *Hermenutic Phenomenology: The Philosophy of Paul Ricoeur* (Evanston, IL: Northwestern University Press, 1971), 56.
4. Frantz Fanon, *Black Skin, White Masks* (New York: Grove Press, 1967), 225.
5. Maurice Merleau-Ponty, *The Phenomenology of Perception*, trans. Colin Smith (New York: The Humanities Press, 1970). The discussion of the body is developed in Part I.
6. Rollo May, *Love and Will* (New York: Dell, 1969), 229.
7. Merleau-Ponty, *The Phenomenology of Perception*, 206.
8. Ibid., 146.
9. Cleaver, *Soul on Ice*, 171.
10. Fanon, *Black Skin*, 110.
11. Merleau-Ponty, *The Phenomenology of Perception*, 167.
12. Fanon, *Black Skin*, 138.
13. George Kent, *Blackness and the Adventure of Western Civilization* (Chicago: Third World Press, 1972), 173.
14. The term "epidermalization" was first used in a phenomenological sense by Professor Thomas Slaughter, of the Afro-American Studies Department at Rutgers, in his unpublished paper, "Epidermalizing the World."
15. Fanon, *Black Skin*, 134
16. Ibid., 110.
17. Merleau-Ponty, *The Phenomenology of Perception*, 138.
18. Richard Wright, *The Outsider* (New York: Harper & Row, 1953), 159.

Afterword: The Black Body: Under the Weight of White America's Microtomes

George Yancy

> And already I am being dissected under white eyes, the only real eyes. I am *fixed*. Having adjusted their microtomes, they cut away slices of my reality. I am laid bare.
>
> —Frantz Fanon

> It was this Africanism, deployed as rawness and savagery, that provided the staging ground and area for the elaboration of the quintessential American identity.
>
> —Toni Morrison

AMERICA AND THE BLACK BODY: IDENTITY POLITICS IN PRINT AND Visual Culture is a dialectically grounded text that dares to imagine America through the site of the black body. By doing so, the text complicates official (white) metanarratives about so-called happy Negroes and benevolent white masters. A radically different America emerges when voices that have been systematically silenced begin to speak. Indeed, a different America emerges when white voices transgress the very conditions that ground their identities by naming and deconstructing problematic representations that continue to sustain and perpetuate white supremacy. The act of imagination itself is dialectical, capable of complicating and seeing beyond the present configuration of racial relations, epistemic orders, cultural arrangements, and racial representations. Moving through sites of cultural practices that signify the black body over and against the national (white) body, how the black body is marked through unconscious white fears, and the complex, tension-filled, and contradictory visions of the black body, *America and The Black Body* neither sacrifices reality for fiction nor renders hope of a radically different American future unimaginable in the face of an ineluctable nihilism. *America and The Black Body* points to a present and a future that is metastable, capable of being radically new through the affirmation of a powerful process of unforgetting, remembering differently, and anticipating anew.

The Black/White Dialectic

The above two epigraphs that frame this afterword speak to the dialectical relationship between the white body and the black body and thereby is in stream with a central theme of this current collection. Frantz Fanon and Toni Morrison are cognizant of the interconnection between the iconographic force of whiteness and blackness within the larger white imaginary that informs this iconography. The white imaginary is able to "play in the dark," to use Morrison's turn of phrase, creating a presumptive metaphysical binary that renders blackness sinister, criminal, evil, savage-like, and hypersexual, while whiteness is rendered supreme, innocent, good, and civilized. To imagine America through the lens of these racial tropes reveals the social ontological Manichean space within which black and white bodies move and have their being. It is within this space that blackness has been historically constructed as problematic; indeed, black people are so-called problem people. It is not the case that their problems exist external to their being. Rather, black people are *ontologically* a problem people. It is their essence to function as obstacles to their own social success, ontological upsurge, and existential fruition. This depiction of blackness as inherently problematic is fueled by a racist narrative that attempts to secure and maintain the ego-maintenance of whites as they continue to live in bad faith. In short, whites are able to distance themselves from their own racist practices, persuading themselves "that savagery is 'out there.' "[1]

Whiteness is parasitic upon blackness. Hence, black people, as Morrison might say, are "convenient in every way, not the least of which is self-definition."[2] She understands how this parasitism is operative in American literature, and how blackness functions as the site of white self-definition. She argues that concepts such as autonomy, authority, newness and difference, and absolute power within the context of black enslavement are "made possible by, shaped by, activated by a complex awareness and employment of a constituted Africanism."[3] The denigration of the black body is the fulcrum around which the normative construction of the white body turned. Hence, the white body as normative is constituted through the negative designation of the black body as deviant. In other words, the affirmation of the white embodied self is constituted through the not-me qua black body. As Morrison writes, "Black slavery enriched the country's creative possibilities. For in that construction of blackness *and* enslavement could be found not only the not-free but also, with the dramatic polarity created by skin color, the projection of the not-me."[4] It is whiteness as the site of so-called racelessness that is purchased "through the presence of the racial other."[5] In America, whiteness is the so-called master norm, the universal, the standard against which nonwhite bodies are particularized as raced, as ersatz, as trouble. James Baldwin was aware of this parasitism when he argued that in this country white people "will have quite enough to do in learning how to accept and love themselves and each other, and when they have achieved this—the Negro problem will no longer exist, for it will no longer be needed."[6]

Locating the racial logic of the process of white parasitism within the context of early American film, James Snead writes, "American films do not merely feature this or that debased black image or this or that glorified white hero in isolation, but rather they correlate these images in a larger scheme of semiotic valuation."[7] Within the context of this larger semiotic valuation, blackness and whiteness stand opposed. However, it is whiteness as the overarching master narrative that sustains the opposition, a form of opposition that sublates blackness and yet nevertheless preserves blackness as *marked* and as the vehicle through which whiteness continues to exist as unmarked and normal. As Kalpana Seshadri-Crooks writes, "The system of race as differences among black, brown, red, yellow, *and white* makes sense only in its unconscious reference to Whiteness, which subtends the binary opposition between 'people of color' and 'white.'"[8] Regarding the concept of white parasitism, Snead further observes, "When we consider *The Birth of a Nation* or *Gone With the Wind*, for example, the mechanisms of racial mythification are clear—the dominant 'I' needs the coded 'other' to function."[9] For Snead, mythification, which involves "the replacement of history with a surrogate ideology" that promotes a "natural" order of white superiority and black inferiority, reinforces bad faith. "For the viewer," according to Snead, "the pleasure of recognizing this ranking displaces the necessity of verifying its moral or actual validity."[10] Whiteness, in short, is constructed as a universal value in terms of which phenotypic embodied whites subordinate their freedom; that is, whites invest in what they have created and yet conveniently elide the fact that they are its source.

The act of subordinating one's freedom vis-à-vis whiteness as an absolute value is reminiscent of what occurs within the context of colonial epistemic orders. In his preface to Fanon's *The Wretched of the Earth*, Jean-Paul Sartre characterizes the colonizer as undergoing a process of reification. He writes, "This imperious being, crazed by his absolute power and by the fear of losing it, no longer remembers clearly that he was once a man; he takes himself for a horsewhip or a gun."[11] In this way, the colonizer subordinates his freedom to that which is deemed absolute and the "natural" order of things. The colonizer becomes fixed. Paulo Friere notes that colonizers "develop a series of methods precluding any presentation of the world as a problem and showing it rather as a fixed entity, as something given—something to which people, as mere spectators, must adapt."[12] Human agency is no longer a factor in the outcome of history; rather, one must watch passively as history unfolds according to "inexorable" laws of colonial domination. In stream with Morrison's conceptualization of the projection of the not-me, Albert Memmi writes, "Far from wanting to understand him as he really is," the colonizer strips the colonized of any recognizable human form through "a series of negations."[13] Hence, the black body is *not* beautiful, *not* civilized, *not* moral, *not* intelligent—indeed, *not* white. Dialectically, the white body—in this case, the colonizer—is constituted through a series of affirmations. Observing how the colonizer/colonized (white/black) relationship is defined in terms of correlative terms, Fanon writes, "The feeling of inferiority of the colonized is the correlative to the European's feeling of superiority. Let us have the courage to say it outright: It is the racist who creates his inferior."[14]

An *abstract* ontology fails to capture the being of black embodiment in white America. It is within the context of the existential and the historical that black embodiment must be understood; for it is within antiblack *concrete* existential and historical terms that the black body undergoes processes of erasure. Further sharpening the importance of the dialectic between white and black, Fanon notes, "For not only must the black man be black; he must be black in relation to the white man."[15] Hence, within this context, "in relation to" signifies deep interstitial dynamics that presuppose a social matrix that is preconstituted with racial value. Indeed, "in relation to" suggests constitutive processes that transcend the self; the self's meaning, in fact, is "stretched" beyond self-enclosure, implicating anterior, current, and future realities. Within this context, the embodied black self's meaning is transversal—it is imposed, contested, negotiated, and recreated across time. Within the context of white America, however, the black body is also weighed down by white racist myths and structured by white power and hegemony. The interpellation of the black body as a site of white fear and trembling is predicated upon the constitutive acts of white subjectivity. Hence, the black body has *become* the object of white fear and brutality *in relation to* various historically informed habituated modes of being white in the world.

The reality of broken bones, torn flesh, being attacked and brutalized by white lynch mobs, castration, mutilation, rape, and torture, are practices that form the historical landscape of black bodies in white America. When the black body is made the center of the analysis of

America's historical legacy, America undergoes a process of transmogrification, revealing a history steeped in horror and terror. To challenge the myth and decenter the metanarrative of America as the land of hope and "salvation" can be done without, as bell hooks says, "evoking a simplistic essentialist 'us and them' dichotomy that suggests black folks merely invert stereotypical racist interpretations so that black becomes synonymous with goodness and white with evil."[16] Blacks have endured a history of white terror. This lived experience informs black subjectivity, particularly as black people were victims of this history and had to create repertoires of resistance against existential devaluation. Cornel West writes, "Two hundred and forty-four years of slavery and nearly a century of institutionalized terrorism in the form of segregation, lynching, and second-class citizenship in America were aimed at precisely this devaluation of black people."[17] Exploring indelible memories that have structured her epistemological standpoint, hooks writes, "Returning to memories of growing up in the social circumstances created by racial apartheid, to all black spaces on the edges of town, I reinhabit a location where black folks associated whiteness with the terrible, the terrifying, the terrorizing."[18] The association of whiteness with terror vis-à-vis the black body is not limited to a bygone past, but exists as a contemporary reality within a context where whiteness continues to perform both discursive and nondiscursive acts that demonize the black body, tear it asunder, and delimit its mobility.

"Yeh, and I'm the Flying Nun. Let's go, Nigger!"

Fanon discloses that he "wanted to come lithe and young into the world that was ours and to help to build it together."[19] To come *lithe* into the world is to exist, "to stand out"; it is to undergo moments of existential vertigo in the face of the possibilities of one's being toward the future. But there were white racist myths and narratives that came with their own expectations. While some men—white men—were simply expected to behave like men, Fanon notes, "I was expected to behave like a black man—or at least like a nigger."[20] Like Fanon, many blacks have "shouted a greeting to the world and the [white] world slashed away [their] joy."[21] Fanon understood the interpellative power of naming: " 'Dirty nigger!' Or simply, 'Look, a Negro!' "[22] The use of "nigger" *fixed* Fanon. He "became" *just* a nigger.

Contemporary blacks are constantly under the surveillance of the white gaze, are fixed by white looks that only see "niggers," haunted by white racist naming processes, and subjected to white America's microtomes. Cornel West provides two personal examples of what it was like to have his black body fixed or typified as criminal while "driving Black." He notes, however, that the incidents that he experienced "are dwarfed by those like Rodney King's beating or the abuse of black targets of the FBI's COINTELPRO efforts in the 1960s and 1970s."[23] He recalls that he was stopped three times in his "first ten days in Princeton for driving too slowly on a residential street with a speed limit of twenty-five miles per hour."[24] Also, driving to teach at Williams College from New York, West describes having been stopped on concocted charges of trafficking cocaine. He tried to explain to the police officer that he was a professor of religion. The police officer replied, "Yeh, and I'm the flying Nun. Let's go nigger!"[25] In stream with Ralph Ellison's observations in *Invisible Man*, West is rendered invisible because the white police officer refuses to see him.[26] The white police officer's white gaze militated against his acceptance of West's self-ascription as a professor of religion or a philosopher. Fanon notes, "No exception was made for my refined manners, or my knowledge of literature, or my understanding of the quantum theory."[27] Within the context of America's white microtomes, West asks, "Can genuine human relationships flourish for black people in a society that assaults black intelligence, black moral character, and black possibility?"[28]

The police officer's actions are part and parcel of a larger white racist regime that is designed to control black bodies. West notes, "White supremacist ideology is based first and foremost on the degradation of black bodies in order to control them."[29] It is partly through acts of naming, which involve the reiteration of norms,[30] that militate against the bodily integrity of West and other black bodies. As a "nigger," it is impossible for West to be a professor of religion. After all, to be called a "nigger" presumes the white normative and epistemic framework that constructs one as worthless, stupid, and inferior. Within the encounter with the white police officer, West's voice possesses little or no power. He is stripped, so to speak, of the ability to render actionable his interior knowledge of his own identity. This knowledge is inconsequential vis-à-vis the white officer's authority to recognize a "nigger" when he sees one. As a professor of religion, he is effectively rendered invisible. Yet, he is rendered hypervisible as a drug dealer, which "is a case of seeing without seeing."[31] The white police officer paradoxically "sees" West, but does not *see* him. For the white police officer, the very act of seeing has become calcified vis-à-vis the black body. Seeing and stereotypification are congealed in a single act of misperception and distortion. Robert Bernasconi writes, "Under slavery, Blacks were supposed to appear happy; under segregation, submissive; and today the stereotypes are manipulated in the form of images of the welfare queen, the teenage mother, the gang member [or ganger banger], and the drug addict [and drug dealer]."[32] Bernasconi also adds, "If he is not already known to us [whites], the stereotype intervenes."[33] This does not mean, however, that white myths and stereotypes become completely inoperative in the presence of those blacks with whom whites are familiar—even friends with. White racist habits work insidiously, often appearing in the form of good intentions.

As white, the police officer is the norm. He knows a "nigger" when *he* "sees" one. He also thinks of himself as good, as a protector of the (white) body politic. Dialectically there is something inherently threatening about West's black body, and especially threatening about West's description of himself as a professor of religion. When West asserts that he is a professor of religion, he forges an identity that conflicts with the white police officer's stereotypes of black bodies. Indeed, West's self-knowledge challenges and renders false the white police officer's perception, but the former does not render the latter inconsequential. West, for all intents and purposes, is laying claim to his own gaze, his own subjectivity. Bernasconi writes, "Treating African-Americans as invisible or, more precisely, rendering them invisible was, among other things, a mechanism by which European-Americans could protect themselves from encountering a point of view that conflicted with their own self-understanding."[34] Perhaps experiencing a slippage between the racist stereotype that presumes West (and other black bodies) to be always already guilty of something, and the possibility that what West says about himself is true, the police officer retreats to sarcasm: "Yeh, and I'm the Flying Nun." The police officer subverts West's gaze by hiding behind the truth that as *he* cannot be the Flying Nun, then West cannot be a professor of religion.

The subtext of the officer's caustic "wit" is designed to portray West as an *irony* (etymologically, a dissembler, one who simulates, puts on the appearance of). The racist presumption is that there is no way that a black man can be a professor of religion. History books confirm this. The media confirms this. Perhaps as this white police officer sat on his mother's lap he was taught—even if unconsciously learned—to associate blackness with evil and malevolence, and whiteness with goodness and beauty. Of course, white America attempted to convince black people "that their bodies are ugly, their intellect is inherently undeveloped, their culture is less civilized, and their future warrants less concern than that of other peoples."[35]

In the police officer's view, West's description of himself as a professor of religion is only a fantasy, like the 1960s sitcom *The Flying Nun;* he is engaging in wishful thinking, perhaps a stratagem to fool the police officer who has caught him in an act of "selling drugs." In fact, the police officer sees West as crazy, delusional. It is during times like these that one's other identities (as a professor of religion or philosophy, for example) are rendered null and void by white America's negative valuation of blackness. It is as if the figure of a black man who is a professor of religion becomes an obscene image, one that registers cognitive dissonance for the white police officer. To be black *and* to be a professor of religion—even if true—is to synthesize two mutually opposed identities that conjure up something comparable to Frankenstein's monster. Hence, a black professor of religion is not simply an exception, but a *monstrous* exception, a freak of nature, something grotesque and fit for teratology. West's body has undergone an act of violence. Black bodies are totalized vis-à-vis a white racist epistemology that leaves no ontological surplus for the black body *to be* other than what the white imagery "dictates." West is not approached by the white police officer as an other, as a site of alterity that belies stereotypification; rather, West remains within the space of white mastery. He becomes a site of "reduplication of the [white] self."[36]

Within this context, the white police officer constructed West as the embodiment of criminality. One might argue that West functioned as the site of "an imagined Africanist persona," a fiction according to which the white police officer enacted his racist aggression and nomination through an a priori suspicion of the black body. The black body is stereotypically *the* threat. Dialectically the white police officer is *the* guarantor of (white) safety. Recall that West was in Princeton for only ten days and was stopped three times. He was not speeding, but driving "too slowly" on a residential street. Despite the fact that West drove within the speed limit of twenty-five miles per hour, he was still stopped. So, even as West obeys the law, his black body is always already guilty, against the law. The white police officer's racist stereotype renders the legal integrity of West's "driving while black" suspect. West might agree with Fanon where the latter writes, "the movements, the attitudes, the glances of the [white] other fixed me there, in the sense in which a chemical solution is fixed by a dye."[37] Such stereotypical constructions can take their toll on the black body in the form of embodied "psychic scars and personal wounds."[38] Imagine the trauma of being constantly stopped, of having one's identity distorted, "being for the white other" a constant threat. Black mobility and spatiality are controlled and policed against the backdrop that it is white people who are free and ontologically expansive, who may come and go as they please.

The desire to come lithe into the world is belied by the social reality that one's blackness will always be under surveillance, watched, and controlled. After running some associational tests with whites, Fanon relates that he would assert the word "Negro." He observed that "Negro brought forth biology, penis, strong, athletic. Potent, boxer, Joe Louis, Jesse Owens, Senegalese troops, savage, animal, devil, sin."[39] Not only does the black body signify a zone of criminality, danger, and avoidance, but it also signifies perversity—a site of specific *sexual* perversity, promiscuity, and power. On this score, both black men and black women were historically constructed as sexually deviant. As Joy James notes, "Part of the racialized attraction or aversion for 'the black' in a society obsessed with race, sex, and violence is the appeal of exotica tinged with racial savagery and perversity."[40] Because of the presumptive possible eruption of the black body's sexual drives, the black body had to be controlled, even if not guilty; lines had to be reinforced; borders had to be policed. Pointing to the logic of borders, Robyn Wiegman writes that "lynching figures its victims as the culturally abject—monstrosities of excess whose limp and hanging bodies function as the specular assurance that the racial threat has not simply been averted, but rendered incapable of return."[41]

"How many generations had to bow to his genital fantasies?"

Within the American context where black sexuality assumes the character of perversion, black women's bodies have been traumatized, brutalized, objectified, and reduced to oversexed "objects" in relation to white America's obsession with its own sense of moral innocence and purity. The Jezebel caricature, for example, allowed white men to "play in the dark" and hide behind a fiction as they refused to value black women as deserving of rights and inviolability. This caricature also enabled white women to evade the fact that the sexual circuits of desire were actually initiated and controlled by white men vis-à-vis the black female body. Enslaved, sold, beaten, and raped, black women had very little agency over their bodies. Given the pervasiveness of white male hegemony, black women's bodies were vulnerable to racist insult, physical assault, and torture. Mythologized as being hypersexual and possessing unavoidable sexual power and seductiveness, the black female body as fantasy became the vehicle through which white men were able to flee from their own freedom, their own sense of guilt. After all, within the context of enslavement, how could one rape a "possession"? Think here of the young Celia in *Celia, A Slave*.[42] From the moment that Robert Newsom purchased her, he raped her. Think of her young body being physically torn apart, violated by a white sadistic pedophile. Think of her young body as a site of sustained trauma, penetration, and violent entry. Newsom could have easily married a white woman. He bought Celia as he bought a piece of land. He owned her by law. It was Newsom's racial status that guaranteed—as if sanctioned by nature—his "right" to possess the black female body. And though she was eventually hanged for killing him, she was his *thing* to have power over, his *thing* of white desire, and his *thing* of white nomination. As Hortense Spillers writes, "Let's face it. I am a marked woman."[43] As marked, the black female body is invested in. She is the Mammy figure of indefatigable patience; the Sapphire figure who can be evil and conniving; the "hole" that has no bottom; the quintessential breeder; and the site of untamed desire and salaciousness.

White myth making around the black female body is inextricably linked to the larger African diaspora, that space of rupture, dispersion, and displacement. The presence of white hegemony, the black female body as property, the pervasive phenomenon of sexual abuse, and the experience of trauma constitute significant motifs, although by no means exhaustive, that are indicative of the reality of black diasporic women's existential experiences. These four motifs function as interlocking, synergistic elements that had a profound negative impact on the somatic and psychic constitution of diasporic black women. These were shared *embodied* experiences that often exceeded description. In Gayl Jones's *Corregidora*, for example, the black female body's somatic integrity is shattered under white oppressive sexual exploitation. From the perspective of white males, black women are referred to as "good little pieces."[44] Within the text, memory functions as a site of trauma and liberation as blues singer Ursa Corregidora, the protagonist, must keep alive the memory of black female sexual exploitation in her family history. Memory functions as a site of evidence of and indictment against the crimes committed against their bodies. It is the Portuguese slave master Corregidora who refers to his black female slaves' genitalia as "his pussy."[45] Ursa's Great Gram shared what it meant to live under the regime of whiteness, to be a prisoner of Corregidora's desire: "He would take me hisself first and said he was breaking me in."[46] Moreover, he feels "entitled" to have black women sexually abused by other white men. In *Corregidora*, the rape of Ersa's Great Gram and Grandmama by Corregidora is tragic. He not only sexually abused them, but engaged in incest with Grandmama (for she was his daughter) and made money from other white men sexually abusing her.

What is also tragic is that Ursa's mother is the product of incest. Hence, technically, although Grandmama is Ursa's mother's mother, she, Grandmama, is also Ursa's mother's sister. This also makes Ursa's Grandmama her aunt. Language seems to implode here. Think of how cancerous the memory of this had to be. Think of "how many generations had to bow to his genital fantasies?"[47] And, yet, the narrative had to be told. The Corregidora women had to do battle through the medium of traumatic memory. Rather than a politics of muted speech, the Corregidora women sought resistance through speech and memory.

Referring to the state of Virginia's official recognition of slavery in 1661, Joy James notes that free or enslaved African women were referred to as "nasty" and "beastly."[48] Such racial tropes promoted acts of violence against black women's bodies. Like the Corregidora women, the act of *voicing* is a powerful means of militating against institutional silencing and social amnesia. However, the history of silencing around the racist denigration of black female bodies is not limited to the past. In the recent case of Megan Williams, there was no national outcry and indignation, no massive news coverage. In both real and reel time, Williams was silenced. In September 2007, six whites (three men and three women) held Megan Williams, a twenty-year-old black woman, prisoner in a trailer in West Virginia. According to Williams, her captors raped her, poured hot water and hot wax on her body, forced her to drink out of the toilet and to eat feces (possibly dog, rat, and human), cut off and yanked out her hair, forced her to lick their toes, taunted her with racial slurs, cut her ankle and stabbed her thigh, and forced her to perform oral sex on one of the white women. She was told that she was being treated this way because she was colored/black, according to Williams. She was forced to bow to their (white) genital fantasies. This violent scene is indicative of the history of whiteness as terror. I would argue that the scene became one of spectacle as the six whites gazed upon the despised and violated black body. Forced to eat feces and drink from a toilet, the racist scene replicated the scene of a lynching: white racist pleasure, masochism, and dominance. It was not enough that Williams' body was sexually violated. She had to be reduced to an eater of feces and a drinker of urine. In short, she was made to mimic white fantasies of the black body as nasty and animalistic.[49] As T. Denean Sharpley-Whiting writes when referring to the tragic situation of the so-called Hottentot Venus, the six white spectators/perpetrators reinforced and reinscribed Williams's "position in the Manichaean social world as a primitive savage."[50]

In Summary

As in the case of the Corregidora women, the memory of the horrible acts visited upon Megan Williams and the racist stereotypification of Cornel West as a criminal must be kept alive. In this way, the process of imagining America is not obfuscated through the substitution of reality for ideology. Imagining America through the site of black embodiment speaks to America's tragic history. Yet, even as the arc of America's moral urgency around ending white racism is long, imagining America as *otherwise* speaks to America as a possibility, as an open ended experiment in which our collective sense of belonging cannot be constituted through acts of fiat alone. As Patricia Williams writes, "Ours must be a world in which we know each other better."[51] As long as "blackness signifies the realm of the always known, as well as the not worth knowing," America as a site of endless possibility will be seriously truncated. To see the other in oneself, as oneself, it is important that white America troubles the relation of the white self to whiteness as the master signifier,[52] and it is important that whites trouble the security of an identity that is predicated on the denigration of the black body. Rather than a "transgressive refusal to know,"[53] white people might then profoundly invest in knowing better.

Notes

1. Toni Morrison, *Playing in the Dark: Whiteness and the Literary Imagination* (New York: Vinatge Books, 1992), 45.
2. Ibid., 45.
3. Ibid., 44.
4. Ibid., 38.
5. Ibid., 46.
6. James Baldwin, *The Fire Next Time* (New York: The Modern Library, 1995), 21.
7. James Snead, *White Screens/Black Images: Hollywood for the Dark Side* (New York: Routledge, 1994), 4.
8. Kalpana Seshadri-Crooks, *Desiring Whiteness: A Lacanian Analysis of Race* (New York: Routledge, 2000), 20 (Emphasis added).
9. Snead, *White Screens/Black Images*, 4.
10. Ibid.
11. Jean-Paul Sartre, preface, in Frantz Fanon *The Wretched of the Earth* (New York: Grove Press, 1963), 16.
12. Paulo Friere, *Pedagogy of the Oppressed* (New York: The Continuum Publishing Company, 1997), 120.
13. Albert Memmi, *The Colonizer and the Colonized* (Boston: Beacon Press, 1991), 83.
14. Frantz Fanon, *Black Skin, White Masks*, trans. Charles Lam Markmann (New York: Grove Press, Inc., 1967), 93.

15. Ibid., 110.
16. bell hooks, *Killing Rage: Ending Racism* (New York: Henry Holt and Company, 1995), 37.
17. Cornel West, *Race Matters* (Boston: Beacon Press, 1993), 85.
18. hooks, *Killing Rage*, 39.
19. Fanon, *Black Skin, White Masks*, 112–13.
20. Ibid., 114.
21. Ibid., 114–115.
22. Ibid., 109.
23. West, *Race Matters*, x–xi.
24. Ibid., x.
25. Ibid., x.
26. Ralph Ellison, *Invisible Man* (New York: Vintage Books, 1995), 3.
27. Fanon, *Black Skin, White Masks*, 117.
28. West, *Race Matters*, 86.
29. Ibid., 85.
30. John T. Warren, *Performing Purity: Whiteness, Pedagogy, and the Reconstruction of Power* (New York: Peter Lang, 2003), 29.
31. Robert Bernasconi, "The Invisibility of Racial Minorities in the Public Realm of Appearances," in *Race*, ed. Robert Bernasconi. (Malden, MA: Blackwell Publishers, Inc., 2001), 288.
32. Ibid.
33. Ibid.
34. Ibid., 295.
35. West, *Race Matters*, 85.
36. Robert J. C. Young, *White Mythologies: Writing History and the West*, 2nd ed. (New York: Routledge, 2004), 48.
37. Fanon, *Black Skin, White Masks*, 109.
38. West, *Race Matters*, 85.
39. Fanon, *Black Skin, White Masks*, 166.
40. Joy James, *Shadowboxing: Representations of Black Feminist Politics* (New York: St. Martins Press, 1999), 127.
41. Robyn Wiegman, *American Anatomies: Theorizing Race and Gender* (Durham, NC: Duke University Press, 1995), 81.
42. Melton A. McLaurin, *Celia, A Slave: A True Story* (New York: Avon Books, 1993).
43. Hortense J. Spillers, "Mama's Baby, Papa's Maybe: An American Grammar Book," in *Feminisms: An Anthology of Literary Theory and Criticism*, ed. Robyn R. Warhol & Diane Price Herndl (New Brunswick, NJ: Rutgers University Press, 1997), 384.
44. Gayl Jones, *Corregidora* (Boston: Beacon Press, 1997), 10.
45. Ibid., 54.
46. Ibid., 11.
47. Ibid., 59.
48. James, *Shadowboxing*, 128.
49. See "Six Held in West Virginia Torture Horror," http://www.thesmokinggun.com/archive/years/2007/0911071logansix1.html.
50. T. Denean Sharpley-Whiting, *Black Venus: Sexualized Savages, Primal Fears, and Primitive Narratives in French* (Durham, NC: Duke University Press, 1999), 14.
51. Patricia Williams, *Seeing a Color-Blind Future: The Paradox of Race* (New York: Farrar, Straus and Giroux, 1997), 5.
52. Seshadri-Crooks, *Desiring Whiteness*, 36.
53. Williams, *Seeing a Color-Blind Future*, 27.

Contributors

LAURA DOYLE is Professor of English and Director of Undergraduate Studies at the University of Massachusetts-Amherst. She has been awarded an ACLS Fellowship (1991), a Five College Women's Studies Research Associateship (1991), a Rockefeller Fellowship in Intercultural Studies at Princeton (1993), and most recently, the Outstanding Teacher Award at the University of Massachusetts-Amherst (2003). Doyle's book publications include *Bordering on the Body: The Racial Matrix of Modern Fiction and Culture* (1994, recipient of the Narrative Society's Perkins Prize); as editor, *Bodies of Resistance: New Phenomenologies of Politics, Agency, and Culture* (2001); and as co-editor, *Geomodernisms: Race, Modernism, Modernity* (2005). She has published numerous essays on race and narrative, on authors ranging from Aphra Behn and Laurence Sterne to Harriet Wilson, Pauline Hopkins, Virginia Woolf, William Faulkner, and Nella Larsen. She also has a special interest in the existential phenomenologist Maurice Merleau-Ponty, whose work influences much of her writing on the body and culture.

SIMONE C. DRAKE is a post-doctoral fellow at Ohio University in the Department of English. She writes on African diaspora and black cultural studies with a focus on gender and geography. She is the author of "Gendering Diasporic Migration in Erna Brodber's *Louisiana*" (2007). The chapter included here is part of a book-length manuscript that analyzes paradigm shifts in contemporary black women's writing. She lives in Columbus, Ohio with her husband and two sons.

MARINA FEDOSIK received her BA in English and French at Minsk State Linguistic University, and her MA in English at the University of Delaware. She has done research on Ishmael Reed and Harlem Renaissance authors. Her current research examines post colonial, global, and feminist approaches to contemporary American literature. She is currently completing her Ph.D. dissertation, "Representations of Transnational Adoption in Literature and Film" at the University of Delaware.

ALLISON E. FRANCIS is an assistant professor and the English department coordinator at Chaminade University of Honolulu. Her fields of study include Vodou in Haiti, African American and Caribbean women's literature, and representations of the African American body in media culture. She is a performance poet who has appeared at numerous venues in the United States and the United Kingdom. She has published poetry and a number of essays on the performance of the body in Vodou and Caribbean women's writing, including a critical essay on the slave narrative *The History of Mary Prince*, in *Swinging her Breasts at History: Language, Body and Caribbean Women's Texts* (2006), edited by Moira Inghilleri. Currently, she is working on a book-length manuscript of the nineteenth-century Jamaican nurse and entrepreneur, Mary Seacole.

CAROL E. HENDERSON is Associate Director of Black American Studies and Associate Professor of English and Black American Studies at the University of Delaware, Newark campus. Her recent publications include an essay entitled "The Ties that Bind: Speaking the Sistahood" in *In-Between: Essays and Studies in Literary Criticism*, Chanakyapuri, New Delhi, India (2008), and an edited book, *James Baldwin's* Go Tell It on the Mountain: *Historical and Critical Essays (2006)* that includes a number of her own pieces, as well as *Scarring the Black Body: Race and Representation in African American Literature* (2002). In addition to numerous articles in professional journals and critical volumes, she has a forthcoming essay, "King Kong Ain't Got Sh** On Me: Allegories, Anxieties, and the Performance of Race in Mass Media" in *The Journal of Popular Culture*. She is currently at work on a monograph entitled *The Hottentot Venus Revisited: Visions, Revisions, and Literary Responses*, and another edited volume entitled *Imagining the Black Female Body*.

CHARLES JOHNSON is the Pollock Professor of English, author of the novels *Middle Passage*, *Ox-herding Tale*, and *Faith and the Good Thing;* a story collection: *The Sorcerer's Apprentice* (nominated for a PEN/Faulkner award), and *Being and Race: Black Writing Since 1970*, a critical study. He is also a screenwriter and book reviewer, and for many years served as fiction editor of *Seattle Review*. He received the 1990 National Book Award (fiction) for *Middle Passage*, a Guggenheim Fellowship, a Writers Guild Award, two Washington State Governor's Awards for literature, and numerous other prizes and honorary degrees. In 1998 he received a John D. and Catherine T. MacArthur Fellowship ("genius" grant).

DAVID FARRELL KRELL is professor of Philosophy at DePaul University, and author of *Of Memory, Reminiscence, and Writing* (1990) and of

Infectious Nietzsche (1996). He is also editor of *Basic Writings: From Being and Time to the Task of Thinking/Martin Heidegger* (1993).

THERESE M. RIZZO is an assistant professor at the University of North Carolina, Pembroke. She has published in *Studies in the Humanities* (2007) and has presented work on the emergence of African American elitist societies in post-Reconstruction literature, the American Race Woman in fin-de-siecle New Woman authors, and the erotics of sentimental submission at conferences, including North-East MLA and Mid-Atlantic Women's Studies Association. Her current work focuses on trickster figures in nineteenth-century American (Con)texts and connects the use of submission, manipulation, and trickery in American sentimental minority authors such as Frederick Douglass, Pauline Hopkins, and Onoto Watanna.

ELIZABETH R. SCHROEDER received a BA in History and Theology from Valparaiso University in 2001 and an MA in American Studies from Lehigh University in 2003. Currently, she is a doctoral candidate in the Department of American Studies at Saint Louis University. Her dissertation focuses on emerging racial geographies and African American artistic and cultural production during the Chicago Black Renaissance, 1932–54.

RICHARD SCHUR is Associate Professor of Interdisciplinary Studies at Drury University. His research focuses on the areas of critical race theory, African American literature, hip-hop studies, and intellectual property law. He is the author of *Parodies of Ownership: Hip-Hop Aesthetics and Intellectual Property Law* (2009). Currently, he is editing a collection (with Lovalerie King) tentatively entitled *Justice Unveiled: African American Culture and the Law.*

KATRINA D. THOMPSON is Assistant Professor of History and African American Studies at Saint Louis University. Her research examines racial imagery, culture, entertainment, popular culture and mass media in the United States. She has been awarded the Erskine A. Peters Fellowship at the University of Notre Dame (2006) and the W. Burghardt Turner Fellowship (2000–2006) at Stony Brook University. She has presented at several national and international conferences.

HENRY B. WONHAM is Professor of English and Department Head at the University of Oregon. He is the author of several books on American literature, including *Charles W. Chesnutt: A Study of the Short Fic-*

tion and, more recently, *Playing the Races: Ethnic Caricature and American Literary Realism.*

George Yancy teaches in the Department of Philosophy at Duquesne University. He is the author of *Black Bodies, White Gazes: The Continuing Significance of Race* (2008). His influential edited books include: *Philosophy in Multiple Voices* (2007), *White on White/Black on Black* (2005), which was a *Choice* Outstanding Academic Title Award winner, *Narrative Identities: Psychologists Engaged in Self-Construction* (2005, with Susan Hadley), *What White Looks Like: African-American Philosophers on the Whiteness Question* (2004), *The Philosophical i: Personal Reflections on Life in Philosophy* (2002), *Cornel West: A Critical Reader* (2001), *African-American Philosophers, 17 Conversations* (1998), which also won a *Choice* Outstanding Academic Title Award, and *Critical Perspectives on bell hooks* (2009, with Maria del Guadalupe Davidson). In 2008, Yancy won the Duquesne University McAnulty College and Graduate School of Liberal Arts Faculty Award for Excellence in Scholarship.

Index